# POETIC ETHICS IN PROVERBS

The book of Proverbs' frequent use of binary oppositions – righteous and wicked, wise and foolish – has led many to assume that its vision of the moral world is relatively simplistic. This study demonstrates that Proverbs in fact presents a remarkably sophisticated response to ethical questions of profound concern to the Israelite sages who crafted the book: What motivates human beings? How do they learn? How does the power of desire shape human character? Anne W. Stewart analyzes Proverbs' multifaceted collection of images and metaphors to reveal their complex understanding of the development of the moral self, which suggests that character formation requires educating all of the senses and not simply the cognitive faculties. One of few works to make explicit connections between the poetic form of Proverbs and its pedagogical function, *Poetic Ethics in Proverbs* will appeal to all those interested in literary approaches to the Bible.

ANNE W. STEWART is Director of External Relations at Princeton Theological Seminary. Her essays have appeared in the *Journal for the Study of the Old Testament*, the *Harvard Theological Review*, the *Women's Bible Commentary*, and the *Encyclopaedia of the Bible and Its Reception*.

# POETIC ETHICS IN PROVERBS

*Wisdom Literature and the Shaping of the Moral Self*

ANNE W. STEWART

*Princeton Theological Seminary*

CAMBRIDGE
UNIVERSITY PRESS

# CAMBRIDGE
## UNIVERSITY PRESS

32 Avenue of the Americas, New York, NY 10013-2473, USA

Cambridge University Press is part of the University of Cambridge.

It furthers the University's mission by disseminating knowledge in the pursuit of education, learning, and research at the highest international levels of excellence.

www.cambridge.org
Information on this title: www.cambridge.org/9781107119420

First published 2016

Printed in the United States of America by Sheridan Books, Inc.

*A catalog record for this publication is available from the British Library.*

*Library of Congress Cataloging in Publication Dat*a
Stewart, Anne W., 1983– author.
Poetic ethics in Proverbs : wisdom literature and the shaping of
the moral self / Anne W. Stewart, Princeton Theological Seminary.
pages  cm
ISBN 978-1-107-11942-0 (hardback)
1. Bible. Proverbs – Criticism, interpretation, etc.  2. Hebrew poetry,
Biblical.  3. Ethics in the Bible.  I. Title.
BS1465.52.S74  2015
223'.706–dc23        2015026749

ISBN 978-1-107-11942-0 Hardback

# Contents

# Contents

# Acknowledgments

Without counsel plans fail, but with many advisors they succeed.
(Prov 15:22)

I am deeply grateful for the many advisers whose wise counsel has shepherded this project to its completion. This work grew out of my doctoral dissertation at Emory University, and I am indebted to the members of my committee. Joel LeMon provided helpful feedback and thoughtful questions. Christine Roy Yoder has for many years been for me a valued source of wisdom on all matters of biblical literature, theological education, and life itself. And I could not have found better or wiser advisers than Carol Newsom and Brent Strawn. They have consistently modeled for me how to pursue excellence in scholarship while cultivating the virtues of generosity, collegiality, and good humor.

I also wish to thank the many other wise voices who have commented on versions of this work, including William Brown, Joel Kaminsky, Timothy Sandoval, and Nicole Tilford. Their insight has sharpened my thinking, and where errors remain, the sages of Proverbs would no doubt chastise me for failing to heed the counsel of others.

Finally, and most importantly, words cannot express my deep appreciation and love for my parents, Richard Stewart and Dr. Mary Simmonds. This work is dedicated to them, my first and best teachers of wisdom.

CHAPTER I

# Poetry, Pedagogy, and Ethos

The subject is also demanding of the clarity only the Muses'
grace can give – which doesn't seem, after all, out of place.
Think of how doctors will give young patients bitter concoctions
but first touching the rim of the cup with a drop of honey
to try to beguile the lips and the tongue so that the child
may drink down the nasty juice of the wormwood or whatever,
deluded but not betrayed, for the motive is to do him
good and restore him to health. Just so, it is my intention
to set forth my argument in sweet Pierian song,
touching it with the drops of the Muses' sweetest honey
the better to engage your mind with hexameter verses
so that you may discover the world and how it is made, and come
to a better understanding of the true nature of things.[1]

Form and content are not just incidentally linked, as they are so frequently in philosophical writing today. Form is a crucial element in the
work's philosophical content. Sometimes, indeed ... the content of the
form proves so powerful that it calls into question the allegedly simpler
teaching contained within it.[2]

Using the metaphor of a honeyed cup, Lucretius describes the function
of didactic poetry to instruct by pleasing. As articulated in *De Rerum
Natura*, Lucretius's project relies on the vehicle of poetry to bring lucidity
and delight to his exposition of Epicurean philosophy. Like medicine dis-
guised with honey, so the sublimities of poetry will delight the mind and
the senses, aiding the student to ingest its teaching. Martha C. Nussbaum
observes that for Lucretius and several of his contemporaries, form is crucial to the philosophical content that they deliver. "Literary and rhetorical

---

[1] Lucretius, *De Rerum Natura: The Nature of Things, A Poetic Translation* (trans. David R. Slavitt;
Berkeley: University of California Press, 2008), I.853–65 [40].
[2] Martha C. Nussbaum, *The Therapy of Desire: Theory and Practice in Hellenistic Ethics* (Martin
Classical Lectures 2; Princeton: Princeton University Press, 1994), 487.

I

strategies," she insists, "enter into the methods at a very deep level, not just decorating the arguments," but shaping the very conception of philosophical argument in order to engage the student.[3]

While not a work of philosophy, Epicurean or otherwise, the book of Proverbs is a similar testament to the close relationship between form and function. Although its poetic form has often been treated by scholars as incidental to its content, mere icing on the proverbial cake, in fact that form is central to the book's content and its didactic purpose. Many studies have pursued the "medicine" that Proverbs prescribes, but this monograph seeks to study the "honey" with which it is dispensed, in the process finding that the honey is indeed part of the prescription. As Patrick D. Miller writes about the psalms, "Meaning and beauty, the semantic and the aesthetic, are woven together into a whole, and both should be received and responded to by the interpreter. To ignore the beauty in pursuit of the meaning is, at a minimum, to close out the possibility that the beauty in a significant fashion contributes to and enhances the meaning."[4]

Within Proverbs, the meaning to which this form contributes is nothing less than the subject and the function of the book as a whole: the cultivation of wisdom and the formation of wise character in its student. While other studies have commented on Proverbs' conception of character, this work gives attention to the relationship between the formation of character and the form of poetry. As I will argue, the didactic poetry of Proverbs is intimately connected to its pedagogical function, a feature that is illumined by comparison with other examples of didactic poetry, such as *De Rerum Natura*.

## The Poetry of Character and the Character of Poetry

From its opening words, the book of Proverbs presents itself as a manual of instruction for the student to acquire the necessary discipline and virtues to follow the wise course (1:2–7). Proverbs speaks in the language of character. It offers various models to the student, some to be emulated, such as the wise (חכם) and the discerning (מבין), and some to be avoided, such as the fool (אויל) and the dunce (כסיל). As these characters are presented throughout the book, they embody certain virtues or vices of character.[5]

---

[3] Ibid., 486.

[4] Patrick D. Miller, *Interpreting the Psalms* (Philadelphia: Fortress Press, 1986), 30.

[5] Virtues of character include wisdom (חכמה), righteousness (צדקה), and savvy (ערמה), all of which are attributes of those characters that are marked positively in the book. On the other hand, vices of character include foolishness (אולת), evil (רע), and deceit (מרמה), features of negative characters.

While the concept of character is pervasive throughout the book, there has been a robust discussion in wisdom scholarship concerning the nature of character formation and the degree to which Proverbs even grants the possibility. John Barton, on the one hand, argues that Israelite wisdom views character "as fixed and unchanging, almost at times as predetermined."[6] Consequently, in his view while Proverbs describes various dispositions of character, its binary oppositions of wise versus foolish and righteous versus wicked indicate that humans are either one type or the other but cannot become either type in greater degrees.[7] On the other hand, William P. Brown insists that Proverbs not only describes various characters, but also functions to shape character within the student.[8] In conversation with character ethics, Brown draws attention to the ethical language of the book and the way in which its profile of certain literary characters (e.g., woman Wisdom and the strange woman) both illumines and cultivates a normative sense of character within the social community. Brown's approach accounts for the indication that virtues of character must be cultivated continually. The explicit addressee of the book is a simpleton (פֶּתִי), whose character must be shaped in accord with wisdom, and thus the book promises to help its student acquire the virtues of shrewdness, knowledge, and prudence (1:4–5). Even the wise person must seek more wisdom (1:5), for formation is a process that does not end. Conversely, vices of character must be ardently avoided, because sinners and fools also promise to shape a person's character, although the end result will of course be negative (see 1:10–19).

The poetry of Proverbs makes an important contribution to the way in which the book seeks to shape character. Indeed, through its poetic form, Proverbs appeals to the whole human person, attending to his emotions, motivations, desires, and imagination, not simply his rational capacities. In so doing, the book indicates that character formation

---

Some attributes could be categorized as virtues *or* vices of character, depending on how they are exercised. Shrewdness (מְזִמָּה), for example, is a positive feature to which the student should aspire (3:21; 5:2); it is a capacity of discretion that woman Wisdom herself possesses (8:12), and in this sense, it is presented as a virtue of character. However, it is also an ability to devise secret schemes (24:8), prompting suspicion from others (14:17) and condemnation from God (12:2). In this sense, it is a character vice.

[6] John Barton, *Understanding Old Testament Ethics: Approaches and Explanations* (Louisville: Westminster John Knox, 2003), 67. See the discussion of Barton's argument in Chapter 2.

[7] He states: "there are no Laodicean moralists in the Wisdom literature. Everyone is either good or bad, wise or foolish" (ibid.).

[8] See William P. Brown, *Character in Crisis: A Fresh Approach to the Wisdom Literature of the Old Testament* (Grand Rapids: Eerdmans, 1996); revised as *Wisdom's Wonder: Character, Creation, and Crisis in the Bible's Wisdom Literature* (Grand Rapids: Eerdmans, 2014).

is more than an intellectual project and, consequently, demands more than appeal to logical reasoning. Robert Lowth suggested that the sublime nature of the poetic form is integral to its pedagogical function, for unlike history or philosophy, "poetry addresses her precepts not to the reason alone; she calls the passions to her aid: she not only exhibits examples, but infixes them in the mind. She softens the wax with her peculiar ardour, and renders it more plastic to the artist's hand."[9] Indeed, the poetry of Proverbs uses a variety of poetic tools in fashioning in the student certain "habits of virtue."[10] Vivid metaphors, perplexing sayings, and arresting images characterize the book, and attention to these literary features will be an essential component of a study of character formation in Proverbs.

The attention to how the poetics of Proverbs function to shape character will also make contributions to the study of biblical Hebrew poetry, at large, and the genre of didactic poetry, in particular. Robert Alter insists that "one of the many gaps in the understanding of biblical poetry is a failure of those who generalize about it to make sufficient distinctions among genres."[11] While the study of Hebrew poetry has blossomed in recent years, much work remains to be done concerning the features of particular genres of biblical poetry, and this study seeks to address part of that gap. In fact, Proverbs is a particularly rich book to study in this respect because it contains several genres of poetry and makes use of a diverse set of poetic features.

## Overview of Chapters

Part I provides a methodological foundation for the work that follows. In Chapter 2, I consider the character ethics approach as it has been practiced in biblical studies and how it has informed recent scholarship on the book of Proverbs. I argue that while the character ethics approach is a very helpful lens through which to study Proverbs, the form of Proverbs also challenges certain central assumptions of character ethics, especially the primacy of narrative in literary form and in the understanding of the human person.

---

[9] Robert Lowth, *Lectures on the Sacred Poetry of the Hebrews* (trans. G. Gregory; 2 vols.; London: Ogles, Duncan, and Cochran, 1816), 1:12.

[10] Lowth adds that the poet teaches "by the beauty of imagery, by the ingenuity of the fable, by the exactness of imitation, he allures and interests the mind of the reader, he fashions it to habits of virtue, and in a matter informs it with the spirit of integrity itself" (ibid., 1:13).

[11] Robert Alter, *The Art of Biblical Poetry* (New York: Basic Books, 1985), ix.

A central assumption of this work is that the poetic form of Proverbs makes a critical difference to interpretation of the book and to its pedagogical orientation, and the poetic form of Proverbs is the subject of Chapter 3. This chapter surveys the poetic features of Proverbs and considers the genre of its poetry in relation to the nature of biblical Hebrew poetry more broadly. I examine the poems in chapters 1–9 as didactic poetry, which can be profitably studied alongside didactic poems of other cultures. Recent critical work on the genre of didactic poetry in the classical tradition proves to be an especially helpful conversation partner for illumining some of the central features of the didactic poem in Proverbs. At the same time, however, I argue that Prov 1–9 shares many features in common with the genre of the Hebrew love lyric, and the Song of Songs is a fitting comparison.

In Part II, I examine four different ways in which Proverbs talks about and seeks to shape its students' character, which I term the models of *mûsār* ("discipline"): rebuke, motivation, desire, and imagination. In my analysis, "model" refers simply to patterns of language and thinking in Proverbs that are clustered around these four themes. These models are not mutually exclusive, nor are their bounds rigid. In fact, there is often a great deal of overlap between them. However, they are useful heuristic categories to illumine distinct ways that Proverbs talks about character and implicitly conveys certain assumptions about the nature of the human person.

In Chapter 4, I consider the model of rebuke, which includes references to both physical and verbal correction. The book is filled with both sayings about such correction and the content of that correction. In this respect, it uses the resources of its poetic form to function as verbal rebuke that provokes the student to follow a particular course. I use this model and its emphasis on discipline as a lens through which to view Proverbs' understanding of the moral self, arguing that it advances a perspective that I term "educated moral selfhood," which assumes both internal and external agency in the formation of a moral self. Chapter 5 treats the extensive language of motivation in the book and the ways in which this functions to highlight central values of the sapiential worldview. This model indicates that Proverbs views its students as self-interested creatures who stand to be influenced by a variety of motivational forces.

The prominence of motivation as a means of character formation points to a related, although distinct, model of desire. In Chapter 6, I explore the pervasiveness of this theme in the book, extending from food to wine to wealth to women, and I consider the relation between desire and the moral self. One of the primary claims of Proverbs, I argue, is that the things that humans desire shape their character and, consequently, a significant facet of the book's pedagogy is built on not only describing helpful and harmful desires but in shaping the student's desires in accord with wisdom. Chapter 7 considers the profoundly imaginative nature of moral reasoning in the book. In conversation with recent work on the imagination in cognitive science and ethics, I survey several of the imaginative structures in the book, including moral prototypes and metaphor, and suggest that Proverbs' manner of thinking is not nearly as simplistic as many scholars have presumed. Throughout these chapters, I intentionally linger over the poetic features of selected poems because it is in and through the poetic form that Proverbs' pedagogy unfolds. Consequently, by way of conclusion, in Chapter 8 I return to the question of character ethics and consider the way in which the poetic form of Proverbs offers an important critique of the narrative orientation of character ethics.

## Character, Knowledge, and the Moral Self

The relationship between character, knowledge, and virtue within Proverbs reveals some of the primary underlying moral and intellectual assumptions of the book, although their precise relationship is the subject of dispute. Michael V. Fox, for example, finds the ethics of Proverbs to be akin to the claim of Socratic ethics that all virtue is one.[12] Socratic ethics holds as a central premise that virtue is knowledge, that is, "knowledge of the good is both a necessary and sufficient condition to being good and doing the good."[13] Furthermore, knowledge of the good – moral knowledge – is the knowledge of what constitutes well-being, and to know this good is to desire the good and to do the good. Conversely, while knowledge is virtue, ignorance is vice. Fox contends that this notion is shared by Proverbs, for the fundamental problem, according to the sages, is ignorance, and, consequently, the solution is knowledge, that is, wisdom. Wisdom is moral knowledge, and the one who has wisdom knows the good, desires the good, and does the good.[14] Christopher B. Ansberry, on the other

---

[12] See Michael V. Fox, *Proverbs 10–31: A New Translation with Introduction and Commentary* (AB 18B; New Haven: Yale University Press, 2009), 935–45.

[13] Ibid., 937.

[14] Here Fox is reading the book as a whole. He argues that there were different conceptions of wisdom in the three different redactional stages he identifies (stage 1 represented by the sayings in Prov 10–29; stage 2 by the "lectures" of Prov 1–9; and stage 3 by the "interludes" in chapters 1–9). In the first stage, he suggests that wisdom was not associated with moral virtue but was instead a purely

hand, argues that Aristotelian ethics, as articulated in *Nicomachean Ethics*, is a more useful heuristic model. In particular, he suggests that Aristotle's notion that knowledge must be accompanied by a virtuous disposition – character – is a more adequate model for Proverbs because, within the book as a whole, "a virtuous disposition is the fundamental prerequisite for the acquisition of wisdom."[15] Ansberry's most noteworthy critique is of the Socratic principle that no one does wrong willingly and that, accordingly, lack of knowledge is the fundamental cause of vice. Ansberry argues that within Proverbs a corrupt moral disposition – a fault of character – is often the cause of vice, which coheres with Aristotle's contention that "unethical behavior is not simply the product of ignorance."[16] He cites the fool (אֱוִיל), the wicked (רָשָׁע), and the scoffer (לֵץ) as examples of characters for whom "ignorance is simply the by-product of their moral disposition."[17] Fox, on the other hand, would argue that their activity is the result of their lack of knowledge, which consequently perverts their character. To some extent, this dispute of the relationship between knowledge and character is a question of "which came first, the chicken or the egg?" Character and wisdom are inseparably intertwined in Proverbs, and it is difficult to discern the priority of one over the other. Just as wise and righteous character leads to knowledge, so it evidences the prior acquisition of knowledge. Fox's view, however, is more compelling because he accounts for wisdom as the fundamental category in the book,[18] although Ansberry

---

practical faculty that enabled a person to live successfully. It is not until the lectures of Prov 1–9 that wisdom and righteousness are conflated such that wisdom encompasses moral virtue.

[15] Christopher B. Ansberry, "What Does Jerusalem Have to Do with Athens? The Moral Vision of the Book of Proverbs and Aristotle's *Nicomachean Ethics*," *HS* 51 (2010): 161. Ansberry argues that this dynamic is especially evident in the sentence literature. He argues that the polarities of righteous/wise and wicked/fool are co-referential; each pair of terms has the same referent, but not the same meaning. The combination of these moral and intellectual traits in a person "suggests that the moral vision of Proverbs is comparable to the ethical theory of Aristotle, for both identify the necessity of moral character and practical wisdom for virtuous behavior" (ibid., 162).

[16] Ibid., 164.

[17] Ibid. He explains: "the ignorance of these personages is not attributed to their intellectual aptitude; rather it is associated with their moral character, which perverts their reason" (ibid.). Ansberry argues that the אֱוִיל delights in evil (10:23), hates discipline and correction (15:5), and lacks self-control (12:16). The רָשָׁע is greedy (10:3), violent (10:6), deceitful (12:5), and cruel (12:10), and the לֵץ is arrogant and resists correction (14:6). These characters thus evidence perverse dispositions, not simply a lack of knowledge, he claims. But Ansberry does not prove that their disposition is anything other than the consequence of lack of knowledge. Ansberry notes that the arrogance of the לֵץ "prevents him from acquiring wisdom, even if he chooses to seek it" (ibid., 165), yet one could say that lack of knowledge is both the symptom and the cause of the scoffer's disease.

[18] It is hard to find an example in Proverbs in which a person clearly has knowledge yet does not act in accord with it, which would be the situation to discredit Fox's point. Fox could counter all of Ansberry's examples with the claim that the character's moral perversion arises from his lack of knowledge.

has a legitimate critique about aligning wisdom solely with knowledge and "intellectual aptitude."[19]

My analysis will not adjudicate Proverbs' precise relationship to classical models of virtue, but it may shed certain light on this debate in examining the diverse ways in which Proverbs conceptualizes character and the grounds of knowledge. This inquiry will also raise the significance of the diverse means of knowing in the book, including desiring, loving, hating, tasting, hearing, and even smelling. The emotions and the senses are important elements of knowledge in Proverbs; intellectual knowledge alone is not enough to make one wise; it must be accompanied by and displayed in one's right desires and emotions.

Finally, through its multifaceted means of formation, Proverbs indicates a more complex view of the human person than has often been acknowledged. One of the primary aims of this study is to consider the moral and intellectual assumptions of the book, particularly with reference to its view of the moral self. What does the way in which Proverbs conceptualizes character formation reveal about its understanding of human beings, including their nature, aptitude, and capacity for wisdom? Does it presume that the moral self – that is, the individual's capacity to think and to choose and to act in accord with moral reasoning or wisdom – is innate and develops by an internal aptitude or is amenable to external influence?[20] I will argue that Proverbs indicates that the moral self requires both the external influence of discipline and an innate receptivity to appropriate that discipline. Within Proverbs, the formation of the moral self is a function of the whole human person, a task of mind and heart.[21]

[19] Ansberry, "What Does Jerusalem Have to Do with Athens?" 165.
[20] For approaches to these kinds of questions, see Michael V. Fox "Who Can Learn? A Dispute in Ancient Pedagogy," in *Wisdom, You Are My Sister: Studies in Honor of Roland E. Murphy, O.Carm., on the Occasion of His Eightieth Birthday* (ed. Michael L. Barré; CBQMS 29; Washington, DC.: The Catholic Biblical Association of America, 1997), 62–77; Jacqueline E. Lapsley, *Can These Bones Live? The Problem of the Moral Self in the Book of Ezekiel* (BZAW 301; Berlin: Walter de Gruyter, 2000); Carol A. Newsom, "Models of the Moral Self: Hebrew Bible and Second Temple Judaism," *JBL* 131 (2012): 5–25.
[21] On this point, see Christine Roy Yoder, "The Shaping of Erotic Desire in Proverbs 1–9," in *Saving Desire: The Seduction of Christian Theology* (ed. J. Henriksen and L. Shults; Grand Rapids: Eerdmans, 2011), 148–62; see also Chapter 6 for further discussion and bibliography.

# PART I

# Character and Poetry

# CHAPTER 2

# Character Ethics and the Shaping of the Self

[T]he idea of character constitutes the unifying theme or center of the wisdom literature, whose raison d'être is to profile ethical character.[1]

Character is very much social in its constitution. It is inseparable from the culture within which it is found and formed. In significant ways, character reflects, even incarnates, the moral culture.[2]

Character incarnates the moral culture. That is, the concept of character displays certain values that a society privileges and its assumptions about what it means to be human. For this reason, the study of character is inevitably a study of the larger moral culture in which it is rooted. Accordingly, the book of Proverbs, a text infused with questions of character, provides a window into the moral culture of the sages who compiled it. How did they conceptualize character? How did they think it was best formed? What were the prospects and obstacles for the development of the moral self, in their view? While these questions are often not answered explicitly within the book – Proverbs is not a work of moral philosophy, strictly speaking – the book's rich reflections on character do illumine certain central assumptions about the human person and the nature of the self, as well as the potential and limits of character formation. The concept of character within Proverbs is inextricably tied to the moral culture of the sapiential tradition.

But what is the nature of the moral culture reflected in the book of Proverbs? And what method of inquiry would provide a lens through which to examine it? The character ethics approach provides one of the most fruitful avenues for exploring such questions. Informed in various

[1] William P. Brown, *Character in Crisis: A Fresh Approach to the Wisdom Literature of the Old Testament* (Grand Rapids: Eerdmans, 1996), 21.
[2] James Davison Hunter, *The Death of Character: Moral Education in an Age without Good or Evil* (New York: Basic Books, 2000), 15.

degrees by traditions in moral philosophy, literary criticism, and theological ethics, character ethics is an umbrella term that broadly refers to approaches that are interested in the moral claims of a text, its rhetorical strategies, and the ways in which it participates in the formation of character.

Character ethics has been a particularly important avenue of inquiry for wisdom literature. In his seminal 1996 study *Character in Crisis: A Fresh Approach to the Wisdom Literature of the Old Testament*, William P. Brown applied this approach to the Israelite wisdom tradition, offering new insight about the concept of the self in biblical literature. Brown used the lens of character ethics to reconcile the anthropocentric and theocentric poles of the wisdom tradition. Brown speaks of wisdom's anthropocentric framework of the self as moral agent and insists that "wisdom begins and ends with the self, in recognition that knowledge of God cannot be divorced from human knowledge of the self."[3] His approach starts with the anthropocentric notion of the individual's character but also incorporates a theocentric dimension, considering the self in relation to God and community. He argues that "to alter one's perspective of God and the world is to shape and reshape character, the goal of sapiential rhetoric."[4] Within Brown's approach, character ethics has both a literary and a moral dimension. He draws attention to the way in which the book intends to shape normative character through profiling paradigmatic literary characters – such as woman Wisdom, the strange woman, and the father – who act as either ideals of or foils for normative character. Brown also offers insight on the pedagogical process of Proverbs, which aims to cultivate discernment within the student by presenting "situationally oriented, open-ended sayings, designed to exercise one's mental and moral faculties and thereby enable the moral agent to size up ethically demanding situations and to act appropriately."[5] Thus, not only does he attend to identifying the virtues and the nature of character in the book, but he also draws attention to the didactic strategies of the text to inculcate desirable character in the student.

The nexus of character and creation in Israelite wisdom is the concept of wonder, Brown argues in the revised edition of *Character in Crisis*, entitled *Wisdom's Wonder: Character, Creation, and Crisis in the Bible's Wisdom Literature* (2014).[6] In this updated monograph, Brown insists that

[3] Brown, *Character in Crisis*, 3.
[4] Ibid., 8.
[5] Ibid., 14.
[6] William P. Brown, *Wisdom's Wonder: Character, Creation, and Crisis in the Bible's Wisdom Literature* (Grand Rapids: Eerdmans, 2014).

wonder – the emotion of awe that impels desire and discovery – is what animates the search for wisdom and the formation of character in each of the wisdom books. Wonder is a "bewildered curiosity" that encompasses both a disorienting perplexity and an insatiable desire to seek under-standing.[7] Even as it may be unsettling, wonder draws one close to the awe-inspiring object, and thus wonder "marks the awakening of desire, the desire to inquire and understand."[8] Brown draws attention to the pro-found role of emotion and desire in the formation of character and the direction of the will toward wise ends.

Yet not all scholars find the character ethics approach befitting to bib-lical literature and Proverbs, in particular. John Barton, for one, is sus-picious of the degree to which the Hebrew Bible operates with notions of virtue and character that are central to most articulations of the char-acter ethics approach.[9] The character ethics approach is largely informed by virtue ethics, the branch of moral philosophy that is concerned with the question of how one ought to live. It is rooted in Aristotle's discus-sion of the nature of virtue as an acquired condition of character, achieved through both instruction and habit.[10] The role of character formation is thus emphasized in virtue ethics because the development of a person's practical wisdom (*phronesis*) requires not only absorbing the content of instruction but also developing a reflective capacity to understand the reasons for action.[11] Yet Barton argues that both the legal and wisdom traditions in the Hebrew Bible are less interested in particular moral dis-positions that inform continual decision making than they are in present-ing static moral types. He states: "Ethical choice is a once-for-all affair which sets one's feet either on the way to life or on the way to death: there are no half-measures. This does not seem to me very like what a virtue

---

[7] Ibid., 20–21.

[8] Ibid., 23.

[9] See John Barton, *Understanding Old Testament Ethics: Approaches and Explanations* (Louisville: Westminster John Knox, 2003), 65–74.

[10] Aristotle, *Nicomachean Ethics* (trans. Roger Crisp; Cambridge: Cambridge University Press, 2000), 1103a [23]. In *Nicomachean Ethics*, Aristotle defines virtue as "a mean between two vices, one of excess, the other of deficiency" (ibid., 1107a [31]).

[11] Julia Annas explains: "In classical virtue ethics, we start our moral education by learning from others, both in making particular judgments about right and wrong, and in adopting some people as role models or teachers following certain rules. At first, as pupils, we adopt these views because we were told to, or they seemed obvious, and we acquire a collection of moral views that are fragmented and accepted on the authority of others. For virtue ethics, the purpose of good moral education is to get the pupil to think for himself about the reasons on which he acts, and so the content of what he has been taught" (Julia Annas, "Virtue Ethics," in *The Oxford Handbook of Ethical Theory* [ed. David Copp; New York: Oxford University Press, 2007], 517).

ethic is asserting about human character."[12] Barton claims that the notion of moral formation is foreign to the Hebrew Bible, asserting that "Hebrew culture differs from Greek on precisely this issue: the Hebrew Bible does not operate with any idea that one can grow in virtue but sees virtue as something one either has or lacks."[13] To the contrary, he finds that "[w]hat the Bible thinks about is not moral progress but *conversion*,"[14] citing the mandates in the prophets and other texts to turn from one's sin. This, he suggests, is opposed to the idea of incremental progress toward virtue that is the concern of virtue ethics. Furthermore, Barton insists that the Bible presents a norm-bound ethics based on divine law, which is more akin to a deontological than a virtue-based ethic. Its moral vision, then, is not about living virtuously, but rather law obedience as a moral obligation.[15]

Barton's critique is particularly strident with respect to the book of Proverbs, one of his main exemplars of the alleged disconnect between virtue ethics and the biblical text. Barton argues that character and moral decisions informed by character are not of concern to biblical wisdom literature. Instead, he thinks wisdom views moral dispositions as innate and predetermined. Consequently, there is no process of moral decision making or need for moral formation. Barton argues that one's acts and decisions are predicated on one's given disposition, and while the text describes these dispositions, its aim is not to cultivate a greater degree of virtue in a person. He asserts, "there are no Laodicean moralists in the Wisdom literature. Everyone is either good or bad, wise or foolish. Living the good life appears to be an absolute, with no gradations or variations."[16]

At first glance, Proverbs may appear to confirm Barton's analysis. It does present the wise and the foolish as two opposing perspectives. However, although an underlying sense of order and coherence rooted in binary oppositions does pervade the book, Proverbs does not proclaim a set of rigid moral axioms, but instead presents a host of scenarios indicating that experience does not always align with idealized order. Accordingly, the book is very much interested in gradations, variations, and the particularity of moral decision making. Moreover, its overt aim is to cultivate greater degrees of virtue in the student, preparing him to make wise decisions in a variety of situations. No matter the advanced state of the sage,

---

[12] Barton, *Understanding Old Testament Ethics*, 67. Barton cites as evidence of his position the "two-ways" tradition in biblical and post-biblical texts (e.g., Deut 30:15; Ps 1; the *Didache*).
[13] Ibid., 67.
[14] Ibid., 68; emphasis in original.
[15] Ibid., 70.
[16] Ibid., 67.

one never fully possesses wisdom, which is the concept that subsumes all virtues in Proverbs.[17] One is always on the path to wisdom, never having finally arrived.[18] It is therefore quite possible to make progress in the development of moral character, and, in fact, such progress is of critical importance precisely because of the nature of moral character – it is not innate and given but must be acquired and cultivated. For this reason, discipline is a central motif in the book. Fools can indeed make progress toward wisdom, but not unless they submit themselves to discipline.[19] Barton posits that "the Old Testament Wisdom literature ... seems to me to inhabit a cruder world of thought, where character is indeed all important but is seen as fixed and unchanging, almost at times as predetermined."[20] To the contrary, however, instruction is so important in Proverbs because character can and must be cultivated, and this is why the character ethics approach is such a helpful resource for reading the book of Proverbs.

## Character Ethics and Biblical Studies

In recent years, a flurry of scholarship in biblical studies has attended to the interface between character, community, and ethics in the biblical text. In the history of biblical studies, ethics has often been a subject of limited interest to scholars. In fact, Cyril S. Rodd relates that in the 1950s, he was warned that there was no future in the subject of Old Testament ethics![21] While earlier forays into the subject of ethical analysis of biblical texts

---

[17] See Michael V. Fox, *Proverbs 10–31: A New Translation with Introduction and Commentary* (AB 18B; New Haven: Yale University Press, 2009), 942. For a discussion of the relationship between wisdom and virtue, see chapter 1.

[18] Contra Barton, who proclaims: "There is no doubt that, taken at face value, Proverbs eschews most ideas of moral progress" (Barton, *Understanding Old Testament Ethics*, 67). Note that the parental voice of Proverbs constantly implores the student to pursue wisdom (e.g., 2:1–5).

[19] Barton's comment that there is no guidance in the Bible "on many virtues such as humility, gentleness, or forbearance" (ibid., 69) is quite curious in this regard. Proverbs repeatedly talks about the requisite disposition of the student so that he may gain wisdom, and humility in particular is of vital importance if he is to submit himself to the discipline and instruction of the parent (e.g., 4:1; 15:5; 19:20).

[20] Ibid., 67. Barton may be overly influenced by the legal material in his discussion of the ethics in wisdom literature. He draws the broad conclusion that "the general style of Old Testament ethics is that in certain areas life is closely regulated by divine decree so that human freedom to explore moral possibilities is fiercely circumscribed" (ibid., 69). While this may be a more defensible claim with regard to the law, Proverbs presents a far different case. Indeed, the book is built around exploring different "moral possibilities" as it presents various situations, character profiles, and speaking voices. To be sure, it sanctions certain actions and rejects others. Yet it builds its case not by divine fiat, but by presenting a diverse array of situations that forces the student to determine the wisest outcome by considering multiple courses of action. For example, see the discussion in chapter 7 of the function of presenting alternative viewpoints for the cultivation of the student's imagination.

[21] Cyril S. Rodd, *Glimpses of a Strange Land: Studies in Old Testament Ethics* (OTS; Edinburgh: T&T Clark, 2001), ix.

tended to emphasize the role of law obedience or general moral codes,[22] its most recent manifestation in the field represents a shift toward articulating the particularity of various texts, narratives, characters, virtues, and visions of the moral world.[23] There is no singular method that unites works of this approach. Indeed, scholars who profess an interest in character ethics employ a variety of methods with a variety of genres of text. As Brown notes, the character ethics approach is "more a shared outlook than an established methodology."[24] And in fact, the extent of the shared outlook is broad indeed. Some of these works have been rather comprehensive in scope, seeking the contours of ethical reflection across the canon. For example, Bruce Birch emphasizes the moral function of the canonical narrative for contemporary Christian communities in *Let Justice Roll Down: The Old Testament, Ethics, and the Christian Life*.[25] In *Old Testament Ethics: A Paradigmatic*

[22] The earliest comprehensive work of "Old Testament ethics" was Johannes Hempel, *Das Ethos des Alten Testaments* (BZAW 67; Berlin: Verlag von Alfred Töpelmann, 1938; 2nd ed., 1964). Hempel argued that there were diverse ethical traditions in Israel, from the norms of semi-nomadic peasants and city-dwellers conveyed in various customs to those of the tribal confederation enshrined in the legal code and the concept of covenant. He traced the diachronic development of such traditions and suggested that one can see a general movement from a collective social outlook to greater emphasis on the individual's duty of religious obligation, moral decision making, and personal responsibility. See also Johannes Hempel, *Gott und Mensch im Alten Testament* (BWANT 3.2; Stuttgart: Kohlhammer, 1926); idem, "Ethics in the OT," *IDB* 2:153–61. Walther Eichrodt also commented thoroughly on ethics in his *Theology of the Old Testament* (trans. J. A. Baker; 2 vols.; OTL; Philadelphia: Westminster, 1967), 2:316–79, in which he argued that Israel's ethical norms were guided ultimately by religious belief in God, but also by a popular morality rooted in society and historical experience. See also his *Man in the Old Testament* (trans. K. and R. Gregor Smith; SBT; London: SCM Press, 1951; repr. 1959). Common to these approaches is an interest in delineating an ethical system, a conviction that one can discern some central principle(s) shared by the diverse texts of the Bible, as well as diachronic analysis that seeks to trace the development of such principles over time. Hempel and Eichrodt were, of course, certainly not the first to ponder the relationship between the biblical text and ethics. In both the Jewish and Christian interpretive traditions, the Bible has long served as a normative source of ethical reflection. For example, in the Protestant tradition, John Calvin highlighted the primary import of biblical law as its function to guide and train one morally.

[23] Those who decidedly oppose any attempt to systematize or define an "Old Testament ethic" include Barton, who is no less optimistic about the prospects for Old Testament ethics despite rejecting the possibility of drawing systematic or comprehensive conclusions (John Barton, *Ethics and the Old Testament* [Harrisburg: Trinity Press International, 1998]; idem, *Understanding Old Testament Ethics*), and Rodd, who insists that "the presentation of the ethics within a systematic frame distorts the ethics themselves" (Rodd, *Glimpses of a Strange Land*, 3). Rodd argues that if "Old Testament ethics is to be viewed as a living reality these features must not be concealed under a general principle or abstract pattern" (ibid.). The most one can hope for, Rodd offers, is "glimpses of occasional features of Old Testament ethics" (ibid., 4), and thus his book is organized by independent chapters that do not produce a systematic whole or diachronic survey. See also John Rogerson, *Theory and Practice in Old Testament Ethics* (ed. M. Daniel Carroll R.; JSOTSup 405; New York: T&T Clark, 2004).

[24] William P. Brown, ed., *Character and Scripture: Moral Formation, Community, and Biblical Interpretation* (Grand Rapids: Eerdmans, 2002), xi.

[25] Bruce Birch, *Let Justice Roll Down: The Old Testament, Ethics, and the Christian Life* (Louisville: Westminster John Knox, 1991; see also Bruce Birch and Larry Rasmussen, *Bible and Ethics in the Christian Life* (rev. ed.; Minneapolis: Augsburg, 1989).

*Approach,* Waldemar Janzen presents various ethical paradigms within the Bible, working from the starting point of paradigmatic characters developed in biblical narratives.[26] While he eschews a rigid systemization of the canon, he in effect seeks to account for the biblical text as a cohesive entity.[27] Similarly, Christopher J. H. Wright avoids a rigid system, organizing thematically his study *Old Testament Ethics for the People of God.*[28] However, he suggests that the "ethical triangle" of God, Israel, and the land constitutes "the three pillars of Israel's worldview, the primary factors of their theology and ethics,"[29] which functions as a kind of organizational system for his understanding of ethics in the Bible. In New Testament studies, Richard B. Hays's *The Moral Vision of the New Testament: Community, Cross, New Creation: A Contemporary Introduction to New Testament Ethics* stands out as a work that offers descriptive evaluation of character, community, and the moral life across the New Testament canon, as well as prescriptive conclusions about contemporary ethical issues.[30]

At the same time, other studies under the character ethics umbrella have consciously avoided making comprehensive claims, instead attending to the interface of character and the moral life in a particular book, tradition, or text. Jacqueline E. Lapsley, for example, studies the tension between two visions of the moral self in Ezekiel in *Can These Bones Live? The Problem of the Moral Self in the Book of Ezekiel.*[31] Gordon J. Wenham attends to the ethical implications of narrative in the books of Genesis and Judges in *Story as Torah: Reading the Old Testament Ethically.*[32] Numerous essays have focused on the formation of character, the ethics of reading, or visions of the good in discrete texts.[33]

What unites these diverse works is an interest, however broadly defined, in the moral claims that a text makes, the way in which those

---

[26] Waldemar Janzen, *Old Testament Ethics: A Paradigmatic Approach* (Louisville: Westminster John Knox, 1994).

[27] Janzen's final chapter discusses the connection between the Old Testament paradigms and the "paradigm of Jesus."

[28] Christopher J. H. Wright, *Old Testament Ethics for the People of God* (Downers Grove, IL: InterVarsity Press, 2004).

[29] Ibid., 19.

[30] Richard B. Hays, *The Moral Vision of the New Testament: Community, Cross, New Creation: A Contemporary Introduction to New Testament Ethics* (New York: HarperCollins, 1996).

[31] Jacqueline E. Lapsley, *Can These Bones Live? The Problem of the Moral Self in the Book of Ezekiel* (BZAW 301; Berlin: Walter de Gruyter, 2000).

[32] Gordon J. Wenham, *Story as Torah: Reading the Old Testament Ethically* (OTS; Edinburgh: T&T Clark, 2000).

[33] For example, see the essays in Brown, *Character and Scripture,* and M. Daniel Carroll R. and Jacqueline E. Lapsley, eds., *Character Ethics and the Old Testament: Moral Dimensions of Scripture* (Louisville: Westminster John Knox, 2007).

claims are developed through the rhetorical devices of the literature, and how those claims impinge on the formation of character. For some scholars, this is a largely descriptive task that centers on the ancient world, while for others it has implications for contemporary communities of faith. Thus Hays states of his own work that "the goal of this entire project is to encourage the church in its efforts to become a scripture-shaped community, to allow its life to be more fitly conformed to the stories narrated in the New Testament."[34] Lapsley's conclusions, on the other hand, primarily contribute to a greater understanding of the conceptions about selfhood in ancient Israel. Whatever the scope of inquiry or the trajectory of their conclusions, the diverse works of character ethics have proven to be a fruitful avenue of research in biblical studies, prompting new attention to the relationship between literature, character, and ethical reflection.

Part of the reason that there is such diversity among character ethics approaches within biblical studies is that these works are informed differently by various theoretical, philosophical, and theological frameworks. Some are tied closely to moral philosophy. Influential in this regard has been Alasdair MacIntyre's work *After Virtue: A Study in Moral Theory*, which argued that the language of contemporary moral philosophy was bankrupt, having come unmoored from its historical foundations.[35] MacIntyre called for a return to the Aristotelian tradition as a helpful alternative in articulating the nature of morality,[36] and his conception of virtue and selfhood has in many ways framed the conversation about moral selfhood in biblical studies and beyond.[37] Theologian Stanley Hauerwas has also had enormous influence on the scope of character ethics within biblical studies. Like MacIntyre, he draws upon Aristotle's conceptions of

---

[34] Hays, *The Moral Vision of the New Testament*, 463.

[35] Alasdair MacIntyre, *After Virtue: A Study in Moral Theory* (2nd ed.; Notre Dame: University of Notre Dame Press, 1984).

[36] Nussbaum questions the extent to which MacIntyre's notions cohere with Aristotle, however. She argues that MacIntyre downplays the role of reason and ignores the centrality of deliberation and reflection in Aristotle's thought. For this reason, she describes MacIntyre as "a neo-Aristotelian of a very peculiar stripe, one who does not really approve of some of the central aspects of Aristotle's thought" (Martha C. Nussbaum, "Virtue Ethics: A Misleading Category?" *The Journal of Ethics* 3.3 [1999]: 197–98). See also Nussbaum's critique of MacIntyre's reading of Aristotle in his later monograph (Martha C. Nussbaum, "Recoiling from Reason" [review of Alasdair MacIntyre, *Whose Justice? Which Rationality?*], *New York Review of Books*, December 7, 1989).

[37] See, for example, M. Daniel Carroll R., "'He Has Told You What Is Good': Moral Formation in Micah," in *Character Ethics and the Old Testament: Moral Dimensions of Scripture* (ed. M. Daniel Carroll R. and Jacqueline E. Lapsley; Louisville: Westminster John Knox, 2007), 103–18. Carroll R. cites MacIntyre's work frequently and finds MacIntyre's analysis of the role of practices and competing visions of justice in a society to be particularly illuminating for the book of Micah.

virtue to construct his own account of character and moral rationality. Hauerwas is particularly interested in the social and theological context of the Christian church, and his numerous scholarly works explore the formative nature of narrative within Christian community.[38] He argues that the church is a community that lives by the stories of the Gospel, telling them not only to give rationale to its members' actions, but to help them live in a manner congruent with its values. Hauerwas insists that "[w]e cannot account for our moral life solely by the decisions we make; we also need the narrative that forms us to have one kind of character rather than another."[39] Hauerwas has been particularly influential in pressing the interrelationship between character, community, and narrative, that is, the stories that a community tells about itself. His impact is clear in the work of Hays and Brown, who attend to the narrative scope of biblical traditions and their relation to ancient and modern communities. Finally, many character ethics approaches are also influenced by narrative ethics, which attends to the interface between particular texts of narrative fiction and the virtues that they endorse and cultivate. Here Martha C. Nussbaum and Wayne C. Booth have been instrumental in the work of many biblical scholars who bring together literary and ethical criticism in the evaluation of ancient texts.[40]

---

[38] See, for example, Stanley Hauerwas, *Character and the Christian Life: A Study in Theological Ethics* (San Antonio, TX: Trinity University Press, 1975; repr. 1985); idem, *A Community of Character: Toward a Constructive Christian Social Ethic* (Notre Dame: University of Notre Dame Press, 1981); and Stanley Hauerwas with Richard Bondi and David B. Burrell, *Truthfulness and Tragedy: Further Investigations in Christian Ethics* (Notre Dame: University of Notre Dame Press, 1977).

[39] Stanley Hauerwas with David B. Burrell, "From System to Story: An Alternative Pattern for Rationality in Ethics," in Hauerwas et al., *Truthfulness and Tragedy*, 20. Richard Bondi argues that Hauerwas does not go far enough in establishing the link between character and narrative. Bondi thus offers a more thorough phenomenology of the self as he insists that "the proper topic of the language of character is the self in relation to the world" (Richard Bondi, "The Elements of Character," *JRE* 12.2 [1984]: 212). Bondi insists that such a phenomenology of the self must be accompanied by a "phenomenology of storytelling in community" because the stories of a community – not only the normative story but also the stories of various individuals within the community – guide how the self is formed in relation to its social context. "Looking at where and how stories are told in a given community," he explains, "gives us a way to see the role both of stories and of the various members of the community in the formation of character" (ibid., 212–13). Such is the task of character ethics, according to Bondi.

[40] See Wayne C. Booth, *The Company We Keep: An Ethics of Fiction* (Berkeley: University of California Press, 1988); Martha C. Nussbaum, *Love's Knowledge: Essays on Philosophy and Literature* (New York: Oxford University Press, 1990); idem, *Upheavals of Thought: The Intelligence of Emotions* (Cambridge: Cambridge University Press, 2001). For a brief analysis of Nussbaum's work and its relevance for biblical studies, see John Barton, "Reading for Life: The Use of the Bible in Ethics and the Work of Martha C. Nussbaum," in *The Bible in Ethics: The Second Sheffield Colloquium* (ed. John Rogerson, et al.; JSOTSup 207; Sheffield: Sheffield Academic Press, 1995), 66–76.

## Character Ethics and Narrative

Character ethics in its many forms in biblical studies privileges the concept of narrative, and the thread of narrative that runs through most of these studies is a legacy of the works in moral philosophy and theological ethics by which they are informed. While the term narrative can imply many different things, it is a central conceptual category whose implicit assumptions often remain unexpressed. For example, within the work of Nussbaum and Booth, "narrative" refers to a work of literature. It is the subject of study that merits both literary and ethical analysis, including narrative fiction but also poetry and drama.[41] For Hauerwas and MacIntyre, the concept of narrative has broader implications, for they argue that narrative is a fundamental feature of character itself and the comprehension of human action.

Whether construed as a form of literature or a model of selfhood, the concept of narrative shapes the character ethics approach in significant ways. It informs many underlying assumptions about the construction of the moral self. The book of Proverbs, however, raises a question about the adequacy of these concepts of narrative. It provides a counterpoint to the way in which Hauerwas and MacIntyre understand selfhood, and its literary form also calls attention to the distinctive literary function of poetry, which has a different mode of developing a concept of character and a different role in the shaping of the self than a narrative text. But before turning to the distinctiveness of Proverbs, we must examine the significance of narrative for the concept of selfhood.

### Narrative and Selfhood

Narrative is such a pervasive concept within moral philosophy and theological ethics because it is fundamental to how many thinkers understand the nature of character. For MacIntyre, the concept of narrative is a cipher for the intelligibility of the self. Selfhood, he states, is "a concept of a self

---

[41] Both Booth and Nussbaum do consider poetic texts in some capacity (see Wayne C. Booth, "Ethics and Criticism" in *The New Princeton Encyclopedia of Poetry and Poetics* [ed. A. Preminger and T.V.F. Brogan; New York: MJF Books, 1993], 384–86; Nussbaum, *Upheavals of Thought*, especially chapters 12 and 15 on Dante and Walt Whitman, respectively), though they are less interested in the technical features of the poetry than the larger story contained in the poetic form. Nussbaum, for example, argues that the emotions have a cognitive dimension that is "in part narrative in form, involving a story of our relation to cherished objects that extends over time.... This, in turn, suggests that in order to talk well about them we will need to turn to texts that contain a narrative dimension, thus deepening and refining our grasp of ourselves as beings with a complicated temporal history" (ibid., 2–3).

whose unity resides in the unity of a narrative which links birth to life to death as narrative beginning to middle to end."[42] Furthermore, he insists that "[n]arrative history of a certain kind turns out to be the basic and essential genre for the characterization of human actions."[43] MacIntyre argues that human action can only be adequately understood in light of the person's intentions, which are revealed through her personal narrative and the narratives of the communities of which she is a part. MacIntyre aims to refute a view common in philosophical circles that separates individual human actions from their larger contexts. To the contrary, he asserts that actions are only intelligible as part of narrative settings.

According to MacIntyre, the self is the subject of a narrative. "Thus personal identity," he explains, "is just that identity presupposed by the unity of the character which the unity of a narrative requires. Without such unity there would not be subjects of whom stories could be told."[44] In other words, character is intelligible by the larger narrative in which it takes shape. Moreover, the self is also a part of the narratives of others, for "[t]he narrative of any one life is part of an interlocking set of narratives."[45] In this way, one can hold others to account, even as others can hold him to account, and this dynamic interaction further supports the creation of narratives. As MacIntyre explains, "this asking for and giving of accounts itself plays an important part in constituting narratives."[46]

Central to MacIntyre's conception of narrative is a temporal sequence in which meaning arises from the connection between events and the orientation toward a particular end or *telos*. Thus "narrative" for MacIntyre takes on an even more specific iteration as a particular kind of plot – a quest. He explains: "[t]he unity of a human life is the unity of a narrative quest. Quests sometimes fail, are frustrated, abandoned, or dissipated into distractions; and human lives may in all these ways also fail. But the only criteria for success or failure in a human life as a whole are the criteria of success or failure in a narrated or to-be-narrated quest."[47] This quest is oriented toward the *telos* of the good.

Thus, MacIntyre views character through the lens of narrative plot, insisting that the unity of a person's character is only visible in the unity of a narrative, from beginning to middle to end. MacIntyre is rebutting what

[42] MacIntyre, *After Virtue*, 205.
[43] Ibid., 208.
[44] Ibid., 218.
[45] Ibid.
[46] Ibid.
[47] Ibid., 219.

he finds to be a deficiency in a certain type of individualism in which one's actions are unconnected to any sense of self or in which the individual is not connected to larger communities. MacIntyre insists, to the contrary, that character is inevitably embedded in the narrative trajectory of a person's life and in the narrative(s) of the community of which that person is a part. He argues that this notion is central to the Aristotelian conception of virtue, for the virtues are exercised not in episodic situations but in the unity of a person's life, ultimately directed toward the *telos* of the good. As he explains, "the liquidation of the self into a set of demarcated areas of role-playing allows no scope for the exercise of dispositions which could genuinely be accounted virtues in any sense remotely Aristotelian. For a virtue is not a disposition that makes for success only in some particular type of situation."[48] For MacIntyre, narrative is vital to his conception of selfhood. It is temporal and organized by a causal plot. Actions are only intelligible as part of a larger narrative sequence. Consequently, one must tell stories about oneself and evaluate the stories of others in order to reach understanding. In this sense, narrative is an evaluative category for character.

One of the primary critiques of MacIntyre's approach is the varied ways in which he employs the concept of narrative. According to L. Gregory Jones, MacIntyre operates with multiple definitions of narrative, not all of which are consistent with one another.[49] Jones delineates at least seven distinct uses of the concept of narrative within *After Virtue*, including as a sense of self, the stories and texts that a self or community tell about themselves, and as a larger epistemological claim about the construction of moral traditions. Even as he draws attention to certain inconsistencies in MacIntyre's claims, Jones consents to the core of MacIntyre's argument that there is a narrative quality to human life that is morally significant. This notion, Jones points out, is dependent upon a particular understanding of historicity that is oriented toward a *telos*, which MacIntyre believes is fundamental to making sense of human life and also presupposes a normative tradition that provides such a *telos*.[50]

Hauerwas, who builds upon MacIntyre's work, likewise emphasizes narrative as a vital conceptual category for rationality and personhood. In an essay written with David B. Burrell, Hauerwas indicates that character only takes on meaning in narrative. This is because "character is

---

[48] Ibid., 205.
[49] L. Gregory Jones, "Alasdair MacIntyre on Narrative, Community, and the Moral Life," *Modern Theology* 4 (1987): 53–69.
[50] Ibid., 57.

the cumulative source of human actions. Stories themselves attempt to probe that source and discover its inner structure by trying to display how human actions and passions connect with one another to develop a character."[51] Hauerwas and Burrell are responding to a trend in moral philosophy that they find disturbing. They argue that the "standard account of moral rationality," which seeks objectivity in moral judgments, is inadequate because it places too much emphasis on particular decisions or moral quandaries and separates the moral agent from his very self.[52] Contrary to this view, they insist that "[i]t is exactly the category of narrative that helps us to see that we are not forced to choose between some universal standpoint and the subjectivistic appeals to our own experience. For our experiences always come in the form of narratives that can be checked against themselves as well as against others' experiences."[53] Echoing MacIntyre, Hauerwas and Burrell argue that one's selfhood is shaped through narrative, "for I have learned to understand my life from the stories I have learned from others."[54]

For Hauerwas, the term narrative conveys "a connection among elements (actions, events, situations) which is neither one of logical consequence nor one of mere sequence. The connection seems rather designed to move our understanding of a situation forward by developing or unfolding it."[55] That is, "[i]t is not the mere material connection of happenings to one individual, but the connected unfolding that we call *plot*."[56] Moreover, the plot structure of narrative makes it particularly apt to capture the essence of character. Thus, for Hauerwas and Burrell "[i]t is that ordering [of narrative], that capacity to unfold or develop character, and thus offer insight into the human conditions, which recommends narrative as a form of rationality especially appropriate to ethics."[57] In their analysis, narrative is a particular plot structure that is a mode of rationality, a way of making sense of character and human experience.

For both Hauerwas and MacIntyre, narrative does much conceptual work for their understanding of character and personhood. So much so, in fact, that they both make exclusive claims for narrative as the defining form of selfhood. Thus MacIntyre insists that "narrative history of a certain kind turns out to be the basic and essential genre for the characterization

---

[51] Hauerwas and Burrell, "From System to Story," 29.

[52] Ibid., 18, 24.

[53] Ibid., 21.

[54] Ibid.

[55] Ibid., 28.

[56] Ibid.

[57] Ibid., 30.

of human actions."[58] Hauerwas similarly concludes: "character and moral notions *only* take on meaning in narrative."[59]

However, not all traditions share the notion that human life *qua* human life is fundamentally narrative. Jones points out that, for example, traditions with a cyclical view of time, such as Hinduism, would likely qualify or reject the notion that human life is narrative.[60] A tradition that believes in reincarnation would not see death as a narrative end. Some cultures may not relate their lives through the medium of narrative. As one example, Jones cites the work of anthropologist Renato Rosaldo, who reported great difficulty in eliciting life stories from members of the Ilongot tribe that he was studying, concluding that members of the group were not "accustomed to telling stories in any form."[61]

The Hebrew Bible provides a helpful point of reference in this conversation, for it contains different models of selfhood, not all of which are narrative in scope. Within Proverbs, for example, character is not fundamentally conceptualized by the unity of a linear narrative plot. To the contrary, the construction of character emerges in discrete episodes. Its coherency is evidenced by responses in particular situations, not from its place in a larger linear frame. In both its short sayings and longer poems, the book presents character in situations that are usually disconnected to any larger plot or sequence of events. The way in which Proverbs conceptualizes selfhood, which will be explored in Part II, is closely connected to its non-narrative literary form, and here too the book stands to make a substantial contribution to the character ethics conversation.

### Narrative and Literature

One of the essential insights of character ethics approaches is that literary form is closely tied to rhetorical function, and on this point, too, the influence of a concept of narrative runs deeply through the work of prominent thinkers who have influenced biblical studies. Nussbaum and Booth, among others, have drawn attention to the ability of literature to shape character in a particular way. Nussbaum observes that "literary forms call forth certain specific sorts of practical activity in the reader that can be

---

[58] MacIntyre, *After Virtue*, 208.
[59] Hauerwas, "From System to Story," 15; emphasis added.
[60] Jones, "MacIntyre on Narrative," 58.
[61] Ibid., 58; see Renato Rosaldo, "The Story of Tukbaw: 'They listen as He Orates,'" in *The Biographical Process: Studies in the History and Psychology of Religion* (eds., Frank E. Reynolds and Donald Capps; The Hague: Mouton Publishers, 1976), 121–22.

evoked in no other way..., as Proust insists, a certain sort of self-scrutiny requires a certain sort of text, namely a narrative text, for its evocation."[62] For this reason, Nussbaum finds moral philosophy, when it attends to philosophical writing alone, inadequate to account for the full range of human personal and social life. Abstract and emotionless philosophical writing, she notes, calls up "a correspondingly narrow range of responses and activities in the reader."[63] On the other hand, works of narrative fiction depict a range of emotional and cognitive activities and accordingly shape them in the reader. "Narratives are constructs that respond to certain patterns of living and shape them in their turn," she explains. "So we must always ask what content the literary forms themselves express, what structures of desire they represent and evoke."[64] Consequently, Nussbaum insists that literary form and content are inseparable; one must attend to both in order to understand the import of the text. In her various works, Nussbaum considers a variety of narrative fictions and explores the link between their aesthetic forms and the desires, emotions, and virtues that they ensconce in the reader.

Similarly, Booth argues that narrative fiction implants or reinforces certain patterns of desire within the reader, for insofar as the reader continues to turn the page and read more of the book, she seeks more of what is offered. "We acquire, from the stories we are told," he insists, "a 'desire to become a different kind of desirer,'"[65] and in this way, literature transforms the reader, at least for the time she spends with the book, into one who desires what it presents.[66] Booth uses the metaphor of friendship to speak of the relationship between literature and its readers. He suggests that all narratives offer a particular kind of friendship to their readers, whether a friendship simply of pleasure, of profit or gain for one of the parties, or as a good in its own right, irrespective of pleasure or profit.[67] The task of the ethical critic is to determine the kind of friendship a narrative offers and whether that friendship will be helpful or harmful to the reader, asking of literature, "Do you, my would-be friend, wish *me* well,

[62] Martha C. Nussbaum, "Narrative Emotions: Beckett's Genealogy of Love," *Ethics* 98.2 (1988): 229.
[63] Ibid.
[64] Ibid., 252–53.
[65] Booth, *The Company We Keep*, 272.
[66] For example, Booth demonstrates how the multitude of philosophical allusions within James Joyce's *Ulysses* make the reader want to be one who readily understands the allusions and possesses knowledge equal to the narrator. Moreover, the narrative does not simply make one aspire to think like a philosopher, but for the duration of the narrative the reader actually becomes one who does think as a philosopher, for she is "being steered through a course that in fact constitutes a stream of philosophical consciousness" (ibid., 275).
[67] Ibid., 173.

or will you be the only one to profit if I join you?"[68] Ethical criticism, Booth explains, consists of "any effort to show how the virtues of narratives relate to the virtues of selves and societies, or how the ethos of any story affects or is affected by the ethos – the collection of virtues – of any given reader."[69] Booth suggests that every narrative contains the potential to shape the reader after its own desires, which is why engaging the "friendship" of a particular narrative can be helpful or harmful to the reader, for the way in which the ethos of the narrative shapes the ethos of the reader can have implications for the reader's character in her life beyond the story. He explains:

> Whenever we embrace the patterns of desire of any narrative ... we become figured, not only by the specific figures of thought and figures of speech that a given world entails ... but more profoundly by cumulative inter-relationships of figurings that make up the temporal narrative experience itself. It transforms (distorts, twists, figures) the life we might have lived during the hours we spend with the narrative, and it thus becomes a *substitute* for – or, better, a replacement of, and consequently a radical criticism of – that unlived life.[70]

In the work of Booth and Nussbaum, the concept of narrative refers to forms of literature that shape readers in particular ways. In their perspective, literature is equally an art form and a moral force in the formation of character.

Here again, the book of Proverbs offers an engaging conversation partner, for its literary form is central to its function of character formation. Booth and Nussbaum consider a broad array of literature under the designation "narrative." However, as literary genres, narrative and poetry operate with different tools and, consequently, convey meaning differently. A significant shortcoming of much scholarship on character ethics, both within and outside of biblical studies, has been an oversight of the unique contributions of poetry to the formation of readers. With respect to the book of Proverbs specifically, neglecting the poetic form causes one to miss the effect of the text's literary artistry upon the formation of the student. It is precisely in and through its poetry that Proverbs forms the student, as will be argued extensively in Part II.

---

[68] Ibid., 178.
[69] Ibid., 11. Booth defines virtue as "the whole range of human 'powers,' 'strengths,' 'capacities,' or 'habits of behavior'" (ibid., 10). By his understanding, virtue does not necessarily imply a positive moral judgment. He defines ethos simply as an individual's character or "collection of habitual characteristics" (ibid., 8).
[70] Ibid., 339.

Both the narrative model of selfhood and the attention to the narrative features of literature have influenced approaches to character ethics within biblical scholarship. In particular, the concept of narrative has shaped the conclusions that many biblical scholars have drawn about the book of Proverbs and the wisdom tradition, more broadly. Brown, for example, suggests that Proverbs is characterized by a meta-narrative in which the character of the silent son is schooled in his home by the father in chapters 1–9, leaves the confines of home to enter the "winding alleyways of public engagement in the larger community,"[71] represented by the proverbial sayings in chapters 10–29, and finally returns home having found the ideal wife (31:10–31). Thus he finds that "the narratival shape of Proverbs fleshes out, socially and ethically, the primordial journey of the male from child to adult as he finds union with his mate."[72] Brown does acknowledge that Proverbs is not a narrative in literary form, and he takes issue with the character ethics of Hauerwas in precisely this regard. Brown explains that "for Hauerwas, the very formation of character involves the self's integration into a particular narrative."[73] Brown critiques Hauerwas on the grounds that character formation is more complex. "It is a reductive mistake," he insists, "to identify that which shapes character as a specific genre, let alone the *only* genre."[74]

Yet even though Brown is correct to push Hauerwas on this point, his work does not entirely move away from a narrative structure, and there are several problems with this narrative scheme. First, the literary form of the book is poetry, not prose. Although the longer poems in chapters 1–9 do include some narratival elements, as a whole they do not follow a linear narrative pattern.[75] Moreover, it is not clear that the character of the son is any more or less wise by the end of chapter 9, and his character does not reappear explicitly at the end of the book. Proverbs does not operate with a narrative scheme. Its poetic form, though not without narrative elements, does not privilege the typical tools of narrative, such as a linear plot, extensive development of literary characters, or connections between various events. Rather, the text employs personification, rich imagery, and complex metaphors as it describes brief episodes, profiles

---

[71] Brown, *Character in Crisis*, 152.
[72] Brown, *Wisdom's Wonder*, 66.
[73] Brown, *Character in Crisis*, 17.
[74] Ibid., 18.
[75] That is, while some of the poems contain narratival elements, such as the vignette about the youth who approaches the strange woman's house in chapter 7, neither the book as a whole nor individual collections tell a coherent story with a narrative arc from beginning to end. The narrative arc does not function as a structuring device, as it does in prose.

certain characters in momentary snapshots, and appeals to the emotional tenor of its audience.

While the insights of the character ethics approach shed important insight on the book, Proverbs demands attention to the unique features of its poetry. Accordingly, it challenges the centrality of narrative to the character ethics project. Proverbs offers a model of a text that is not narrative in literary form and that operates with a non-narrative conception of selfhood. These features of the text bear further exploration. The following chapter will consider the form and function of Proverbs' poetry, while Part II will examine what particular elements of Proverbs' pedagogy reveal about its conception of selfhood.

# CHAPTER 3

# Form Criticism and the Way of Poetry in Proverbs

The end of writing is to instruct. The end of poetry is to instruct by pleasing.[1]

The human mind has, in the course of its history, found and cultivated many different ways of assimilating and recording intellectual perceptions. When we approach the teachings of Israel's wise men, one peculiarity must strike us at once, a peculiarity which unites them above and beyond their great differences in form and content; they are all composed in poetic form, they are poetry. And in no circumstances can that be considered to be an insignificant, external feature. Indeed, this peculiarity cannot be separated from the intellectual process as if it were something added later; rather, perception takes place precisely in and with the poetic composition.[2]

Gerhard von Rad insisted that the poetic form is crucial to the function of Proverbs, for form cannot be separated from content. Yet despite von Rad's astute observation, too often biblical scholars have neglected the poetic aspects of the form of Proverbs or considered it to be incidental to the content and larger rhetorical purpose of the book.[3] To be sure, there has been no lack of form-critical endeavors with regard to the book, but even so, such studies frequently lose sight of the poetic forest for the mechanical and syntactical trees. That is, rigorous attention to form has often obscured the vividness and dynamism of Hebrew poetry. William

---

[1] Samuel Johnson, "Preface to Shakespeare (1765)" in *Johnson on Shakespeare: Essays and Notes* (ed. Walter Raleigh; London: Henry Frowde, 1908), 16.

[2] Gerhard von Rad, *Wisdom in Israel* (trans. James D. Martin; London: SCM Press, 1972; repr., Harrisburg: Trinity Press International, 1993), 24.

[3] But see the recent introductory text by Craig G. Bartholomew and Ryan P. O'Dowd, which includes a chapter on "The Poetry of Wisdom and the Wisdom of Poetry" that serves as a basic orientation to wisdom poetry and argues that the poetic form of the wisdom books is vital to its meaning (Craig G. Bartholomew and Ryan P. O'Dowd, *Old Testament Wisdom Literature: A Theological Introduction* [Downers Grove, IL: InterVarsity Press, 2011], 47–72).

McKane, for example, says of the instruction genre that its function "is to communicate clearly and authoritatively, and it sacrifices the literary effectiveness of imaginative language in order to avoid its ambiguities and achieve a pedestrian clarity."[4]

Yet the sophisticated poetry of Proverbs merits admiration as much or more for its vivid language, appeal to emotion, and figurative speech, as for its adherence to particular forms. In fact, these features are central to its pedagogical function. As von Rad asserted, "perception takes place precisely in and with the poetic composition."[5] Thus, understanding *how* the poetry engages in this thinking process is as crucial to grasping its function as analysis of the content or formal features.

This is not to say, however, that form criticism offers little benefit. To the contrary, form-critical approaches have raised many important questions for the poems and sayings in the book. In which genre(s) do they participate? What features do they share with wisdom texts in the wider ancient Near East? In what setting were they composed, edited, and circulated? When, why, and to what extent did they undergo editorial expansion? Indeed, form criticism has dramatically enriched the study of ancient literature and the book of Proverbs, in particular.

At the same time, the multiplicity of form-critical studies in the past century of scholarship has produced a certain degree of confusion, for there is often disagreement about the number of forms that can be meaningfully distinguished and their relevance to the setting and composition history of the book. Philip Johannes Nel, for example, who insists that there are only two basic sentence forms in the book, argues that those who introduce more categories confuse the diversity of stylistic devices with a multiplicity of genre and do nothing to provide form-critical clarity. Rather, only "a kaleidoscopic and confusing variation in terminological usage comes to view."[6]

With regard to the sayings in Proverbs 10–30, form-critical categories have served various functions from classification to conclusions about composition history and connection to wisdom traditions in the ancient Near East. Otto Eissfeldt was the first to make a firm distinction between the popular proverb (*Volkssprichwort*) and the "artistic wisdom saying" (*Kuntspruch*).[7] He argued that most of the sayings in the book fell into

---

[4] William McKane, *Proverbs: A New Approach* (OTL; Philadelphia: Westminster Press, 1970), 22.

[5] von Rad, *Wisdom in Israel*, 24.

[6] Philip Johannes Nel, *The Structure and Ethos of the Wisdom Admonitions in Proverbs* (BZAW 158; Berlin: Walter de Gruyter, 1982), 7.

[7] Otto Eissfeldt, *Der Maschal im Alten Testament. Eine wortgeschichtliche Untersuchung nebst einer literargeschichtlichen Untersuchung der משׁל genannten Gattungen "Volkssprichwort"* (BZAW 24; Giessen: Töppelmann, 1913), 12–13.

the latter category, although one can find vestiges of popular proverbs in the book, marked by their brevity, general human interest, and use of assonance. Building on Eissfeldt's work, William Oesterley developed a three-stage theory of the composition of the book, asserting that the various stages corresponded to the different types of sayings.[8] In the first stage, the single-line sayings were compiled, followed by the two-line saying, "which demands more thought," and then finally in the third stage the "more elaborate treatment of the distich which takes the form of a miniature essay," especially found in chapters 1–9.[9]

Basic distinctions between one- and two-line sayings continued to dominate form-critical discourse for the next generation of scholarship. At the same time, however, growing interest in the relationship between Israelite wisdom and the wider ancient Near Eastern wisdom traditions sparked greater consideration of the generic categories and social setting reflected in related literature. The publication of the Egyptian *Instruction of Amenemope* in 1923 inaugurated a new era in the form-critical study of Proverbs and prompted many scholars to search for other parallels in form and genre to the material in the book.[10] McKane, for example, included in his Proverbs commentary an extensive discussion of "international wisdom," on which he drew regularly in his form-critical comments on Proverbs.[11] The most suggestive parallels have come from Egyptian instruction texts, such as *Amenemope, Ptahhotep,* and *Any,* as well as Babylonian and Sumerian proverbs and the Aramaic text *Ahiqar.*[12]

---

[8] William Oesterley, *The Book of Proverbs* (New York: E. P. Dutton and Company, 1929).

[9] Ibid., xii. Also see Johannes Hempel, who noted that certain sections of the book contained a higher percentage of statements (*Mahnwörter*) to admonitions (*Aussagewörter*) (3% in Prov 10ff., 9% in Prov 25ff., and 75%, in Prov 22:17ff., according to his calculations) and reasoned that the higher occurrence of statements, especially in 22:17–24:22, represented a later stage of development (Johannes Hempel, *Die althebräische Literatur und ihr hellenistisch-jüdisches Nachleben* [Wildpark-Potsdam: Akademische Verlagsgesellschaft Athenaion, 1930], 175).

[10] E. W. Budge, *Second Series of Facsimiles of Egyptian Hieratic Papyri in the British Museum* (London: British Museum, 1923), plates I–XIV. Adolf Erman was one of the earliest proponents for the dependence of Prov 22:17–24:22 on the Egyptian text. He argued that *Amenemope* had been revised for Israelite readers, and he suggested several emendations to make the Hebrew text conform more closely to the Egyptian text, especially in 22:17–24:22 (Adolf Erman, "Eine ägyptische Quelle der 'Spruch Salomos,'" *SPAW, Phil.-hist. Klasse* 15 [1924]: 86–93). For a more recent review of the evidence, see Nili Shupak, "The Instruction of Amenemope and Proverbs 22:17–24:22 from the Perspective of Contemporary Research," in *Searching Out the Wisdom of the Ancients: Essays Offered to Michael V. Fox on the Occasion of His Sixty-Fifth Birthday* (eds. Ronald L. Troxel et al.; Winona Lake: Eisenbrauns, 2005), 203–20; see also Harold C. Washington, *Wealth and Poverty in the Instruction of Amenemope and the Hebrew Proverbs* (SBLDS 142; Atlanta: Scholars Press, 1994), 135–45.

[11] McKane, *Proverbs,* 51–208.

[12] For a brief overview, see Michael V. Fox, *Proverbs 1–9: A New Translation with Introduction and Commentary* (AB 18A; New York: Doubleday, 2000), 17–23; Roland E. Murphy, *Wisdom*

Ancient Near Eastern parallels have also sparked discussion concerning the form and function of the proverbial collection as a whole. Glendon Bryce, for example, suggested that Prov 25:2–27 is a "wisdom book" that existed originally as a separate work, a form recognizable from Egyptian literature.[13] Bryce's conclusions were both thematic – he argued that the context of advice to a young man at court constituted the unifying motif of the book – and structural, for he noted certain stylistic features that appeared to tie the work together.[14] Other scholars also explored possible organizational schemes of the proverbial collections within the book, drawing particular attention to sound play, word repetition, and repeated themes throughout the various collections. While some, such as Raymond C. Van Leeuwen and Knut M. Heim,[15] have found a fair degree of cohesion and organization in various parts of the book, others continue to insist that there is little, if any, deliberate structure that can be discerned.[16]

These distinctions have produced abundant theories although little consensus, and the situation is no less complex in relation to the longer poems of chapters 1–9. R. N. Whybray, one of the first scholars to give sustained form-critical attention to this section of the book, argued in his 1962 Oxford dissertation, "The Concept of Wisdom in Proverbs I–IX,"

---

*Literature: Job, Proverbs, Ruth, Canticles, Ecclesiastes, and Esther* (FOTL 13; Grand Rapids: Eerdmans, 1981), 9–12. See also Miriam Lichtheim, *Late Egyptian Wisdom Literature in the International Context: A Study of Demotic Instructions* (OBO 52; Göttingen: Vandenhoeck & Ruprecht, 1983); Edmund I. Gordon, *Sumerian Proverbs: Glimpses of Everyday Life in Ancient Mesopotamia* (Philadelphia: University Museum, University of Pennsylvania, 1959); idem, "A New Look at the Wisdom of Sumer and Akkad," *BO* 17 (1960): 122–52.

[13] He compared it to the *Wisdom of Sehetepibre*, from the Middle Kingdom, and the *Kemyt*, although he also notes a Babylonian text comparable in nature, the *Wisdom of Shube'awilum* (Glendon Bryce "Another Wisdom-'Book' in Proverbs," *JBL* 91 [1972]: 145). He argued that both the Egyptian texts and Prov 25:2–27 have as their aim the "intention to indoctrinate" and privilege the king as next to God in the capacity for revelation (ibid., 155).

[14] Bryce argued that the work was comprised of an introduction, conclusion, and two main sections, one dealing with the king and the other with a cast of wicked characters. He discerned a series of wordplays and key words throughout each section and across the sections (ibid., 151–55).

[15] Raymond C. Van Leeuwen, *Context and Meaning in Proverbs 25–27* (SBLDS 96; Atlanta: Scholars Press, 1988); Knut Martin Heim, *Like Grapes of Gold Set in Silver: An Interpretation of Proverbial Clusters in Proverbs 10:1–22:16* (BZAW 273; Berlin: Walter de Gruyter, 2001).

[16] Fox, for example, proclaims that "[i]t is far-fetched to imagine editors compiling proverbs according to grand and detailed designs. It is implausible that an editor would write down all the proverbs on little bits of papyrus or parchment and move them around until they fit into tidy, well-organized groupings and larger, well-designed structures, with certain repeated words and phrases ... being located in exactly the right places" (Michael V. Fox, *Proverbs 10–31: A New Translation with Introduction and Commentary* [AB 18B; New Haven: Yale University Press, 2009], 481). See also Murphy, who is likewise skeptical about the intentional organization of the collections, although he acknowledges that certain groupings of sayings may constitute limited interpretive contexts (Murphy, *Wisdom Literature*, 63).

that the chapters consisted of ten "discourses" spoken in a school context by a teacher whose purpose was to exhort the student to obey certain instructions.[17] The original discourses, Whybray argued, were characterized by a common form that shared remarkable similarities with the Egyptian instruction genre.[18] Similarly, Bernhard Lang argued that Prov 1–7 is comprised of ten discourses, although, guided mainly by the hortatory address to the son, he identified different units than did Whybray.[19] William McKane termed the units "instructions," although the characteristic features he defined share much in common with Whybray's.[20]

[17] R. N. Whybray, "The Concept of Wisdom in Proverbs I-IX" (D.Phil. diss., Oxford, 1962); subsequently published as *Wisdom in Proverbs: The Concept of Wisdom in Proverbs 1–9* (SBT 45; London: SCM Press, 1965).

[18] Whybray refuted André Robert and others who argued that these texts reflect direct influence from Israelite texts such as Deuteronomy or the prophets. While there is some overlap, Whybray conceded, such as the appeal to "bind" the father's instruction on the heart, on the whole he found the parallels with Egyptian texts such as the *Instruction of Amenemope* to be far more compelling (Whybray, *Wisdom in Proverbs*, 37; cf. André Robert, "Les Attaches Littéraires Bibliques des Prov. i–ix," *RB* 43 [1934]: 42–68, 172–204, 374–84; *RB* 44 [1935]: 344–65, 502–25). Nonetheless, Whybray also insisted that the book firmly reflects an Israelite context, chiefly in its use of the divine name, the attribution to Solomon, and the address to all students who will listen, as opposed to a particular class of young men, as in the Egyptian material (Whybray, *Wisdom in Proverbs*, 52). Whybray also pointed to additional differences between the Egyptian instructions and Israelite discourses, such as a lack of appeal to the antiquity of the tradition and less detailed content in the Israelite wisdom than in its Egyptian counterparts (ibid., 70).For the relationship between Israelite and Egyptian wisdom, see also Christa Kayatz, *Studien zu Proverbien 1–9: Eine form- und motivgeschichtliche Untersuchung unter Einbeziehung ägyptischen Vergleichmaterials* (WMANT 22; Neukirchen-Vluyn; Neukirchener Verlag, 1966), which is a comparative study of Proverbs 1–9 and Egyptian wisdom. While Kayatz highlighted the similarities between Israelite and Egyptian wisdom, Franz-Josef Steiert, on the other hand, said that there were key differences between Proverbs and the Egyptian material, especially between the concepts of Maat and Wisdom (Franz-Josef Steiert, *Die Weisheit Israels – ein Fremdkörper im Alten Testament? Eine Untersuchung zum Buch der Sprüche auf dem Hintergrund der ägyptischen Weisheitslehren* [Freiburger theologische Studien 143; Freiburg: Herder, 1990], 214–19). He followed Robert in emphasizing the dependence of Proverbs on Israelite religious traditions in Deuteronomy, Isaiah, and Jeremiah, although he did not conclude that there was as much textual dependence as Robert argued (ibid., 219–45).

[19] Bernhard Lang, *Die weisheitliche Lehrrede. Eine Untersuchung von Sprüche 1–7* (SBT 54; Stuttgart: KBW, 1972), 28. Whybray's divisions are much more selective; he often rearranges the order of verses or parts of verses and omits large sections of the text, for he wishes to conform them to what he believes was the original shape of the discourse form. Lang, on the other hand, tends to follow the contours of the extant text and largely bases his divisions on the hortatory address to the son (compare Whybray, *Wisdom in Proverbs*, 39–50; and Lang, *Die weisheitliche Lehrrede*, 29). Lang also distinguished between these units and the "didactic poems" in Prov 1:20–33; 8; 9:1–6 (ibid., 29).

[20] McKane named the form of imperative address and the function of exhortation and persuasion, demonstrated particularly through motive clauses, as key elements of the instruction (see McKane, *Proverbs*, 1–10). McKane argued that the Egyptian instruction genre was appropriated by Israel in the age of Solomon. At that time, he stated, it had a similar function as in Egypt, the training of a specialized, elite class of court officials. However, in Israel the instruction soon developed a different purpose than in Egypt as it became "a method of generalized mundane instruction and thereafter a way of inculcating Yahwistic piety" (ibid., 10). McKane's larger point was that the instruction

Roland E. Murphy also proposed "instruction" as a meaningful form, but he emphasized that in chapters 1–9 they have a longer form than both the instructions in the rest of the book and the Egyptian instructions that they resemble.[21] Like Lang, he identified coherent poems in Prov 1:20–33; 8:1–36; 9:1–6, which he designated as "wisdom speeches." Michael V. Fox is one of the few scholars who classifies the form of these chapters differently. He prefers the term "lectures," which he argues more aptly captures their nature, that of a father lecturing his son about moral behavior.[22]

To what end does this panoply of form-critical distinctions lead? When form criticism is extended to questions of genre, the implicit goal is usually to identify the form's salient features in order to categorize the text appropriately. In this sense, genre implies a fairly strict classification, a notion that arises from the form-critical goal of identifying original textual units and the oral setting they presumably reflect.[23] Such assumptions lead Whybray, for example, to posit that the discourses of Prov 1–9 belong to the category of (Egyptian) instruction, rooted in an oral educational context, not to the category of an Israelite legal text such as Deuteronomy, anchored in Israelite religious institutions. In this sense, his understanding of discourse as a particular genre prompts him to identify features common to a set of texts, thus drawing categorical boundaries around them.[24]

genre itself was not indicative of a late date of chapters 1–9, for the differences between Egyptian and Israelite instruction indicated to him that the genre underwent its own development in the Israelite tradition.

[21] Murphy, *Wisdom Literature*, 50–51.

[22] Fox, *Proverbs 1–9*, 45. See also Richard J. Clifford, who likewise uses the term "lectures" (Richard J. Clifford, *Proverbs: A Commentary* [OTL; Louisville: Westminster John Knox, 1999]). Fox divides each lecture into three components: (1) exordium, the introduction to the lesson consisting of an address to the son, an exhortation to hear the teaching, and a motivational clause; (2) lesson; and (3) conclusion, which includes a memorable capstone to reinforce the content of the lesson. Fox draws the three components from classical Greek rhetoric, in which the components of an oration are termed *exordium, propositio,* and *peroratio* (Fox, *Proverbs 1–9*, 45). He maintains that such features are common to Egyptian and Mesopotamian instruction literature, as well, although he finds that these components occur in different distribution than in the Israelite material. Fox suggests that in foreign instruction literature these features are usually found in the work as a whole, rather than in each individual discourse (ibid., 46). While some scholars, such as Kayatz, have used the similarity between Israelite and Egyptian instruction to support an early date of Prov 1–9, Fox, like McKane before him, draws attention to the distinct differences between the two to suggest that the Israelite material represents considerable development in form and thus is not proximate in date (ibid., 47).

[23] For a thorough treatment of the salient questions of form criticism and the history of the method, see Martin J. Buss, *Biblical Form Criticism in Its Context* (JSOTSup 274; Sheffield: Sheffield Academic Press, 1999).

[24] For a discussion of various conceptions of genre, see Carol A. Newsom, "Spying Out the Land: A Report from Genology," in *Seeking Out the Wisdom of the Ancients: Essays Offered to Honor Michael V. Fox on the Occasion of His Sixty-Fifth Birthday* (ed. Ronald L. Troxel et al.; Winona Lake: Eisenbrauns, 2005), 437–50.

The problem with this classificatory notion of genre is that it tends to obscure the unique particularities of a specific text in an effort to highlight the features it shares with other texts. Moreover, the categorical bounds tend to be quite rigid, ignoring the ways in which texts may not entirely align with the category or may participate in multiple categories at once.[25] This is not to discount the value of classification entirely – this kind of study has illumined profound links with wisdom traditions in the ancient Near East. Yet this classificatory scheme can encourage a univocal vision of the book that overlooks pertinent features.

One feature of Proverbs that such genre distinctions tend to overlook entirely is the poetic form of the text. While some scholars may note that the text is comprised of poetic lines, this feature is not directly relevant to typical definitions of the instruction genre and thus is often incidental to their analysis.[26] Yet, as von Rad so aptly insisted, the poetic form is by no means an incidental feature of the text, and a clearer understanding of its features and rhetorical function will illuminate another genre in which the text participates: didactic poetry.

Rather than categorization of types, a more pressing issue is the function of the sayings. How do they make meaning? What does form have to do with pedagogy? The full import of these questions cannot be explored apart from the poetic features of the sayings. Their didacticism resides in the various ways in which they employ such features as parallelism, imagery, sound play, and word play, a point that will be explored later. Form-critical study of the sayings has contributed important insights, but

---

[25] The notion of genre implicit in Whybray's and others' work on the instruction genre is that of a classificatory scheme in which a particular text belongs to the genre by virtue of its conformity to certain characteristic features. Newsom notes that genre theorists have increasingly found this notion wanting, for "classificatory schemes are by their very nature static, whereas genres are dynamic" (ibid., 439). The classification of texts obscures the way in which they participate to varying degrees in genres and, in so doing, actually change the nature of the genre or produce new genres. Newsom suggests that one productive model of genre for biblical studies may be, following Jacques Derrida, "thinking of genre in relation to a text's rhetorical orientation so that rather than referring to texts as belonging to genres one might think of texts as participating in them, invoking them, gesturing to them, playing in and out of them, and in so doing, continually changing them" (ibid.).

[26] Thorough consideration of the poetics of chapters 1–9 is absent from the work of Whybray and McKane, for example. Murphy does note that there are certain signs of units of poetry, citing Patrick W. Skehan's notion of alphabetizing poems of twenty-two or twenty-three lines in chapters 2–7 (Murphy, *Wisdom Literature*, 52; cf. Patrick W. Skehan, "The Seven Columns of Wisdom's House in Proverbs 1–9," in *Studies in Israelite Poetry and Wisdom* [CBQMS 1; Washington, DC: The Catholic Biblical Association of America, 1971], 9–14; repr. and rev. from *CBQ* 9 [1947]; see also idem, "Wisdom's House," in *Studies in Israelite Poetry and Wisdom*, 27–45; repr. and rev. from *CBQ* 29 [1967]). However, Murphy does not draw any larger implications of this observation for the pedagogical or rhetorical function of the text.

it has not been as helpful in discerning the didactic dynamics within and between the lines of the sayings themselves.

## Proverbs and the Genre(s) of Biblical Hebrew Poetry

Defining poetry is often a vexed question, and the matter of Hebrew poetry is no different. Historically, Hebrew poetry has been defined in relation to what have been considered its central features: meter and parallelism.[27] However, both of these categories have proved problematic. Although several scholars have attempted to discern a characteristic meter of Hebrew poetry, this has never been a successful enterprise. And parallelism, while a prominent feature of many Hebrew poems, is not a conclusive indicator of poetry, for it is present in texts that belong to different genres, such as lists and legal texts.[28] Furthermore, parallelism is not a consistent feature of all Hebrew poems.[29]

The problems surrounding parallelism as a reliable measure of poetry have led some scholars to question the extent to which poetry is a valid genre for biblical literature at all. James L. Kugel notes that biblical Hebrew does not even have a word for "poetry," and he insists that the notion of a strict distinction between poetry and prose is a "Hellenistic imposition"

---

[27] Robert Lowth presumed that biblical poetry must have had a distinctive meter, although it was lost to contemporary readers. He argued that such meter is evidenced by the relatively even length of most poetic verses, which can be discerned through syntactical structure, including parallel phrases. It is important to note that although Lowth is most widely known for his threefold classification of parallelism, he did not define Hebrew poetry based strictly on its parallel structure. Rather, Lowth's discussion of parallelism was an attempt to prove that the prophetic writings were metrical and thus poetry. See lecture 19 in Robert Lowth, *Lectures on the Sacred Poetry of the Hebrews* (trans. G. Gregory; 2 vols.; London: Ogles, Duncan, and Cochran, 1816), 2:34.

[28] One might consider lists and legal texts also to be poetic, depending on one's definition of poetry. Note the phenomenon of "list poems" or catalog verse. (See the discussion and examples in Larry Fagin, *The List Poem: A Guide to Teaching & Writing Catalog Verse* [New York: Teachers & Writers Collaborative, 2000].) Even so, however, a text such as an ancestral list is distinct from, for example, Ps 136, although both are highly parallelistic in syntax. Yet Ps 136 has a high density of other poetic tropes that are missing in the list.

[29] Contra the arguments of T. H. Robinson, who suggested that even when parallelism is not explicitly present, it still influences the form of the line, otherwise the text is not poetry: "Parallelism is not merely a matter of style.... It is the principle which controls the form which every line of Hebrew poetry takes, and although in our existing poems it may exhibit various types, and even be, in its strictest sense, absent from individual lines, yet the outward form which it produces is still there, and unless there is some trace of it we cannot speak of a passage of Hebrew being poetic at all" (T. H. Robinson, "Basic Principles of Hebrew Poetic Form," in *Festschrift Alfred Bertholet zum 80. Geburtstab gewidment von Kollegen und Freunden* [ed. Walter Baumgartner et al.; Tübingen: J.C.B. Mohr (Paul Siebeck), 1950], 444).

on these texts.[30] Rather than a sharp divide between poetry and prose, Kugel argues that texts are situated on a continuum of heightened language.[31] While some texts clearly fall closer to one side of the spectrum than the other, Kugel claims that to maintain only two categories – poetry and prose – is artificial, for "the 'middle ground' between these extremes is important, and will forever elude a biblical critic equipped only to recognize the maximum of heightening or its total absence."[32]

Robert Alter, on the other hand, does not find the situation to be nearly so dire. While he concedes that there are instances in which the boundary between prose and poetry is ambiguous, Alter rejects Kugel's premise that one cannot make meaningful distinctions between the two.[33] Alter maintains that the category of parallelism is an important structural feature of Hebrew poetry, and he explores its dynamics at the level of individual lines and larger units. He finds that Hebrew poetry does have discernible structures and characteristic means of expression that distinguish it from prose.[34]

The problems associated with defining Hebrew poetry by meter or parallelism have led F. W. Dobbs-Allsopp to suggest that the line is the

---

[30] James L. Kugel, *The Idea of Biblical Poetry: Parallelism and Its History* (New Haven: Yale University Press, 1981), 69.

[31] See also Adele Berlin, who agrees with Kugel that there is "a continuum of elevated style in the Bible," which she suggests is characterized by relative degrees of parallelism and terseness. She explains, "It is not parallelism per se, but the predominance of parallelism, combined with terseness, which marks the poetic expression of the Bible. And since the difference between poetic and less-poetic sections is a matter of degree, we would not expect different *kinds* of parallelism in 'prose' and 'poetry,' but only different perceptions of their dominance" (Adele Berlin, *The Dynamics of Biblical Parallelism* [rev. and enl. ed.; Grand Rapids: Eerdmans, 2008], 5). S. E. Gillingham also argues that "there are in fact no clear-cut distinctions between prose and poetry in Hebrew" (S. E. Gillingham, *The Poems and Psalms of the Hebrew Bible* [Oxford: Oxford University Press, 1994], 19). While she proposes four general features that are characteristic of Hebrew poetry – terseness, figurative language, ambiguity of meaning, and "the evocation of a response" – she notes that these occur in prose texts, as well (ibid., 21–23).

[32] Kugel, *The Idea of Biblical Poetry*, 94. He elaborates: "what is called biblical 'poetry' is a complex of heightening effects used in combinations and intensities that vary widely from composition to composition even within a single 'genre.' No great service is rendered here by the concept of biblical poetry, since that term will, if based on the various heightening features seen, include compositions whose genre and subject are most unpoetic by Western standards, and since it will imply a structural regularity and design that are simply not there" (ibid.).

[33] Robert Alter, *The Art of Biblical Poetry* (New York: Basic Books, 1985), 6.

[34] For example, see Alter's comparison of the prose and poetry versions of the story of Jael and Sisera in Judg 4–5 (ibid., 43–49). Among other things, he notes that while the prose uses dialogue to define action and relationships between the characters, the poetry uses the sequencing of various images to draw attention to particular detail and to build and intensify the effect from line to line. While he is careful to say that one is not superior to the other, he insists that "the different formal logics of the two media lead to strikingly different imaginative definitions of the same narrative data" (ibid., 47).

fundamental feature of Hebrew verse.[35] At the same time, however, he insists that it must be accompanied by a density of other poetic features, for "the line, without which there can be no verse, is by itself insufficient to identify a specific instance of discourse as poetic, biblical or otherwise."[36] Dobbs-Allsopp thus defines Hebrew poetry as: "a nonmetrical form of discourse arranged as verse and characterized above all by terseness, verbal inventiveness, and a discernible poetic diction and texture."[37] This definition has the advantage of accounting for the pervasiveness of parallelism without making it an exclusive category of definition. The line is an individual unit that is set apart, and it is the density and configuration of other features that alert the reader to the presence of the line. In much of the Western literary tradition, lines of poetry are represented graphically, with each line of poetry written on a separate row of text, but graphic display is not a prerequisite for the presence of lines.[38] Rather, lines may be bounded by a variety of oral/aural, syntactical, and structural indicators. In an alphabetic acrostic, for example, the alphabet provides a structuring device to mark the beginning of the individual lines of the acrostic. Likewise, parallelism can serve the same function to mark the bounds of lines. In Dobbs-Allsopp's understanding, parallel structure points to the presence of lines, but it is the line, not parallelism per se, that distinguishes poetry from prose. Parallelism is also put into perspective as a feature that occurs alongside many others in Hebrew poetry, such as wordplay, terseness, and vivid imagery. However, Dobbs-Allsopp's approach can also be a rather subjective measure of

---

[35] Dobbs-Allsopp notes that almost all premodern poetry was set in verse, and thus, with few exceptions, despite the diverse forms and cultural contexts of poetry, "the line is the single differentia of poetry on which almost all critics and poets agree" (F. W. Dobbs-Allsopp, "Poetry, Hebrew," *NIDB* 4:551).

[36] Ibid.

[37] Ibid., 554. By "verbal inventiveness," he means that "its language routinely seems denser and more intense, with increased instances of wordplay and other tropes, ambiguity, allusion, etc." (ibid., 552). That is, Hebrew poetry often has a higher concentration of rare words or rare meanings of words, abrupt transitions in subject matter, and certain syntactical or grammatical conventions that are uncommon in prose.

[38] Many biblical poems are represented graphically in lines in the Masoretic tradition. For a discussion of the linear arrangement of poems in texts from Qumran, see F. W. Dobbs-Allsopp, "Space, Line, and the Written Biblical Poem in Texts from the Judean Desert," in *Puzzling Out the Past: Studies in Northwest Semitic Languages and Literatures in Honor of Bruce Zuckerman* (ed. Marilyn J. Lundberg et al.; Culture and History of the Ancient Near East 55; Leiden: Brill, 2012), 19–61. Dobbs-Allsopp presents manuscript evidence to indicate that the Qumran scribes did use spacing and other means of formatting (dots, strokes, etc.) to indicate the presence of lines, which he argues arose out of ancient Levantine scribal practices.

poetry, for the bounds of lines are not always evident,[39] and it leaves to the interpreter to judge in what particular density certain features must occur to distinguish poetry from elevated prose.

A succinct, clear, incontrovertible definition of Hebrew poetry remains elusive because of the diversity of poetry in the Bible. It is nearly impossible to offer a definition of Hebrew poetry that is sufficient for all instances of biblical poetry, for it would either be too general to be meaningful or too specific to encompass all of the instances of poetry. In my judgment, Dobbs-Allsopp has advanced the most adequate starting point in the poetic line, yet even he cannot provide a foolproof measuring stick, as if poetry were a matter of scientific calculation. While I agree with Alter that one can make reasonable distinctions between poetry and prose, one must always make an argument for the presence of poetry. In many cases, this is a relatively straightforward prospect. Many psalms, for example, are designated as מירים, "songs" (e.g., Pss 30; 45; 46; 48; 65–68, etc.), marking them as a genre distinct from Hebrew prose. For other texts, however, it is a more complex question. For example, Ellen F. Davis suggests that Genesis 1 should be read as a "liturgical poem," drawing attention to its structure, choice of words, and rhythm.[40] This is a contestable claim, of course, and many modern translations render this text in paragraph form as prose.[41] Whether poetry or prose, one must be informed by the conventions of language and form in the Bible and in the wider ancient Near East, as well as the features of particular genres.

Proverbs is poetry in the sense that it is highly stylized discourse that makes extensive use of sound play, vivid imagery, and paratactic syntax, and is organized in lines, as demonstrated by the end-stops created by its parallel structure, word choice, and syntax. Consider, for example, the unit in Prov 3:13–18, which makes extensive use of sound play in binding its lines together, most noticeably with the recurring /a/ sound of many of its words.

---

[39] For example, see Dobbs-Allsopp and Tod Linafelt's analysis of several different ways to lineate Qoh 3:1 (Tod Linafelt and F. W. Dobbs-Allsopp, "Poetic Line Structure in Qoheleth 3:1," *VT* 60 [2010]: 249–59).

[40] Ellen F. Davis, *Scripture, Culture, and Agriculture: An Agrarian Reading of the Bible* (New York: Cambridge University Press, 2009), 42–65.

[41] Compare NJPS and NRSV. NRSV depicts Gen 1:27 as a poem, rendering it in line form with blank space between the lines, clearly setting it off from the surrounding material. But see also Michael Fishbane, who characterizes Gen 1:1–2:4a as a "highly stylized" narrative that is "nonpoetic in formulation" (Michael Fishbane, *Text and Texture: Close Readings of Selected Biblical Texts* [New York: Schocken, 1979], 15).

¹³אַשְׁרֵי אָדָם מָצָא חָכְמָה וְאָדָם יָפִיק תְּבוּנָה:

¹⁴כִּי טוֹב סַחְרָהּ מִסְּחַר־כָּסֶף וּמֵחָרוּץ תְּבוּאָתָהּ:

¹⁵יְקָרָה הִיא מִפְּנִיִּים וְכָל־חֲפָצֶיךָ לֹא יִשְׁווּ־בָהּ:

¹⁶אֹרֶךְ יָמִים בִּימִינָהּ בִּשְׂמֹאולָהּ עֹשֶׁר וְכָבוֹד:

¹⁷דְּרָכֶיהָ דַרְכֵי־נֹעַם וְכָל־נְתִיבוֹתֶיהָ שָׁלוֹם:

¹⁸עֵץ־חַיִּים הִיא לַמַּחֲזִיקִים בָּהּ וְתֹמְכֶיהָ מְאֻשָּׁר:

Beyond simple repetition of vowel sounds, other poetic devices, such as rhyme scheme, sound play, and parallelism, contribute to the sense of rhythm and function to mark the bounds of lines. For example, verse 17 is held together by word repetition (דרכיה דרכי), parallelism (דרכיה// נתיבותיה; נעם// שלום), rhyme of the parallel terms, and repetition of the sounds /ā/, /ê/, /ō,ô/, /n/, and /m/ (*dĕrākêhā darkê-nōʿam wĕkol-nĕtîbôtêhā šālôm*). The unit as a whole is marked by sound and root repetition in its opening and closing words: אשרי and מאשר.

In a general sense, the poetry in Proverbs shares many of its features with other biblical poems. Psalm 30, for example, also marks its lines with parallel structure, sound play, and word repetition. However, Proverbs is also unlike the poetry of Ps 30 in many respects. It is not addressed directly to the deity. Further, Ps 30 has particular generic conventions as a thanks-giving psalm that it does not share in form or theme with the poetic units in the book of Proverbs. Even this brief comparison exposes both the possibilities and the limits of defining Hebrew poetry as such. While one can recognize features common to these texts, it would also obscure their differences merely to categorize Proverbs and the Psalms as poetry in distinction from prose.⁴² For this reason, it is more helpful to consider particular genres of biblical poetry rather than poetry versus prose. Hebrew poetry is not a single, static genre, but is represented by texts that participate to varying degrees in a wide array of poetic genres.

---

⁴² See the sentiment of J. P. Fokkelman, who insists that "a correct perception of poetry is based on the art of reading. Competent reading, and the right kind of experience, I consider more essential than drawing up a definition of the art of poetry" (J. P. Fokkelman, *Reading Biblical Poetry: An Introductory Guide* [trans. Ineke Smit; Louisville: Westminster John Knox, 2001], 15).

Alter suggests that "one of the many gaps in the understanding of bib-lical poetry is a failure of those who generalize about it to make sufficient distinctions among genres," and he offers his work as "an initial effort to correct that tendency of amalgamation."[43] Alter's call to resist the "tendency of amalgamation" has not been taken up sufficiently in biblical studies, but it will be one of the main goals of this project to redress this situation with respect to the book of Proverbs. Alter suggests that the pressing question is not whether Proverbs is poetry, but what *kind* of poetry does Proverbs con-tain? What genres of poetry, biblical or otherwise, present useful points of comparison for understanding the nature of poetry in the book as a whole?

## Proverbs and/as Didactic Poetry

Nearly a century ago, S. R. Driver argued that Hebrew poetry, on the whole, can be classified as either lyric or gnomic. He explained that lyric poetry is characterized by the poet's personal emotions or experiences, while gnomic poetry makes general observations about human life and society.[44] Yet he was also quick to note that the line between these two types is not always clear. Lyric poetry, he argued, "may assume a pare-netic tone, giving rise to an intermediate form which may be called *didactic*," and he cites Prov 1–9 as a key example of this phenomenon.[45] Robert Lowth also classified Proverbs as didactic poetry, a designation that encompassed both the longer poems of chapters 1–9 and the shorter say-ings of the rest of the book. Lowth found the first part of the book to contain some of the finest poetry in the Bible, for "the diction is polished and abounds with all the ornaments of poetry; insomuch, that it scarcely yields in elegance and splendor to any of the sacred writings."[46]

The insights of Driver and Lowth are at once both suggestive and prob-lematic. The terms "lyric" and "didactic" derive from the classical Greek and Latin tradition, and while it is useful heuristically to consider the fea-tures that Proverbs' poetry may share with lyric and didactic poetry, it

---

[43] Alter, *The Art of Biblical Poetry*, ix.

[44] S. R. Driver, *An Introduction to the Literature of the Old Testament* (rev. ed.; New York: Charles Scribner's Sons, 1920), 360.

[45] Ibid., 361.

[46] Lowth, *Lectures*, 2:164. Lowth's notion of didactic poetry appears to refer primarily to its pedagogi-cal function, for he distinguishes between the *didactic* and the *poetical* "species" of Hebrew poetry. The former "expresses some moral precept in elegant and pointed verses, often illustrated by a com-parison either direct or implied," while the latter is "adorned with all the more splendid colouring of language, magnificently sublime in the sentiments, animated by the most pathetic expression, and diversified and embellished by figurative diction and poetical imagery" (Lowth, *Lectures*, 1:98). According to Lowth, the poetry in Prov 1–9 is both didactic and poetical.

is finally difficult to say that it fits entirely within these generic categories. Unlike classical lyric poetry, Proverbs is not rooted in musical composition. Unlike didactic poetry, as understood in the classical tradition, Proverbs does not feature a characteristic metrical pattern. However, neither of these genres is restricted to its manifestation in the classical tradition, and when they are understood in a larger framework as genres of poetry that are active in a variety of contexts and cultures, they prove to be a fruitful lens through which to view Proverbs' poetry. Just as many scholars have found productive insights in the comparison of the Egyptian instruction genre with Proverbs, so too, holding Proverbs alongside other genres of poetry yields helpful points of similarity. Depending on the date of the texts in question, the Egyptian material may be closer to Proverbs in terms of chronological proximity. Yet we have as much to learn about the rhetorical tools of Proverbs and their pedagogical function by examining other genres of literature that, while not necessarily contiguous in time or place, nonetheless share prominent features.

At its most basic level, didactic poetry aims to teach something to the reader and thus figures, either implicitly or explicitly, the relationship between author and reader as one between teacher and pupil. Willard Spiegelman argues that poetry is a fitting vehicle for pedagogy because "the returns of poetry, in rhythm, sound, and troping, guarantee its effectiveness as an educational instrument."[47] "Pleasure and instruction," he explains, "far from occupying opposing ends of a logical or aesthetic spectrum, sit squarely together in both the poet's intention and the audience's reception of his work."[48] Furthermore, poetry has the ability to convey something about the process of learning as much as the content of instruction. For this reason, Spiegelman suggests that the didactic poem imparts not only "a sharing of enthusiasms and an imparting of knowledge, but also an understanding of a process, whether in the world or in the language by which the poet represents and creates his world. Teaching, in the final analysis, does not take a direct object: the poets teach us *how*."[49]

Viewed in this light, the poetry of Proverbs is not simply a literary form but is a central means by which the sages teach one *how* to think, to discern, and to seek wisdom. The sages of Proverbs also convey the nature of learning through the medium of poetry. Indeed, the *how* of discernment emerges through the images, metaphors, and dynamism of the poetic lines.

---

[47] Willard Spiegelman, *The Didactic Muse: Scenes of Instruction in Contemporary American Poetry* (Princeton: Princeton University Press, 1989), 256.

[48] Ibid., 4.

[49] Ibid., 257.

The poetic features of Proverbs are not incidental to its wisdom, but are instead crucial to the book's didactic function. As Alexander Dalzell remarks of didactic poems, "The poem does not exist for its 'embellishments'; rather, the 'embellishments' enrich and broaden our understanding of the subject."[50] In other words, the features of poetry are in fact themselves didactic strategies. These features – including parallelism, sound play, terseness, parataxis, and figurative language – are integral to Proverbs' pedagogical ends.

## Didactic Strategies in Proverbial Sayings

### Parallelism

Parallelism is one of the characteristic marks of Hebrew poetry, and nowhere is this more evident than in the proverbial sayings. However, classifying types of parallelism only takes one so far. The more pressing question is the ends to which the sayings deploy parallelism. Proverbs is a fitting case study of the dynamism of poetic parallelism, for while parallelism is an essential component of the proverbial form, it is used to a variety of different ends throughout the book. It is a stable, although not a static, trope. Parallelism is an essential tool of the proverbial saying, a main factor in how it makes meaning.[51] Within Proverbs, parallelism can promote emphasis, qualify a statement, expand a statement, create a comparison, produce disjunction, or sharpen the "wit" of a saying with an element of surprise. For example, Prov 12:5, an evenly balanced couplet, is marked by two halves that mirror each other in number of words, syntax, and sound, and use parallelism to contrast the righteous and the wicked: מחשבות צדיקים משפט תחבלות רשעים מרמה, "plans of (the) righteous – justice // counsels of (the) wicked – deceit." Each word in the first half of the line is the same part of speech and similar in sound to its corresponding term in the second half. The rhyme and balanced syntax hold the two halves together, even as the sense holds the two apart. Bare of any conjunctions, particles, or other extraneous features, the saying starkly opposes the

---

[50] Alexander Dalzell, *The Criticism of Didactic Poetry: Essays on Lucretius, Virgil, and Ovid* (Toronto: University of Toronto Press, 1996), 130.

[51] See the extensive study of parallelism and variant repetition in Knut Martin Heim, *Poetic Imagination in Proverbs: Variant Repetitions and the Nature of Poetry* (BBRSup 4; Winona Lake: Eisenbrauns, 2013). Heim concludes that, given the range and complexity of parallel structures in Proverbs, one must analyze specific examples of parallelism rather than categorizing by types (e.g., synonymous, antithetic, synthetic). Heim finds parallelism and repetition to be highly sophisticated poetic structures in the book that function differently in different contexts. In fact, he argues, "often the imprecise nature of the parallelism allows a range of complex and highly productive implications and inferences that immensely enrich meaning and significance" (ibid., 637).

righteous and the wicked. Yet in so doing, it subtly introduces an element of irony, for the paths that are so opposed sound strikingly similar. On the one hand, the parallelism promotes a dichotomous view of the righteous versus the wicked, yet on the other hand, the remarkable overlap in sound and syntax perhaps suggests that there is a finer distinction between the two paths, requiring careful discernment. One must listen closely to hear the difference between מרמה and מִשְׁפָּט.

A similar feature occurs in Prov 13:7, יֵשׁ מִתְעַשֵּׁר וְאֵין כֹּל מִתְרוֹשֵׁשׁ וְהוֹן רָב, "there is one who acts rich but (has) nothing // one who acts poor but (has) great wealth." Again, the two halves of the verse present opposing scenarios, yet their parallel sounds מתעשר//מתרושש, as well as ואין//והון, subtly underscore the larger point of the saying. That is, appearances may be deceiving, even to the point of concealing an opposite truth. The one who appears rich may in fact have nothing, while the one who appears poor may possess great wealth. Careful discernment is required to know the true nature of a situation. So too, the very sounds of this proverb prompt the reader or listener to reconsider the entire saying and the distinction between sound and sense. Such sound play may even spark a double take: was that מתעשר or מתרושש, ואין or והון? As the sounds of the saying echo, the reader herself must discern carefully, thus proving the point that one must look closely to "read" the situation, whether מתעשר or מתרושש.

Proverbs 13:14 uses parallelism to expound on the statement in the first half of the line: תּוֹרַת חָכָם מְקוֹר חַיִּים לָסוּר מִמֹּקְשֵׁי מָוֶת, "the instruction of the wise – a fountain of life // to turn from snares of death." While the first half of the verse could stand alone as a sense unit, the second half explicates in what respect the instruction is a *fountain of life*. The second half of the verse does not mirror as closely the first half in syntax and sound as does the example previously provided. However, the strong contrast between the final word of each half – *life* and *death* – binds the entire saying together. Furthermore, the saying implicitly contrasts the first and last phrases of the entire verse – *instruction of the wise* and *snares of death* – which become the frame of the whole saying. Parallelism thus operates at the micro- and macro-levels of this verse, heightening the contrast between particular words and phrases, even as the second half does not oppose but advances the meaning of the first. In this way, the saying comes to mean more than the first half would have meant by itself.[52]

---

[52] See also Heim's analysis of the parallel structure in this verse in comparison to its near twin in Prov 14:27: "the fear of YHWH – a fountain of life//to turn from snares of death" (Heim, *Poetic Imagination in Proverbs*, 353–58).

While well-balanced parallel lines can contribute to a sense of symmetry not only in the saying itself but in the world that is described, parallelism can also deploy elements of surprise to communicate disjuncture.[53] Proverbs 13:7, for example, begins מִתְעַשֵּׁר יֵשׁ, "there is one who acts rich,"[54] and one expects this half of the saying to conclude with some explanation of or commentary on the person's wealth. Instead, however, the saying immediately overturns the sense – וְאֵין כֹּל, "but he has nothing." Likewise in the second half of the saying, the statement מִתְרוֹשֵׁשׁ, "one who acts poor," is quickly qualified: וְהוֹן רָב, "but he has great wealth." In this case, the ordered form of parallelism conveys a disorder in the world. The symmetry in syntax conceals an asymmetry in sense.

## Sound Play

The high degree of sophisticated sound play in the sayings is no accident but is crucial to their function and staying power as proverbs. What makes a proverb "stick" is not only its wisdom, but its wit. Sound play, word choice, rhyme schemes, and rhythm are all important aspects of this. For a modern example, consider Shakespeare's famous saying "a rose by any other name would smell as sweet." This is a functional proverb in contemporary culture, quoted and recognizable by many English speakers. Shakespeare's words persist, yet a saying such as "if a rose were called an angiosperm it would still have the same odor" falls flat, even though it expresses the same sentiment. The rhythm and alliteration of Shakespeare's saying is central to its proverbial function – not only to communicate a piece of wisdom, but to encapsulate it in a form that lends itself to terseness, memorability, and repetition.

The extensive use of sound play within the sayings has been widely recognized, although it is often tied to form-critical conclusions with less regard for its particular didactic function. In the 1930s, Berend Gemser went so far as to say that some form of paronomasia, whether alliteration, assonance, rhyme, or the like, could be found in almost every verse of Proverbs![55] More recently, Thomas P. McCreesh has done an extensive study of sound in Proverbs, *Biblical Sound and Sense: Poetic Sound Patterns in Proverbs 10–29.*[56] Like many of his predecessors, McCreesh was specifically interested in detecting sound patterns that might indicate a larger

---

[53] For a discussion of "disjointed" proverbs, that is, those proverbs whose couplets are not clearly linked, see Michael V. Fox, "The Rhetoric of Disjointed Proverbs," *JSOT* 29 (2004): 165–77.

[54] The roots עשר and רוש occur in the *hitpaʿel* and *hitpoʿlel*, respectively, only here.

[55] Berend Gemser, *Sprüche Salomos* (Tübingen: J.C.B. Mohr, 1937), 7.

[56] Thomas P. McCreesh, *Biblical Sound and Sense: Poetic Sound Patterns in Proverbs 10–29* (JSOTSup 128; Sheffield: JSOT Press, 1991).

organizational structure among the collections.[57] While the conclusive results of such a study are mixed, one of the most helpful elements of McCreesh's approach is that he considers both sound and content, the relationship between form and meaning, rather than simply patterns of repeated consonants, words, or grammatical forms. In addition, he examines not only play between individual words and sounds, but also between phrases and in larger patterns, as well as the use of sound to punctuate the syntax or content of the sayings. For example, Prov 29:12, ‑עַל מַקְשִׁיב מֹשֵׁל דְּבַר־שָׁקֶר כָּל־מְשָׁרְתָיו רְשָׁעִים ("A ruler who attends to deceitful speech – all of his advisors are wicked"), issues not an if-then condition, but a simple statement. McCreesh argues that the building sound patterns emphasize the progression from deed to consequence, thus providing a movement that otherwise is missing.[58] In Prov 20:9, מִי־יֹאמַר זִכִּיתִי לִבִּי טָהַרְתִּי מֵחַטָּאתִי ("Who can say, *I have cleansed my heart, I am cleansed of my sin*?"), the constant repetition of /i/ vowels underscores an implicit judgment in the rhetorical question, suggesting that only a self-righteous person could proclaim such things. With the יִ‑ suffix attached to nearly every word, "in effect, the proverb is repeatedly saying: 'me ... me ... me!' "[59]

## Terseness and Vocabulary

Samuel Taylor Coleridge defined poetry as the best words in the best order,[60] and indeed, a hallmark of any poetry, in distinction from prose, is its terseness and deliberate choice of words. The grammatical forms that are the glue of Hebrew prose – conjunctions, prepositions, direct object and relative clause markers – fall away in poetry. Only the best, most essential words will do. Because of its terseness, a poem relies on other features to carry it forward and serve as structuring devices, such as parallelism, sound play, and parataxis. Furthermore, it relies on the words

---

[57] While McCreesh suggests that Proverbs is highly intentional literature, written by scribes who were skilled in the use of language, he also argues that the analysis of sound is relevant, particularly in the case of proverbs, even apart from any question of the author's intention. He insists that there is a natural appeal of poetic sound patterns in language: "Sounds, even without conscious effort, naturally attract like sounds and can still contribute to the structure of the saying" (McCreesh, *Biblical Sound and Sense*, 52).

[58] Note the /m, š/ sequence in the opening two words (מֹשֵׁל מַקְשִׁיב) and the final two words (מְשָׁרְתָיו רְשָׁעִים), as well as the sequence /(q, k), š/ that links the descriptive words in the first half (מַקְשִׁיב ... שָׁקֶר) with those in the second (כָּל־מְשָׁרְתָיו) (ibid., 54).

[59] Ibid., 74. McCreesh also notes several other sound plays in this verse, including the repetition of חי, מ, and ר, all of which tie together each half of the line and the saying as a whole.

[60] "I wish our clever young poets would remember my homely definitions of prose and poetry; that is, prose, – words in their best order; poetry, – the best words in their best order" (Samuel Taylor Coleridge, *Poems of Coleridge* [ed. Arthur Symons; Whitefish: Kessinger Publishing, 2004], 14).

themselves to strike a chord within the reader and to produce rhetorical effect. Thus, poetry may evidence a higher occurrence of unusual, vivid, or obscure words. Such vocabulary choices can lend memorability and ambiguity to a poetic line, causing the reader to slow down and negotiate the multivalent or unfamiliar meaning of the term. As a modern example, note Billy Collins's poem "Snow Day," in which he describes his pet bounding through the snow by saying, "the dog will porpoise through the drifts."[61] While "porpoise" will be a term familiar to most readers as a large, aquatic mammal, it is used here as a verb and calls to mind an image of a dog diving through the snow drifts as a porpoise in a great sea. With one term, the poet captures an image that otherwise could have taken several words to describe. The term itself is at once both familiar and odd, prompting the reader to reconsider its meaning.

While terseness and unusual word choice are features of poetry in general, they can serve particular pedagogical ends in proverbial sayings. In fact, terseness and unusual vocabulary are prominent features of proverbial sayings in all cultures. For example, the British proverb "many a little makes a mickle," which means that many small things become a large thing ("mickle"), is short in form, held together by rhythm, alliteration, and rhyme, and uses the rare term "mickle."[62] All of these features distinguish the saying as a proverb, setting it apart from ordinary speech, and the unusual term "mickle" requires additional interpretation, prompting the hearer to consider carefully the import of the saying.

Such features are also prominent in Israelite proverbs. Indeed, the book of Proverbs has one of the highest incidences of *hapax legomena* in the Hebrew Bible.[63] Its obscure language often makes translation difficult, a problem only compounded by the brevity of the poetic lines. While parallelism is often an aid to discerning the meaning of rare words, the absence of lengthy

---

[61] Water imagery pervades the entire stanza, which reads: "In a while I will put on some boots / and step out like someone walking in water, / and the dog will porpoise through the drifts, / and I will shake a laden branch, / sending a cold shower down on us both" (Billy Collins, "Snow Day" in *Sailing Alone Around the Room: New and Selected Poems* [New York: Random House, 2001], 140–41).

[62] The obscurity of the term "mickle" is also evidenced by the alternative form of this proverb, "many a mickle makes a muckle," which is actually nonsensical because "muckle" is a Scottish pronunciation of "mickle." Those who circulate this form of the saying assume that mickle and muckle have opposite meanings. George Washington, who perhaps brought the alternative saying to America, may be guilty here! (See Wolfgang Mieder, ed.; *A Dictionary of American Proverbs* [New York: Oxford University Press, 1992], 410; see also F. P. Wilson, ed., *The Oxford Dictionary of English Proverbs* [3rd ed.; Oxford: Oxford University Press, 1970], 508).

[63] Frederick E. Greenspahn estimates that only Job, Song of Songs, and Isaiah contain more *hapax legomena* than Proverbs (Frederick E. Greenspahn, "The Number and Distribution of *hapax legomena* in Biblical Hebrew," *VT* 30.1 [1980]: 13).

descriptions or prose particles means that in certain cases, meaning can only be approximated, at best. For example, Prov 21:8, הֲפַכְפַּךְ דֶּרֶךְ אִישׁ וָזָר וְזַךְ יָשָׁר פָּעֳלוֹ, has caused many scholars to make interpretive somersaults concerning the form wāzār. The Masoretic vocalization could be understood as a rare term, perhaps meaning "guilty" or "dishonest,"[64] or as a hendiadys with אִישׁ, that is a man who is a stranger.[65] Others vocalize as wĕzār, thus taking זר as another attribute of the man's way.[66] BHS proposes reading instead אִישׁ כֹּזֵב, a lying man,[67] and Fox omits the term entirely.[68] Plausible arguments can be mounted for each of these alternatives, but when one considers the nature of proverbial poetry, there are strong reasons to resist textual emendation. As McCreesh points out, the form wāzār is linked by sound to the following term, wĕzak, and the antithetical nature of the saying thus indicates that the two should have opposite meanings.[69] Further, these two terms taken together serve as a structuring device for the entire saying, for they "both link and contain in themselves all the important sounds of the proverb," including the repetition of the consonant sounds /z/, /r/, /k/ and the /a/ vowels.[70] Moreover, the presence of a rare term, particularly if it plays on or sounds like a more familiar term, is stronger evidence for its authenticity, not corruption.[71] While it is difficult to solve this riddle definitively (particularly because of its terseness), the nature of proverbial poetry suggests that reading the text in its present form is the best solution, "crooked is the way of a guilty man, but the pure – his work is upright."[72]

---

[64] Perhaps a cognate of either wazara (Arb.), to burden oneself with a crime, or zawira (Arb.) to be dishonest. See HALOT, 259.

[65] See GKC §104.2(e), which attests to the phenomenon of wā- before the tone syllable used to unite two nouns that express one concept.

[66] See the translation of NJPS: "The way of a man may be tortuous and strange, though his actions are blameless and proper."

[67] See also R. B. Y. Scott, Proverbs – Ecclesiastes (AB 18; Garden City: Doubleday & Company, 1965), 123. This suggestion is omitted in BHQ. Driver rewrites the entire line as אִישׁ הֲפַכְפַּךְ דַּרְכּוֹ זָר, "a man crooked of his way is false" (G. R. Driver, "Problems in the Hebrew Text of Proverbs," Biblica 32 [1951]: 185).

[68] He argues that the line is "overlong" and suggests that the word is due to dittography of וְזַךְ (Fox, Proverbs 10–31, 682).

[69] Noting that it is unusual for West Semitic to preserve the original ו, McCreesh posits that wāzār may be "an archaizing, learned or dialectical form coined by the proverb maker for the sake of the sound patterning" (McCreesh, Biblical Sound and Sense, 58).

[70] McCreesh notes that the sounds /š/, /w/, /z/, /r/ at the end of the first half (אִישׁ וָזָר) echo the sounds at the beginning of the second (וְזַךְ יָשָׁר). Further, the /k/ sound in הֲפַכְפַּךְ דֶּרֶךְ is echoed by וְזַךְ, as the /r/ of דֶּרֶךְ is picked up in וָזָר and יָשָׁר (ibid., 59).

[71] Many of the sound patterns McCreesh notices would also be operative should the term be vocalized wĕzār, although his point is tied to the syntactical issue that the content of the saying hinges on the opposition between these two words at the center of the verse.

[72] Although the philological evidence is rather weak, the connection between sound and sense is a more compelling proposal than omitting the word entirely, as does Fox. This translation also

The terseness and often unusual vocabulary is not a detraction from the saying's wisdom or simply an embellishment to an otherwise straightforward point. Rather, such features are an integral part of the function of the saying itself. Terseness lends itself to memorability,[73] and obscure or multivalent vocabulary can prompt the student to engage the wisdom more deeply, seeking understanding beneath the surface of the text. For example, Prov 22:6 states: חנך לנער על־פי דרכו גם כי־יזקין לא־יסור ממנה. Aside from the rather obscure verb חנך,[74] the grammar and vocabulary are relatively simple. The meaning, however, is a more complicated matter. The sense could connote a directive to school a child correctly, that is, *train a child in the right way,*[75] *and he will not depart from it when he is old.* Or it could serve as a warning against indulging a youth in what he prefers,[76] that is, *train a child in the way of his preference, and he will not depart from it when he is old.* Or it could suggest training a child according to his particular age,[77] aptitude,[78] or social position,[79] that is, *train a child in the way appropriate to him, and he will not depart from it when he is old.* If the intent was to make

makes more sense than Fox's proposal: "A man's behavior may be tortuous, (even) while his deeds are pure and upright" (Fox, *Proverbs 10–31,* 682). For the importance of sound play, consider again the proverb "many a little makes a mickle." An alternative saying, "many a little makes a *muckle,*" would not be as effective a proverb, even though the meaning is the same, because the pronunciation "muckle" disrupts the rhythm and assonance with "little." Of course, sound must be matched with content, for "many a mickle makes a muckle," *sounds* like a good proverb, although the sense is lacking.

[73] Recall my revision of the saying "a rose by any other name would smell as sweet" to "if a rose were called an angiosperm it would still have the same odor." Part of the reason that the second version would also fail to "stick" as a proverb is its longer length and clumsier phrasing. Lowth, too, insisted on the terseness of a proverb: "let brevity be admitted as the prime excellence of a proverb. This is, indeed, a necessary condition, without which it can neither retain the name nor the nature. For if the sentiment be diffusely expressed … it is no longer a proverb but a harangue. For the discriminating sentiment must force itself on the mind by a single effort, and not by a tedious process" (Lowth, *Lectures,* 2:166–67).

[74] Elsewhere, the term means to consecrate a structure (Deut 20:5 [2x]; 1 Kgs 8:63 = 2 Chr 7:5), and the nominal form חנכה indicates a consecration (e.g., Num 7:10; Ps 30:1; Neh 12:27). The sense here implies to train, echoing the root's use in the *pi'el* stem in Rabbinic Hebrew, or perhaps to dedicate to a function or task. Note also Arabic *ḥanaka,* meaning to rub a newborn's palate (חך) with oil, which provides an interesting point of comparison to the action toward the young person described in Proverbs, although Hildebrandt is correct to issue caution about the extent to which the term's possible etymology is significant in this case (Ted Hildebrandt, "Proverbs 22:6a: Train Up a Child?" *Grace Theological Journal* 11 [1988]: 5). See also S. C. Reif, "Dedicated to חנך," *VT* 22 (Oct 1972): 495–501.

[75] Alternatively, *school a child in his way,* i.e., God's way, could be a possible, although perhaps unlikely, interpretation.

[76] Similarly, Gersonides (see Fox, *Proverbs 10–31,* 698).

[77] See Franz Delitzsch, *Biblical Commentary on the Proverbs of Solomon* (trans. M. G. Easton; 2 vols.; Edinburgh: T&T Clark, 1874), 2:86.

[78] See Saadiah.

[79] See Hildebrandt, who argues that נער in this saying refers to a young man of high status who is initiated into his role (Hildebrandt, "Proverbs 22:6a," 17–18).

the saying as clear as possible, there would be other ways to communicate the meaning. Yet clarity is not the chief end of a proverbial saying. Instead, its function is not only to convey wisdom but to ensconce the skill of discernment and understanding within the student. As Heim observes, ambiguity within the sayings "deliberately slows down the reading process, opens up multiple windows on reality, and stimulates the interpreter's imagination."[80] One must engage the content and the form of the saying, filling in the gaps that its terseness leaves open for interpretation and exploring the ambiguities of its vocabulary and syntax. In so doing, the student of the saying practices the very discernment such sayings seek to provoke.

*Parataxis*

Parataxis – the juxtaposition of two different lines, expressions, or images – also provokes discernment in the student because it creates an ambiguity or gap between the two that the student must supply. By joining seemingly incongruent elements, certain sayings may elicit an element of surprise. For example, Prov 11:22 states, "a golden ring in a pig's snout – a beautiful woman who turns from good sense" (נזם זהב באף חזיר אשה יפה וסרת טעם). Alter argues that this saying uses a technique frequent to Proverbs of placing the moral of the saying as the second of two images. This sequence then functions as a type of riddle, but "instead of a punch-word the entire second verset becomes a punch-line."[81] Furthermore, the images themselves heighten the effect: "It is a little shocking to contemplate the image of a gold ring in a pig's snout, and that sense of shocking incongruity then carries over strongly from the metaphor to its referent, making us see with a new sharpness the contradiction of beauty in a senseless woman."[82]

But it is not simply the element of surprise that sharpens this saying. Here parataxis, the juxtaposition of the images, fosters an ambiguity that requires discernment in interpretation. The relation between the image of the pig's ring and the beautiful woman is not explicitly spelled out, but the juxtaposition of these two striking images leaves it to the reader to draw the point. In so doing, the saying resists conclusion, allowing more than one possible explanation of their relation. In this respect, many of the sayings in the book delight in ambiguity and multivalency, even as they present stark images and dichotomous characterizations. This very verse,

---

[80]  Heim, *Poetic Imagination in Proverbs*, 640.
[81]  Alter, *The Art of Biblical Poetry*, 176.
[82]  Ibid.

in fact, has prompted quite divergent interpretations from commentators. While some argue that the woman and the pig are objects of comparison, concluding that a woman without sense is no different than "the coarsest and uncleanest of beasts,"[83] others suggest that it is the golden ring, not the pig, that is comparable to the woman's beauty, neither adornment appropriate to its owner. Heim has argued vigorously, against much of the interpretive tradition, that "the proverb is concerned with warning young men against choosing their spouse on the basis of outward appearance only."[84] It is not, he insists, a denigration of the woman. Bruce K. Waltke, on the other hand, draws the opposite conclusion: "Having left whatever sensible judgment of moral behavior this woman once cultivated and/or had, it implies that she has turned herself into a boorish animal in her dress, speech, and behavior. *In fact, she is worse than a pig.*"[85]

At stake in the competing interpretations of this proverb is the use and function of the poetic tools of parallelism, imagery, and parataxis. Heim's interpretation rests on his careful analysis of parallelism in the saying. He notes that golden ring (נזם זהב) is parallel to beautiful woman (אשה יפה). The pig's snout (אף חזיר) and turning from discretion (סרת טעם) modify the main topic of each parallel half, respectively. He then concludes that pig and woman are *not* objects of comparison, given the parallel syntax.[86] Waltke, however, explores the implications of each image, arguing that what makes the first image of a ring in a pig's snout resonate as an unfitting scenario is that with its snout, the pig "roots in mud and swill."[87] Analogously, then, he suggests that the second image is also unseemly because the woman "lacks discretion and implicitly immerses her beauty that adorns her in evil."[88] While each of these interpretations is plausible, it is significant that neither is conclusive because the saying is not definitive. Lacking any comparative element, the saying leaves ambiguous exactly which elements are comparable, and in what respect.[89] Instead,

---

[83] Crawford H. Toy, *The Book of Proverbs* (ICC; Edinburgh: T&T Clark, 1899), 233.

[84] Knut M. Heim, "A Closer Look at the Pig in Proverbs XI 22," *VT* (2008): 21.

[85] Bruce K. Waltke, *The Book of Proverbs: Chapters 1–15* (Grand Rapids: Eerdmans, 2004), 504; emphasis added. Waltke argues that the act of "turning aside" (סור), "represents the woman as an apostate from that which is normative" (ibid.).

[86] Heim, "A Closer Look," 24.

[87] Waltke, *Proverbs*, 503.

[88] Ibid.

[89] For this reason, Waltke's addition of the comparative particle *like* in his translation is not helpful, for it too readily resolves the ambiguity in the Hebrew: "[Like] a gold ring in the snout of a pig [is] a beautiful woman who turns aside from discretion" (Waltke, *Proverbs*, 498). Heim also calls the parallel phrase a simile, which obscures the true ambiguity of the paratactic phrasing (Heim, "A Closer Look," 22).

two descriptive images sit next to each other in parallel lines, and meaning emerges in the interaction between the two lines.[90] The paratactic expression requires the reader to engage the saying and probe its meaning. After all, if these two images – a golden ring in a pig's snout, a beautiful woman lacking sense – were encountered as separate images, one would not necessarily assume they had any bearing on one another, even if they had similar syntax. It is their juxtaposition, even more than their parallelism or imagery, that causes the reader to seek a meaningful relationship between the two.[91]

### Figurative Language

In many respects, figurative language is the lifeblood of the proverbial sayings. Such language, which consists of those tropes that convey an idea or image by means of language put to another use than its common or plain sense,[92] infuses every chapter and lends a vivid liveliness to the sayings. Metaphor is one of the most common tropes in the book, used to color vice, virtue, and a variety of other concepts with striking imagery. For example, Prov 11:30a describes the condition of the righteous in terms of flourishing plant life: "the fruit of the righteous is a tree of life" (פְּרִי־צַדִּיק עֵץ חַיִּים) (see also 11:18b, 28b; 12:3b), while Prov 10:20a states: "the tongue of the righteous is choice silver" (כֶּסֶף נִבְחָר לְשׁוֹן צַדִּיק), using an image of a valuable commodity to convey the surpassing worth of righteous speech.[93] Such comparisons between the righteous and plants or silver are at once striking for both their incongruity – a tongue is not literally money, nor is a person a plant – and their fittingness. As Paul Ricoeur explains of metaphor, it consists "in the reduction of the shock between two incompatible ideas.... What is at stake in a metaphorical statement is making a

---

[90] Cf. Alter's description of proverbial parallelism in which "meaning emerges from some complicating interaction between the two halves of the line" (Alter, *Art of Biblical Poetry*, 164).

[91] Parataxis can also operate at the macro-level across the book as different sayings sit next to each other, each in some sense qualifying the others by virtue of their inclusion in a larger collection.

[92] For example, simile, metaphor, metonymy, and synecdoche. For an overview of the often vexed question of defining trope and figure, see Timothy Bahti, "Figure, Trope, Scheme" in *The New Princeton Handbook of Poetic Terms* (ed. T. V. F. Brogan; Princeton: Princeton University Press, 1994), 90–93; Richard A. Lanham, *A Handlist of Rhetorical Terms: A Guide for Students of English Literature* (Berkeley: University of California Press, 1968), 101–02. See also Albert N. Katz, "Figurative Language and Figurative Thought: A Review," in *Figurative Language and Thought* (ed. Albert N. Katz et al.; New York: Oxford University Press, 1998), 3–43. Here I use the term "trope" to denote figures of thought, as opposed to figures of sound, often termed "schemes."

[93] Note also the use of synecdoche in the phrase "the *tongue* of the righteous" to refer to the speech of the righteous.

'kinship' appear where ordinary vision perceives no mutual appropriateness at all."[94]

It should come as no surprise that figurative language is so prominent in the book, for it is a hallmark of proverbs in a variety of cultures. Paremiologist Wolfgang Mieder points out that not only do proverbs often employ metaphor, but proverbs themselves can be applied in a figurative way.[95] Advising someone, "do not count your chickens before they're hatched," uses a statement that could be understood in a literal or a non-literal fashion, depending upon if the person actually possessed eggs that were about to hatch or just found herself in a situation in which she should not count on an outcome preemptively.

Figurative language is not simply a clever way to say what could be said otherwise. Rather, it communicates ways of conceptualizing the world. The significance of metaphor, in particular, has garnered wide debate among philosophers, linguists, cognitive psychologists, anthropologists, and literary theorists. Since Aristotle, some have understood metaphor as a departure from the normal use of language, a decorative effect more than a generator of new meaning. I. A. Richards observes that "[t]hroughout the history of Rhetoric, metaphor has been treated as a sort of happy extra trick with words, an opportunity to exploit the accidents of their versatility."[96] On the other hand, others have emphasized the power of metaphor to create something new. Ricoeur insists that metaphor is more than an "ornament of discourse," more than an appeal to emotion. Rather, "metaphor says something new about reality."[97] Those who highlight the power of metaphor to offer novel concepts or ways of thinking suggest that figures of speech have cognitive meaning that cannot be paraphrased adequately or communicated otherwise.

George Lakoff and Mark Johnson argue that metaphor is a cognitive activity of conceptual mapping in which an abstract concept is figured in terms of more familiar or concrete knowledge, an activity that influences how people reason and imagine the world.[98] Although their work has not gone without criticism,[99] Lakoff and Johnson present a helpful way of illuminating the

---

[94] Paul Ricoeur, "Biblical Hermeneutics," *Semeia* 4 (1975): 78–79.

[95] Wolfgang Mieder, *Proverbs: A Handbook* (Westport: Greenwood Press, 2004), 8.

[96] I. A. Richards, *The Philosophy of Rhetoric* (New York: Oxford University Press, 1965), 90.

[97] Ricoeur, "Biblical Hermeneutics," 80. He adds, "Metaphor is nothing other than the application of a familiar label to an object which first resists and then surrenders to its application" (ibid., 86).

[98] George Lakoff and Mark Johnson, *Metaphors We Live By* (Chicago: University of Chicago Press, 1990); see also George Lakoff and Mark Turner, *More Than Cool Reason: A Field Guide to Poetic Metaphor* (Chicago: University of Chicago Press, 1989).

[99] For example, see Anna Wierzbicka, "Metaphors Linguists Live By: Lakoff & Johnson Contra Aristotle," *Papers in Linguistics* 19.2 (1986): 287–313.

implicit assumptions and conceptual webs that undergird common metaphors. For example, they consider the use in contemporary English of the
metaphorical concept TIME IS MONEY,[100] which appears in such metaphors as
"you are *wasting* my time" or "she's living on *borrowed* time" or "that mistake
*cost* me two hours." They argue that this metaphorical concept structures
how we conceive of everyday activities and reflects the values of contemporary, English-speaking, Western culture.[101] In this sense, the metaphors associated with the concept TIME IS MONEY participate in shaping a symbolic
world in which time is prized as a precious commodity, often in short supply.

Similarly, the range of metaphors in the book of Proverbs also may
reveal the construction of a symbolic moral world. For example, there
are several overlapping conceptual metaphors used to describe virtue,
such as VIRTUE IS A PATH, VIRTUE IS A BUILDING, and VIRTUE IS A PLANT.
Accordingly, one can *walk* in uprightness (10:9) or follow the *way* of life
(10:17a); a righteous person is an everlasting *foundation* (10:25), while a
person cannot be *established* in wickedness (12:3); and the *root* of the righteous will not totter (12:3b), for his *fruit* is a *tree* of life (11:30a). Virtue,
of course, could not literally be a path, a building, or a plant – to say
nothing of all three at once! – yet the overlapping metaphors color the
concept of virtue as straight, firm, and fruitful.[102] In this sense, as Ricoeur
explains, "[m]etaphorical interpretation presupposes a literal interpretation which is destroyed. Metaphorical interpretation consists in
transforming a self-defeating, sudden contradiction into a meaningful
contradiction."[103] Consequently, "the metaphorical interpretation gives
rise to a re-interpretation of reality itself, in spite of, and thanks to, the
abolition of the reference which corresponds to the literal interpretation
of the statement."[104] Interpreting figurative language, especially metaphor,
in Proverbs thus provides a window into the symbolic world that the text
creates, for it is through such language that the world is refashioned.[105]

In the following chapters, I will examine various uses of figurative language in each of the models of character formation, guided by the cognitive theories of metaphor that emphasize the role of figurative language in
creating meaning and generating symbolic worlds. This cognitive theory

[100] I follow the practice of Lakoff and Johnson of placing conceptual metaphors in capital letters.
[101] Lakoff and Johnson, *Metaphors We Live By,* 8–9.
[102] See Ricoeur's comments that, "a metaphor never comes alone. One metaphor calls for another and
altogether they remain alive thanks to their mutual tension and the power of each to evoke the
whole network" (Ricoeur, "Biblical Hermeneutics," 94).
[103] Ibid., 78.
[104] Ibid., 84.
[105] For further analysis of conceptual metaphors in Proverbs, see Chapter 7, §4.

is particularly helpful in illuminating the central didactic function of proverbs as they aim to engage the student in new patterns of thought, prompting her to view the world in a new way. As William P. Brown explains, metaphor is particularly well suited to proverbial pedagogy, for "metaphors are sparing of words yet capable of prompting reflection in ways that compel the reader or listener to regard the topic in a new or different light. In other words, metaphors *teach*, and they do so by reorienting the readers' perception."[106]

## Didactic Strategies in Proverbs 1–9

While the longer poems in Prov 1–9 share many of the same didactic strategies as the sayings, they also feature unique elements that are developed over the course of the poems, such as the use of alternating voices of address and extended development of the ethos of the addressee as student. In this respect, quite suggestive parallels can be drawn with features of didactic poems in the classical tradition. In the classical tradition, didactic poetry was grouped with epic (hexameter verse) and was associated most closely with Hesiod. As a genre, it has been variously defined and understood.[107] Dalzell provides a general definition of the didactic genre as comprised of poems that "provide, or claim to provide, a systematic account of a subject."[108] Katharina Volk defines the genre as "the self-consciously poetic speech uttered by the persona, who combines the roles of poet and teacher, explicitly in order to instruct the frequently addressed student in some professed art or branch of knowledge."[109] Didactic poetry implies a relationship between author and reader as akin to that between teacher and pupil, and thus a key dynamic of this genre is the relationship between student, teacher, and subject. The particular features and tools of the genre vary considerably depending on the particular context of the poet and the time period of the poetry in question, but general features of the genre include its ability to form the subject position of the reader as a student, enact a process of instruction that appears to happen

---

[106] William P. Brown, "Didactic Power of Metaphor in the Aphoristic Sayings of Proverbs," *JSOT* 29 (2004): 152.

[107] Didactic poetry developed a particularly unfavorable reputation in the Romantic period, from which it perhaps has not yet recovered. For a history of the genre, see David Duff, *Romanticism and the Uses of Genre* (New York: Oxford University Press, 2009), 95–118.

[108] Alexander Dalzell, *The Criticism of Didactic Poetry: Essays on Lucretius, Virgil, and Ovid* (Toronto: University of Toronto Press, 1996), 8.

[109] Katharina Volk, *The Poetics of Latin Didactic: Lucretius, Vergil, Ovid, Manilius* (New York: Oxford University Press, 2002), 40.

concurrently with the development of the poem, and make palatable the subject and the pedagogical process through its poetic features.

Because didactic poetry addresses the reader as student, one of its expressed goals is to shape the ethos of the reader, to inform her character by the instruction it imparts. Volk discusses some of the rhetorical techniques that didactic poetry may use to manipulate the subject position of the addressee. For example, a speaker may address the student as "you," thus situating the reader of the poem as the student, the one to whom the lesson is taught. Or in Lucretius's *De rerum natura*, the repeated use of first-person plural pronouns implicates the reader in a common enterprise of study with the teacher, "[L]et *us* now examine the question."[110]

This didactic stance is also an effective tool in Proverbs because it does not engage the reader in abstract argumentation, but rather it presents the reader with no choice but to take up the position of the student who is addressed directly. This is a very different mode of delivery than an objective report issued by a third-person narrative voice. To the contrary, Proverbs grounds its authority not in an omniscient narrator but in the specific voice of a father addressing his son. As the father, personified Wisdom, and the strange woman speak in the first person, the reader of the poem inevitably falls into the role of student, the one to whom they speak.

Moreover, Proverbs uses the first-person address of a variety of speaking voices to shift the subject position of the student/reader. As various voices call to the student throughout the poems, he becomes situated in different company. Chapter 7, for example, begins by addressing the student as the father's child, "my son, keep my words" (7:1), and the student is presumably by the father's side as the father describes a scene that he observes through his window of a woman lurking in the city (7:6–13). Yet soon the strange woman speaks in the first person and addresses the senseless one directly (7:14–20), thus positioning the son – and the reader – as the חסר־לב to whom she appeals, "Let *us* intoxicate ourselves with love until the morning" (7:18). With a quick shift in speaker's voice, the student/reader has gone from the son of the father to the one led astray by the wayward woman.[111]

A didactic poet may also attempt to differentiate the reader from the student explicitly addressed in the poem. Volk argues that *De rerum*

---

[110] Lucretius, *De Rerum Natura: The Nature of Things, A Poetic Translation* (trans. David R. Slavitt; Berkeley: University of California Press, 2008), I.868 [40].
[111] For a more thorough discussion of Prov 7, see Chapter 6.

*natura* shapes the reader by characterizing its explicit addressee (the student addressed in the poem, Memmius) as foolish so as to prompt the implicit addressee (the reader) to identify instead with the wise teacher. Volk explains that "Lucretius' construction of the poem's student character as a stupid child functions as a kind of psychological trick in the extra-textual interaction of author and reader."[112] As the reader witnesses the exchange between the speaker and his dim-witted student, she is more likely to accept the superior intellect of the teacher. Thus, "with the help of the less-than-ideal intra-textual student, Lucretius creates his ideal extra-textual reader."[113]

Volk draws attention to the ability of didactic poetry to influence the ethos of the reader by placing her in the subject position of the student and shaping her to become one who desires to pursue the course of study offered by the poem. Volk attends to the way in which the particular voice of the speaker can engage the reader, yet she also observes that poets can engage the reader through perspectives other than the direct speaker. A poet may then seek to shape the character of the reader, the implicit addressee, by identification or dis-identification with the ethos of the explicit addressee.

Proverbs also utilizes a variety of speaking voices and perspectives in an effort to shape the ethos of the student. While the father is the dominant voice throughout these chapters, both the strange woman and woman Wisdom also offer their own visions of the world, and in the complex of these three voices, which address the student/reader directly, wisdom takes root. As these voices speak directly to the student, they contribute to shaping the ethos of the student by positioning him in relation to their own speaking voice and to other characters whom they name, such as the fool or the simpleton. At times, the speakers differentiate the student from the fools, the wicked, and the simple. In chapter 1, for example, the father describes a scene of conspiring sinners and urges the student to avoid their snares: "My son, if sinners entice you, do not consent" (1:10). Here the sinners are clearly a group of which the son is not (yet) a part. Yet the father also describes the sinners' appeal to the student in the first person, which implicitly associates the student with the group as if they confronted him directly, for the sinners say to him, "Come with us! Let us lie in wait for blood!" (1:11). By assuming the voice of the sinners, the father enacts their appeal to the student as a means of prompting him

[112] Volk, *The Poetics of Latin Didactic*, 81.
[113] Ibid.

to disavow the temptation. Following the father's address in chapter 1, Wisdom includes the student in her second-person plural address to the simple ones, scoffers, and fools (1:22), yet she concludes her speech by referring to this group in the third person. This subtle switch in address allows the student to be differentiated from the group who is rebuked and instead identify with Wisdom herself.[114] Through the manipulation of various voices and explicit addressees, Proverbs prompts the student – and the implicit student, the reader/listener – to identify with the father and Wisdom but against sinners, fools, and the strange woman, much like the phenomenon that Volk identifies in Lucretius's poem.

Volk suggests that another key aspect of the didactic genre is "poetic simultaneity," the concept that the events or action the poet is describing are unfolding at that very moment. For example, Ovid's *Ars amatoria*, in which a seasoned teacher instructs his students in the art of seduction, begins in the future tense as the poet anticipates his forthcoming song: "The truth will I sing; Mother of Love, favour my design.... We will sing of guiltless delights, and of thefts allowed; and in my song there shall be nought that is criminal."[115] As the teacher moves from topic to topic, the poem presents his speech as simultaneous to the external events of the young men's love affairs. Volk argues that this trait throughout the poem indicates that the speaker is not just providing theoretical guidance to the addressed students but rather gives the impression that the young men "are already following the teacher's advice, and the love affair the persona is describing is at the same time actually taking place."[116] Not only does the instruction unfold as the poem advances, but it also reflects the students' growing skill. Volk notes that the poem speaks of the resounding success of both teacher and student: "the young man who entered his military service at the beginning of Book 1 is now a veritable Achilles ([2.]741–2), while the poet proclaims himself the greatest craftsman of love (*amator*) of all times (735–8)."[117] In fact, Volk argues that in this way the poem is an

---

[114] For a more thorough discussion of Prov 1, see Chapter 4. Sun Myung Lyu observes that while Proverbs speaks *about* the wicked, it does not address the wicked explicitly. This, he concludes, indicates that the intended audience of the book excludes the wicked. In this sense, "the chief opposition lies between the wicked and the rest of the audience rather than between the wicked and the righteous" (Sun Myung Lyu, *Righteousness in the Book of Proverbs* [FAT II; Tübingen: Mohr Siebeck, 2012], 73). Through this rhetoric, the book thus prompts its student to identify himself against the wicked.

[115] Ovid, *The Art of Love* (trans. Henry T. Riley; ed. Walter S. Keating; New York: Stravon Publishers, 1949), 15.

[116] Volk, *The Poetics of Latin Didactic*, 178.

[117] Ibid., 186.

example of a didactic poem that actually "works," for "the reader of the book 'really' does become a *doctus amator,* the teacher's advice is automatically put into practice and has its desired effect."[118]

Proverbs 1–9 has a similar, although not identical, effect as the voices of the father, woman Wisdom, and the strange woman reverberate throughout the chapters. Throughout the nine chapters, woman Wisdom's voice serves as a compass to steer the student on the proper path. Her virtues are compelling because she echoes the advice of the father (see 8:32–36) and embodies the very traits that the father extols in his son. Wisdom has found knowledge and savvy (8:12; cf. 1:4, 2:5, 3:21), possesses counsel and competence (8:14; cf. 3:21), loves those who love her (8:17; cf. 4:6), and walks in the path of righteousness and justice (8:20; cf. 1:3, 2:20). As the student hears her appeal, he finds in Wisdom the virtues that he is admonished to seek. On the other hand, the wife of another man embodies nefarious desire in her speech. The appeal of her character is her erotic allure (7:11–13). She offers sensuous delight (7:16–17) and promises passionate embrace (7:18). She rejects the rival discourse of fidelity (cf. 5:18; 6:32), for her husband is not at home (7:19). Who will know? Her voice makes a valiant appeal to the ethos of the reader, yet her persuasive power is ultimately undermined by the virtues of Wisdom and the father.

With each of these particular voices, Proverbs displays before the student a dispute of character between the father, Wisdom, and the strange woman. By permitting the opposing voices to speak, although ultimately maintaining control of their appeal, Proverbs enacts a process of pedagogy. The poetry itself is the discipline. It exposes the young man to various voices he may encounter, while educating his cognitive and emotional faculties to discern the righteous speaker from the one who is harmful. In this sense, it evidences an aspect of the "poetic simultaneity" that Volk observes in Ovid. The lesson unfolds in each successive poem and engages the student in its pedagogical process. Unlike *Ars amatoria,* however, Prov 1–9 is not one long poem that is held together by an overarching narrative framework. It is not clear that the student is necessarily any wiser at the end of chapter 9 (or the end of the book as a whole). Nonetheless, the poems that comprise these chapters do not merely describe the content of a lesson or a set of moral axioms, but they unfold as the lesson itself, positioning the student as the one who acquires wisdom and discernment.

---

[118] Ibid., 188.

Robert Frost states that poetry "begins in delight and ends in wis-dom,"[119] and indeed, didactic poetry often employs the delightful play of language and imagery to advance its desired end of wisdom. Lucretius uses the metaphor of a "honeyed cup" to describe poetry's function in pedagogy. As a doctor lines a child's cup of medicine with honey so that she will drink it, so poetry constitutes the pleasurable honey that will make the student swallow the teaching: "the better to engage your mind with hexameter verses so that you may discover the world and how it is made, and come to a better understanding of the true nature of things."[120] Dalzell also highlights the capacity of didactic poetry to use its pleasure to advance knowledge of a subject. He affirms that "a didactic poet must conceive of his subject poetically, that is to say, he must develop imagi-natively what is implied in the material of his subject. The poem does not exist for its 'embellishments'; rather, the 'embellishments' enrich and broaden our understanding of the subject."[121] The outward form of poetry is thus crucial to its didactic function.

So too in Proverbs, the use of vivid language and imagery serves to rein-force the pedagogical goal. Proverbs does not issue a dry and staid descrip-tion of the alternatives of wisdom and foolishness before the student. On the contrary, it portrays these paths with rich images of their appearance, smell, taste, and sound, appealing to the range of the student's senses. For example, one can almost taste the allure of the strange woman, whose lips drip with honey and are smoother than oil (5:3). Her bed becomes an object one can touch and smell, for it is covered in fine Egyptian linen (7:16) and sprinkled with myrrh, aloes, and cinnamon (7:17). Both woman Wisdom and the foolish woman invite the simple to a banquet to eat their food and drink their wine (9:4–5, 16–17). Such descriptions are not just literary embellishment, but serve the larger didactic purpose of educating the student's senses and emotions – not just his mind or cognition – to choose the way of wisdom. Within Proverbs, wisdom is not simply a set of precepts that the student must memorize, but rather it is figured as an appealing and desirable object that the student must imbibe, delight in, and even love (2:10; 4:6; 8:17). Those who highlight the discur-sive nature of Prov 1–9 as "lectures" or "instructions" often tend to over-look the significance of such imagery, yet this is a crucial feature of the

[119] Robert Frost, "The Figure a Poem Makes," in *The Robert Frost Reader: Poetry and Prose* (eds. E. C. Lathem and L. R. Thompson; New York: Henry Holt and Co., 2002), 440.
[120] Lucretius, *De rerum natura*, I. 851–65. For an analysis of this passage, see Volk, *The Poetics of Latin Didactic*, 96–99.
[121] Dalzell, *The Criticism of Didactic Poetry*, 130.

text's function as pedagogy. Following the way of wisdom not only makes intellectual sense, it also proves to be enticing, pleasurable, and beneficial for the student.

In sum, considering the ways in which Prov 1–9 participates in the genre of didactic poetry illumines the relationship between its poetic form and its pedagogical function. Didactic poetry involves a constellation between speaker/teacher, reader/student, and subject that seeks to shape the student as one who desires certain knowledge and seeks the pleasure of learning. Within Prov 1–9, the reader is positioned as the student in relation to various characters, some of whom prove wise teachers – the father and Wisdom – and others who present negative enticements. As the student hears the address of various voices throughout the poems alongside the father's guiding commentary, he becomes schooled in discerning the way of wisdom.

Yet didactic poetry is not the only genre in which Prov 1–9 participates. This collection of poems contains some features that have more in common with Hebrew love poetry than with didactic texts, such as legal codes or wisdom psalms. In fact, Prov 1–9 bears a surprising resemblance to the Song of Songs, particularly in its language of desire and its form as a collection of discrete poems that can be read as a unit, and the comparison of these texts suggests another genre that Prov 1–9 invokes: the Hebrew love lyric.

## Proverbs beyond Didactic Poetry

The resonance between Prov 1–9 and the Song is most readily apparent in Proverbs' use of sensual imagery. The strange woman, for example, is described with vivid and alluring language: "For the lips of the strange woman drip honey (כי נפת תטפנה שפתי זרה), and her mouth is smoother than oil (וחלק משמן חכה)" (Prov 5:3). In the Song, the beloved describes the Shulammite likewise: "Honey drips from your lips, O bride (נפת תטפנה שפתותיך כלה); honey and milk are under your tongue" (Song 4:11). Equally provocative language is used by the father of Proverbs to portray the young man's wife. She is "a loving doe, a graceful mountain goat (אילת אהבים ויעלת־חן)" (Prov 5:19a). The father exhorts his son to "let her breasts satisfy you at all times (דדיה ירוך בכל־עת)" (Prov 5:19b). Similarly, the Shulammite's beloved is "like a gazelle or a young stag (דומה דודי לצבי או לעפר האילים)" (Song 2:9). These lovers are also encouraged to become intoxicated with love: "Eat, lovers, and drink! Be drunk with love! (אכלו רעים שתו ושכרו דודים)" (Song 5:1c). Both texts also describe lovemaking with the metaphor of fountains and cisterns.[122] The father advises, "Drink water from your own cistern, flowing water from your own well (שתה־מים מבורך ונזלים מתוך בארך). Your springs will gush forth in the squares with streams (יפוצו מעינתיך חוצה ברחבות פלגי־מים)" (Prov 5:15–16a). And the beloved extols his lover as "a garden fountain, a well of living water (מעין גנים באר מים חיים)" (Song 4:15). Woman Wisdom is compared to fine gold and jewels (Prov 3:14–15), just as the Shulammite (Song 1:10–11) and her beloved (Song 5:11, 14–15). Even the pleasing and peaceful paths of wisdom (דרכיה דרכי־נעם וכל־נתיבותיה שלום, Prov 3:17) may have overtones of love language.[123]

Proverbs employs the language of love and desire for didactic ends. In chapter 4, for example, love imagery and instruction are intertwined:

> Possess wisdom! Possess understanding!
>     Do not forget – do not stray from the words of my mouth!
> Do not abandon her, and she will keep you.
>     Love her! And she will guard you.
> The beginning of wisdom – possess Wisdom!
>     Above all of your possessions, possess Understanding!
> Adore her, and she will exalt you –
>     She will honor you, if you embrace her.
> She will set upon your head a wreath of grace,
>     an incredible crown she will gift you. (Prov 4:5–9)[124]

Here the father urges his son to seek after Wisdom with love, and he envisions mutual affection between Wisdom and the young man: "Hug to her (סלסלה) and she will exalt you" (4:8a). What is at stake for the poetry of Proverbs is not purely intellectual virtue or disdain for the sexual appeal of the strange woman. Rather, the poetry seeks to cultivate one who embodies desire rightly placed, embracing desire as a tool of discipline. The father's instruction to love wisdom is not merely referring to an esoteric kind of love, but it is couched in language of physical affection and desire. "She will honor you if you *embrace* her" (תכבדך כי תחבקנה), the father explains (4:8b).[125] This is what it means to hold fast to discipline (החזק במוסר, 4:13).[126] From the outset, the father's instruction concerning

---

[122] For a discussion of water imagery in the Song, as well as its relation to the larger "imaginative fields" in the book see Jill M. Munro, *Spikenard and Saffron: The Imagery of the Song of Songs* (JSOTSup 203; Sheffield: Sheffield Academic Press, 1995), especially 110–16.

[123] Compare the use of נעם in Song 1:16, "Surely you, my beloved, are handsome and pleasant (הנך יפה רעיתי אף נעים)" and 7:7 (מה־יפית ומה־נעמת). See also Song 8:10: "Then I became in his eyes as one who finds favor" (כמוצאת שלום).

[124] For notes on the translation, see Chapter 6.

[125] See also Prov 5:20, where חבק clearly refers to the physical embrace of a woman.

[126] Note the sound play between חבק in verse 8 and חזק in verse 13.

discipline and fostering wisdom in the son uses the language of desire as part of its appeal.[127] Proverbs seeks to form youth who are shaped by the desire of wisdom. In this sense, Proverbs is love poetry with a pedagogical aim.

Yet Proverbs recognizes that desire can also have a dark side.[128] Proverbs 5 explores the problem of misplaced desire, that is, desire of the strange woman. She is an alluring beauty, her lips dripping with luxurious liquids (5:3). But she is a sharp-edged sword, and the desire of this woman leads to Sheol (5:4–5). The student is advised to avoid "the opening of her house" (5:8), even as the poetry concedes the desirability of her appeal. Yet it is not desire, in and of itself, that is the problem. To the contrary, the student is urged to "rejoice in the wife of your youth" (5:18b-19). The poetry delights in the image of abundant water and gushing streams (5:15–18a), language which even exceeds the oil and honey of the strange woman's charms. Fox notes that "the father depicts his son's wife as ipso facto graceful, lovely, and *sexy*. Let the youth make *her* the object of his desire."[129] While the one who pursues the strange woman rejects discipline (5:12, 23), desire, rightly placed, is not incompatible with the path of the upright.[130]

A hallmark of love poetry is not simply desire but, more specifically, the theme of *unsatiated* desire, and it is a feature common to both the Song and Proverbs. Within the Song, this unfolds as each of the lovers extols the virtues of his or her beloved and expresses a longing to find the other. The Shulammite conveys her unsatisfied desire as she speaks of seeking out her beloved and laments that she cannot find him (Song 3:1–2; 5:6).[131]

---

[127] The sages of Proverbs, Fox argues, insist "that we do more than simply obey the teachings or learn wisdom for utilitarian advantage alone. They insist on an emotional commitment, a desire for learning.... Without love, knowledge is inert. Hence we are required to love wisdom (4:6; 7:4; 29:3; cf. 8:34)" (Fox, *Proverbs 1–9*, 275).

[128] The dark side of desire is also a pressing theme in the Song. For a treatment of the many facets of desire in the Song of Songs, see Carey Ellen Walsh, *Exquisite Desire: Religion, the Erotic, and the Song of Songs* (Minneapolis: Augsburg Fortress, 2000). For a fuller treatment of desire in Proverbs, see Chapter 6.

[129] Fox, *Proverbs 1–9*, 202, emphasis in original.

[130] Note the parallel language as the student is urged to be drunk continually in the love of his wife (באהבתה תשגה תמיד, Prov 5:19b), while he is warned not to be infatuated with the strange woman (ולמה תשגה בני בזרה, Prov 5:20), for such a fool will only be drunk in his great foolishness (וברב אולתו ישגה, Prov 5:23b). For a more thorough discussion of Prov 5, see Chapter 7.

[131] J. Cheryl Exum notes that the poetic form of the Song facilitates the theme of desire for the other: "The poetic preoccupation with conjuring – the drive to overcome absence with presence through language – becomes particularly intense in 3:1–4, where desire is channeled into one overriding concern, seeking and finding the loved one. This is conveyed through an ordered pattern of repetition and variation" (J. Cheryl Exum, *The Song of Songs* [OTL; Louisville: Westminster John Knox, 2005], 134).

This theme has a surprising counterpart within Proverbs, where it is not only a question of the student's desire for Wisdom or the strange woman, but also their desire for him. In this respect, while it is not always an explicitly erotic desire, as in the Song, the rhetoric of Wisdom and the strange woman bears a remarkable similarity to the lover in the Song. For example, in chapter 1, Wisdom cries out in the streets and open places (Prov 1:20); she shouts in the midst of bustling roads and city gates (Prov 1:21). Yet her cries go unanswered; her advances are denied (Prov 1:24). Similarly, the Shulammite shouts for her beloved, vowing to call him in the streets and the open places (Song 3:2a), although she laments, "I sought him but I did not find him" (Song 3:2b). Unlike the Shulammite, however, Wisdom vows to be elusive to those that seek her (Prov 1:28), disdaining those who have spurned her (Prov 1:30). Wisdom's desire is that her affections be reciprocated, but as that desire is unsatisfied, she, in turn, will prove difficult to apprehend.[132]

The theme of desire within Proverbs is complicated by the presence of the strange woman, who also seeks out the young man and urges him to seek her. Proverbs uses the metaphor of desire to display a conflict between woman Wisdom and the strange woman as rivals for the young man's affections.[133] Chapter 7 develops the image of the strange woman as one who dwells in dark corners and is exceedingly difficult to locate: "a foot in the street, another in the squares – beside every corner she lurks" (7:12).[134] Echoing the language of desire heard elsewhere in Proverbs, the strange woman exclaims: "Then I went out to call you (לִקְרָאתֶךָ), to seek your face (לְשַׁחֵר פָּנֶיךָ)! And I found you (וָאֶמְצָאֶךָ)" (7:15). With evocative language, the strange woman woos her suitor and offers satiety in love (7:16–18, 21). Yet the promise of this satiety is destruction. Fools follow

---

[132] Wisdom's speech in chapter 1 has often been associated with prophetic address. Fox compares the image of refusing to be found with God's response to recalcitrant Israel (Hos 5:6, 15) (Fox, *Proverbs 1–9*, 102). Likewise, Carole R. Fontaine notes that "this kind of speech, with its emphasis on divine offer and human rejection, is associated only with God or an authorized intermediary such as a prophet" (Carole R. Fontaine, "Proverbs," in *Women's Bible Commentary: Expanded Edition*, [eds. Carol A. Newsom and Sharon H. Ringe; Louisville: Westminster John Knox, 1998], 155). However, the language of seeking and finding has as much resonance with love poetry, such as that found in the Song.

[133] Note, for example, the contrast in Wisdom's speech that "those who love me I love" (אֲנִי אֹהֲבַי [אֹהֲבֶיהָ] אֵהָב, 8:17), but "all who hate me love death" (כָּל־מְשַׂנְאַי אָהֲבוּ מָוֶת, 8:36). The imagery of death is a direct reference to the strange woman, whose poem in chapter 7 also ends with the word "death" (7:27). Fox notes that "for Proverbs, love and hate are not two emotions among many. They are the polar mind-sets that define the basic shape of a person's character. The wise are typified by love of wisdom and hate of deceit, fools by their perverse loves and hatreds" (Fox, *Proverbs 1–9*, 275).

[134] For notes to the translation and further analysis of Prov 7, see Chapter 6.

her, but the strange woman's path ends in death.[135] Whereas Wisdom makes it more difficult for those who seek her to find her, thus prolonging the satisfaction of desire, the strange woman offers the sure satiety of desire: death. As these two different models of desire play out through the book, the wise student is schooled to seek after a desire that is more difficult to attain.

Neither Proverbs nor the Song has a strong plot that develops over the course of the book and leads to a conclusion, a feature which in fact underscores the theme of unsatiated desire. Instead, both the Song and Prov 1–9 are a series of poems that alternate between various voices; and as a whole, each collection ends without resolution. The Song ends as the beloved bounds off into the hills, the lovers' desire never consummated (Song 8:14).[136] Proverbs 9 ends with the banquet of the foolish woman (9:13–18), not the banquet of woman Wisdom (9:1–6), as one might expect if this were the story of the son developing wisdom, and in fact it is not clear that the son has succeeded in finding wisdom by the end of chapter 9.[137] Neither of these texts is organized by the linear progression of thought that characterizes prose and provides a general trajectory that structures the work as a whole. While there are certain narrative aspects to the poems, they do not form a continuous narrative from beginning to end.[138] In this respect, the poetic form of the texts captures something about the nature of desire. As J. Cheryl Exum explains concerning the Song:

> The Song of Songs is lyric poetry; its progression ... is not linear but rather meandering. It surges forward and circles back upon itself, continuously

[135] In a stunning poetic closure, the entire poem of chapter 7 ends, "going down to the chambers of death" (רְשָׁדוֹת אֶל־חַדְרֵי־מָוֶת, 7:27). See Barbara Herrnstein Smith, *Poetic Closure: A Study of How Poems End* (Chicago: University of Chicago, 1968), 102.

[136] Exum writes that the ending of the Song leads the reader back to the beginning, for the missed consummation is in fact the dynamic of the Song itself, "the seeking latent in finding and the finding latent in seeking, the separation prerequisite to union ... It is what the Song leads us to expect to happen, over and over" (Exum, *The Song of Songs*, 262–63). Similarly, Munro observes that the effect of the close of the Song "is to assure us that the Song will never end. The lovers will evermore be engaged in love's game of hide and seek" (Munro, *Spikenard and Saffron*, 89).

[137] In this respect, the book of Proverbs differs from several ancient Near Eastern wisdom texts that couch their instruction in a tale of the education of a particular student. See, for example, the *Instruction of Ankhsheshonqy*, which begins with a narrative explanation of the circumstances leading to the instruction, or the *Instruction of Any*, which ends with a conversation between the student and his father concerning what he has and has not learned.

[138] Such as the Shulammite's report of her dream about searching for her beloved (Song 3:1–4) or the father's description of the scene outside of his window of the strange woman (Prov 7:6–23). Yet, as Alter points out, such elements are more frequently "episodic narrativity" than actual narrative, for when narrative is embedded within poetry, it often does not serve as a plot-structuring device but as an intensification of a particular image or theme (Alter, *The Art of Biblical Poetry*, 61).

and effortlessly repeating its acts of conjuring and reissuing its invitation to the reader.... [T]he poetic rhythm of the Song, ever forward and then returning, reflects the repetitive pattern of seeking and finding in which the lovers engage, which is the basic pattern of sexual love: longing – satisfaction – renewed longing – and so on. The prolonging of desire and of fulfillment stretching across the span of the poem plays an essential part in the Song's effectiveness – its power – as a love poem.[139]

In other words, the Song does not tell a story or make a logical argument about desire, but it uses the poetic form to enact the nature of desire. The nature of desire emerges not as the conclusion to a plot or the logical deduction of an argument, but in a series of snapshots as the theme is teased out over the course of several poems that capture various moments in the lovers' pursuit, from their ecstatic expressions of love to their desperate longing to find the other. The Song relies on the form of lyric poetry to convey the captivating, capricious, consuming, and, ultimately, insatiable nature of desire.

So too in Proverbs, the nonlinear progression of the poetry plays an essential part in its larger pedagogical point. The concept of desire in Proverbs is not limited to erotic desire. Rather, it is also a metaphor for the pursuit of wisdom and the potentially competing attraction of the way of foolishness. Throughout the nine chapters, images of the righteous and the wicked, Wisdom and the strange woman, the path of life and the highway to Sheol, alternate and constantly force the student to negotiate their competing – and desirable – claims. The father could simply state (and sometimes does) that the young man should avoid the strange woman and pursue Wisdom. Yet instead the poetry presents alternative visions of the allure of both women, and thus it builds its argument by offering these contrasting images, intermingled with the father's alternating admonishment and encouragement, not by long discourses on the relative merits or perils of one or the other. In this sense, the poetry enacts the thinking process of the student who is alternately attracted to wisdom and to destructive desires as he learns to discern the beneficial desires from the harmful. Accordingly, when taken as a whole, the poems communicate an essential premise of Proverbs' wisdom: discerning among competing desires is a vital component of discipline. Furthermore, one must continually cultivate the ability to discern wise desires from harmful ones, for the search for wisdom never ends. The wise person must have an insatiable desire for wisdom.

What Exum terms the "meandering" progression of poetry is an important feature by which lyric poetry may make certain arguments. Helen

[139] Exum, *The Song of Songs*, 11–12.

Vendler argues that lyric poems are not simply the domain of emotion and the senses but are capable of intellectual reasoning. She insists that lyric poems frequently evidence a developing thought process and that the reader participates in the "drama" of unfolding thought "as we are worked on by the linguistic processes in view."[140] Vendler articulates the distinction between prose and poetry as a difference in the structure and development of its thought. Unlike prose, poetry does not simply present axioms in a logical, linear fashion, but rather it evidences an active and ongoing thought development that emerges over the course of the poem. The "thinking" of poetry is "always in process, always active. It issues ... in pictures of the human mind at work, recalling, evaluating, and structuring experience."[141] This is why the import of poems cannot be appreciated by paraphrasing their main point, but rather the point "can be grasped only by our *participating* in the process they unfold."[142] For example, in her treatment of Alexander Pope's poem, *Essay on Man,* which parodies the philosophical discussion of the five senses, Vendler discusses the way in which Pope plays with language and infuses the philosophical ideas with a certain whimsicality. In so doing, Pope creates "living thought," Vendler claims, that stands in stark contrast to the "thought embalmed" of his philosophical subject. Vendler insists that Pope creates an *experience* of active thought, which "must advance too swiftly for instant intelligibility: the reader must hang on for the ride, bouncing to the next hurdle hardly having recovered his seat from the last. It is as if the poet wants to say, 'This is what thinking really is like: have you ever known it?' "[143] Although Vendler studies English lyric poetry, a different corpus than Hebrew literature, the dynamic she observes is present to some degree in both the Song and Proverbs. Both of these collections use poetry to advance a larger point about the nature of desire (Song) and its connection to discipline (Proverbs).

Similarly, Robert von Hallberg suggests that lyric poetry is uniquely situated to accommodate vacillations of thought and experience in a way that linear prose is not. In this way, poetry can lead the reader toward more complex thought. Indeed, "one thinks in a poem not so much *of* a truth as *toward* something unpossessed."[144] Thus, "the value of lyrical thinking, and

---

[140] Helen Vendler, *Poets Thinking: Pope, Whitman, Dickinson, Yeats* (Cambridge: Harvard University Press, 2004), 6.
[141] Ibid., 119.
[142] Ibid., emphasis added.
[143] Ibid., 27.
[144] Robert von Hallberg, *Lyric Powers* (Chicago: University of Chicago Press, 2008), 125; emphasis in original.

of poetry in particular, is to lead consciousness toward ever more comprehensive ideograms, or ideas of order and coherence."[145] Proverbs contains an element of such "lyrical thinking," insofar as it presents a kaleidoscope of various speakers, themes, and images, often switching quickly from one to another without clear transition.[146] Within Proverbs, this tool fosters a more comprehensive discernment as the young man encounters, always through the guiding vision of the father, both the sanctioned discourse of wisdom and the rival discourse of the strange woman, sinners, or other disreputable characters. He thus becomes patterned as one who is able to resist the temptations of the wrong objects and pursue those of value.

In this sense, the poetry of Prov 1–9 presents an unfolding process of pedagogy that schools the reader as a student of wisdom who is alternatively exposed to patterns of wisdom and foolishness. As it vacillates between images of wise and foolish desires, portraits of righteous and wicked characters, and words of uprightness and crookedness, it enacts a process of pedagogy that patterns the student as one who seeks the desires, character, and speech that the text sanctions. In this way, these chapters entertain various moral codes by permitting the voices of different speakers and offering images of the righteous and the wicked alike.[147] In so doing, it in fact guides the student to become his own ethical critic, one who is able to compare various patterns of desire and discern the helpful from the harmful. For this reason, it offers the student tools of analysis not simply to parrot the father's claims, but to discern the path of wisdom amidst a bewildering array of choices in daily life. As Wayne C. Booth suggests, the best "literary friends" are helpful because they "introduce us

---

[145] Ibid., 139. For another way in which poetry involves the reader in the thinking process, note Edward L. Greenstein's discussion of "staircase variation" in Hebrew poetry, in which the first line in the structure is syntactically incomplete until the second or third line. This functions to slow the reader's mental perception: "Since we process incoming speech clause by clause, we must suspend processing until the completion of the clause is presented in the second line. Our perception is kept on edge, so to speak, during such a staircase" (Edward L. Greenstein, "How Does Parallelism Mean?" in *A Sense of Text: The Art of Language in the Study of Biblical Literature: Papers from a Symposium at the Dropsie College for Hebrew and Cognate Learning, May 11, 1982* [JQR Supplement; Winona Lake: Eisenbrauns, 1982], 55). Another form of this staircase variation occurs when the same phrase is repeated in the first and second lines but one of the words or phrases has a different syntactical function in the second line. In this way, Greenstein explains, "we must do a sort of double-take and analyze that word or phrase twice. The phrase serves a double function, but we cannot perceive it in both functions at the same time" (ibid.).

[146] For example, in the first chapter alone there are several shifts of tone and focus, from the highly parallelistic discourse of the purpose of the book in verses 2–6, to the address to the son to listen to parental discipline (1:8–9), the scene of conspiring sinners (1:10–19), and the call of Wisdom (1:20–33).

[147] By "moral code," I mean a value system of a particular person or group. In this text, the strange woman represents one moral code, while Wisdom represents another.

to the practice of subtle, sensitive moral inference, the kind that most moral choices in daily life require of us."[148] Likewise in Proverbs, the father introduces the reader to various desires that constantly require moral discernment as the poetry develops, as if to say (to paraphrase Vendler), "This is what the search for wisdom really is like – have you ever known it?"

## Proverbs and the Genre(s) of Biblical Hebrew Poetry (Again)

To consider the poetic genres in which Proverbs participates opens a new window of analysis than that offered by a form-critical emphasis on the instruction genre. Proverbs 1–9 is sophisticated didactic poetry that also shares prominent features with Hebrew lyric love poetry. Yet its resonance with the Hebrew lyric ultimately serves to advance the text's pedagogical aims. Proverbs 1–9 uses the language of desire and the lyric organization of its thought to contribute to its didactic ends. In so doing, it offers a unique articulation of didactic poetry, which is not necessarily shared by other kinds of didactic poetry. The proverbial collections in Prov 10–29, for example, also participate in the genre of didactic poetry, yet they are not characterized by long poems or sustained speaking voices, although they have a similar didactic goal and also rely on certain poetic features for a pedagogical function. As a whole, the book of Proverbs points to the diversity of forms within a single genre, as well as the often porous bounds of genre. It is no wonder that providing a general definition of Hebrew poetry is such a difficult task. Perhaps the true continuum is not between poetry and prose but between the genres of Hebrew poetry themselves.

[148] Wayne C. Booth, *The Company We Keep: An Ethics of Fiction* (Berkeley: University of California Press, 1988), 287.

# PART II

# *Models of* Mûsār

## Introduction: Proverbs and the Simplicity Thesis

[T]he man of maxims is the popular representative of the minds that
are guided in their moral judgment solely by general rules, thinking that these will lead them to justice by a ready-made patent
method, without the trouble of exerting patience, discrimination,
impartiality – without any care to assure themselves whether they
have the insight that comes from a hardly-earned estimate of temptation, or from a life vivid and intense enough to have created a wide
fellow-feeling with all that is human.[1]

The search for knowledge in every age has only the confidence which
it has been given and is forced to a halt at specific limits. Thus, both
its optimism and its pessimism are of a specific kind. It is bad if the
exegete seizes on one aspect of what is, in all periods, a very lively
process of grasp of meaning and loss of meaning and makes it the
criterion of two major phases in Israel's education system.[2]

If there is such a thing as the truth about the subject matter of
ethics – the truth, we might say, about the ethical – why is there any
expectation that it should be simple?[3]

In *Ethics and the Limits of Philosophy*, Bernard Williams argues that modern moral philosophy is largely reductive and simplistic. Whether deontological, utilitarian, or contractualist in orientation, many approaches to
moral philosophy, he insists, attempt to reduce all ethical deliberation to
one particular pattern in an effort to show that a certain element, such

---

[1] George Eliot, *The Mill on the Floss* (ed. Carol T. Christ; New York: Norton & Company, 1994),
VII.2: 403.
[2] Gerhard von Rad, *Wisdom in Israel* (trans. James D. Martin; London: SCM Press, 1972; repr.,
Harrisburg: Trinity Press International, 1993), 110.
[3] Bernard Williams, *Ethics and the Limits of Philosophy* (Cambridge: Harvard University Press,
1985), 17.

as obligation or one's sense of the good, is primary and that all other ethical considerations can be explained in light of it. Consequently, such expressions of moral philosophy are inadequate to capture the complexity of moral life, and they operate with an impoverished notion of ethical concepts that are overly general, such as "good," "right," or "ought."[4] In contrast to these "thin" ethical concepts, Williams advocates for greater attention to so-called thick or substantive ethical concepts, which are more richly descriptive and evaluative.[5] Thick ethical concepts, such as justice, gratitude, or brutality, are characterized by their specificity. They are "action-guiding," for they are related to reasons for a person's action, and they are "world-guided," in the sense that their application is determined by real conditions of the world.[6] Moreover, thick ethical concepts reflect not only ethical judgments, but also emotional, aesthetic, and prudential responses, calling on the range of human feeling and experience.[7]

In Williams's estimation, reductive approaches to moral philosophy neglect the thick concepts in favor of the thin and in so doing ignore the complexity of moral discourse. A similar dynamic is at work in much scholarship on the book of Proverbs, which often reduces the moral discourse of the book to a simplistic scheme of good versus bad, right versus wrong. James L. Crenshaw, for example, states that within Proverbs, "The wise were righteous, and fools wicked. This surprising conclusion arose from the operative assumption that anyone who strengthened the order upholding the universe belonged to God's forces, while those who undermined this harmony were enemies of the creator."[8] Indeed, many wisdom scholars appear to share George Eliot's withering evaluation of the "men of maxims" insofar as they characterize the Israelite sages who were responsible for Proverbs as dogmatic, rigid, or removed from the human condition, particularly in contrast to the perspectives of Job or Qoheleth.

---

[4] Ibid., 128.

[5] Williams's notion of "thick" concepts is not related to Clifford Geertz's anthropological category of thick descriptions. For an analysis of Williams's thought, see Chloë Fitzgerald and Peter Goldie, "Thick Concepts and Their Role in Moral Psychology," in *Emotions, Imagination, and Moral Reasoning* (ed. Robyn Langdon and Catriona Mackenzie; New York: Psychology Press, 2012), 219–36.

[6] Williams, *Ethics and the Limits of Philosophy*, 140–41.

[7] For example, an act of cannibalism could be termed "disgusting," which is at once an ethical evaluation (eating another human's remains is not natural), an aesthetic response (the sight itself may be repulsive), a prudential judgment (the practice is not hygienic), and even an emotional description (e.g., sparking anger); it provides much more information and evaluation about the act than merely describing it as "bad" or something one ought not to do. For a description of this typology, see Fitzgerald and Goldie, "Thick Concepts," 223.

[8] James L. Crenshaw, *Old Testament Wisdom: An Introduction* (rev. ed.; Westminster John Knox, 1998), 67.

A tacit assumption of much wisdom scholarship is the presumed naïveté, simplicity, or rigidity of the worldview represented by Proverbs, particularly by the sentences of Prov 10–29. While this is certainly not a universal presumption, its pervasiveness is obscured by the implicit ways in which such notions inform certain conclusions about the nature of wisdom, the development of the literary tradition, and the differences among the wisdom books. Thus the frequent caricature of Israelite wisdom indicates that Proverbs represents the so-called traditional wisdom, optimistic in its outlook, which is later challenged by the more pessimistic perspectives of Qoheleth or Job, both of which represent a "crisis" for the wisdom tradition. R. B. Y. Scott, for example, speaking of the various sayings in Proverbs that correlate moral judgments with material consequences, speculates:

> Such doctrinaire teaching must have become firmly lodged in the theological wing of the wisdom teachers to have called forth such a passionate rejoinder in the Book of Job. Job, too, is a wise man, but one whose searing personal suffering has brought him down from the clouds of theorizing to the hard ground of reality. The truth that emerges from his physical and mental torment confronts the mechanical oversimplification of scholastic teaching.[9]

While Scott is not speaking of Proverbs as a whole, per se,[10] he implies that the book contains a kind of wisdom that is characterized by a "mechanical oversimplification" that is divorced from reality, caught instead in the lofty "clouds of theorizing." And Scott is certainly not alone in this presumption. Walther Zimmerli spoke of wisdom's "naïve optimism and the unhistorical approach to life as necessary emanations from this basic rationalistic attitude."[11] Similarly, William McKane found the YHWH sayings in Proverbs[12] to be frequently characterized by a strict dichotomy between the righteous and the wicked that is detached from reality:

> The extreme tidiness of the doctrine is an indication of its sterility and its disengagement from mundane realities. This is not old wisdom but

[9] R. B. Y. Scott, *The Way of Wisdom in the Old Testament* (New York: Macmillan, 1971), 139; Scott also notes that "Qoheleth, too, was a wise man in revolt against the traditional doctrine of retribution," although Qoheleth's objections were based on different grounds than were Job's (ibid., 140). Yet both Job and Qoheleth "are wise men in revolt against the unexamined assumptions of their colleagues" (ibid.).

[10] He cites Prov 10:3 and 15:25 as representative examples of a doctrine of retribution, which he suggests that Job's friends maintain "with a rigidity that drives the sufferer to distraction" (ibid., 139).

[11] Walther Zimmerli, "Concerning the Structure of Old Testament Wisdom," in *Studies in Ancient Israelite Wisdom* (ed. James L. Crenshaw; New York: KTAV, 1976), 199; trans. by Brian Kovacs of "Zur Struktur der alttestamentlichen Weisheit," *ZAW* 51 (1933): 177–204.

[12] McKane's "class C;" see William McKane, *Proverbs: A New Approach* (OTL; Philadelphia: Westminster Press, 1970), 11.

the theory of a kind of Yahwistic piety which is condemned to emptiness because it has disengaged itself from the realities of life and has left all problems behind.[13]

Scott, Zimmerli, and McKane presume that Proverbs contains a wisdom that is removed from reality and is more theoretical than practical, which at first glance may be a surprising conclusion given Proverbs' typical subject matter of daily life. Yet such assumptions are informed by a developmental trajectory from Proverbs to Job and Qoheleth, which are presumably the more "practical" books insofar as they deal more explicitly in the contingencies and vagaries of daily life, according to many commentators.[14] Such distinctions between the wisdom books are also frequently expressed in terms of the "optimism" of Proverbs in distinction to the "pessimism" of Job and Qoheleth. Katharine Dell, for example, succinctly explains the relationship between Proverbs and Job thus:

> While Proverbs maintained an optimistic belief in the doctrine of retribution, Job is seen to be a refutation of this. Job represents the experience of the righteous man to whom suffering unexpectedly came.... Did this not show that the exhortations to lead a good life in order to expect material rewards found in Proverbs were bankrupt?[15]

The developmental scheme of Israelite wisdom has produced the mistaken assumption that there is a simplicity to Proverbs' wisdom that Job and Qoheleth find inadequate because they press wisdom's limits and more adequately explore the complexities of life. It is widely acknowledged that there are certain limits even within Proverbs' wisdom, a point pressed by Gerhard von Rad.[16] Yet even those scholars who note that the wisdom of Proverbs does acknowledge certain ambiguities and contradictions nonetheless often persist in rendering the book's worldview as rather simplistic in orientation. Dell, for example, although she points to some

---

[13] Ibid., 16.

[14] For a survey of the general trajectory from the naïve optimism of Proverbs to the "mature skepticism" of Job and Qoheleth, see Elizabeth Faith Huwiler, "Control of Reality in Israelite Wisdom," (PhD diss., Duke University, 1988), 12–31. For an analysis of the way in which Proverbs has been undervalued in wisdom scholarship, see Peter T. H. Hatton, *Contradiction in the Book of Proverbs: The Deep Waters of Counsel* (Burlington: Ashgate, 2008), 17–45.

[15] Katharine J. Dell, *"Get Wisdom, Get Insight": An Introduction to Israel's Wisdom Literature* (Macon: Smyth & Helwys, 2000), 32.

[16] See von Rad, *Wisdom in Israel*, 97–110. For an extensive treatment of the limits of wisdom and the function of those limits in the Israelite wisdom tradition, particularly the book of Job, see Charles Davis Hankins, "Job and the Limits of Wisdom" (PhD diss., Emory University, 2011).

ambiguity in the sayings,[17] indicates that learning wisdom is ultimately rather simple, according to Proverbs:

> There is a just and individual accounting system in operation. *It is a simple choice to be made by the one who wishes to learn* – either that such people can take the path of wisdom that is smooth and straight and leads to all good things or they can take the path to folly which is full of pitfalls and covered with thorns. There are material rewards associated with these two paths: wealth is the result of wisdom, poverty comes to the unsuspecting fool.[18]

More recent treatments of Proverbs have emphasized greater complexity in the book, although the shape of these arguments often reveals the continued pervasiveness of the notion that Proverbs' worldview, at least as represented by the proverbial sayings, is fundamentally simplistic.[19] For example, in his 2011 monograph *Be Wise, My Son, and Make My Heart Glad: An Exploration of the Courtly Nature of the Book of Proverbs*, Christopher B. Ansberry labels the wisdom contained in Prov 10–24 as "rudimentary" in comparison to the rest of the book.[20] Reading the book as a whole, he suggests that the moral worldview of the book grows in complexity as the collections advance. In Prov 10:1–15:33, the stark polarities between the righteous and the wicked and the wise and the fool provide a simplistic ethical framework to orient the student, which is then made more complex in the later collections. According to Ansberry, the simplicity of the initial presentation is founded in the antitheses between righteous/wise and wicked/fool, for they "present a static, bipolar world in which all people belong to one of two distinguishable groups based on their behavior."[21] He explains that "[t]he simplistic character of this scheme does not mean the complex is an artificial construct. Rather the indefinite character-consequence connection serves as a foundational

---

[17] Dell names ambiguity as one of the themes of Proverbs. She explains that even as there is a picture of an ordered world within the book, "there was seen to be an ambiguity in events.... Sometimes experience was contradictory – and the proverbs make allowance for this" (Dell, *Get Wisdom, Get Insight*, 17).

[18] Ibid., 19; emphasis added.

[19] An important exception to this trend is found in William P. Brown's essay "The Pedagogy of Proverbs 10:1–31:9" in *Character and Scripture: Moral Formation, Community, and Biblical Interpretation* (ed. William P. Brown; Grand Rapids: Eerdmans, 2002), 150–82. Brown argues that there are developments in theme and rhetorical forms as the proverbial collections of the book advance. Brown insists that "the tendency to view the proverbial as pedagogically simplistic is inaccurate, if not prejudicial" (ibid., 151).

[20] Christopher B. Ansberry, *Be Wise, My Son, and Make My Heart Glad: An Exploration of the Courtly Nature of the Book of Proverbs* (BZAW 422; Berlin: De Gruyter, 2011).

[21] Ibid., 77.

building block for the thematic development that takes place throughout
the successive sections of the document."[22]

Similarly, Tomáš Frydrych highlights the polarity at the heart of
Proverbs' worldview,[23] and he indicates that it is a vital part of the book's
paradigmatic construction, "a consciously simplified picture of reality."[24]
On the whole, Frydrych finds that Proverbs depicts an ordered, predictable world in which the wise prosper and fools suffer.[25] Yet he indicates
that the book hints toward a subtle recognition of the limits of wisdom
and the complexities of reality. At first glance, he explains, "the world
which emerges is very black and white: the wise prosper and the fools
come to destruction, over and over again.... A closer reading shows that
indeed some exceptions are at least implied, if not explicitly stated."[26]
Drawing attention to references to fools who prosper or righteous ones
who suffer, as well as significant gaps between the parallel lines of some
sayings, Frydrych argues that "there are both explicit and implicit indica-
tions that the proverbial sages were aware that the picture of the world
they paint is not entirely accurate."[27] He further explains that such gaps
may be part of the explicit rhetorical purpose of the book, giving knowledge to the simple: "it is the stated intention of the book to foster the ability to scrutinise different perspectives, suggesting that there is legitimate
wisdom even outside Proverbs."[28]

Frydrych helpfully points to the pedagogical function of the ambiguities and limits indicated within Proverbs, yet he also does not go far
enough in thoroughly rebutting the supposed naïveté of the book. He
does reject the notion that its simplicity results from a total removal from
reality, for "if, from our contemporary experience, the book appears to
be very naïve, we must resist the temptation to see it is a product of a
primitive or dogmatic mind."[29] But instead he indicates that its simplicity

---

[22] Ibid.
[23] Frydrych defines "worldview" as "an overall and comprehensive set of beliefs about the world and
one's place in it which informs, if not dictates, one's behaviour" (Tomáš Frydrych, *Living under the
Sun: Examination of Proverbs and Qoheleth* [VTSup 40; Leiden: Brill, 2002], 10).
[24] Ibid., 51. Frydrych understands both Proverbs and Qoheleth as paradigmatic constructions, which
he defines as "a simplification [of] reality with a two-fold purpose, carrying with it a systematic
error, which, however, is considered insignificant for the particular purpose; a paradigm is intended
for specific users and is to be applied under specific conditions; the primary function of a paradigm
is to predict the real system" (ibid., 22).
[25] Ibid., 32.
[26] Ibid., 37.
[27] Ibid., 38.
[28] Ibid., 38–39.
[29] Ibid., 39.

comes from reality itself. He suggests that the worldview of Proverbs arises from a relatively simple, peaceful world in which the family is the central organization and the power of a centralized government is quite limited.[30] In other words, Frydrych suggests that the wisdom contained in Proverbs originates from a fairly idyllic social context, and thus it may be realistic to its context, although perhaps appear naïve with respect to contemporary contexts or even differing socioeconomic contexts of other Israelite wisdom texts. While Frydrych dates Qoheleth to the Hellenistic period, he suggests that the origin of Proverbs' worldview is in a pre-monarchic period. He explains, "Once this perspective is accepted, some of the persistently criticised naiveté of the book disappears, for in such a setting the wicked would indeed more often than not suffer and the righteous prosper, simply due to the economic forces at work in such a small and interdependent community."[31] The simplicity of the book is still an essential premise of Frydrych's conclusions.

One of the fundamental flaws in the "simplicity thesis"[32] is the presumption that the style of the literary form of Proverbs corresponds to a simplicity of moral worldview. It is an implicit assumption of much of the scholarship surveyed here that the terseness of the proverbial sayings and the binary oppositions throughout the book indicate a rigidity and lack of complexity in the sages' moral worldview. Thus Scott can speak of "mechanical oversimplification," and Ansberry of the "static, bipolar world" that is allegedly envisioned. However, one should not be too quick to draw such conclusions. As we have already seen, the form of Proverbs

---

[30] Ibid., 168. Yet he also suggests that the repeated emphasis on the importance of the family and the constant assurances that the wicked will falter and the righteous prosper may also indicate a world in which those elements of order are perceived as under threat (ibid., 148).

[31] Ibid., 213. While he indicates that the literary form likely developed in the monarchic period, Frydrych believes that the final form represents only a limited development from the worldview codified in the pre-monarchic wisdom. Gradually, such views became more removed from present reality: "As the monarchy settled in and developed, the increasing socio-economic changes would have meant that the harmonious life pictured by the ancient sages would have been more and more remote from daily reality, yet, a heritage passionately held onto by successive generations of wise men" (ibid., 214). In a much later period, the perspective of the pre-monarchic period would have served a different function, he suggests: "The book then would not have been seen as depicting the world that was, but the world that could have and ultimately should have been, a world worth striving for, offering hope by pointing back to a time when the righteous prospered and the joy of the wicked was quickly snuffed out" (ibid., 214–15). This evolutionary scheme of the worldview becoming more complex over time is overly anachronistic and cannot be substantiated by the text, which is notoriously difficult to date in any case.

[32] I use the term "simplicity thesis" for the sake of convenience to refer to the general notion that Proverbs has a simplistic, rigid, or naïve view of reality, particularly in comparison to other Israelite wisdom texts. I do not mean to imply that those with whom I associate this idea are of one mind about it or, in some cases, even claim this concept explicitly.

is sophisticated poetry that employs complex word plays and rhyme schemes, as well as an array of figurative language and rich imagery. Its terseness is not indicative of simplicity. Furthermore, both in its literary form and pedagogical function, the book suggests a keen awareness of the complexity of moral reasoning.

## The Models of *Mûsār* in Proverbs

Within Proverbs, the formation of the student's capacity for such complex forms of moral reasoning is tied to the concept of *mûsār*, "discipline." *Mûsār* is at the heart of the book's purpose, as stated from its opening words: to know wisdom and *mûsār* (1:2), to acquire the *mûsār* of sagacity (1:3) (הַשְׂכֵּל). The student of the book is enjoined to hear it (1:8) and warned that fools despise it (1:7). Throughout the book, it is invoked as instruction that one must grasp (4:13), correction that the wise imbibe, even love (13:29), and a lesson that leads to life (6:23; 10:17). As Michael V. Fox explains, *mûsār* is more than practical teaching but is "a moral insight or a quality of moral character."[33] The term is frequently paired with תּוֹכַחַת, "chastisement," and thus associated most commonly with verbal correction. And yet it is also a conceptual category in the book that refers to the task of formation. It is not simply the lesson itself or the action of correction, although the term at times refers to both of these, but it is more broadly the nature of the education that the sages advance. In this sense, it is a multifaceted concept that extends to various modes of intellectual, emotional, and moral development.

Behind the concept of *mûsār* is a sophisticated moral psychology that presumes the complexity of the human person. Accordingly, *mûsār* is a task not only of verbal or physical correction, but of training the student's intellect, emotion, and perception such that his faculties are equipped for navigating the world. Thus the effect of *mûsār* is not described simply as intellectual assent to certain principles, but rather it is a process of acquiring right perception, the proper perspective to see and experience the world. As Prov 15:32 advises, "one who ignores discipline hates himself, but one who listens to reproof gains a heart (לֵב)." In this sense, the pursuit of *mûsār* is connected to an evaluative faculty.

Accordingly, *mûsār* is not a monolithic concept in the book, but it can be separated into at least four discrete models, which I term rebuke,

---

[33] Michael V. Fox, *Proverbs 1–9: A New Translation with Introduction and Commentary* (AB 18A; New York: Doubleday, 2000), 34; cf. 59.

motivation, desire, and imagination. Each model speaks about formation in a particular way, uses certain rhetorical tools to enact formation within the student, and also operates with implicit assumptions about the nature of learning and of human beings. The model of rebuke, for example, encompasses threats of physical punishment and explicit verbal correction, as well as observations about the efficacy of rebuke and advice for those who administer it. It uses the resources of language to make rebuke more immediate to the student and to position the student alternatively as an object of its rebuke and as the onlooker of the rebuke another receives, a dynamic that will be explored in more detail in Chapter 4. These four models are not clearly distinguished by the book itself, but are heuristic categories that I propose to clarify the complexity of pedagogy in the book. While ultimately they often work together, it is useful to consider them separately, for they contain different assumptions and often use different means of appeal. In the following chapters, I will consider the dynamics of each model in turn, while suggesting its implications for the question of moral psychology in Proverbs.

# CHAPTER 4

# *The Model of Rebuke*

Instruct him then in the sayings of the past
May he become a model for the children of the great,
May obedience enter him,
And the devotion of him who speaks to him,
No one is born wise.[1]

But an offspring can make trouble:
If he strays, neglects your counsel,
Disobeys all that is said,
His mouth spouting evil speech,
Punish him for all his talk!
They hate him who crosses you,
His guilt was fated in the womb;
He whom they guide can not go wrong,
Whom they make boatless can not cross.[2]

The fault in every kind of character comes from not listening.
Thoth has placed the stick on earth in order to teach the fool by it.
He gave the sense of shame to the wise man so as to escape all punishment.[3]

An unbroken horse turns out stubborn and an unchecked son turns out headstrong.... Bow down his neck in his youth, and beat his sides while he is young, or else he will become stubborn and disobey you, and you will have sorrow of soul from him. Discipline your son and make his yoke heavy, so that you may not be offended by his shamelessness.[4]

Pedagogy and moral development were of central concern to the wisdom traditions in Israel and the wider ancient Near East, and there are multiple perspectives in this literature about the methods and prospects of

---

[1] *Instruction of Ptahhotep* 38–42 in Miriam Lichtheim, *Ancient Egyptian Literature: A Book of Readings* (3 vols.; Berkeley: University of California Press, 1973–80), 1:63.
[2] *Instruction of Ptahhotep* 210–220, Lichtheim, *Ancient Egyptian Literature*, 1:67.
[3] *Instruction of Papyrus Insinger* 9.5-7, Lichtheim, *Ancient Egyptian Literature*, 3:192.
[4] Sir 30:8, 12–13.

education. The *Instruction of Ptahhotep* advocates that a recalcitrant child must be punished, yet it offers little hope that punishment will effect any real change in the student since his "guilt was fated in the womb." Ben Sira also insists on the need for physical correction, but his advice is founded on the conviction that exercising discipline prevents the child from developing according to his shameless nature. It must be administered with zeal because it can shape the student positively. At the heart of these ancient perspectives on the methods of discipline is a more fundamental question about human nature. While each of the texts cited above assumes that all people require instruction because no one is born wise, they reveal different assumptions about human aptitude and the potential for acquiring wisdom, as indicated in their comments about the purpose and efficacy of punishment. According to *Ptahhotep*, while fools must be punished, they have no hope of becoming wise because their condition has been divinely ordained from the womb and cannot be reversed. *Papyrus Insinger* indicates that the gods have bestowed humans with different capacities – some shameless and some shameful – although it leaves open the potential that the rod might benefit the fool, for "the stick and the shame protect their owner from the fiend."[5] In the *Instruction of Any*, the scribe appeals to the natural world, reasoning that just as animals can be trained to do tasks they did not do in the wild, so too humans can be educated regardless of their nature. Any replies to the protest of his son: "The fighting bull who kills in the stable, he forgets and abandons the arena; he conquers his nature, remembers what he's learned, and becomes the like of a fattened ox. The savage lion abandons his wrath, and comes to resemble the timid donkey. The horse slips into its harness, obedient it goes outdoors. The dog obeys the word, and walks behind its master. The monkey carries the stick, though its mother did not carry it."[6] Similarly, Ben Sira uses

---

[5] *Instruction of Papyrus Insinger* 9.11, Lichtheim, *Ancient Egyptian Literature*, 3:192. But also note the saying, "It is the god who gives the heart, gives the son, and gives the good character. The fate and the fortune that come, it is the god who determines them" (9.19–20, Lichtheim, *Ancient Egyptian Literature*, 3:192–3). This sentiment is fairly similar to the idea in the *Instruction of Ptahhotep* that character comes from the deity. However, this section of *Papyrus Insinger* also places some responsibility on the father to give proper instruction: "A statue of stone is the foolish son whom his father has not instructed" (8.22, Lichtheim, *Ancient Egyptian Literature*, 3:192). Cf. the scribe Any's reply to the protest of Khonshotep in the *Instruction of Any*, discussed later.

[6] *Instruction of Any* 10.1–4, Lichtheim, *Ancient Egyptian Literature*, 2:144. For a discussion of the nature of the dispute between Any and his son in the epilogue of this instruction, see Michael V. Fox, "Who Can Learn? A Dispute in Ancient Pedagogy," in *Wisdom, You Are My Sister: Studies in Honor of Roland E. Murphy, O.Carm., on the Occasion of His Eightieth Birthday* (ed., Michael L. Barré; CBQMS 29; Washington, DC: The Catholic Biblical Association of America, 1997), 62–77. Fox suggests that there are three main viewpoints of education in Egyptian wisdom: that some people cannot learn, that everyone can be taught, and that teaching requires the correct approach,

the metaphor of an untrained horse to describe the undisciplined student, suggesting that all are shameless and will inevitably become embarrassments to their family if the parent does not intervene.

The book of Proverbs also participates in a conversation about the purpose of education, the methods of pedagogy, and the nature of human beings. The book is filled with the content of instruction and commentary on the tools of education, such as rod and rebuke, as well as the process and outcomes of learning, including a student's receptivity or recalcitrance and the consequences of each. Although it does not always frame the related issue of human moral psychology in explicit terms, behind the poems and sayings of the book are certain operative assumptions about human nature. The threat of the rod, for example, presumes that humans are, in part, motivated by fear.

While the presence of pedagogical language in Proverbs has long been noted and hardly deserves further comment, it has not been sufficiently connected to the rather complex moral psychology that it presumes. Indeed, the pervasiveness of binary character oppositions in the book has led many scholars to presume that its moral psychology is similarly binary and simple. One is either wise or foolish, righteous or wicked. Thus James L. Crenshaw argues that "all people fell into one or the other category. In the view of the sages, no middle ground existed for those who participated in folly, or in wisdom, only minimally."[7] Similarly, John Barton insists that, within wisdom literature, "[e]veryone is either good or bad, wise or foolish. Living the good life appears to be an absolute, with no gradations or variations."[8] Crenshaw and Barton imply that Proverbs' language is more useful for identifying in which category a person falls than for shaping a person's character to any degree. While Barton acknowledges that the book of Proverbs may have been used for "some kind of moral training," he maintains that its language only underscores the fixed, unchanging nature of character, for instruction will only make the wise wiser while fools will continue to persist in their folly.[9]

Yet the importance of formation in Proverbs' pedagogy, as well as the diverse means by which formation is discussed and enacted in the book,

---

according to the disposition of the student. He suggests that Khonshotep's arguments in the epilogue of *Any* are an example of the third view (ibid., 73–77).

[7] James L. Crenshaw, *Old Testament Wisdom: An Introduction* (rev. and enl. ed.; Louisville: Westminster John Knox, 1998), 67.

[8] John Barton, *Understanding Old Testament Ethics: Approaches and Explanations* (Louisville: Westminster John Knox, 2003), 67.

[9] Ibid.

points to a more complex understanding of the human person than has often been acknowledged. As the book promotes the value of discipline, appeals to the motivation of wealth, and describes the appeal of the strange woman in provocative and alluring terms, just to name a few examples, its rhetoric presumes that humans are complexly motivated by an array of both positive and negative stimuli. Furthermore, it indicates that formation is a lifelong process that can occur for good or for ill, although it also admits of innate impediments to formation that external influence cannot overcome. To understand more adequately the connection between Proverbs' pedagogy and its moral psychology, one must examine its language in more detail.

## The Model of Rebuke

Rebuke is at the heart of Proverbs' pedagogy. It is a central theme that encompasses corporeal correction and verbal reprimand, as well as commentary on the nature of discipline, its efficacy, and advice for those who dispense it. The model of rebuke extends from physical correction, which is administered by striking (נכה)[10] with the rod (שבט), to rebuke (גערה) and reproof (תוכחות/יכח), terms which are used for verbal admonishment.[11] The force and effect of physical and verbal rebuke are largely similar. If anything, verbal rebuke is the stronger of the two.[12] In fact, it can pierce receptive ears more powerfully than can the rod (17:10). Outside of wisdom literature, גערה is a divine prerogative that has the power to overturn nature (Isa 50:2), uncover the world's foundations (2 Sam 22:16; cf. Ps 18:16; see also Job 26:11), and overwhelm that which is in its path (Isa 51:20; Ps 80:17).[13] While rebuke carries a slightly different nuance in Proverbs, as a tool of correction it likewise holds the potential to disrupt foundations. In this case, however, it is the orientation of foolishness that is the target. The wise are those who have been disrupted by rebuke, those who have listened and received wisdom (e.g., 29:15), while fools persist

---

[10] Also note references to מהלמות, "beatings" (18:6; 19:29).

[11] Although usually used for verbal rebuke, תוכחות and גערה can carry implications of physical punishment, especially when connected to God's wrath (see Isa 51:20; Ezek 5:15; 25:17).

[12] This is not to say, however, that striking with the rod is necessarily a benign punishment. The rod (שבט) is a firm staff that can be used as an instrument to wound severely or kill (see 2 Sam 18:14; 23:21). For a discussion of the various uses of the rod, including as a threshing tool, a shepherd's staff, and a scepter, see H.-J. Zobel, "שֵׁבֶט *šēbeṭ*," *TDOT* 14:304–05.

[13] When used of God, גערה has a resonance of a battle cry against enemies, a meaning that is absent in Proverbs. See the discussion in A. Caquot, "גָּעַר *gāʿar*; גְּעָרָה *gᵉʿārāh*; מִגְעֶרֶת *migʿereth*," *TDOT* 3:50–52.

in their error. Within Proverbs, the goal of rebuke, in whatever form it comes, is to orient the student toward the characters and practices that the community sanctions. In this capacity, it is one means of shaping the character of the student.

The purpose of corporeal correction is neither to wound nor to inspire undue terror or hatred.[14] In fact, the rod is framed as a tool of parental love, even a safeguard from death (23:14). References to physical discipline are usually reserved for fools, scoffers, and the senseless.[15] Proverbs 10:13, for example, states that "wisdom is found on the lips of the intelligent, but a rod is ready for the back of the senseless." Words alone are not effective on certain characters, and thus the rod, perhaps a more rudimentary means of communication, is required. Discipline takes physical form as fools or senseless ones, whose natural inclination is not to seek wisdom, must be beaten into submission. Thus Prov 26:3 observes, "a whip for a horse, a bridle for a donkey, and a rod for the back of fools." As an animal requires a whip and bridle, so too the foolish student requires the rod to guide him toward the way of wisdom and to incite the action that the teacher desires.[16] In this respect, the rod is a tool of training, not one of punishment, per se. The importance of the rod should also not be neglected for the ordinary student. Because rebuke is a tool for inculcating

---

[14] Yet note Prov 20:30 חברות פצע תמריק ברע ומכות חדרי־בטן. Reading with Kethib (Q: תמרוק), "Blows that wound cleanse from evil and strike at the inner parts." Fox reads with Qere but points as a Qal form of the verb מרק, "to polish" (cf. Jer 46:4), and he reads MT בָּרָע as בְּרָע, the "mind" or "thoughts" (Michael V. Fox, *Proverbs 10–31: A New Translation with Introduction and Commentary* [AB 18B; New Haven: Yale University Press, 2009], 678–79; cf. Berend Gemser, *Sprüche Salomos* [Tübingen: J.C.B. Mohr, 1937], 61). An argument could be made for either reading. To support his reading of ברע, Fox notes that the effect of cleansing or scouring is on the surface that is rubbed, not on what is rubbed out. One could also note that nowhere else does Proverbs indicate that evil can be removed from a person, nor does it consider the wicked to be recipients of discipline (see the following note). In any case, the reference to wounds inflicted by punishment is rare.

[15] The rod or discipline is not linked explicitly to the wicked (but cf. 9:7–8, which testifies to the futility of rebuking the wicked). The need for the rod is a reflection of one's lack of knowledge, and the wicked are beyond its reach. The relation, or lack thereof, between the wicked and rebuke accords well with Sun Myung Lyu's observation that the wicked are not part of the audience of Proverbs. While the book speaks about the wicked, it does not address them directly (Sun Myung Lyu, *Righteousness in the Book of Proverbs* [FAT II; Tübingen: Mohr Siebeck, 2012], 73). The wicked are an important part of rebuke within Proverbs, however, in the sense that they are the object of the negative characterization of the father as they are described throughout the book. This is, in effect, a kind of rebuke against the wicked, but the goal is not to give knowledge to the *wicked*, but rather to give knowledge to the students in the audience. The audience learns from observing the figurative rebuke of the wicked.

[16] One can also find this sentiment in Egyptian texts. For example, see *Papyrus Lansing*, in which a student comments on the utility of rebuke and even likens himself to a horse, presumably in his submission and eagerness to serve the teacher: "I grew into a youth at your side. You beat my back; your teaching entered my ear. I am like a pawing horse" (*Papyrus Lansing* 11.2–3, Lichtheim, *Ancient Egyptian Literature*, 2:172). The rod is a form of engendering receptivity to the instruction.

wisdom, it is important that the father utilize it to foster wise character in his son, for "one who spares his rod hates his son, but one who loves him seeks discipline for him" (13:24).[17]

While the sayings in Proverbs are of unanimous opinion about the suitability of physical rebuke for fools, scoffers, and the senseless, there are mixed opinions concerning the efficacy of this brand of correction on such characters.[18] Proverbs 22:15 states that the "rod of discipline" (שבט מוסר) holds the ability to remove the foolishness lodged in a young person's mind. But the usefulness of physical discipline depends on the particular type of fool. Physical discipline is appropriate for the dunce (כסיל) because his obtuseness prevents him from hearing verbal rebuke. Although he spurns *words* of correction (e.g., 23:9; 26:4), he may understand the more rudimentary communication inspired by the rod (19:29; 26:3). However, even physical discipline is wasted on the אויל. Proverbs 27:22, for example, expresses little optimism about the potential of physical rebuke to prompt significant change in the fool, for "even if you crush the fool (אויל) in a mortar with a pestle amidst the grain, his folly will not leave him" (see also 17:10). The innate recalcitrance of אוילים makes them impervious to rebuke, even when inflicted with the rod.

Likewise, the efficacy of verbal rebuke depends on the disposition of the recipient. Fools – both כסילים and אוילים – are unable to hear reproof with profit. In fact, they hate rebuke and reject it, failing to see any redeeming value in it (1:25, 30; 5:12; 12:1). Those who have receptive ears, however, welcome rebuke, even love it (9:8), because they see it for what it is: not a punishment but a guide, not an end in itself but a means to greater

---

[17] Verse 24b is difficult to translate: ואהבו שחרו מוסר. The verb שחר means "to search for" and is used elsewhere in the book to refer to the search for wisdom (1:28; 7:15; 8:17; 11:27). One could also translate "searches out discipline for him." *HALOT* glosses as "searches him out for a beating," i.e., the father beats him from time to time. NRSV translates, "those who love them are diligent to discipline them," while NJPS states, "he who loves him disciplines him early." Fox notes that in Rabbinic Hebrew, the stem can mean "to do something early" (cf. the nominative form *šaḥar*, dawn). Thus Ramaq translates, "will discipline him every dawn" (Fox, *Proverbs 10–31*, 571). Fox himself translates, "he who loves him disciplines him zealously" (ibid., 570).

[18] Chapters 1–9 do not contain any explicit references to physical correction, although the motif of verbal rebuke figures prominently in this part of the book. William P. Brown argues that in Prov 1–9, "instruction or discipline is not so much an external force as a matter of internal suasion" (William P. Brown, "To Discipline without Destruction: The Multifaceted Profile of the Child in Proverbs," in *The Child in the Bible* [ed., Marcia J. Bunge; Grand Rapids: Eerdmans, 2008], 76). He points to Wisdom as a companion to the student (7:4), one who "comes wielding not the rod of discipline but the power of persuasion, and of the most intimate kind" (ibid.). However, Wisdom also has strong words and stinging rebuke for those who rebuff her call (see discussion of Prov 1, later); at times she does reveal the rod of discipline, at least rhetorically. See also Brown's interesting discussion of Wisdom as a child in Prov 8, which he interprets as "a way to bond with her audience, her 'children' (v. 32), by revealing her own childlike nature" (ibid., 79).

wisdom. "A fool (אויל) rejects the discipline of his father," reports Prov
15:5, "but one who hears reproof becomes savvy." Herein lies the paradox
of rebuke: its goal is to orient the student toward wisdom so that he can
avoid the way of foolishness and the company of fools. However, without
an innate receptivity to correction, the fool can never profit from rebuke.
His nature prevents him from obtaining the very medicine he needs.

Rebuke governs many social interactions, and Proverbs also addresses
the productive exchange of rebuke in the community. One can profit
from rebuke not only by receiving it oneself, but by witnessing the rebuke
of others. So Prov 19:25, "Strike a scoffer and the simple becomes savvy;
reprove the discerning and he discerns knowledge." Furthermore, rebuke
requires wise disciplinarians to dispense it with the well-being of the
whole community in mind, either engaging and correcting fools or recognizing the futility for some beyond its reach (e.g., 26:4–5). Part of wisdom
is the ability to discern what kind of rebuke is suitable to which student,
as well as those on whom rebuke would be wasted. Proverbs 9:7–8 advises,
"Whoever corrects a scoffer receives abuse; whoever rebukes the wicked,
a wound. Do not rebuke a scoffer, lest he hate you; reprove the wise, and
he will love you."

In some sense, the book of Proverbs as a whole is the functional equivalent of rebuke. Not only does it contain a wealth of commentary on
receiving and administering rebuke, but it is also filled with the content of
verbal correction, which includes admonitions to avoid certain behaviors,
characters, or activities, such as the warnings about the strange woman
(e.g., 5:8) or injunctions about proper court behavior (e.g., 25:6–7). Such
sayings mark the actions that lie beyond the bounds of sanctioned behavior and provide a kind of preemptive rebuke, teaching the student to identify certain actions as foolish or wicked even before he may be tempted to
engage in them. In fact, the example of fools is itself a form of discipline.
Proverbs 16:22 states: "Insight is a fountain of life to its owner, and the
discipline of fools is folly." The discipline of fools (מוסר אולים) is the lesson
they provide in their folly, from which a person with insight will profit.[19]

---

[19] Fox understands מוסר אולים to refer to the education that fools impart to others: "Fools teach
folly not only in formal instruction but also in the bad examples they set" (Fox, *Proverbs 10–31*,
620). For another interpretation, see Roland E. Murphy, who translates: "A fountain of life,
a possessor of insight, but folly, the discipline of fools" (Roland E. Murphy, *Proverbs* [WBC 22;
Nashville: Thomson Nelson, 1998], 117). He understands the saying to mean that folly is discipline
for fools in the sense that their own foolishness punishes them. Alternatively, he suggests that it
may imply that "to administer discipline is folly, since the fools cannot and will not be taught; any
attempt to instruct them is useless" (ibid., 123; see also William McKane, *Proverbs: A New Approach*
[OTL; Philadelphia: Westminster Press, 1970], 490).

Moreover, the vivid depictions of various unseemly characters throughout the book are a form of rebuke, implicitly cautioning the student to
avoid such miscreants and their wicked ways. Proverbs acknowledges that
the observation of rebuke delivered to another can be as valuable as that
which is received directly. As the father or woman Wisdom issue negative
commentary on certain characters, these effectively function as the figurative rebuke of another, from which the student who listens carefully will
gain wisdom.

Rebuke is a means of educating the student in the right perceptions of
the world, according to the sages. It calibrates one's "moral aesthetic,"[20]
such that he views the world in its proper dimensions, foresees the opposite horizons of wisdom and foolishness, and desires the things that lead
toward wisdom. Every negative comment about the fool, every warning to
avoid the wicked, and every cautionary tale that ends with death or Sheol
is thus part of conditioning the student to view the world from the same
perspective as the instructor. For this reason, rebuke as a model of character formation signifies more than simply the means of correction, whether
words or physical discipline, but it is about conveying a particular moral
worldview. As such, the model of rebuke is ultimately about the acquisition of knowledge and the establishment of moral norms. Rebuke functions to identify deviants from the sanctioned bounds.

In this sense, the purpose of the model as a whole is encapsulated by
the Hebrew term מוסר, "discipline," which refers both to the content of
correction and the knowledge that such correction facilitates. Discipline
is the ultimate end of all rebuke. Although correction of waywardness
and foolishness is a means of rebuke, whether verbal or physical, its primary goal is the acquisition of knowledge that orients all of one's faculties
toward the way of wisdom. Discipline is the concept that encompasses
both the means of rebuke and the knowledge it endows. Within Proverbs,
the term מוסר is used to describe both physical rebuke (22:15) and verbal
correction, although it can also denote the lesson that one learns through
rebuke (4:13).[21] In this sense, discipline is not something that is simply
received, but knowledge that must be actively sought after. For this reason,

[20] A term borrowed from Fox, who defines it as "a sense of harmony, a sensitivity to what is fitting and right, in all realms of attitude and behavior" (Fox, *Proverbs 10–31*, 973).
[21] Fox notes that discipline is always used of authoritative correction delivered from a superior to an inferior. It is a lesson intended to correct a moral fault, as opposed to a practical fault. The goal of discipline is thus "a moral insight or a quality of moral character" (Michael V. Fox, *Proverbs 1–9: A New Translation with Introduction and Commentary* [AB 18A; New York: Doubleday, 2000], 34; see also ibid., 59).

one must "bring your mind to discipline, your ear to words of knowledge" (23:12; see also 4:13; 23:23).

## The Poetics of Rebuke

While the content of the book addresses many facets of rebuke, the poetic form of Proverbs is also a vital component in the way in which rebuke is realized as a model of character formation. Attending to the poetry illumines how the book marshals the resources of language to underscore and develop its assumptions about the role of rebuke in shaping the student, as well as its value and purpose. An exhaustive survey is beyond the scope of this chapter, but I will consider a poem from chapter 1 and three sayings from the latter part of the book to illustrate the connection between content and form. How the poem makes meaning illumines a vital feature of rebuke and also contributes to enacting the formative value of rebuke in the student.

*Proverbs 1:20–33*

20 Wisdom[22] – in the street she cries out; in the squares she raises her voice.

21 Over the commotion,[23] she calls; at the openings of the city gates she speaks her words.

---

[22] The line could also be translated, "Wisdom calls out in the street ..." yet I choose to set off the word in order to lend extra emphasis to the term in translation. By placing חכמות as its opening word, the poem draws the ear and the eye (literally and figuratively) directly to woman Wisdom. The plural form חכמות is here used as a singular in reference to personified Wisdom. The plural form is also used of woman Wisdom and paired with a singular verb in Prov 9:1 and Sir 4:11 (but cf. Prov 24:7, where חכמות takes a plural participle, ראמות). P. Joüon and T. Muraoka consider this form to be a "plural of majesty," analogous to אלהים or אדנים to refer to the singular subject God (P. Joüon and T. Muraoka, *A Grammar of Biblical Hebrew* [2nd ed.; Rome: Gregorian & Biblical Press, 2009], §136d; 88M*k*). The expected plural form is חֲכָמוֹת, not חָכְמוֹת, but Joüon and Muraoka suggest that the form was vocalized this way on account of the singular form חָכְמָה (ibid., §88M*k*). W. F. Albright proposed that the form could be explained as a Phoenicianism from a Canaanite form *ḥukmatu* (W. F. Albright, "Some Canaanite-Phoenician Sources of Hebrew Wisdom," in *Wisdom in Israel and in the Ancient Near East: Presented to Professor Harold Henry Rowley* [eds., M. Noth and D. Winton Thomas; VTSup 3; Leiden: Brill, 1955], 8).

[23] בראש המיות, literally: "at the head of the bustling." Fox translates, "at the bustling crossroads," explaining that המיות is elliptical for bustling *roads*. He envisions the point at which various roads diverge at the city gate (Fox, *Proverbs 1–9*, 97). Yet the verbal root can refer to a wide variety of noisy and turbulent places, emotions, and characters, including the tumult of sparring nations (Ps 46:7), the noise of one's enemies (Ps 83:3), the bark of a dog (Ps 59:7), the churning of one's innards (Jer 31:20; cf. Ps 42:6), and the rushing of stormy water (Ps 46:4). The term is used as an adjective for the strange woman and the foolish woman (Prov 7:11; 9:13). In the context of Prov 1, the word likely refers to the noise of the crowds, the activity on the roads and in the public square, and even the foolish murmuring of scoffers and sinners (cf. Prov 1:11, 22). Translating המיות simply as "commotion" leaves the ambiguity of the image intact.

22 "How long, simple ones, will you love simplicity, will scoffers desire scoffing, will fools hate knowledge?

23 Turn to my reproof!²⁴ That I might engulf you with my spirit,²⁵ enlighten you with my words.

24 Yet I called and you rejected – I extended my hand and no one inclined.

25 You let loose²⁶ all of my counsel and my reproof you did not receive.

26 As for me, I will laugh in your disaster; I will jeer when your moment of dread comes –

---

²⁴ The meaning and significance of the phrase תשובו לתוכחתי has been disputed. I read the second-person imperfect form with imperatival force, as Wisdom's call for the simple to heed her reproof (see also Fox, *Proverbs 1–9*, 99). Murphy, however, prefers to understand the form as an indicative, describing the past failing of the simple, who have turned away from Wisdom. תשובו, Murphy argues, "is not an invitation to repent, but part of wisdom's indictment" (Roland E. Murphy, "Wisdom's Song: Proverbs 1:20–33," *CBQ* 48 [1986]: 458; cf. NIV translation: "If you had responded to my rebuke, I would have poured out my heart to you."). Murphy argues that nowhere in the poem "does Wisdom invite the audience to conversion" (ibid., 460). Further, he states that given the tone of the poem, in which Wisdom describes the past infidelity of the fools and the destruction that is sure to come to them, "an invitation to listen to her reproof (as some would understand v 23) does not make sense" (ibid.).
The model of rebuke illumines the interpretation of this crux. Contrary to Murphy's view, within Proverbs rebuke is elsewhere always an invitation to greater wisdom. Whether or not the recipient has the disposition to hear rebuke favorably and learn from it depends, of course, on the individual student, yet within Proverbs rebuke always has inherent potential to be a tool of charac-ter formation, should it be wisely received. It is not simply an opportunity to berate a person's past failings. Murphy points to Wisdom's lengthy description of past infidelity and impending destruc-tion (1:24–27), reasoning that this is no invitation; rather, Wisdom has ruled out the possibility for change and is already anticipating the demise of the fools. To the contrary, however, this is exactly how rebuke works within Proverbs, for even if the recipient of such rebuke cannot profit from a description of his errors and anticipation of the consequences, it can still provide wisdom to the receptive ears of those who will learn from observing a negative example. Finally, Murphy points to the repetition of the root שוב in verse 32 (משובת פתים), where it clearly refers to a turning *away* of the simple, suggesting that these two uses are synonymous and function as an *inclusio* (ibid., 459). However, this repetition is part of the poem's ironic reversal, a technique it uses to contrast Wisdom's invitation with the demise of those who reject her. Although she calls for the simple to turn (תשובו, v. 23), it is their turning *away* (משובה, v. 32) that leads to their death. Although she called them (קראתי, v. 24), when they call (יקראנני, v. 28), she will not answer. While they rejected her counsel (עצתי, v. 30), they will be sated on their own counsels (מעצתיהם, v. 31). The poem uses the repetition of these roots (שוב,קרא,עצה) to contrast Wisdom's gesture toward the simple with their refusal to heed her call.

²⁵ In the *hipʿil*, the root נבע means to "allow to gush out," usually referring to words or speech (Pss 19:3; 59:8; 78:2; 94:4; 119:71; Prov 15:2, 28). It is used with רוח only in this occurrence, although the term is used in parallel with דבר in the following phrase. The sense of the image is that Wisdom will not only speak her mind and share her thoughts, but will let them loose with fervor. I choose to translate אביעה as "I will engulf" to convey this image and to capture the sound play with "enlighten" (אדיעה) in the following phrase.

²⁶ The root פרע means to let free or leave unattended; it is often used with respect to disheveled or loose hair (see Lev 10:6; Judg 5:2). In Proverbs, the root means to ignore or be unconcerned with (Prov 4:15; 8:33; 13:18; 15:32; see also 29:18), which is congruent with its meaning here. However, as a description of personified Wisdom, perhaps there may be a slight resonance of dishonoring a

*27* When your moment of dread comes like a devastating storm[27] and your disaster enters like a whirlwind; when distress and debacle come upon you –

*28* Only then will they call for me – but I will not reply. They will seek me, but not find me.

*29* Since they hated knowledge and the fear of YHWH they did not choose.

*30* Not at all did they receive my counsel! Spurned all of my reproof!

*31* They will eat from the fruit of their way and from their own counsels be sated!

*32* For the turning away of the simple kills them, and the ease of fools destroys them.

*33* But one who listens to me will dwell securely and be at ease[28] from dread of trouble."

This poem employs its poetic tropes to didactic effect. The rhyme schemes, parallelism, and imagery are not simply rhetorical flourishes, but underscore and advance the content of instruction. The heightened image of dread in verse 27, for example, brings into sharp relief the potential consequence of wayward ways. It elaborates the image of impending dread at the end of verse 26 (בבא פחדכם) with three parallel phrases. The first phrase, בבא כשואה פחדכם, mirrors the previous image while adding the detail that dread will come as a devastating storm. The following phrase, ואידכם כסופה יאתה, alludes to the image of disaster in verse 26a (אידכם) and specifies that it will come like a whirlwind, a term whose sound nicely resonates with כשואה in the previous phrase. Finally, the third phrase of the triplet, בבא עליכם צרה וצוקה, builds the theme of dread to its height, a point which it underscores by the similarity in sound between צרה and צוקה, as well as with סופה. Taken together, verses 26–27 contain a chiastic structure whose capstone is the third image of verse 27.[29] Furthermore,

woman by letting down her hair (cf. Num 5:18), thus the translation "let loose." This point should not be pushed too far, yet the poetic depiction of Wisdom as a spurned woman invites some play with language. In English, the description "let loose" also nicely contrasts with the frequent injunction throughout Proverbs to "keep" Wisdom's or the parent's instruction.

[27] Reading with Qere, כשואה (K: כשאה). Note the sound play with כסופה in the following phrase.

[28] The rare root שאן indicates a condition of silence or repose without fear (see Job 3:18; Jer 30:10; 46:27; 48:11). There is an ironic sound play with the parallel term in the preceding line, ושלות, which I have tried to capture with the translations "to be at ease" (ושאנן) and "ease" (ושלות). The fools' ease, however, connotes a complacency that is accompanied by an unjustified lack of concern for the consequences of their waywardness.

[29] That is, A: אשחק באידכם (v. 26a); גם־אני (v. 26b); B: אלעג בבא פחדכם (v. 26b); B₁: בבא כשואה פחדכם (v. 27a); A₁: ואידכם כסופה יאתה (v. 27b); C: בבא עליכם צרה צוקה (v. 27c).

the use of a triplet line where couplets have predominated draws extra attention to this line. The reader must dwell on the image of dread as the expected rhythm of couplets is broken. In effect, developing the image of disaster functions as the metaphorical "rod" of Wisdom's rebuke.

The poetic nature of this text has not always garnered the attention it deserves. As the first instance of direct speech by Wisdom in the book, interpreters have often focused on the role of personified Wisdom, with various commentators suggesting that she is figured as a prophet,[30] a divine mediator,[31] a preacher,[32] a teacher,[33] or a counselor.[34] Each of these perspectives has certain merits, yet, as Phyllis Trible has argued, because these various dimensions of Wisdom's character "have their being in a poetic mode, the poem itself is primary for understanding."[35] Trible suggests that this poem, a veritable "work of art," contains a tight chiastic structure, both at the level of individual lines and in the poem as a whole, which is indicative of the posture Wisdom assumes toward her audience.[36] Trible notes that in the beginning of the poem, Wisdom addresses all humanity, as highlighted by the double parallel structure of verses 20–21, which emphasize Wisdom's position in public spaces. By the conclusion, however, Wisdom speaks in the third person of a single figure (שֹׁמֵעַֽ לִ֑י, v. 33), suggesting that Wisdom's focus narrows from a general invitation to singular acceptance of her call.[37] Trible finds the switch between

---

[30] André Robert was the first to suggest that Wisdom's words here contain great similarity to a prophetic oracle (André Robert, "Les Attaches Littéraires Bibliques de Prov. i–ix," *RB* 43 [1934]: 172–81). Following Robert, many scholars have suggested that this text is influenced by prophetic material, likely the book of Jeremiah, and that here Wisdom is figured as a prophet. See especially Christa Kayatz, *Studien zu Proverbien 1–9: Eine form- und motivgeschichtliche Untersuchung unter Einbeziehung ägyptischen Vergleichmaterials* (WMANT 22; Neukirchen-Vluyn; Neukirchener Verlag, 1966), 122–29; Scott L. Harris, *Proverbs 1–9: A Study of Inner-Biblical Interpretation* (SBLDS; Atlanta: Scholars Press, 1995), 87–109.

[31] Bruce K. Waltke, "Lady Wisdom as Mediatrix: An Exposition of Proverbs 1:20–33," *Presbyterion* 14.1 (1988): 1–15.

[32] Gemser characterizes Wisdom in chapter 1 as a preacher, yet he suggests that she has "prophetic talent," though does not quite issue a call to conversion (Gemser, *Sprüche Salomos*, 16–17).

[33] McKane emphasizes her role as a teacher, as opposed to a prophet, although he also refers to her as a preacher (McKane, *Proverbs*, 272–77).

[34] P. A. H. de Boer, "The Counsellor," in *Wisdom in Israel and in the Ancient Near East: Presented to Professor Harold Henry Rowley* (eds., M. Noth and D. Winton Thomas; VTSup 3; Leiden: Brill, 1955), 52.

[35] Phyllis Trible, "Wisdom Builds a Poem: The Architecture of Proverbs 1:20–33," *JBL* 94 (1975): 509.

[36] Trible outlines the text as follows: A: vv. 20–21 (introduction); B: v. 22 (address to untutored, scoffers, and fools); C: v. 23 (declaration of disclosure); D: vv. 24–25 (reason for announcement); E: vv. 26–27 (announcement of judgment); D₁: vv. 28–30 (result of announcement, "with interruption"); C₁: v. 31 (declaration of retribution); B₁: v. 32 (address about untutored and fools); A₁: v. 33 (conclusion) (ibid., 511).

[37] Ibid., 518.

second- and third-person descriptions of the fools and their company to reflect Wisdom's "ambivalence about the people," shifting from proximity to distance in her relationship to the audience.[38]

However, the shifting voices of address in the poem are less reflective of Wisdom's "ambivalence" toward the audience than they are of the very nature of rebuke as a model of character formation. As discussed earlier, rebuke in Proverbs involves both personal reproof that one receives and an ability to learn from the reproof that others receive. One needs not only a receptivity to rebuke, but also the ability to hear rebuke directed toward others. In fact, as the poem unfolds, it subtly shapes the student both as a simpleton who receives directly Wisdom's reproof and as an onlooker who can profit from the rebuke another receives. The poem begins in an omniscient voice, describing Wisdom in the third person. But as Wisdom's address begins, the student (i.e., the listener or reader) is implicitly incorporated with the company of the simple who cling to their simplicity: "How long, simple ones, will *you* love simplicity?" (v. 22). As Wisdom's speech continues in the second-person address, the student shares the blame of shunning Wisdom personally, for although she calls to him, "*you* rejected me" (v. 24). Likewise, the impending doom threatens to come upon the student and the simple alike, as the second-person plural suffixes provide a constant refrain: *your* disaster, *your* moment of dread. As Carol A. Newsom observes, the reader "discovers himself in the text as always, already at fault. And the fault is recalcitrance before legitimate authority."[39] The dynamics of the poetry further underscore this point. In verses 26–27, for example, the repetition of כם־ (five times) and בבא (three times) highlights in both sound and sense the relentless approach of disaster to *you*.

גם־אני באידכם אשׂחק אלעג בבא פחדכם
בבא כשׁאוה פחדכם ואידכם כסופה יאתה בבא עליכם צרה וצוקה

This repetition serves as a structuring device, highlighting the parallel phrases, and it also drives the point. In other words, it insists that disaster is "coming, coming, coming to you, you, you, you, *you*." The point is not neatly summarized, but developed to powerful effect by the use of language.

Yet even as such language situates the student among the simple, the poem also differentiates the student from those who receive Wisdom's

[38] Ibid., 512.
[39] Carol A. Newsom, "Woman and the Discourse of Patriarchal Wisdom: A Study of Proverbs 1–9," in *Gender and Difference in Ancient Israel* (ed. P. Day; Minneapolis: Augsburg Fortress, 1989), 146.

rebuke. Just when the rebuke of Wisdom is most direct and would seem most unbearable, the student is offered reprieve in the shift to a third-person description of the wayward group. By verse 28, this group is referenced in the third person. "*They* will call me," Wisdom explains, "but I will not answer." At this point in the poem, the student once again becomes an observer of commentary. This time Wisdom elaborates on the consequences that will follow the simple and the fool. Now, however, Wisdom's words are no longer addressed directly to the fools and their compatriots but to the student. The rebuke now serves not as a direct warning to those engaged in wayward behavior but as a cautionary tale to those who have yet to stray from Wisdom's words. The last line of the poem shifts the address yet again from the description of a negative group to the lone one who listens to Wisdom (וְשֹׁמֵעַ לִי, v. 33). Strikingly, this is not addressed to the student directly. Many other poems in chapters 1–9 include a direct appeal to "my son," leaving the reader no choice but to take up the subjective position of the one who hears and imbibes the instruction. Yet Wisdom refers here only to "one who listens to me," thus ultimately leaving to the student to determine his receptivity. In this way, the poem leads the reader through the experience of direct rebuke and indirect rebuke addressed to another, then leaving to the student whether he will be one who heeds Wisdom's words – or not.

Contra Newsom, Michael V. Fox argues that "the reader does not identify with the fools but views them at a distance, with contempt."[40] Fox suggests that Wisdom's direct address to the fools and simpletons is merely a foil, for they are not the intended recipient of her words. It is only when Wisdom speaks of these characters in the third person that she is addressing her "real audience," the reader. Although Fox attempts to draw a line rather sharply between his and Newsom's reading of the text,[41] in fact they are both correct. The ingenuity of this poem is that it can position the student *both* as the one who is at fault, colluding with simpletons and fools, *and* as the one who stands apart from the crowd yet within earshot of Wisdom's rebuke, privileged to Wisdom's evaluation of the consequences that await fools, on the one hand, and a careful listener, on the other. In the way that it unfolds, this poem thus seeks to shape the character of the student as one who gains wisdom from receiving rebuke directly and from witnessing the rebuke of another, for "when a scoffer is punished, the simple becomes wise" (21:11a).

[40] Fox, *Proverbs 1–9*, 102.
[41] Ibid., 101.

## Rebuke in the Sayings

While the model of rebuke is developed at length in this poem, the terseness of the sayings in chapters 10–29 do not preclude poetic development of the concept of rebuke. Indeed, attention to the figurative language employed by these sayings reveals central assumptions about the nature of rebuke. With memorable images and word play, the sayings enliven rebuke in the eye and the ear, as well as in the mind.

### Proverbs 25:12

Ring of gold and ornament of glisten – reproof of a wise one upon a listening ear.

נזם זהב וחלי־כתם מוכיח חכם על־אזן שמעת

The terse, paratactic construction of this saying leaves to the interpreter the task of discerning the relationship between the precious objects and מוכיח חכם, yet one should not be too quick to dismiss the aptness of the comparison, nor to flatten its complexity in translation. Although many have understood this saying as a rather straightforward comment concerning the value of a teacher's rebuke, the nature of the poetry facilitates multiple interpretations that are consistent with the model of rebuke. An awareness of the nuances of rebuke in the book opens other possible meanings, even as this particular saying sheds further light on the nature of rebuke.

The ambiguity of the saying turns on the interpretation of מוכיח חכם. Taken together, the words can indicate a wise person who reproves[42] or, similarly, a wise act of reproving, thus "wise reproof."[43] In this interpretation, the emphasis falls on the act of primary rebuke delivered to a receptive student. However, חכם could also be interpreted as the object of מוכיח, that is, as the one *to whom* reproof is given. In other words, the worth of "one who reproves a wise person" is measured in precious objects. Similar syntax in Prov 28:23 clearly yields this construction: מוכיח אדם אחרי חן ימצא ממחליק לשון, "One who reproves a person finds more favor in the end than one whose tongue flatters."[44] If one reads Prov 25:12 similarly, then the saying is not simply a commentary on rebuke, but on giving instruction to the wise, a

---

[42] See Fox, *Proverbs 10–31*, 783; and Murphy, *Proverbs*, 187.

[43] Cf. NJPS: "a wise man's reproof."

[44] The interpretation of אחרי is problematic. Literally, the form means "after me," which makes little sense. Fox emends to אחר, "another [man]" (Fox, *Proverbs 10–31*, 830). Cf. Vulgate, which interprets as "afterwards," *qui corripit hominem gratiam postea inveniet apud eum.* LXX has ὁ ἐλέγχων ἀνθρώπου ὁδοὺς, "the one who reproves the *ways* of a man," perhaps from ארח, not אחר.

notion that is an important part of the model of rebuke (1:5; 19:25; 21:11). In either case, the translation "reproof of a wise person," which can imply reproof that is issued *by* or issued *to* the wise, leaves such ambiguity intact.

The metaphors used in this saying also reveal significant aspects of the nature of rebuke. The golden decorations indicate that reproof is an object of high value, a point which accords with other sayings that speak of rebuke as something to be treasured (e.g., 13:18). A second implication of the earring metaphor is that rebuke is also an object of adornment. As a gold ring hangs on an ear,[45] so does reproof decorate the receptive ear. This point underscores the value of rebuke itself, but it also may carry a slightly different connotation, perhaps ascribing worth to the student who is rebuked. Glistening rings are befitting to a listening ear, a synecdoche for the receptive student. In other words, reproof is a mark of honor and adds beauty, just as golden decorations are a mark of wealth and embellish the wearer's appearance.[46] Through its use of metaphor and syntactical construction, this saying at once deftly praises both the instructor who delivers rebuke wisely and the instructed one who hears rebuke with profit, both the value of rebuke itself and the value of the student to whom it is delivered.

> *Proverbs 26:3*
>
> A whip for the horse, a bridle for the donkey, and a rod for the back of fools.
>
> שׁוֹט לסוס מתג לחמור ושבט לגו כסילים

> *Proverbs 26:11*
>
> As a dog returns to its vomit, a fool repeats his folly.
>
> ככלב שב על־קאו כסיל שונה באולתו

These sayings use imagery from the animal world to comment on the nature of discipline and the fool. The two lines, which come from a series of sayings on the fool in chapter 26,[47] express somewhat conflicting sentiments concerning the prospect of educating the fool. The first saying borrows its metaphors from the domain of animal training.[48] The fool

---

[45] A נזם can decorate the ear (Gen 35:4; Exod 32:3) or the nose (Gen 24:47; Isa 3:21). While an ear ring is not explicitly specified here, the image matches nicely with the reference to the ear in the second half of the saying.

[46] See also Prov 3:12, which indicates that rebuke is a mark of divine love.

[47] For a discussion of 26:1–12 as a unit, see Raymond C. Van Leeuwen, *Context and Meaning in Proverbs 25–27* (SBLDS 96; Atlanta: Scholars Press, 1988), 87–106.

[48] Compare the Syriac version of the Aramaic Proverbs of Ahiqar, which uses metaphors of agricultural cultivation and animal training to speak of discipline: "My son, spare not thy son from stripes; for the beating of a boy is like manure to the garden, and like a rope to an ass, and like a tether on the foot of an ass" (cited in Brown, "To Discipline Without Destruction," 70).

is akin to a horse or donkey, possessing inferior intelligence (cf. Ps 32:9) yet also able to be trained. While the comparison is, on the one hand, rather disparaging of the student, on the other hand it does operate with the assumption that fools can be schooled, although to learn they require a method appropriate to their nature. Furthermore, the comparison between whip, bridle, and rod indicates an important element of physical rebuke – it is not a tool primarily intended for punishment. Rather, it is both a means of inciting the student toward a desired end, as a whip prompts the horse to respond more promptly to the rider's command, and a tool of submission, much as a bridle is an instrument for guiding the animal to obey the will of another rather than his own.[49] The rod as a tool of discipline is thus about integrating the student into a hierarchical social structure in which he respects and takes direction from his superiors, surrendering his foolish – brutish – instincts.

The animal simile in the second saying expresses more skepticism about the possibility of correction. The consonance between שׁב and שׁונה highlights the comparable element between dogs and fools: their predictable and repetitive action. The end rhyme of קאו and באולתו underscores exactly why such repetition is so problematic. Each returns to something repulsive, although presumably it is not repulsive in the consumer's eyes. Here is yet another example of the fool's distorted perception. Folly looks appetizing to the fool, and thus he continues to engage in it. The comparison between vomit and folly would never occur to the fool because his distorted perception prevents him from seeing its true nature. The saying has both a descriptive and didactic function. It describes the nature of the fool while it serves as a cautionary word to the discerning ear. Not only does it temper the notion that fools can be educated, but it also warns against joining the company of fools. By painting the nature of folly in such vivid terms, the saying renders the nature of the fool to be as repulsive as the dog's activity to which it is likened.

Taken together, these sayings indicate a certain tension concerning the discipline of fools. As horse and donkey can be trained, so can the fool. As no reason or rod will dissuade the dog, so the fool's nature cannot be altered. Fools present both an opportunity for discipline and an intractable problem, requiring discernment on the part of those

[49] See also Prov 29:15, "Rod and rebuke give wisdom, but a boy set loose shames his mother." Fox suggests that an animal metaphor is also behind this saying, interpreting the rod as a shepherd's rod. He explains, "Some are controlled by the shepherd's rod and protected, others are 'let loose' ... to go astray" (Fox, *Proverbs 10–31*, 839). Beating with the rod is thus "a means of control rather than punishment" (ibid.).

who administer discipline. Should one answer a fool according to his folly – or not (26:4–5)? The book does not issue ironclad dictums but offers observations that leave to the interpreter (and the disciplinarian) the task of evaluation. At the crossroads of these views are deeper assumptions about the nature of human beings and the formation of the moral self.

## The Model of Rebuke and the Moral Self

In her monograph *Can These Bones Live? The Problem of the Moral Self in the Book of Ezekiel*, Jacqueline E. Lapsley argues that there are two primary models of moral selfhood in the Hebrew Bible.[50] The dominant model of moral selfhood, which she calls "virtuous moral selfhood," is grounded in the notion that humans are inherently capable of making moral choices. She suggests that this assumption lies behind much of the rhetoric in the Hebrew Bible, for "the emphasis on the human capacity to freely make choices that accord with the divine will, the urgency of the call to choose responsibly, and the gravity of the consequences of choosing rightly or wrongly – these characteristics pervade and are central to these Israelite traditions," including narrative, priestly, wisdom, prophetic, and covenant traditions.[51] This is not to say that humans always succeed in choosing rightly, of course, yet their failure is attributed to a corrupted will. As Lapsley puts it, "Refusal to orient one's will to do the right thing constitutes a failure in the proper *use* of one's moral equipment, not a defect in the equipment itself."[52] On the other hand, the less prevalent model, "neutral moral selfhood," implies that humans are not capable of such moral choice. While humans are still held accountable for their actions, this model presumes that there is a deep failure in the nature of humanity.[53] Indeed, "[t]he incapacity of people to orient themselves to the good is a problem of fundamental moral equipment; it is a flaw at the most basic level of the moral self."[54]

Lapsley is quick to acknowledge that while virtuous moral selfhood is the dominant model in the Hebrew Bible, the two models can interact.

---

[50] Jacqueline E. Lapsley, *Can These Bones Live? The Problem of the Moral Self in the Book of Ezekiel* (BZAW 301; Berlin: Walter de Gruyter, 2000).

[51] Ibid., 44.

[52] Ibid., 10.

[53] She notes that even in the "neutral" model, "human beings are still *moral* persons, that is, they are still held accountable for their choices and actions: nowhere in the HB are humans depicted as dumb wood, not to be held responsible for their decisions" (ibid., 9).

[54] Ibid., 10

In the book of Jeremiah, for example, she finds the virtuous model to be evident in the prophet's repeated calls for the people to repent, implicit in which is the assumption that although the Israelites have erred, they know what is right and are capable of returning to faithfulness (e.g., Jer 3:13–14). At other times, however, the extreme corruption of the people causes Jeremiah to express pessimism that humans are capable of moral choice after all (e.g., Jer 13:21; 17:9). Lapsley suggests that one can glimpse a view of neutral moral selfhood in Jeremiah's appeal to "unilateral divine action to resolve the moral conundrum created by that incurable corruption."[55] Lapsley presents Ezekiel as the prime example of a text drawing on both of these models, although ultimately the book crafts a new vision of the moral self in which God grants a new moral identity to humans, which is grounded not in action but in knowledge of God and of the human condition.[56]

Within Proverbs, however, the question of moral selfhood is rather different. If Lapsley is correct, in most of the Hebrew Bible, the presenting issue of moral selfhood is whether or not humans have an inherent capacity for moral action. Do they possess, in Lapsley's terms, the right "moral equipment"? As Lapsley sets up the models, it is a question of whether the origin of moral selfhood is internal or external – an innate capacity of humans or something that can only come from outside the agent. At first glance, it may appear that Proverbs simply contains both of these models in tension, with certain sayings expressing optimism about the ability of humans to choose wisely and others more suspicious about the capacity of some humans, particularly fools and the wicked, to do so at all.[57] However, Proverbs offers a more complex model which simultaneously presumes both internal and external agency while it promotes the cultivation of the moral self.

Proverbs reflects a third model of moral selfhood in the Hebrew Bible, one that might be termed "educated moral selfhood," insofar as the book indicates that one's moral selfhood must be disciplined into being.[58] Proverbs implies that moral equipment is innate, but exists in potential only. The origin of moral selfhood is both with the external aid of discipline, which serves to orient one's concept of the good toward wisdom,

---

[55] Ibid., 58.
[56] Ibid., 186.
[57] Lapsley does not discuss Proverbs at any length, although she suggests that it is an example of a text in which both models exist in tension (ibid., 44, n. 1).
[58] Thus age is prized more than youth in Proverbs (e.g., 16:31; 17:6). See Brown, "To Discipline without Destruction," 65–66.

*and* with an internal capacity to receive and profit from discipline. A comparison with the other models makes the distinction clear. According to the model of virtuous moral selfhood, the primary problem with humanity is a failure to align one's will and action with what one knows to be good, while in the neutral model it is an inherent inability to act according to the good at all. By contrast, in the model of educated moral selfhood, the primary problem resides in a misalignment between one's perceptions of the good and the reality of wisdom, a gap that can only be rectified by discipline but also requires an innate receptivity to correction. For this reason, the book constantly enjoins the student to hear the instruction of the parent and learn from rebuke, just as it insists that the parent must administer discipline consistently, wisely, and thoroughly (e.g., 13:24). What is at stake is the formation of the student's moral self.

The character of the simpleton (פתי) crystallizes the conundrum of moral selfhood. The simple one is infatuated with his own simplicity (1:22), unable to foresee dangerous circumstances (22:3b = 27:12b), susceptible to the influence of nefarious company (7:7–27; 9:16), and subject to a waywardness that will ultimately result in his demise (1:32). And yet the book is not entirely pessimistic about the formation of the פתי. Indeed, the education of the פתי is one of its main ends (1:4). The simple have an innate receptivity to external influence, which is both to their credit and their detriment. For this reason, they are able to profit from discipline, even discipline delivered to others (19:25; 21:11). However, the simpleton's receptivity can result in his harm should he imbibe the wrong counsel. "A simple one believes every word" (14:15a), which is why he is liable to be swayed by smooth talkers but is also not beyond the purview of correction. Only by ingesting discipline in ever greater degrees will he learn to discern the words of wisdom from the words of foolishness. In this respect, the development of his moral selfhood presupposes an inherent malleability, which is why the stakes of discipline are so high. Without proper discipline, his moral self will be shaped in the likeness of sinners, fools, and the wicked, but if he is shaped by discipline, he will learn to deploy his innate receptivity toward the further acquisition of wisdom.

The character of the fool or "dunce" (כסיל), on the other hand, presents the consequences of uneducated moral selfhood. Lacking any inherent receptivity, the fool's moral selfhood is shaped by his own internal perceptions. Proverbs indicates that the primary problem with the dunce is both his intractability and a distortion in his perceptions, emotions, and desires. It is not that the fool knows the good but chooses to do otherwise.

Instead, his moral equipment is skewed such that he does what he imag-
ines to be good, failing to understand its harmful consequences. Proverbs
14:8 reports that, "the wisdom of the savvy discerns his way, but the foolishness of fools is deceit" (חכמת ערום הבין דרכו ואולת כסילים מרמה). The fools'
lack of wisdom deceives them, and they do not understand their own way.
The fool also suffers from a confusion of desire: he loves what he should
hate, such as folly (12:23; 15:14), and hates what he should love, such as
knowledge and understanding (1:22; 18:2). It is not that fools choose the
crooked path or pursue the wrong desires knowing them to be evil. Rather,
they walk according to flawed perception and choose what is straight and
pleasurable in their own eyes. Their "moral equipment," in other words, is
not lacking entirely – as in the model of "neutral moral selfhood" – but is
severely impaired.

The solution to such distorted sensibilities is discipline, but nowhere
does Proverbs promise that discipline will be effective for the fool.
Indeed, administering discipline to a fool only results in frustration to
the teacher. For the fool's distorted perception extends to discipline itself.
Failing to see the utility of discipline, he spurns words of advice, placing
more trust in his own insight (23:9; 28:26). At the same time, however,
the book indicates that corporeal correction is appropriate for fools, perhaps as the only means that may catch their attention when words fail.
So Prov 22:15, "Folly is bound in the heart of a boy – the rod of discipline
removes it from him," which testifies to the importance of early interven-
tion. Yet the fool persists in foolishness (26:11). There is a malfunction in
his moral equipment because he rejects the tool that would calibrate it
properly: discipline.[59]

Being a wise person or a fool is not a simple matter of either-or, but
is a result of the converging influences of one's internal propensities and
certain external forces of formation. Part of the underlying complexity
of moral formation is the complexity of human motivation. Proverbs
does not assume that the student is motivated solely by a pure desire
for wisdom and aversion to foolishness. His moral equipment is not
innately calibrated to such measures. Rather, the desire for wisdom
must be cultivated, often by appeal to the more mundane motivations
of wealth and renown. The language of rebuke is in many respects an
appeal to negative motivation, implicit in which is the notion that
humans are prompted partly by fear and a desire to avoid pain. Thus

---

[59] This problem is even more pronounced in the case of the אויל, who rejects discipline outrightly
(1:7; 15:5) and is thus impervious to correction, whether with words or the rod.

certain warnings end with threat of death or peril. The rod, while not a tool of punishment, does hold the potential to injure. However, Proverbs also attends to a range of positive motivations that endeavor to increase the student's receptivity to wisdom. Accordingly, the means for educating the moral self include an appeal to a breadth of human motivations, both positive and negative, and this model will be the subject of the next chapter.

CHAPTER 5

# The Model of Motivation

The world of Old Testament ethics is very much a world of sticks and carrots, threatening punishment for sin and promising blessing for righteousness.[1]

In the Hebrew Bible, morality is motivated. John Barton argues that there is a threefold scheme of motivation in the Hebrew Bible, consisting of past, present, and future motivations.[2] Past motivations arise from the rationale that one should act morally as a grateful response to God's past acts of mercy or deliverance. This idea is a frequent motif in the law and the prophets, where the history of God's faithfulness is recounted as a claim on God's people for their obedience. For example, Deut 5:15 provides the following rationale for observing the Sabbath: "Remember that you were a slave in the land of Egypt, and YHWH your God brought you out from there with a strong hand and an outstretched arm. *Therefore*, YHWH your God commanded you to keep the Sabbath day." The motivation for obedience here is grounded in a past action of God. Other texts offer present motivations, which Barton understands as an appeal to the inherent goodness of the law or moral act.[3] One ought to obey the law because it is good, even delightful.[4] Barton claims that this perspective appears most frequently in the psalms, which often appeal to the inherent beauty and perfection of the law. Thus Psalm 19 proclaims: "The law of YHWH is perfect, restoring the soul; the statutes of YHWH are sure, making wise the

---

[1] John Barton, *Ethics and the Old Testament* (Harrisburg: Trinity Press International, 1998), 82.
[2] Ibid., 82–96.
[3] Ibid., 95.
[4] Barton explains that this is a slightly different perspective than the belief that no motivation is necessary. Although the idea of present motivation does not place significant emphasis on the benefits that may accrue to the individual, "it thinks that there *is* a reward for well-doing, but that this is inherent in living a law-abiding life, and makes the well-doer happy even if there are no external benefits" (ibid.; emphasis in original).

simple; the precepts of YHWH are straight, making the heart rejoice; the commandment of YHWH is pure, lighting up the eyes" (Ps 19:8–9).

Finally, Barton posits that future motivation, the appeal to promised benefits, is the "most common device for encouraging good conduct" in the Hebrew Bible.[5] "The idea that well-doing brings a divine blessing, and wrong-doing a divine curse, seems to have been wholly uncontroversial in the world Israel inhabited," he argues, and he finds evidence of this perspective in the law, the prophets, and especially in the wisdom tradition. This view of future motivation leads Barton to conclude that Proverbs holds a fairly rigid and simple view of the world. He argues that the wisdom writers believe that "the consequences of an action for good or ill are somehow bound up with the action itself, and come about more or less automatically.... [I]t is not an open question whether good or ill will result from doing this or that, but a foregone conclusion."[6] Consequently, "[i]t is this sense that we always know in advance that good behaviour will lead to prosperity and bad behaviour to adversity which produces the somewhat dogmatic character of wisdom literature, so offensive to many modern readers."[7]

Barton is surely correct that much of the ethical import of Proverbs is based in the appeal to future motivation, but it is not clear that it implies as dogmatic a view as he suggests. To the contrary, the pervasive and sophisticated appeal to motivation within Proverbs points to a complexity in the understanding of the human person. It is not that humans are moral automatons who act only on the premise that good outcomes are the inevitable result of good behavior, as the act-consequence scheme posits.[8] If

---

[5] Ibid., 82.
[6] Ibid., 86.
[7] Ibid.
[8] Klaus Koch advanced the *Tat-Ergehen Zusammenhang* as a doctrine of retribution in his influential essay, "Is There a Doctrine of Retribution in the Old Testament?" trans. Thomas H. Trapp, in *Theodicy in the Old Testament* (ed. James L. Crenshaw; IRT 4; Philadelphia: Fortress, 1983), 57–87; trans. of "Gibt es ein Vergeltungsdogma im Alten Testament?" *ZTK* (1955): 1–42. Koch argued that reward and punishment are inherent in good and bad deeds, and thus the evil person falls victim to his own evil, without the interference of God. This view has a robust history and is still held by many scholars, although it has also been either nuanced or thoroughly critiqued by others (see Gerhard von Rad, *Wisdom in Israel* [trans. James D. Martin; London: SCM Press, 1972; repr., Harrisburg: Trinity Press International, 1993], 124–37; Bernd Janowski, "Die Tat kehrt zum Täter zurück: Offene Fragen im Umkreis des >>Tun-Ergehen-Zusammenhangs<<," *ZTK* [1994]: 247–71; Lennart Boström, *The God of the Sages: The Portrayal of God in the Book of Proverbs* [ConBOT 29; Stockholm: Almqvist & Wiksell International, 1990], 90–139; Michael V. Fox, *Qohelet and His Contradictions* [JSOTSup 71; Sheffield: Almond Press, 1989], 132–37; Raymond C. Van Leeuwen, "Wealth and Poverty: System and Contradiction in Proverbs," *HS* 33 [1992]: 25–36; Samuel L. Adams, *Wisdom in Transition: Act and Consequence in Second Temple Instructions* [Supplements to the Journal for the Study of Judaism 125; Leiden: Brill, 2008]).

this were true, any evidence to the contrary would be devastating to such a premise. Nor is it the case that the approach is pure dogma, removed from a notion about the workings of reality. Rather, the use of motivation in Proverbs hinges on the convergence of a strong conviction about the operative structure of order in the world, as well as an understanding of human psychology. Even as Proverbs seeks to educate its student about the fundamental, and reliable, nature of order, its appeal to motivation suggests that it accommodates the reality of human self-interest. In fact, Proverbs treats this seriously as a powerful force in character formation.

## The Model of Motivation

Although rebuke is a prominent theme within Proverbs, its pedagogy includes both a carrot and a stick. Indeed, in many sayings, these are two sides of the same coin, and the incentives of the wise course are presented jointly with cautionary tales about the foolish course. Proverbs 15:4, for example, admonishes the student that "a healing tongue is a tree of life, but crookedness in it shatters the spirit." Alongside the father's injunctions to avoid certain behaviors and his threats of physical correction or certain danger, he also promises great reward for those who adhere to the right course. Such incentives, used as an integral strategy of character formation, are part of Proverbs' model of motivation. This model includes both the explicit motivational statements in the book, as well as its extensive use of motivational symbols to mark the desirability and value of certain sanctioned activities and concepts.[9] Behind the use of various forms of

[9] For the purpose of this discussion, I will consider the book as a whole. Fox argues that there is a distinct difference in the motivations in chapters 10–29 versus chapters 1–9. He states that in the sayings of chapters 10–29, most likely chronologically earlier than chapters 1–9, all of the benefits are practical and worldly. There are no religious benefits; benefits do not come from YHWH. Rather, these chapters are primarily concerned with practical benefits in the realm of daily life (Michael V. Fox, *Proverbs 10–31: A New Translation with Introduction and Commentary* [AB 18B; New Haven: Yale University Press, 2009], 927). In chapters 1–9, however, he finds more discussion of the ethical or religious benefits and less interest, if any, in the practical, specific benefits of wisdom. While some of the promised rewards are the same, he argues that they "lack some of the utilitarian benefits" associated with the motivations in the sayings (ibid., 932). Fox may make this distinction too sharply, for there are benefits in the sayings connected to YHWH (e.g., 15:25; 20:22), as well as certain practical benefits in chapters 1–9 (e.g., 3:10, 23–24). Yet the use of motivational symbols is more pronounced in chapters 1–9, and the practical benefits in chapters 1–9 mostly come from the realm of life, safety, and honor. The language of material wealth is more often used as a motivational symbol than as explicit motivation, i.e., used to mark what is desirable more than promised as an expected outcome. In general, one might say that there is a more pronounced rhetorical and metaphorical use of both rebuke and motivation in Prov 1–9. Even so, these chapters are thoroughly infused with motivation, and thus I will consider the book as a whole in sketching the contours of motivation as a model of character formation.

motivation are profound assumptions about the nature of human beings, namely, that they are complexly motivated by a variety of negative and positive stimuli and, consequently, are self-interested creatures who can be formed by appeal to human desire.

## What Is Motivation?

At its most basic level, motivation is simply a rationale or incentive to pursue a certain course. It has proven a particularly important category for the study of ancient legal texts, many of which issue motive clauses to support the law in question. For example, Exod 20:12 offers a motivation of longevity for the command to honor one's parents: "Honor your father and your mother *so that your days may be long upon the land.*" Accordingly, within biblical studies the concept of motivation often refers to specific grammatical and syntactical features of a text. Yet when the study of motivation is limited to particular syntactical constructions, an underlying logic of motivation in many texts is often lost. While Proverbs does contain many motivational clauses, what is in focus here is not the grammatical construction but instead the underlying rationale or incentive offered for the student to undertake a certain practice or listen to a particular instruction. At times such motivations are issued explicitly, although at other times they must be inferred.

Proverbs contains a rich array of motivations, but for heuristic purposes they can be organized into four primary paradigms: wealth, honor, protection, and life. Each paradigm contains a set of related motivations that appeal to particular human desires, and certain motivations can often serve more than one paradigm. These are not sharply defined or mutually exclusive categories, and it is helpful to think of each of these paradigms as part of a larger, overarching network of motivation in the book. In addition, each of these paradigms also has a negative counterpart. While wealth constitutes a positive motivation, for example, the fear of poverty conversely provides a negative motivation for the student to avoid particular company or actions. Even as attaining honor serves as a positive motivation, the threat of shame or lack of renown is its negative correlate. Indeed, positive and negative motivations are often closely tied by the parallel structure of individual sayings, such as Prov 10:7, "[T]he memory of the righteous is for a blessing, but the name of the wicked will rot." In this saying, the first half of the line appeals to the positive motivation of a particular honor that will follow the righteous, as the second half of the line alludes to a negative incentive to avoid the degradation that comes with a wicked reputation. While this discussion will focus on the positive motivations in Proverbs, they are not unrelated to the negative motivations that are implicit in much of the language of rebuke in the book.[10]

## What Is Moral Motivation?

Israelite sages were not the only ones to wrestle with the profound influence of motivation. The role of motivation in ethical action and decision making has long occupied moral philosophers, who have proposed different explanations for the formation of such motivations and their relevance to moral belief and moral character. Within moral philosophy, the concept of *moral* motivation refers specifically to the motivational force of moral judgments, and there is broad debate concerning whether and to what degree moral beliefs motivate corresponding action. While the approaches to motivation are numerous, for heuristic purposes they can be categorized into at least four distinct approaches.[11] The *instrumentalist* approach, one of the most pervasive perspectives (often called the Humean perspective), insists that belief alone is insufficient for moral motivation.[12] Rather, it argues that motivation begins with intrinsic desires, such as the desire for pleasure or the desire for a loved one's well-being. When such intrinsic desires are matched with beliefs about what will bring about the desire in question, a person is thus motivated to take the appropriate action. In other words, "motivation on the instrumentalist's view is a matter of having non-intrinsic desires ... to do what is believed to be instrumental to (or a realization of) an intrinsic desire."[13] That is, if I have an intrinsic desire to feel pleasure and then come to the belief that giving to charity will bring me pleasure, I will develop a non-intrinsic desire to make a charitable contribution. My motivation to give arises from my intrinsic desire to feel pleasure, not my belief that giving to charity is good. On the other hand, the *cognitivist* approach argues that motivation begins

[10] For a discussion of the model of rebuke, see Chapter 4, which considers the way in which the descriptions of negative characters and actions function as figurative rebuke, implicitly warning the student against imitating the negative example. Put differently, such descriptions function as negative motivations, i.e., disincentives, to carry out such behavior and act in a similar manner.

[11] See the typology in Timothy Schroeder, Adina L. Roskies, and Shaun Nichols, "Moral Motivation" in *The Moral Psychology Handbook* (ed. John M. Doris, et al.; New York: Oxford University Press, 2010), 74–78.

[12] For example, see Bernard Williams, *Moral Luck: Philosophical Papers 1973–1980* (New York: Cambridge University Press, 1981), 101–13.

[13] Schroeder, et al., "Moral Motivation," 75.

with belief, independent of one's desires.[14] In my example, the motivation to give to charity comes solely from my belief that it is a good thing to do; any desire for pleasure is purely ancillary. The *sentimentalist* view suggests that the emotions play a primary role in motivating moral behavior, and in fact, for an act to be moral, it should be accompanied by certain emotions.[15] For example, my emotion of compassion may elicit charitable giving, thus making my act morally motivated. Finally, the *personalist* approach, associated with the tradition of virtue ethics, is the most holistic of the four. It proposes that the motivation for moral action comes from good character, which encompasses one's knowledge, desires, emotions, and habits.[16] It is distinct from the instrumentalist view in insisting that character is not able to be reduced to intrinsic desires.

Proverbs undoubtedly has much to say about motivation, yet in what respect does it address *moral* motivation? How does motivation play a role in moral character and behavior? While this is not a question that the sages of Proverbs asked directly, at least as reflected in the final form of the text, these philosophical perspectives do highlight certain operative assumptions in the book that bear further exploration. There is a complex relationship between intrinsic desires, acquired knowledge, emotion, perception, and character, all of which relate to the primary role of motivation as one impetus of formation. Each of the paradigms of motivation reveals not only the *presence* of motivation, but also its vital and varied role in influencing moral character and action.

## Paradigms of Motivation in Proverbs

### Wealth

The language of wealth, which has been one of the most widely recognized and commented upon motivations in Proverbs, would at first glance appear to provide evidence of an instrumentalist view of moral motivation. For example, Prov 10:4b states, "[T]he hand of the diligent brings wealth," which implicitly suggests that wealth will come to the industrious. This type of logic seems akin to an instrumentalist perspective, in which certain intrinsic desires – such as wealth – when joined with a belief about particular actions or traits that might endow this desire – such as diligence – foster

---

[14] For example, see Thomas Nagel, *The Possibility of Altruism* (Princeton: Princeton University Press, 1978).

[15] Schroeder, et al., "Moral Motivation," 77.

[16] See Rosalind Hursthouse, *On Virtue Ethics* (Oxford: Oxford University Press, 1999), 141–60.

secondary motivations for sanctioned behavior. However, the desire of wealth serves more than utilitarian function within Proverbs.

Wealth itself is inherently neither good nor evil; it animates the desires of sinners (1:10–19) and also colors the path of wisdom (3:14). Its ends can be destructive or regenerative, depending on the path toward which it leads. Given the power of wealth's allure, Proverbs appeals to the motivation of wealth in its effort to shape the character of its student. The book does not call on the student to reject the desire of wealth. To the contrary, its rhetoric encourages the student's desire, while reframing that desire in the larger context of the book's moral claims. For example, Prov 10:20 states that "the tongue of the righteous is choice silver, but the mind of the wicked of little worth" (כסף נבחר לשׁון צדיק לב רשׁעים כמעט). The saying turns on the assumption that choice silver is a valuable commodity and something worthy of acquisition; being "of little worth," by contrast, is an undesirable economic condition. Yet the saying, while it assumes the value of silver, is not a literal directive to accumulate wealth, but borrows imagery from the economic realm as a metaphor for righteous speech. In this way, the desire of wealth is reframed, although not discounted, in a larger moral issue of righteousness.

The motif of wealth is not limited to material gain, but also includes images of luxury, which suggests that motivation involves more than a calculation of strictly economic benefit. Luxurious objects or fineries have financial value, yet they do not mark purely utilitarian merit. Beyond their economic measure, these images point to beauty and sensory appeal. Proverbs 20:15, for instance, uses precious objects to mark the exceeding value of wise speech: "There is gold and abundant jewels (רב־פנינים), but lips of knowledge are a precious vessel." With the metaphor of a rare object, the saying implies not only the value of wise language (cf. 10:20) but also its rarity, even its beauty, exceeding fine jewels. It is not simply that such speech has a value that could be measured in currency, but also that it has qualities that set it apart from what is commonly encountered. Similarly, Prov 1:9 uses images of luxury as motivational symbols to speak of parental teaching. A father's discipline and a mother's instruction are "a wreath of grace for your head, and a necklace for your throat." These metaphors suggest that listening to such instruction does not simply repay dividends in economic value, but promises to adorn the student, marking him with outward signs of distinction, ornamentation, and value. While the motif of luxury is certainly related to wealth, it offers an additional dimension by introducing implications of beauty and aesthetic appeal, not only economic value.

The extensive language of wealth, with its related images of luxury and value, is not only indicative of a particular kind of motivation, but it also reveals fundamental values of the sapiential worldview. Proverbs is not primarily concerned with issuing economic advice. Rather, as Timothy J. Sandoval has argued, "the rhetoric of desirable wealth in Proverbs is much more intimately linked to the book's overall effort to construct a particular moral identity for the hearer or reader; its attempt to form a wise person."[17] Sandoval, who has undertaken one of the most extensive surveys of the language of wealth and poverty in Proverbs, suggests that there are both literal and figurative uses of such language in the book. Wealth is a subject of direct instruction and social commentary, but it is also a motivational symbol that is used to persuade the listener of the exceeding value of wisdom.[18] "When it comes to the discourse of wealth and poverty," he emphasizes, "it is important to remember that the sages are less concerned with offering observations and primarily concerned with communicating their fundamental values."[19]

Sandoval's study is enormously helpful because he issues a call to read Proverbs with greater literary sophistication, insisting that the use of motivational tropes cannot be reduced either to a strict act-consequence nexus, in which profit inevitably accrues to the wise, or to the ideology of a social elite.[20] In drawing attention to the extensive use of the figurative language of wealth in the book, Sandoval advances the conversation beyond purely literal readings, which have often struggled to account for the seemingly disparate uses of wealth imagery in the book.[21] Instead, as Sandoval points out, the figurative use of wealth as a motivational symbol is a rhetorical tool used to enculturate the student into a particular view of reality. The notion that wealth marks objects of moral value is reflective not of personal experience, per se, but of a deeply held belief about the order of

---

[17] Timothy J. Sandoval, *The Discourse of Wealth and Poverty in the Book of Proverbs* (Biblical Interpretation Series 77; Leiden: Brill, 2006), 70. For other treatments of the language of wealth and poverty in Proverbs, see also R. N. Whybray, *Wealth and Poverty in the Book of Proverbs* (JSOTSup 99; Sheffield: Sheffield Academic Press, 1990); Harold C. Washington, *Wealth and Poverty in the Instruction of Amenemope and the Hebrew Proverbs* (SBLDS 142; Atlanta: Scholars Press, 1996); Van Leeuwen, "Wealth and Poverty."

[18] Sandoval suggests that there are three distinct, although related, discourses of wealth and poverty in the book. The discourses of social justice and social observation contain literal observations and commentary about desirable practices and social relations, while "wisdom's virtues discourse" employs figurative language to persuade the listener of the ultimate value of wisdom and its associated virtues (Sandoval, *The Discourse of Wealth and Poverty*, 69–70).

[19] Ibid., 66.

[20] See Sandoval's discussion in ibid., 61–66.

[21] Ibid., 31–39.

the world, in which the very structures of the cosmos confirm virtue and obstruct vice.[22]

In other words, it is not that the language of motivation is – *of necessity* – based in literal, first-hand experience of, for example, wisdom as a trove of riches. Rather, these motivations are part of schooling the student in a particular way of looking at the world. It portrays certain sanctioned concepts or characters not only as wise or righteous, but as *desirable* and conducive to the student's own well-being. Like rebuke, then, the model of motivation is also about the acquisition of knowledge, based on certain underlying assumptions about the coherence of order in the world. And indeed, this is a pervasive aspect of the book that is not limited to the language of wealth.

## *Honor*

Honor, whether a literal conferral of rank or privilege or a figurative symbol of esteem or approval, highlights the role of emotion and social relationship in moral motivation. Honor is related to wealth in the sense that the wealthy enjoy privileged social standing, and thus one of the motives for attaining wealth is to gain honor. But honor is not restricted to what is gained through material prosperity. Honor also encompasses social respect that may come from displaying one's wisdom or enjoying divine blessings (e.g., 3:33; 10:7; 11:26; 13:15). Honor includes parental pleasure, which is a particularly potent motivation as the father extols the son to follow his command in order to bring joy to his parents (e.g., 10:1; 15:20; 23:24, 25; 29:3). Within these sayings, the motive for obedience is not solely the inherent wisdom of the instruction, but also the honor that it will bring to the student's parental teachers. The repeated emphasis on bringing honor to – and avoiding the disgrace of – one's parents and teachers serves as a potent emotional motivation and is part of educating the student's emotional perceptions and responses. Accordingly, the stakes of heeding discipline are frequently framed in terms of the emotions of the parent, as in Prov 10:1, which implicitly connects honorable behavior with joy and shameful behavior with grief: "A wise son – a father rejoices; but a foolish son – the grief of his mother" (see also, e.g., 15:20; 17:21).

---

[22] Sandoval explains that for the sages of Proverbs, "to act righteously and wisely is to align oneself with the structures of creation; to act foolishly and wickedly is to oppose the organization of reality. Hence the book's assured claims about the prosperity of the wise and righteous and the demise of the foolish and wicked. ... The 'truth' of the sages' act-consequence rhetoric thus has to do primarily with how one *perceives* the world" (ibid., 64; emphasis in original).

As a motivational symbol, honor points to the cultural value placed on seniority and the social hierarchy, values which are also linked to the ultimate motivation of life, particularly the longevity of life, fostered through the practice of wisdom and righteousness. Proverbs 16:31, for example, states: "[A] glorious crown – gray hair, found on the way of righteousness." The saying does not mean to say that gray hair is literally a crown, but it uses one attribute of motivation, the crown as an outward symbol of honor, to reframe old age as honorable and link it to the larger moral concern of righteousness. In this way, the saying orients the student's desire for honor toward the ultimate desire of the way of righteousness. This saying also illustrates the way in which multiple motivations can operate within one saying, for it appeals not only to honor, but also to an image of luxury with the metaphor of gray hair as a resplendent adornment.

### Protection

The paradigm of protection, which includes the promises of safety, security, and stability, highlights slightly different values in the book, including a penchant for order and equilibrium. Within the sapiential worldview, there is a conception that wealth affords a certain stability that can protect one against economic distress (e.g., 18:11), so this motivation is also related to the paradigm of wealth. However, it is distinct insofar as the motivations within this paradigm concentrate more on a condition of safety than of comfort, financial or otherwise. Safety constitutes protection from trouble, as in woman Wisdom's vow that the one who listens to her will dwell securely (ישכן־בטח), untroubled by the terror of evil (1:33). Part of the appeal of personified Wisdom is her ability to preserve the one who seeks her. This motif is operative in the metaphor WISDOM IS A GUARDIAN, which is evident in the father's promise that Wisdom will protect (שׁמר) and keep (נצר) the one who seeks her (4:6). This metaphor is also active in the many sayings that suggest that understanding, instruction, or certain attributes will act as guardians on behalf of the student (e.g., 6:22–23; 13:6; 14:3). Proverbs 2:11–12, for example, states:

> Shrewdness will protect you; insight will keep you –
> To deliver you from the way of evil, from the one speaking waywardness.

> מזמה תשמר עליך תבונה תנצרכה
> להצילך מדרך רע מאיש מדבר תהפכות

These lines are part of a larger instruction that extols the virtue of heeding the father's counsel and provides a litany of metaphors that appeal to protection. Within this instruction, the motif of protection is grounded in the fear of YHWH, for God is a shield for the upright (מגן להלכי תם, 2:7). Related to safety is the motivation of security, although it implies not only protection from trouble but a stable condition derived from a source of strength, such as wealth (10:15; 18:11), the fear of YHWH (14:26–27; 18:10), or righteous character (12:21).

The motivation of stability undergirds security and safety, and its frequency in the book underscores the fundamental values of order and social stability. It is a pervasive motivation in the book, for it also relates to wealth and honor. Part of the appeal of possessing wealth or social standing within the community is that it insulates one from disequilibrium. While the foolish and the wicked are tossed about by the winds of trouble and the unexpected events that reality brings (e.g., 12:7; 13:6; 14:11; 24:16), the wise and the righteous are preserved from the grave problems such events can cause. As Prov 10:25 proclaims, "[W]hen the whirlwind passes over, the wicked is no more, but the righteous is an everlasting fountain." While the wise or righteous may experience ill effects from unforeseen events, they will not be affected in the same detrimental way. Stability thus proves to be a primary motivation in the appeal for the student to seek wisdom and righteousness, for these virtues ensure that he has some measure of protection from harm. This motif underscores the overarching value of order and the preservation of tradition within Proverbs. Within the Psalms, by contrast, protection more often has to do with deliverance from one's enemies or preservation from anguish. For example, Ps 27:1–3 proclaims:

> YHWH is my light and my deliverance; whom will I fear? YHWH is the stronghold of my life, whom will I dread? When evildoers approach me to devour my flesh, my adversaries and my enemies, they indeed stumble and fall. If an army encamped against me, my heart would not fear. Even if a war rose up against me – in this I trust.

The emphasis here is on the present personal threat of the psalmist's enemies. Yet in Proverbs, the motif of protection is more about the maintenance of order and keeping one's life in alignment with that order.

### Life

While wealth has garnered the most critical attention of all of the motivations in Proverbs, the language of wealth cannot be viewed in isolation from the larger network of motivations of which it is a part, including the paradigms of honor and protection. Yet all of the motivations in Proverbs ultimately lead to some aspect of life, which is the most common motivation in the book.[23] The promise of a successful life, characterized by its length, prosperity, and security, is the driving motivation in the book, an umbrella under which other motivations of wealth, luxury, honor, and protection take their place. At times, the motivation of life is a literal promise of longevity, as in Prov 16:15a, which suggests that a king's favor will prolong one's days, for "in the light of the king's face is life." In Prov 3:1–2, the father issues the promise of life as a motive for attending to his teaching: "My son, do not forget my teaching, let your mind keep my commandments, for they will bestow on you length of days, years of life, and well-being" (cf. 9:11; 10:2, 15; 11:19; 12:28; 13:3; 21:21). But the motif of life also functions as a motivational symbol, pointing to the value of other objects. Thus, Wisdom, the righteous, and worthy speech are described as a "tree of life" (3:18; 11:20; 15:4), while wisdom, wise teaching, righteous speech, and the fear of YHWH are called a "fountain of life" (10:11; 13:14; 14:27; 16:22). Within the paradigm of life, healing is a related motivation, as in Prov 4:22, in which the father proclaims that his words are "life to those who find them, and healing to his entire flesh." The parallel structure of the saying highlights the relationship between healing and life, for listening to wise instruction is the balm that allows one to attain wholeness and vitality.

The motivation of life encompasses images of satiety, insofar as satisfaction and abundance are marks of success and contentment, and these too indicate aspects of the sages' fundamental values.[24] Proverbs 12:11 indicates that "one who works his land will be sated with food (יִשְׂבַּע־לֶחֶם), but one who seeks vanities lacks sense (חֲסַר־לֵב)." Satiety and healing mingle in Prov 16:24 to advance two different features of speech: "Pleasant words are a honeycomb – sweet to the soul and healing to the bones." Similarly, Prov 24:13–14 appeals to the student's sweet tooth as a metaphor for wisdom: "Eat honey, my son, for it is good – sweet drippings on your palate! Know this: such is wisdom for your soul (נֶפֶשׁ); if you find it, there is a future, and your hope will not be cut off."[25] Both sayings rely on the literal

---

[23] Also noted by R. N. Gordon, "Motivation in Proverbs," *BT* 25 (1975): 54. See also Roland E. Murphy, "The Kerygma of the Book of Proverbs," *Int* 20 (1966): 3–14. Zoltán S. Schwáb characterizes the kind of life that is the reward of virtue within Proverbs as "happiness," which he explains "can be comprised by the material benefits, like long life and riches, the social benefits, like honour, but it also expresses something of the peaceful, content mindset that is mirrored in many of these verses" (Zoltán S. Schwáb, *Toward an Interpretation of the Book of Proverbs: Selfishness and Secularity Reconsidered* [Winona Lake: Eisenbrauns, 2013], 126).

[24] For a more complete treatment of satiety and its relation to desire, see Chapter 6.

[25] For notes on the translation and more discussion of these verses, see Chapter 6.

desirability of sweet honey, yet the pedagogical function of the sayings hinges on their figurative use of such objects to mark the value of speech and wisdom, respectively. Moreover, such language of satiety and healing points to a larger conception of the nature of life as the sages envision it. Wisdom does not mean doing without, necessarily, nor does it require a vow of poverty or asceticism. To the contrary, satiation and abundance provide the metaphors for the satisfaction of the way of wisdom.

The attention to life in all of its facets accords with the book's purpose as an instruction manual in wise living (1:2–6) and also underscores the prime value of order and social stability. While the promise of life does refer to longevity, it also connotes human flourishing that comes from wisdom, discipline, righteous speech, and the fear of YHWH. The vision of life in the book coheres with the values that are central to the sages' understanding of order in the world. Life is not a neutral term in Proverbs, as if one could have a good life or a bad life. The negative counterpart to life is death (e.g., 2:18; 5:5, 23; 7:27; 10:21; 16:25; 19:16). Life constitutes the sages' vision of the dividends of wisdom, righteousness, and the fear of YHWH; it is the ultimate motivation.

## The Form of Motivation

The form of motivation has long drawn scholarly attention, particularly in discussion of the relationship between wisdom and law. For the most part, motivation has been understood in terms of its grammatical and syntactical form. In 1953, Berend Gemser cataloged the motive clause, a subordinate clause introduced by a particle, as a grammatical feature of biblical literature found in legal, prophetic, and wisdom texts.[26] Gemser argued that motive clauses were unique to Israel, and he categorized four different types of motives: explanatory, ethical, cultic or theological, and historical.[27] Rifat Sonsino, on the other hand, pointed to the presence of motive clauses in some ancient Near Eastern texts, although he affirmed that their presence was far more frequent in the biblical material.[28] In considering

---

[26] Berend Gemser, "The Importance of the Motive Clause in Old Testament Law" in *Congress Volume, Copenhagen 1953* (VTSup 1; Leiden: Brill, 1953), 50–66.

[27] Ibid., 55–56. Gemser posited a connection between law and wisdom based on the motive clause, suggesting that proverbial sayings may have served a function in conveying legal judgments. He pointed to certain similarities in motive language between Proverbs and legal texts, as well as anthropological data from African societies (ibid., 64–66).

[28] Rifat Sonsino, *Motive Clauses in Hebrew Law: Biblical Forms and Near Eastern Parallels* (Chico: Scholars Press, 1980), 153–75.

the content of the motivations, Sonsino identified that motive clauses are variously oriented toward one of four categories: divine authority, historical experience, fear of punishment, or the promise of well-being.[29] While his interest was mainly in motivational clauses within legal codes, he noted the frequent presence of motive clauses in wisdom literature and posited that this was one, although not the only, influence on the form in the legal material.[30] Henry Postel's investigation of the motive clause concentrated specifically on Prov 10–29.[31] Like Gemser, Postel relied on the formal features of Hebrew syntax, although he found different categories of motives: consequential, explanatory, and theological.[32]

Gemser, Sonsino, and Postel based their data and conclusions on the presence of a particular grammatical form, but as Ted Hildebrandt has pointed out, restricting such analysis to outward form impoverishes the understanding of motivation in Proverbs.[33] Hildebrandt argues that many sayings in Proverbs have motivational intent, even if they do not conform to the syntactical features of the motive clause, and he insists that "[w]hen looking at motivation in the sentences it is imperative to penetrate below the surface motive clauses in order to isolate how the sages actually motivated."[34] Using a structural analysis of the sayings in Prov 10–15, Hildebrandt argues that motivation is implicitly operative in most of the sayings. In Prov 10:1, for example, a positive character (בן חכם) is linked to a positive consequence (ישמח־אב), while a negative character (בן כסיל) is linked to a negative consequence (תוגת אמו). Although it does not employ an explicit motivational clause, Hildebrandt adds, the saying "acts as a motivation drawing the son to be wise and driving him from becoming foolish. Its motivational force is unleashed by exposing the son to the emotive consequences, whether joy or sorrow, that his character will have on his parents."[35] Hildebrandt finds eight different structural categories of

---

[29] Ibid., 109–110.

[30] He suggests that the basic model for the motive clause in legal codes may have been a direct influence of wisdom literature, but the authors of the legal codes "did not, however, limit their motivations to those which are basically prudential in nature and reflective of the daily experiences of the people, but also made frequent references to the historic events of the past and used them as the motivation for a number of laws. In other cases, especially in priestly laws, they also chose to justify many legal prescriptions by means of formula-type motivations ... which are unlike the motive clauses found in wisdom instructions" (ibid., 123).

[31] Henry John Postel, *The Form and Function of the Motive Clause in Proverbs 10–29* (PhD diss., University of Iowa, 1976).

[32] Ibid., 151–69.

[33] Ted Hildebrandt, "Motivation and Antithetic Parallelism in Proverbs 10–15," *JETS* 35 (1992): 433–44.

[34] Ibid., 436.

[35] Ibid., 437.

motivation in Prov 10–15, although character → consequence is by far the most frequent.[36] Moreover, Hildebrandt notes that most of the sayings employ antithetical parallelism, and he draws models from modern psycholinguistics to account for this feature, suggesting that "antithesis provides a perfect psycholinguistic structure for doubling the motivational potency of the sentences by combining in an additive sense approach and avoidance motivations."[37] That is, the nature of a binary saying allows simultaneous appeal to both positive (approach) and negative (avoidance) motivation, offering the student a clear choice between the alternative ways of wisdom and foolishness.[38]

Hildebrandt's study is quite helpful in framing motivation in Proverbs more broadly than simply grammatical or syntactical forms, and in fact, motivation is more pervasive than even structural analysis reveals. In addition to the relevant forms that Gemser, Postel, Hildebrandt, and others have identified, motivation is implicit in the book's imagery and figurative language. The individual sayings, longer poems, and larger collections provide the tuition in motivation that appeals to the breadth and diversity of human motives, all the while reframing those motives in the light of wisdom, righteousness, and the fear of YHWH in an effort to shape the character of the student. To consider the form and function of motivation in Proverbs, I will consider a selection of sayings from Prov 10, as well as two longer poems from chapter 3.[39]

*Proverbs 10:1–7*

1  *The Proverbs of Solomon*
   A wise son – a father rejoices; but a foolish son – the grief of his mother.
2  Troves of wickedness will not profit; but righteousness delivers from death.
3  YHWH will not let the righteous soul starve, but he will disrupt[40] the desire of the wicked.

---

[36] The other categories Hildebrandt identifies are: Character → Act (CA); Character → Evaluation (CE); Act → Consequence (AS); Item → Consequence (IS); Item → Evaluation (IE); Act → Evaluation (AE); and Appearance → Reality (PR) (ibid., 437–38).

[37] Ibid., 438–39.

[38] Ibid., 440.

[39] This discussion is necessarily selective and not exhaustive. Proverbs 10 receives special attention here because it provides a particularly nice example of the diversity of motivations within a short span of collected sayings. As the opening of the second proverbial collection, it also provides a hermeneutical lens for the material that follows. With the frequency and variety of motivations to which it appeals, it orients the reader toward an important conceptual category in the book.

[40] Literally, to "push away" or "thrust out" (הדף).

*4* A lazy palm produces poverty, but the hand of the diligent brings wealth.

*5* One who harvests in the summer – savvy son; one asleep in the harvest – shameful son.

*6* Blessings for the head of the righteous; but the mouth of the wicked conceals violence.

*7* The memory of the righteous, a blessing; but the name of the wicked rots.

Even without explicit motivational clauses, each of the sayings operates with an implicit motivational model. Were each of these sayings to be analyzed with Hildebrandt's structural analysis, a similar pattern would emerge. All employ parallelism to present opposing topics and comments.[41] For example, verse 4 offers that a lazy palm (–) leads to poverty (–), while diligent hands (+) bring wealth (+). The first half of the line pairs a negative character attribute, laziness, with a negative result, poverty, while the second half pairs a positive character attribute, diligence, with a positive result, wealth. Both halves employ a character → consequence scheme. The saying simultaneously cautions the student to reject one kind of character ("avoidance," in Hildebrandt's terms), while embracing another ("approach"). It thus turns on the negative and positive implications of the motivation of wealth, appealing to the student's desire to gain wealth and avoid its absence. The other sayings here could be analyzed similarly. In each case, attention simply to grammatical form alone would be insufficient to understand the pervasiveness of motivation to the underlying logic of the lines.

These sayings utilize motivation to make implicit directives, although they refrain from issuing explicit commands. Unlike certain sayings that operate in the model of rebuke, which offer stark imperatives addressed explicitly to the student (e.g., 20:13a, "Do not love sleep lest you be impoverished"), these sayings present the desired character or quality as an observational statement colored by a particular motivation. It is a different rhetorical model. Rather than a command to "be diligent!", Prov 10:4 employs a condition that it assumes the student will find desirable, wealth, and suggests that such will be the profit of diligent behavior.

This motivational model has caused some scholars to posit that there is a rigid act-consequence nexus in Proverbs, in which certain outcomes are considered to be guaranteed to the one who follows the sanctioned

---

[41] See Raymond C. Van Leeuwen, *Context and Meaning in Proverbs 25–27* (SBLDS 96; Atlanta: Scholars Press, 1988), 48–52.

path.[42] However, such sayings are not necessarily based in empirical reality, and one misunderstands the pedagogical and rhetorical function of the motivation by insisting that it must reflect the sages' personal experience.[43] On the contrary, such motivational statements are part of schooling the student in the virtues that the sages value by using the conditions and motivations that hold cultural currency, such as wealth, honor, and social standing.

What is even more striking is the diversity of motivations to which even this short sampling appeals. The first seven sayings of the collection appeal to five different motives: parental favor (v. 1), wealth (vv. 2, 4), satiety (v. 3), renown (vv. 5, 7), and blessing (v. 6). The chapter as a whole alludes to at least four other motives, including safety (10:9), life (10:11, 16, 17, 25, 27), security (10:15, 29, 30), and joy (10:23, 28, 32).[44] As the beginning of the second part of the book, Prov 10 provides a hermeneutical orientation toward the proverbial collections that follow, and motivation proves a vital element of its pedagogy. Indeed, almost every saying in this chapter alludes to some kind of motivation, thus providing a signal to the reader that it will be an important category in the following material.

Moreover, the sum of these motivations indicates a more complex view of the human than has often been suggested. Even as the individual sayings are frequently built on binary oppositions between two opposing character types, as a whole the collection of sayings indicates that a variety of motives inform human action. There is more to the equation than simply whether one is wise or foolish, righteous or wicked. Christopher B. Ansberry has argued that Prov 10–15 presents a simplistic pattern to introduce the student to certain social and moral values: "The general, bifurcated worldview and the facile description of the character-consequence connection present the fundamental structure of

[42] For example, Barton proclaims that "Proverbs insists (often against the evidence) that good things come to good people, evil things to evil ones" (Barton, *Ethics and the Old Testament,* 85).

[43] See Fox's refutation of empiricism in Proverbs (Fox, "Essay 8: Knowledge," in idem, *Proverbs 10–31,* 963–67). Fox notes that it is a common scholarly consensus that wisdom epistemology in Proverbs is empirical. He explains, "Wisdom empiricism is understood to mean that the sages gained and validated their knowledge by looking at the world, observing what was beneficial and harmful, and casting their observations in the form of proverbs and epigrams" (ibid., 963). However, he argues, human experience is not a direct source of wisdom in Proverbs. Although it may provide some of the ingredients of wisdom, direct experience is not the final arbiter of what is true. Instead, Fox insists that there is an underlying system of assumptions about wisdom, which he terms a "coherence theory of truth." Daily observation may support the assumptions of this epistemology; however, this experience is not the *source* of the posited coherence.

[44] The motives of wealth and satiety reappear in 10:22 and 10:21, 24, respectively. In addition, note the use of silver as a motivational symbol to describe righteous speech (10:20).

the socio-moral order and provide the addressee with an elementary paradigm of the wise life."[45] Yet while Ansberry is correct to highlight the function of Prov 10–15 in orienting the student to particular values and a sense of order, it is not clear that the character-consequence model is really so facile after all.

The various motivations that animate these sayings indicate not a rigid axiom but a more subtle perspective in which character, consequence, motive, and context are complexly intertwined. For example, even within chapter 10 there is contradictory advice about the value of diligence, for verse 4 indicates that it will bring wealth (see also v. 5) while verse 22 states that no labor can increase wealth, which is a gift of YHWH. Although the second saying does not necessarily condemn diligence, it qualifies the idea that diligence inevitably leads to wealth. A strict act-consequence or character-consequence model does not account adequately for this more judicious outlook. Furthermore, both sayings turn on the motivation of wealth, yet they appeal to it differently. While the first saying highlights wealth as an incentive for the student to embody a particular character, the second saying subordinates that motive to a theological framework, although it does not discredit it entirely.

There is an additional complexity indicated by what these sayings leave unsaid, a function of the terse poetic lines. Proverbs 10:2, for example, does not indicate that wickedness will reap no financial benefits. The phrase אוצרות רשע implies that outward signs of wealth may indeed accrue either to those of unsavory character or by unethical means.[46] Yet this symbol of wealth will not prove profitable, perhaps implying it will provide only fleeting wealth (cf. 21:6) or invite plunder (cf. Jer 50:37). The second half of the line, however, qualifies the economic imagery of the first half. By ascribing to righteousness the ability to deliver from death, the saying indicates that what is truly at stake is not wealth versus poverty, but life versus death. When the two halves of the line are read together, it appears that troves of wickedness do not profit in the sense that they, unlike righteousness, cannot protect from death. In this way, the second part of the saying reframes the first half of the line and even reframes motivation itself.[47] The desire for wealth may motivate the

---

[45] Christopher B. Ansberry, *Be Wise, My Son, and Make My Heart Glad: An Exploration of the Courtly Nature of the Book of Proverbs* (BZAW 422; Berlin: De Gruyter, 2011), 77.

[46] The terse expression אוצרות רשע leaves to the interpreter to discern the relationship between the two terms. "Troves of wickedness" could imply either wealth that *belongs to* the wicked or troves *acquired by* wicked practices.

[47] For a discussion of the various ways in which parallel couplets in Hebrew poetry function together to create meaning that resides in neither couplet alone, see David J. A. Clines, "The Parallelism of

wicked to acquire it by any means necessary, although such iniquitous practice is ultimately futile and does not lead to wealth, a point that offers negative motivation for the wise student to avoid this trap. Yet the second half of the line qualifies the motivation of wealth in the larger framework of life and death. One motivation must be weighed against another. This is not a rigid outlook in which only good accrues to the righteous and only bad consequences follow the wicked. Nor does it imply that motivation is purely a force for good. Rather, it indicates that motivation itself may present a rather vexed problem, leading to vice or proving illusory in the end.

*Proverbs 3:1–12*

*1* My son, do not forget my instruction, and let your heart guard my commandments.

*2* For length of days and years of life and peace it will add to you.

*3* Fidelity[48] and truth will not abandon you. Bind them upon your throat!

Write them on the tablet of your mind!

*4* Thus find favor and high value[49] in the eyes of God and human.

*5* Trust YHWH with all of your mind, but on your own insight do not depend.

Greater Precision: Notes from Isaiah 40 for a Theory of Hebrew Poetry," in *Directions in Biblical Hebrew Poetry* (ed. Elaine R. Follis; JSOTSup 40; Sheffield: JSOT, 1987), 77–100.

[48] Hebrew חסד can connote a variety of qualities, including love, mercy, faithfulness, and loyalty, or acts thereof. For a full treatment, see Katharine Doob Sakenfeld, *The Meaning of Hesed in the Hebrew Bible: A New Inquiry* (HSM 17; Missoula: Scholars Press, 1978). In Proverbs, חסד often implies characters or acts that are faithful to and reflective of wisdom and order (see 14:22; 20:28; 31:26). Fox argues that חסד is kindness in act or attitude that is always delivered from a superior to an inferior, adding that it is not mandatory but a charitable benevolence (Michael V. Fox, *Proverbs 1–9: A New Translation with Introduction and Commentary* [AB 18A; New York: Doubleday, 2000], 144). Thus he argues that in this verse the term "can only be God's kindness toward the pupil, not the pupil's toward others" (ibid.). In this context, he interprets kindness as the gift of life, "which is at once a divine grant and a natural outcome of human wisdom, and yet is not something that God is *obligated* to bestow" (ibid.; emphasis in original). I agree that qualities beyond the student's own are likely in view here, although the translation "kindness" may not be strong enough to convey the association with wisdom and order. Thus, חסד ואמת protect the king, and חסד is the very foundation of his reign (20:28). With חסד ואמת, iniquity can be removed (16:6). The one who pursues חסד finds life and honor (21:21). I choose to translate "fidelity," implying faithfulness to order and the practices that sustain it. The father's instruction offers a reliable guide to order such that the son might receive fidelity and come to embody it.

[49] שכל usually means "insight" or "success." Here, however, it connotes a worth that one receives in another's eyes. Fox translates "high regard," explaining that it indicates the way another person views the subject (Fox, *Proverbs 1–9*, 147). Murphy translates the term as "high esteem" (Roland E. Murphy, *Proverbs* [WBC 22; Nashville: Thomson Nelson, 1998], 18). I choose the translation "high value" to communicate the value the student will hold in others' eyes, a motivation of social esteem, but also to maintain an allusion to the other meaning of the term שכל, success.

*6* In all of your ways, know him,[50] and he will make straight your paths.

*7* Do not be wise in your own eyes. Fear YHWH and turn from evil!

*8* It will be healing for your body[51] and tonic for your bones.

*9* Honor YHWH with your wealth and with the first of your produce.

*10* Your storehouses will be filled to satiety, and your presses will burst new wine.

*11* The discipline of YHWH, my son, do not reject! Do not detest his reproof!

*12* For YHWH reproves the one he loves – as a father takes pleasure in a son.

At first glance, this unit is not as clearly a discrete poem as some of the other units in chapters 1–9, and in fact, the Masoretic tradition separates it into three units (3:1–4, 5–10, 11–12). But when one recognizes the alternating pattern of rebuke and motivation, it is clear that the lines have been carefully crafted as one unit, each line building on the next to comprise an encomium to discipline that employs both rebuke and motivation.[52] The final two verses mark a significant shift in the poem that conveys a deeper significance to the pattern of rebuke and motivation as it gives the addressee a new identity as a son of the divine father, not only the human

---

[50] The LXX has αὐτήν, a feminine singular pronoun. Johnson argues that the LXX understands the referent not as wisdom but as the idea of trust or confidence, implied by the translation of verse 5, in which the Greek renders πεποιθὼς for Hebrew בטח. He suggests that the verbal form's connection to the feminine noun πειθώ, "persuasiveness," implies that the verse is an injunction to know security or confidence (Timothy Johnson, "Implied Antecedents in Job XL 2b and Proverbs III 6a," *VT* 52 [2002]: 281–82). This is an interesting proposal, although Wisdom seems the more likely antecedent given the second half of the line, which indicates that "she" will make one's paths straight, which is a power elsewhere ascribed to Wisdom or YHWH.

[51] MT has לשרך, "for your navel," but the LXX reads τῷ σώματί σου, reflecting לבשרך or לשארך, a reading also supported by Syriac. The Vulgate, however, supports MT: *umbilico*. In the case of either reading, the image is of healing for one's physical body. Paul Overland, who argues that this unit is dependent on Deut 6:4–9, suggests that the image also implies healing of one's mind (cf. Deut 6:5, ואהבת את יהוה אלהיך בכל־לבבך ובכל־נפשך): "In biblical poetry, 'navel' and 'bones' refer to the core of one's being, not to merely anatomical parts. To enjoy health in these parts of one's being is to experience the satisfaction of psychological desire at a most profound level" (Paul Overland, "Did the Sage Draw from the Shema? A Study of Proverbs 3:1–12," *CBQ* 62 [2000]: 430). G. R. Driver proposes a noun "health" from the root שרר, "to be strong" (G. R. Driver, "Problems in the Hebrew Text of Proverbs," *Bib* 32 [1951]: 175); see also William McKane, who translates likewise (William McKane, *Proverbs: A New Approach* [OTL; Philadelphia: Westminster Press, 1970], 293).

[52] For an analysis of the unity of Prov 3:1–12, see Overland, "Shema," 425–27. Fox considers the unit to comprise one "lecture" (Fox, *Proverbs 1–9*, 153–54). See also Arndt Meinhold, "Gott und Mensch in Proverbien III," *VT* 37 (1987): 468. But compare Crawford H. Toy, who argues that verses 11–12 are a later editorial insertion, possibly intended as a "modification of the preceding paragraph, to explain cases in which worldly prosperity does not follow rectitude" (Crawford H. Toy, *The Book of Proverbs: A Critical and Exegetical Commentary* [ICC 13; Edinburgh: T&T Clark, 1899], 64).

father. These verses turn the focus explicitly from the *father's* instruction to *YHWH's* discipline and reproof.[53] They thus serve as a fitting capstone to the entire unit, which has commanded the son to turn toward YHWH and offered various motivations for doing so. The final motivation is slightly different than the previous ones. It is not a promise of a benefit that will follow, but a rationale for valuing divine discipline. The final line frames discipline as indicative of divine love and appeals to the motive of parental pleasure, for YHWH loves the one he disciplines as "a father takes pleasure in a son." The addressee of the poem is now positioned not just as the father's son, but as God's son.[54] The motive of parental pleasure is thus ultimately realized by the affection and esteem the son will foster not just in the human father but in God (cf. 3:4).

Motivation is the glue that holds together this poem, and the diversity of motivations referenced within testify to the interrelationship of each of the paradigms. Within the twelve lines, there are at least eight different motivations: longevity, peace, renown, divine blessing, healing, satiety, abundance, and parental pleasure. These motivations include each of the four major paradigms in Proverbs – wealth, honor, protection, and life – and several lines play on multiple motivations at once. The vow that one's storehouses will be full (3:10), for example, alludes to material wealth but also promises satisfaction or satiety (cf. 10:2). Yet as a very visible symbol of wealth, it may also appeal to the motivation of social standing and esteem in the community.

Moreover, the constant appeal to motivation in this unit demonstrates how the two models of rebuke and motivation can work in concert. They are not mutually exclusive pedagogical models, for, as seen here, they interact seamlessly. The motivations lend added impetus and urgency to the father's commands, while the commands concentrate the motivations toward the goal of wisdom, fidelity, and the fear of YHWH, thus implicitly steering the student away from the danger of motivations unchecked: the unbridled accumulation of wealth or the pursuit of social esteem unaccompanied by the esteem that comes from God alone.

---

[53] Yet God has been in view since the appeal in verse 4. At first glance, these verses may appear to be only loosely related to the preceding verses. Fox seems to equivocate when he says that "[i]n terms of content, there is undoubtedly a certain shift in topic, but unless we take vv 11–12 as a stray epigram or a later addition, it must be joined to Lecture III" (Fox, *Proverbs 1–9*, 152). The MT divides verses 11–12 as a separate section. Yet reading the lines as poetry and giving attention to the pattern that the lines establish reveals that these verses are not a misfit or a strong shift in topic, but a fitting conclusion to the poem.

[54] The repetition of בן ties the final two verses to the beginning. Note the repetition of בני, the first word of the unit (3:1), in verse 11, as well as בן, the second-to-last word of the entire unit (3:12).

*Proverbs 3:13–18*

*13* Fortunate[55] is the man[56] who finds Wisdom and the man who obtains Insight.

*14* For her profit is better than silver's profit and better than gold, her inventory.[57]

*15* She is more valued than precious jewels,[58] even all of your desirables do not equal her.

*16* Length of days is in her right hand; in her left, fortune[59] and honor.

*17* Her ways are lovely ways, and all of her paths, peace.

*18* A tree of life she is to those who seize her, and those who grasp her – "Fortunate."[60]

This poem takes the model of motivation to new heights in playing with both literal and figurative levels of motivation, many of which turn on the polyvalency of the term יקרה. While the poem implicitly appeals to certain literal motivations, including longevity and social esteem, it makes extensive use of figurative language to portray the value of Wisdom. Here motivational symbols are not literal promises of what Wisdom offers, per se, but instead convey her surpassing value. Just as with the literal motivations in other texts, what is striking is the diversity of motivations to

---

[55] The term אשרי is often translated "happy" or "blessed," although it may have more to do with being praiseworthy, commendable, or noteworthy. Thus the *pi'el* of the root אשר, which can have a declarative sense, "to call fortunate," occurs in parallel with הלל, "to praise" (see Prov 31:28; Song 6:9), and can be used to mark one's social standing, as in Job 29:11, "for the ear heard and commended me" (כי אזן שמעה ותאשרני). I choose the translation "fortunate," to convey the sense of being commendable. The English term also nicely foreshadows the economic metaphors that dominate the second line of the poem. For an analysis of אשרי, see C. L. Seow, "An Exquisitely Poetic Introduction to the Psalter," *JBL* 132 (2013): 275–93.

[56] Hebrew אדם is not necessarily restricted to males but can refer to humanity, more broadly (Gen 1:27). A male student is likely in view here given the book's rhetorical orientation toward "my son," although women too are capable of pursuing wisdom (e.g., the "woman of valor" praised in Prov 31:10–31). While the more inclusive term "human" is preferable, in English it makes ambiguous the antecedent of the feminine singular suffix in the following line: "*her* profit." In Hebrew, however, the antecedent is clearly one of the feminine singular nouns in this line: חכמה and תבונה. I thus choose to translate אדם as "man" so as not to create an ambiguity that is not present in the Hebrew text.

[57] תבואה is literally a yield or produce derived from the harvest (see Exod 23:10; Deut 14:22). I choose the English translation "inventory" in order to capture the sound play with תבונה, "insight," in the previous line.

[58] Reading with Qere: מפנינים (K: מפניים).

[59] I translate the term for wealth, עשר, as "fortune" in order to capture the sound play with אשרי (v. 13) and מאשר (v. 18).

[60] The form מאשר is a *pu'al* participle of אשר, which has the declarative sense "to call fortunate" in the *pi'el*. In order to preserve the terseness of the poetic line and its play with the first word of the poem, אשרי, I have translated "Fortunate," that is, the name that the person in question is called by others.

which the poem appeals. Wisdom is first figured in economic terms. Her profit and produce outweigh silver and gold. The following line continues the economic metaphor, mirroring the comparative syntax (טוב מן...יקרה מן) and expressing Wisdom's value in terms of expensive objects (פנינים), yet it introduces another undertone. It is not Wisdom's purely economic value that is significant, as if this were simply a utilitarian appeal. Rather, the rest of the line makes clear that she is valuable (יקרה) not only in economic terms, but also in terms of beauty and desirability, exceeding precious jewels and even anything desirable that one possesses. In this way, יקרה, which can connote financial value (cf. 1:13; 12:27; 24:4) but also non-economic preciousness or rareness (cf. 1 Sam 3:1; Pss 36:8; 116:15), functions as a poetic hinge that enhances the economic metaphor of the previous line and extends it into different senses of value. Multiple aspects of the Hebrew term are at play when it is read both with the preceding line and the line of which it is a part.

The final lines of the poem move away from economic language to various aspects of life as motivational symbols, and this movement again demonstrates the interrelationship of the paradigms and the way in which they are used to advance the poem. Verse 16 heightens the personification of Wisdom by describing long days, riches, and honor as items she holds in her hands.[61] These images are perhaps implicitly literal motivations, suggesting that the one who follows Wisdom will enjoy their fruits, but in the larger context of the poem, they further heighten the value of Wisdom. In this sense, they are motivational symbols that tie Wisdom's value to the image of flourishing life. The following line employs the metaphor of Wisdom's path, describing it as lovely (נעם) and full of peace. The image of loveliness hearkens back to verse 15, where Wisdom is figured in relation to fine jewels and desirable objects, while the reference to peace highlights the images of well-being in the previous line.[62] The final line of the poem blends an implicit directive with additional motivations. Declaring that Wisdom is a tree of life to those who seize her, the line implicitly counsels the student to make Wisdom, who surpasses all desirable objects, to be his prime object of desire, for then she will become a tree of life to him.[63]

---

[61] See Christa Kayatz, who argues that the image of Wisdom holding objects in her hands is influenced by Egyptian images of Maat (Christa Kayatz, *Studien zu Proverbien 1–9: Eine form- und motivgeschichtliche Untersuchung unter Einbeziehung ägyptischen Vergleichmaterials* [WMANT 22; Neukirchen-Vluyn; Neukirchener Verlag, 1966], 105).

[62] Compare Prov 3:2, where שלום is used in parallel with the same phrase, ארך ימים, as well as years of life (שנות חיים).

[63] The "tree of life" was a widespread mythological image in the ancient Near East. See Othmar Keel, *Goddesses and Trees, New Moon and Yahweh: Ancient Near Eastern Art and the Hebrew Bible*

The tree of life imagery thus functions both as a motivational symbol, a figurative image that portrays Wisdom's relation to life and well-being, and as an implicit motivation, suggesting that life will indeed come to those who seek her. The final word of the poem shifts the attention from Wisdom to her followers and appeals to the motivation of social renown, suggesting that they will also be recognized as commendable. Those who seek Wisdom will be called fortunate (מְאֻשָּׁר), a fulfillment of the opening line: fortunate (אַשְׁרֵי) is the one who finds Wisdom.

Yet the figurative language coursing throughout this poem is not merely literary embellishment but is crucial to the poem's pedagogical function of shaping the student's conception of motivation. As a litany of motivational symbols for Wisdom, the poem portrays her as exceeding in value and desirability even the literal motivations with which she is figured.[64] Consequently, it reframes these motivations in light of Wisdom. Even as it bases its appeal in the assumption that wealth, jewels, and longevity are legitimate objects of pursuit that the student already values, it subordinates these motivations and uses them to paint Wisdom herself as the ultimate motivation. That is, the poem does not suggest that fine jewels or wealth have no value. Indeed, it is their inherent value that makes them fitting comparisons to Wisdom. Yet it is clear that their value, however great, pales in comparison to Wisdom's own, for "all of your desirables do not equal her" (3:15). The use of motivational symbols is thus an important aspect of the model of motivation, for it tempers the potential danger of human motivation, the pursuit of goods for their own ends. Thus the sinners depicted in chapter 1 were motivated solely by the pursuit of wealth, a mistake they might have avoided had they viewed the motivation of

---

(JSOTSup 261; Sheffield: Sheffield Academic Press, 1998), 20–57. For a discussion of the tree of life imagery in Proverbs and wisdom literature, see Ralph Marcus, "The Tree of Life in Proverbs," *JBL* 62 (1943): 117–20. Marcus, noting similar language in 1 Enoch, 4 Ezra, and Rev 2, suggests that while the mythological associations with the tree of life are preserved to a late date in Jewish and Christian eschatological literature, the term serves "only as a secularized term or faded metaphor in Jewish Wisdom literature" (ibid., 120). He attributes this to a tendency in this literature to equate "life" and "health," as well as a tendency in wisdom literature "to reclaim some of the older mythological terminology from the eschatologists" and to present Wisdom and Torah as "this-worldly rather than other-worldly" concepts (ibid.). Fox also argues that in the book, "the tree of life is devoid of mythological significance and serves only as a figure for vitality and healing" (Fox, *Proverbs 1–9*, 159). While I agree that strong mythological significance is missing here (see also Prov 11:30; 15:4), some undertones may yet be operative, highlighting the function of personified Wisdom as something that sustains.

[64] For a discussion of the use of figurative language in vv. 14–16, see Sandoval, *The Discourse of Wealth and Poverty*, 79–83. Contra those who interpret the use of economic imagery in this passage as a literal promise of wealth for the student, Sandoval points out that the use of personification to speak of wisdom is itself a figurative trope that provides a hermeneutical orientation toward other figurative language in the passage (ibid., 82).

wealth in the larger framework of wisdom. While Proverbs recognizes the potency of motivation, it is always a tool used toward a greater good.

## The Model of Motivation and the Moral Self

Even this selective examination of the abundance and range of motivations in Proverbs makes clear that this is by no means an incidental category in the book, but is a fundamental aspect of the book's pedagogy. Moreover, its pervasiveness suggests implicit assumptions about the task of instruction and the nature of human beings. Proverbs recognizes that humans are complexly motivated, and thus it offers a variety of motivations in its appeal. Furthermore, although there are acknowledgments that motivations can lead one astray, the book does not question the underlying power and validity of motivation itself. Nowhere does it call on the student to reject certain material motivations unconditionally. Rather, it takes for granted the notion that humans are not disinterested creatures, and it models its pedagogy accordingly. Consequently, the appeal to wisdom is colored by an abundance of literal motivations and figured with an array of motivational symbols. Indeed, rarely is wisdom its own reward. It is certainly the *highest* reward – and the wise person values it above all else – but the extensive discourse of motivation indicates that a host of positive consequences commend the pursuit of wisdom. The way of wisdom is appealing, and one chooses it not solely out of high ideals or the fear of straying away, but also because it is desirable. Thus, the sanctioned course is lined with silver, gold, and jewels (at least metaphorically); it brings wealth and long life, healing and safety. The use of such tropes is not simply literary embellishment but, again, suggests an awareness of the complexity of human motivations. In other words, Proverbs does not appear terribly interested in the question of disinterested piety, a topic that animates other wisdom texts, such as the book of Job. It takes as its starting point the fundamental assumption that self-interest is a powerful and productive force in the cultivation of character.[65]

---

[65] See also Schwáb's comparison between Proverbs and the moral theology of Thomas Aquinas, which holds a primary place for human self-interest in the cultivation of the virtuous life. Schwáb notes that Proverbs and Thomas emphasize happiness as the end of human life and allow room for the reward of basic human needs as indispensable toward that end. Yet Thomas is more cautious in touting the value of riches and honor than is Proverbs, Schwáb argues, although Proverbs also acknowledges that these material rewards can lead one astray (see Schwáb, *Toward an Interpretation of the Book of Proverbs,* 126–28).

Within Proverbs, motivation is a potent tool in the formation of the moral self. As discussed in the previous chapter, Proverbs advances a view of moral selfhood that I term "educated moral selfhood," which presumes both external and internal agency in the cultivation of the moral self. The model of motivation presents an additional factor in moral formation. It suggests that it is not only a matter of matching the right internal disposition with the proper discipline, as if cultivating the moral self was as simple as pairing a receptive student with the correct knowledge. Rather, the pervasive presence of motivation in the book implies that one's receptivity to knowledge may be influenced positively by a host of motivational appeals, even as knowledge may reframe the very concept of motivation. Here again, another complexity emerges in Proverbs' view of the human. It is not simply a matter of having wisdom or not, being receptive to discipline or not. Rather, desires for such things as wealth, security, or longevity can influence one's native receptivity. Consequently, the book appeals to motivation as a pedagogical tool to encourage the student to follow the sanctioned course and to make the pursuit of knowledge itself a motivating force.

## Proverbs and Moral Motivation

Finally, to return to an earlier question, to what degree are the motivations in Proverbs considered *moral* motivations? How do they relate to moral character and virtue? The four philosophical approaches to moral motivation discussed previously – instrumentalist, sentimentalist, cognitivist, and personalist – provide useful points of comparison. While it is not my intent to fit Proverbs soundly into one of the four categories, these philosophical approaches do highlight certain operative assumptions found in the book. At first glance, the cognitivist approach may seem most congenial to Proverbs if one assumes that knowledge of the good, that is, knowledge of wisdom, is a sufficient and necessary condition for being wise and acting wisely. In this perspective, motivation comes from knowledge. This would indeed seem to be the case in such sayings as Prov 4:7, "The beginning of wisdom is – acquire wisdom!" in which wisdom itself is the motivation to seek wisdom. Michael V. Fox comes close to the cognitivist view when he suggests that there is a Socratic quality to Proverbs' ethics. He argues that like Socrates, who emphasized the supremacy of cognition in determining moral behavior, so too "the sages of Proverbs intellectualized virtue by making it a species of knowledge. Virtue is an act of cognition."[66] Yet even as knowledge is certainly a major concern of the book, the model of motivation in Proverbs does not base its appeal solely in knowledge. Certainly, Proverbs aims to *provide* a certain kind of knowledge as it orients the student to the structures of order in the world, but it also assumes prior motivations for such things as pleasure and prosperity.

For this reason, the instrumentalist view may be closer to what we find in Proverbs insofar as intrinsic desire is considered to be a vital component in shaping human action and character. When desires are joined with knowledge, they become positive motivations for the student to act in accord with wisdom. For example, Prov 20:13, "Do not love sleep, lest you become impoverished; open your eyes and be sated with food," implicitly appeals to the intrinsic desires of wealth and satiety. Joined with the knowledge that laziness may produce impoverishment, these desires become motivations that can lead to industry. The saying does not imply that the motivation for hard work comes from its innate value, irrespective of the benefit it may bring and the satisfaction to the student's natural desire.

Proverbs also recognizes that the emotions have motivational force, and this element is particularly evident in the appeal to honor in so many of the poems and sayings. Furthermore, the book makes clear that the pursuit of wisdom involves a *love* for wisdom and, conversely, *hatred* of foolishness (e.g., 4:6; 8:31). In this respect, it may bear a certain similarity to a sentimentalist view of moral motivation, for right action is often linked to right emotion within the book. Yet this perspective, too, is inadequate to account for the full range of motivations and their attendant implications. On the other hand, given the primary importance of character in the book, one might also posit that Proverbs holds much similarity to the personalist view. Indeed, knowledge, desire, motivation, and character are always intertwined in Proverbs, such that it is impossible to reduce questions of morality in the book to knowledge or motivation or desire or emotion in isolation from the others. Rather, these factors work in

---

[66] Fox, *Proverbs 10–31*, 943. Fox argues that knowledge is closely linked to desire, yet in the Socratic comparison, desire of the good is a *consequence* of knowledge, not an intrinsic element of motivation. He explains: "Desire, Socrates believes, is directly consequent on a calculation of benefits.... The identification of knowledge with virtue thus effectively intellectualizes desire" (ibid., 936). For an argument that Socrates' philosophy actually has much more room for the influence of the emotions, desires, and appetites and is not as "intellectualist" as often thought, see Thomas C. Brickhouse, and Nicholas D. Smith, *Socratic Moral Psychology* (Cambridge: Cambridge University Press, 2010).

concert to shape moral character, a point which will be explored in more detail in the next chapter.

Motivation is not simply a rhetorical device within Proverbs, but it is a primary mode of character formation. The book's pedagogy seeks to shape the student's motivations such that material goods such as wealth or luxury become not ends in themselves but symbols of the surpassing value of wisdom, righteousness, and their associated behavior traits. In this sense, it trains the student's motivations toward certain ideals by appeal to innate motivations, such as prosperity, security, and satiety. At the same time, however, Proverbs does not call on the student to abandon such motives completely. Rather, it recognizes these innate motivational forces as a reality of the human condition, and it shapes its pedagogical strategy accordingly.

Proverbs suggests that innate human desires can inform and lead to moral action. While the goal of the book is that the student might gain ever more knowledge and learn to love the way of wisdom, it is not necessary for the student to seek wisdom strictly for its own sake, at least not initially. Rather, he may be motivated by the consequences it will bring to him. In this sense, motivations can indeed become moral motivations.

What is at stake in variant views of moral motivation is the status of innate human desires, and Proverbs' perspective on this issue is indicative of a significant aspect of its moral psychology. While some perspectives view human desires as irrelevant, even detrimental, to moral motivation, others suggest that they can inform, or even serve as the basis of, moral motivation. In Proverbs, it is clear that the model of motivation is closely tied to desire. Desire can lead one astray, but if desire is properly ordered, it can lead one toward wisdom. Proverbs takes for granted that such desires are present; otherwise, appeals to motivation would be ineffective. Moreover, human desire is not inherently bad, but can be used to orient one toward wisdom. However, desire must be directed toward the proper objects. After all, appeals to motivation and desire can come not only from wisdom and wise teaching, but also from more questionable sources. The strange woman, too, appeals to the student's desires as she seeks to motivate him to choose her path (e.g., 7:16–21). For this reason, one's desires must be rightly educated. The education of desire, closely related to the model of motivation, will be the subject of the next chapter.

CHAPTER 6

# The Model of Desire

> [M]utability animates desire even as it thwarts it. Put slightly differ-
> ently, the very nature of desire is what prevents its fulfillment, what
> makes it "impossible."[1]

> All human desire is poised on an axis of paradox, absence and pres-
> ence its poles, love and hate its motive energies.[2]

Desire is central to the human condition; it is the lifeblood of our deepest ambitions, longings, and pleasures, as well as even the most mundane
tasks. Desire animates the magnetic attraction of lovers and the baby
crying of hunger. It governs human pursuits, prompts deep emotions,
and rouses the passions. William B. Irvine declares: "Banish desire from
the world, and you get a world of frozen beings who have no reason to
live and no reason to die."[3] Irvine demonstrates that desire is as vital to
human life as breath. While certain aspects of desire resist explanation –
e.g., there is little rationale control over when and with whom one falls
in love – the pervasiveness of human desire is connected to a variety of
biological, social, and psychological factors, Irvine explains. For example,
one of the most basic desires one experiences on a daily basis is hunger
pangs. There is a physical sensation that is connected to an experience of
lack, which prompts a person to seek the nourishment that will sustain
her. Desire is thus at the root of the basic human need to survive.[4] For

---

[1] Jonathan Dollimore, *Death, Desire, and Loss in Western Culture* (New York: Routledge, 1998), xvii.

[2] Anne Carson, *Eros: The Bittersweet* (Princeton: Princeton University Press, 1986; repr., Champaign: Dalkey Archive Press, 2009), 11.

[3] William B. Irvine, *On Desire: Why We Want What We Want* (New York: Oxford University Press, 2006), 2.

[4] Irvine speaks similarly about the desire for erotic love. He argues that humans have a biological incentive system that is a vestige of the evolution of the species. Because sex is intensely pleasurable, he argues, it provides an innate incentive to engage in an activity that will lead to the propagation of the species (ibid., 145).

this reason, Leon R. Kass insists that "appetite or desire, not DNA, is the deepest principle of life."[5]

At the heart of desire is a paradox between satiation and want, bringing both pleasure and pain, and herein lies the power of desire to sustain and to destabilize. This conundrum is a function of the very nature of desire, which is, simply expressed, a condition of lack.[6] One lacks food and so experiences hunger pangs; one lacks the presence of the lover and so experiences longing. Such lack inspires the pursuit of the absent, which ostensibly will lead to pleasure, the satiation of the desired end. Yet desire, by its very nature, can never be fully satiated, for in the moment of satiation, desire ceases to exist. Once I have eaten a meal, I am no longer hungry; the desire evaporates. But for something to remain continually desirable, it must resist satiation, prolonging the experience of absence, which leads to pain, not pleasure. Satiation is both the goal and the destruction of desire, and thus vibrant desire constantly renews itself by spiraling through experiences of presence and absence. Anne Carson thus insists: "All human desire is poised on an axis of paradox, absence and presence its poles, love and hate its motive energies."[7]

This inherent dynamic of desire is most visible – and perhaps most dangerous and destabilizing – in the realm of erotic love. Sappho depicted desire as a three-fold dynamic between lover, beloved, and whatever separates the two. As Carson explains,

> [W]here eros is lack, its activation calls for three structural components – lover, beloved, and that which comes between them. They are three points of transformation on a circuit of possible relationship, electrified by desire so that they touch not touching. Conjoined they are held apart. The third component plays a paradoxical role for it both connects and separates, marking the two are not one, irradiating the absence whose presence is demanded by eros.[8]

[5] Leon R. Kass, *The Hungry Soul: Eating and the Perfecting of Our Nature* (New York: Free Press, 1994), 48.

[6] See Carson, *Eros*, 10–11. Carson notes that the Greek term *eros* "denotes 'want,' 'lack,' 'desire for that which is missing.' The lover wants what he does not have. It is by definition impossible for him to have what he wants if, as soon as it is had, it is no longer wanting" (ibid., 10). Similarly, Kass, who discusses not erotic desire but hunger and eating practices, notes that there must be an experience of lack for a person to take the action of seeking nourishment. The mere presence of something edible is not enough to make a person eat, but rather "[i]n higher animals awareness of an edible being or object leads to eating only because – and if – hunger or felt lack is present.... What moves an organism to feed is not merely the sensed and registered presence or absence of a certain chemical or edible being in its environment but the *inner needy state* of the organism, for which such an absence is a lack, an absence to be overcome or remedied" (Kass, *The Hungry Soul*, 47; emphasis in original).

[7] Carson, *Eros*, 11.

[8] Ibid., 16.

This alternation of absence and presence makes desire a destabilizing force. In this respect, love is paradoxical at its core, as bitter intersects sweet, as desire proves unattainable. Its paradoxical nature arrests the lover "at a point of inconcinnity between the actual and the possible."⁹ Carson adds that this moment of recognition is invariably one of anguish and attraction: "We love that moment, and we hate it. We have to keep going back to it, after all, if we wish to maintain contact with the possible. But this also entails watching it disappear.... Only a god's desire can reach without lack."¹⁰

This paradox of desire was widely recognized in the ancient world, and erotic love was frequently depicted as destructive and akin to illness. Carson details the way in which the classical Greek poets, even as they celebrate the beauty and pleasure of love, also "represent eros as an invasion, an illness, an insanity, a wild animal, a natural disaster.... No one can fight Eros off."¹¹ Likewise, ancient Egyptian love poetry testifies to both the bitter and the sweet of desire. For example, a love song found on a nineteenth-dynasty papyrus describes the lover's experience of sickness, brought on by the absence of his beloved:

> I will lie down inside, and then I will feign illness.
> Then my neighbors will enter to see, and then (my) sister will come with them.
> She'll put the doctors to shame (for she) will understand my illness.¹²

In a sequence of love poems in P. Chester Beatty I, a twentieth-dynasty Egyptian papyrus, both the male and female voices speak of absence and the conjured presence of the other. The female lover indicates that the very sound of her beloved's voice makes her sick because although he is physically present, she cannot possess him – he remains absent to her: "My brother roils my heart with his voice, making me ill. / Though he is among the neighbors of my mother's house, I cannot go to him."¹³ When she thinks of her beloved, she reports, she loses control over her heart and body:

> My heart quickly scurries away when I think of your love.
> It does not let me act like a (normal) person – it has leapt [out] of its place....
> O my heart, don't make me foolish! Why do you act crazy?
> Sit still, cool down, until the brother comes to you, when I shall do
> many such things.

⁹ Ibid., 75.
¹⁰ Ibid., 75–76.
¹¹ Ibid., 48.
¹² The poem is in a series of love songs found in P. Harris 500. The translation is taken from Michael V. Fox, *The Song of Songs and the Ancient Egyptian Love Songs* (Madison: University of Wisconsin Press, 1985), 13.
¹³ Ibid., 52.

Don't let people say about me: "This woman has collapsed out of love."
Stand firm whenever you think of him, my heart, and scurry not away.[14]

Similarly, her male beloved describes the illness that has avenged his body in her absence:

Seven whole days I have not seen (my) sister. Illness has invaded me,
My limbs have grown heavy, and I barely sense my own body.
Should the master physicians come to me, their medicines could not
ease my heart.
The lector-priests have no (good) method, because my illness cannot be
diagnosed.
Telling me, "Here she is!" – that's what will revive me.
    Her name – that's what will get me up.
The coming and going of her messengers – that's what will revive my heart.
More potent than any medicine is my [sister] for me;
    She is more powerful for me than The Compendium.
    Her coming in from outside is my amulet.
(I) see her – then (I) become healthy.
    She opens her eyes – my limbs grow young.
    She speaks – then I become strong.
I hug her – and she drives illness from me. But she has left me
for seven days.[15]

Even imagining the presence of his beloved through the poem permits the male to speak of his health ("I hug her – and she drives illness from me"), although the poem ends by returning to the theme of absence: "But she has left me for seven days."

In ancient Israel, the Song of Songs stands out as the most sublime articulation of the complexity, allure, and danger of desire. Even as the Shulammite finds great pleasure in seeking after her lover, love proves to be an overpowering force that subjects her to sickness, despair, and even assault (see Song 2:5; 5:7–8). Throughout the eight chapters of the book, the Song reverberates between the lovers' presence and absence, which only serves to fuel desire.[16] Each time the lovers appear close to joining together, they are separated, and one is never certain whether the description of their meeting represents dream or reality. The Song even testifies

---

[14] Ibid., 53–54.
[15] Ibid., 55.
[16] Scholars have long debated whether the Song represents the work of a single hand or a collection of independent poems. J. Cheryl Exum notes that while it is difficult, if not impossible, to assess the book's compositional unity, one can assume the Song's structural unity, as repetition of language and theme occurs throughout the various poetic units (J. Cheryl Exum, "How Does the Song of Songs Mean? On Reading the Poetry of Desire," *SEÅ* 64 [1999]: 60).

to the insatiable nature of desire in its very form, for it ends not with the consummation of love but with the lover bounding over the hills, fleeing like a gazelle (Song 8:14). As J. Cheryl Exum suggests, the poem's resistance to closure "is perhaps the Song's most important strategy for immortalizing love. Closure would mean the end of desiring, the silence of the text, the death of love. Resistance to closure is an attempt to keep love always in progress before us."[17]

Desire's pain and pleasure are held in tension throughout the Song. While the Shulammite extols love's delight, she also laments its intensity and warns of its danger. Three times in the book (Song 2:7; 3:4; 8:4; cf. 5:8) the woman warns the daughters of Jerusalem, "do not rouse, do not stir up love until it pleases!" (אם־תעירו ואם־תעוררו את־האהבה עד שתחפץ).[18] The spirit of her warning is disputed, with some commentators suggesting that the Shulammite, having finally united with her lover, requests that the two not be disturbed.[19] However, there is an element of danger in the strength of her counsel. Her words are neither flippant advice nor friendly supplication but suggest an urgency provoked by the wisdom of experience. In each case, the warning follows a period of illness or persecution experienced through her pursuit of the beloved. The final admonition of the book powerfully evokes the ferocity and insatiable nature of erotic desire:

> For love is as strong as death – passion fierce as Sheol.
> Its flames are flames of fire, a raging flame –
> Mighty waters can't quench love, rivers can't drown it.
> If a man gave his entire wealth for love: utterly scorned![20] (Song 8:6b-7)

כי־עזה כמות אהבה קשה כשאול קנאה
רשפיה רשפי אש שלהבתיה
מים רבים לא יוכלו לכבות את־האהבה ונהרות לא ישטפוה
אם־יתן איש את־כל־הון ביתו באהבה בוז יבוזו לו

---

[17] J. Cheryl Exum, *The Song of Songs* (OTL; Louisville: Westminster John Knox, 2005), 12–13.

[18] Song 8:4: מה־תעירו ומה־תעררו את־האהבה עד שתחפץ.

[19] Fox, *The Song of Songs*, 109. Marvin H. Pope, on the other hand, suggests that the woman is requesting aphrodisiacs: "The love-sick lady's call for raisin cakes and apples is not a rejection of stimulants but a request for them. The adjuration can scarcely be an appeal not to be disturbed or interrupted in the course of love-making before satisfaction has been achieved" (Marvin H. Pope, *Song of Songs: A New Translation with Introduction and Commentary* [AB 7C; Garden City: Doubleday, 1977], 387). Roland E. Murphy counters that the woman's warning "prohibits (artificial) stimulation of love." He asserts that love "has its own laws and is not to be achieved artificially." It can only be enjoyed when it is present by a natural course (Roland E. Murphy, *The Song of Songs: A Commentary on the Book of Canticles or The Song of Songs* [ed. S. Dean McBride, Jr.; Hermeneia; Minneapolis: Fortress Press, 1990], 137).

[20] The antecedent of לו is ambiguous, and it is unclear whether it is the *man* or his *wealth* that would be scorned. This translation leaves the ambiguity intact.

Within the Song, desire is a source of life-giving nourishment *and* a force with a ravenous appetite, equal only to death.[21] It is a mighty force that can never be fully satisfied. For this reason, it compels continued pursuit, even as – in fact, *because* – such pursuit results in continued frustration, which only serves to impel the pursuit. The Song enacts a conception of desire as powerful, enticing, and dangerous; it can be the cause of both intense pleasure and deep pain.

The power, pleasure, and pain of desire provide the pretext for an important didactic model in the book of Proverbs.[22] The book recognizes desire of all kinds as a fundamental reality of the human condition, and it acknowledges the force of desire to motivate the pursuit of various ends. Desire, the sages indicate, can be either help or hindrance to the larger pedagogical aim of discipline, and thus an astonishing portion of the book is devoted to discussing, invoking, and shaping desire. In so doing, it alludes to the paradoxical nature of desire that is likewise present in other ancient literature, although it puts these elements to didactic ends and suggests that desire is a potent force in the shaping of the self.

## The Ubiquity of Desire in Proverbs

While erotic desire is the sole focus of the Song, Proverbs points to the ubiquity of many kinds of desire, both positive and negative, within human life. Erotic desire of course animates several of the poems in chapters 1–9,[23] but

---

[21] For a study of the connection between desire and death in literature from antiquity to modernity, see Dollimore, *Death, Desire, and Loss.*

[22] The centrality of desire to the pedagogy of Proverbs was also recognized by ancient commentators. Gregory of Nyssa, following Origen, suggested that the task of Proverbs was to train the soul to desire virtue. Gregory notes that not only does Proverbs not attempt to dispel the student's desires, but it seeks to encourage, even provoke them. In so doing, it seeks to direct the student's natural desires for corporeal things toward a desire for incorporeal things, namely, Wisdom and God. Thus Wisdom "enjoins on us to fall in love (ἔρος) with divine Beauty" (Gregory of Nyssa, *Commentary on the Song of Songs* [trans. Casimir McCambley; Brookline: Hellenic College Press, 1987], 1:23, 9–12). For a discussion of the various pedagogies of desire in Proverbs, Qoheleth, and, especially, the Song of Songs in the writings of Origen and Gregory of Nyssa, see Martin L. Laird, "Under Solomon's Tutelage: The Education of Desire in the *Homilies on the Song of Songs*," *Modern Theology* 18.4 (2002): 507–25. For discussion of the relationship between *eros* and wisdom by modern commentators, see Gerhard von Rad, *Wisdom in Israel* (trans. James D. Martin; London: SCM Press, 1972; repr., Harrisburg: Trinity Press International, 1993), 166–76; Roland E. Murphy, "Wisdom and Eros in Proverbs 1–9," *CBQ* 50.4 (1988): 600–603; Scott C. Jones, "Wisdom's Pedagogy: A Comparison of Proverbs VII and 4Q184," *VT* 53 (2003): 65–80; and Christine Roy Yoder, "The Shaping of Erotic Desire in Proverbs 1–9," in *Saving Desire: The Seduction of Christian Theology* (eds. J. Henriksen and L. Shults; Grand Rapids: Eerdmans, 2011), 148–62. While these scholars emphasize the erotic dimensions of desire and focus on chapters 1–9, the present chapter endeavors to make broader claims about the nature of desire in the book of Proverbs as a whole.

[23] See discussion in Chapter 3.

references to desire throughout the book encompass a broad range of desires held by a diversity of characters. Desire is not associated with only one type of character, nor is it something that is categorically rejected or embraced. The noun תאוה denotes something that either the righteous (10:24; 11:23) or the lazy (21:25–26) can possess. The act of desiring is a habit of scoffers (חמד, 1:22), the wicked (חמד, 12:12; אוה, 21:10), and the lazy (אוה, 13:4). The text also issues prohibitions against desiring certain objects or activities, ranging from keeping company with evildoers (24:1), to consuming rich food (מטעמות/מטעמת, 23:3, 6), to lusting for the beauty of a foreign woman (נכריה, 6:25). At the same time, the book goes to great lengths to depict other objects, such as wisdom or the love of one's own wife, as inherently *desirable* and worthy of pursuit by the student. Desire thus has a broad semantic and conceptual range within the book that is not confined simply to overt references to desire (תאוה) or the act of desiring (אוה, חמד). Rather, it also encompasses the figuring of desirable objects, as well as descriptions about the pursuit of that which is lacking. The paradoxical, dangerous, destabilizing nature of desire is also an important theme within the book.

Within Proverbs, desire is often conceptualized as bodily appetite.[24] It is hunger and thirst that arises from one's body (נפש, see, e.g., 6:10; 10:3; 13:24; 16:24, 26) and is often linked to the tongue, palate, mouth, lips, or belly (e.g., 10:32; 13:3, 25; 18:21; 24:13). Christine Roy Yoder argues that not only do the sages speak of desire as bodily appetite but, accordingly, they depict desire for anything – not simply food and drink – as hunger and thirst. Thus instruction becomes *fruit* and *produce* of one's mouth (e.g., 12:14; 18:20), and one can *eat* the *fruit* of one's lips, that is, one's words (18:21).[25] Yoder explains that desire is not only an intellectual knowledge of worthy objects or an emotional reaction to what one ought to love, but also a bodily fixation directed toward particular objects.[26] Consequently, she insists, "the sages' persistent attention to orienting the *nepeš*, the palate, the lips, the belly – interwoven with appeals to the *lēb*, the eyes, the ears, the feet, the hands, and so on – suggests a complex portrait of the self and how the self comes to know."[27]

In many respects, the book of Proverbs is a manual of desires, for much of the book turns on identifying *what* humans desire, what they *should*

[24] As discussed by Christine Roy Yoder, "Contours of Desire in Israelite Wisdom Literature" (paper presented at the annual meeting of the SBL, Chicago, IL, 17 November 2012).
[25] Ibid., 5. For a discussion of the use and significance of food metaphors throughout Proverbs, see William P. Brown, "The Didactic Power of Metaphor in the Aphoristic Sayings of Proverbs," *JSOT* 29 (2004): 133–54.
[26] Yoder, "Contours of Desire," 2.
[27] Ibid., 9.

desire, and *where* those desires may lead. The issue of *why* humans desire is not taken up in Proverbs. Rather, it is assumed to be an innate part of the human. Indeed, the absence of strong desires is indicative of a perversion of character, as in the case of the lazy one whose desires are not robust enough to impel him to action: "the lazy one hides his hand in the bowl, too tired to return it to his mouth" (26:15).

Desire functions as an internal source of motivation, and this is both its promise and its problem for the goal of character formation. Desires prompt people to take all sorts of actions, which is a basic assumption on which the entire model of motivation in Proverbs relies.[28] There would be no use in offering motivational incentives if they did not appeal to innate human desires. Wisdom is not figured as soiled rubbish for good reason! She is a woman, a crown, and a jewel, all items viewed as inherently desirable.

Yet a complicating factor for the didactic aim of Proverbs is that such innate motivation can either advance or undermine the cause of discipline. Wealth, for example, which is one of the most complexly figured desires in the book, motivates sinners to lie in ambush (1:10–13) but others to act with diligence (10:4b). Women also prove to be a particularly ambiguous symbol of desire, for even though certain women, such as the strange woman (אישה זרה), the harlot (זונה), the foreign woman (נכריה), the foolish woman (אשת כסילות), and the adulterous woman (אשה מנפאת),[29] represent a danger to the youth, other women are praised

---

[28] See Chapter 5.

[29] The identity of these women, particularly the "strange woman" (אישה זרה), has sparked considerable debate. The interpretation of the strange woman has ranged from foreign goddess, to metaphor of evil, to symbol for the threat of foreign wives, to literal figure. For a survey of the major issues and interpretive possibilities, see Nancy Nam Hoon Tan, *The "Foreignness" of the Foreign Woman in Proverbs 1–9: A Study of the Origin and Development of a Biblical Motif* (BZAW 381; Berlin: Walter de Gruyter, 2008); Claudia V. Camp, "What's So Strange About the Strange Woman?" in *The Bible and the Politics of Exegesis: Essays in Honor of Norman K. Gottwald on His Sixty-Fifth Birthday* (ed. David Jobling, et al; Cleveland: Pilgrim Press, 1991), 17–31; Michael V. Fox, *Proverbs 1–9: A New Translation with Introduction and Commentary* (AB 18A; New York: Doubleday, 2000), 252–62; see also Joseph Blenkinsopp, who discusses the strange woman as a response to the social and economic consequences of exogamy in the early postexilic period (Joseph Blenkinsopp, "The Social Context of the 'Outsider Woman' in Prov 1–9," *Biblica* 72 [1991]: 457–73). In addition, note the argument of Tova Forti, who argues that the strange woman should be understood in a literal fashion as a "mundane, seductive, adulterous, married woman who threatens the safeguarding of the family nucleus," a figure from everyday life (Tova L. Forti, "The *Isha Zara* in Proverbs 1–9: Allegory and Allegorization," *HS* 48 [2007]: 89). This figure should not be read as a metaphor, allegory, or symbol for "the Other," she insists. For such interpretations are "an unsuccessful model in marshaling the biblical text for modern hermeneutic proclivities" (ibid., 100). One of Forti's main arguments against such readings is the genre of Proverbs, which she identifies as a "manual of conduct" that is characterized by its clarity, precision, and concern with practical advice and experience. Symbolic or allegorical readings presume a genre which "conveys a symbolic surplus of meaning beyond the literal level of the referent text"

and the desire for them is encouraged, including the wife of one's youth (5:18–19), the "woman of valor" (31:10–31), and, of course, personified Wisdom.[30] Proverbs recognizes both women and wealth as inherently desirable and incentivizing to the student. Desire, in and of itself, is not necessarily a vice. The problem is not with the desires themselves, per se, but the ends toward which they lead. The trouble with desire thus has less to do with a particular kind of desire than it does the character of the desirer. For this reason, it is necessary to consider the desires of several paradigmatic characters. The central characters in the book, whether the wise, the righteous, the simple, or the fool, each have a unique profile, and the way in which they respond to their desires is indicative of the sages' assessment of their propensity for formation.

## Typologies of Desire

### The Wicked, Fools, and Other Questionable Characters

Two characters in Proverbs, the sinners (חטאים) and the wicked (רשעים), have purely negative desires, and there is no hint that their inclination to desire foolishly can be altered. Their desires may be futile, insofar as they are unsatisfied (13:25), even impeded by YHWH (10:3). Yet their desires also may have dangerous consequences both for themselves and for the larger community, which may be victims of their pursuit for selfish or harmful gains. Sinners seek precious treasure (1:13), while the wicked desire harmful things, such as אולת or רע: "the appetite of the wicked desires evil (נפש רשע אותה־רע); his neighbor finds no favor in his eyes" (21:10; see also 5:23). Furthermore, the internal incentive system of

---

(ibid., 96). Forti issues a worthy caution against too quickly assimilating the figure of personified Folly (9:13–18) with the strange woman as an exact negative correlate of personified Wisdom (see also Fox, *Proverbs 1–9*, 262). Yet the abundance of figurative language in Proverbs indicates a surplus of symbolic meaning, and one needs to look no further than the personification of wisdom itself. Proverbs does counsel against the literal desire of certain women, but desire of and for women also serves an important symbolic role within the book.

For a discussion of the Egyptian parallels to the depiction of women in Proverbs, see Nili Shupak, "Female Imagery in Proverbs 1–9 in the Light of Egyptian Sources," *VT* 61 (2011): 310–23. While she contends that the strange woman and the wife of one's youth do refer to real women in Proverbs, Shupak notes that the line between the literal and the metaphorical is frequently blurred (ibid., 323).

[30] Shupak notes that Egyptian wisdom literature also evidences ambivalence about the nature of women, and in some cases, one woman epitomizes both positive and negative attributes. The *Instruction of Ptahhotep*, for example, refers to the youth's wife as both a fertile field to be tended and a storm wind that must be restrained from power (see *The Instruction of Ptahhotep* 325–38, Shupak, "Female Imagery in Proverbs 1–9," 320).

both the wicked and the sinner is irreparably distorted. While the book acknowledges that these figures are motivated by their desires, these desires lead toward their destruction, and the book makes no effort to direct such desires differently, for these figures are not part of Proverbs' immediate audience.[31] At the same time, however, the desires of these characters do provide a cautionary tale for the student of the book. In this respect, the presentation of their desires serves pedagogical goals. For example, the father's report of the sinners in Prov 1:10–19 revolves around the dynamics of multiple desires. It is a commentary on the deep incentives of wealth and social acceptance, for these are the desires that motivate the sinners to conspire and they are also the desires to which the sinners appeal in cajoling the onlooker. Desire has a powerful magnetism, which the father recognizes, and in presenting the negative consequences of the way in which this group pursues those desires, the father offers a warning to the student.[32]

The desires of the wicked represent not just a moral confusion, but a psychological one. It is not simply that the wicked one seeks out the wrong objects of desire, but he takes intense pleasure in them. As Michael V. Fox notes, the evildoer "not only speaks and does evil, he *delights* in it; he is a moral pervert."[33] Moreover, the pleasure he experiences only serves to magnify the desire, thus prompting an insatiable seeking out of wrong. As Prov 4:16–17 notes, the wicked "do not sleep unless they do evil, and their sleep is robbed unless they make others stumble.[34] For they eat bread of wickedness and drink wine of violence." Sun Myung Lyu observes the "addictive power of evil" to which these verses point. The wicked one, he notes, "simply cannot stop desiring and devising evil even when there is nothing particularly profitable about it."[35] For the wicked, evildoing is the very food and drink they desire, its warped profit the fleeting satisfaction it brings. It is the *absence* of wickedness that brings torment to the wicked. In this sense, the perversion of the wicked is both moral and psychological, for it results from a failure to discern the right path but also a distorted sense of pleasure and pain.

---

[31] See discussion in Sun Myung Lyu, *Righteousness in the Book of Proverbs* (FAT II; Tübingen: Mohr Siebeck, 2012), 73.

[32] Again, it is not necessarily the desires themselves that are the problem. After all, the father too relies on wealth and social acceptance in some measure as incentives for the student to obey his instruction. Thus he vows that honoring YHWH will bring full storehouses (3:10) and that obedience will result in honor (e.g., 3:4).

[33] Michael V. Fox, "The Pedagogy of Proverbs 2," *JBL* 113 (1994): 241.

[34] Reading with Qere: יכשׁילו (K: יכשׁולו).

[35] Lyu, *Righteousness in the Book of Proverbs*, 65.

The problem with the desires of the fool (כסיל), however, is more psychological malfunction than moral confusion.[36] One of the primary faults of the fool is his lack of restraint. He has little control over his reactions and emotions: "A fool pours out his whole spirit (כל־רוחו יוציא כסיל), while the wise one quietly holds it back" (29:11). Similarly, the fool has no control over his desires and thus pursues with vigor whatever is before him. As Prov 21:20 observes, "precious treasure and fine oil are in the wise one's house, but the fool swallows them up." The fool's lack of restraint is particularly manifest in his language, which translates into failure to contain his speech (12:23; 15:2, 7, 14). Such incapacity for self-control is compounded by his inability to discern. Because he has no לב, in Proverbs' terminology, the fool is unable to judge the ramifications of what he pursues.[37] Thus the desires of wisdom and wise things are lost on him. As Prov 17:16 asks, "what good is money in the hand of a fool to buy wisdom when he has no mind (לב)?" Furthermore, the fool suffers from a confusion of emotion. He *hates* the right objects of desire, such as knowledge (1:22) or understanding (18:2), which are things he should, in fact, love (cf. 4:6; 12:1; 29:3).[38]

By contrast, the desires and aversions of the wicked are described in slightly different terms, and the distinctions in description between the wicked and the fool highlight their respective potential for formation. The fool is described primarily in relation to his confused response to certain desires, including the correct desires. That is, he either cannot discern them or has an averse emotional reaction to them. The wicked one, however, is characterized by both the wickedness of his desires, which bring harm not only to himself but to others, and the profound delight he takes in them. In this sense, the desires of the wicked are more sinister and

---

[36] There are less frequent references to the desires of the rogue (אויל) and the brute (בער), making it more difficult to develop a full typology of these characters as desirers. However, like the כסיל, both the אויל and the בער are afflicted with emotional confusion. The rogue hates the objects he should desire, such as wisdom and discipline (1:7; 15:5), just as the brute hates rebuke (12:1). For both of these characters, their hatred further impedes any hope of positive moral formation, for they dismiss the means that would reorient their desires.

[37] Similarly, the חסר־לב desires harmful things or fails to make correct choices when tempted by positive and negative desires because he too lacks the ability to discern the ends of his desires (see 6:32–33; 7:7, 23; 12:11).

[38] Yoder argues that "the fools' distorted emotions are emblematic of misperceiving the world – of moral depravity" (Christine Roy Yoder, "The Objects of Our Affections: Emotions and the Moral Life in Proverbs 1–9," in *Shaking Heaven and Earth: Essays in Honor of Walter Brueggemann and Charles B. Cousar* [ed. C. Roy Yoder et al.; Louisville: Westminster John Knox, 2005], 76). Yoder notes that in chapters 1–9, fools are frequently characterized by what they hate. Accordingly, "their moral universe is upside down, characterized by *antipathy* toward God, wisdom, other people, and even themselves" (ibid.; emphasis in original).

symptomatic of moral depravity. The desires of the fool, while certainly misguided in the view of the book, have their problematic origin in a faulty faculty of restraint and a confusion of emotion. For this reason, fools are potentially amenable to formation, although the prospects are dim, while the wicked are simply beyond the pale of correction.

The chronic problem of the simpleton's (פתי) desires stems from mental and emotional naïveté. Infatuated with his own simplicity (1:22), the simpleton's horizon of discernment is problematically small. Consequently, the simpleton is depicted as inherently susceptible to being swayed, which can either be to his favor or his detriment. The simple has the potential to desire rightly, yet without the proper guidance, his character is shaped by the influence of negative desires. Indeed, chapters 1–9 present the simpleton in the crosshairs of desire, enticed by the call of Wisdom (1:28) and also among the youth near the strange woman's house (7:7).[39] Both woman Wisdom and the foolish woman lure the simple to join their respective banquets (9:4, 16). In effect, the voices of these women present a contest of desire for the student, offering two similar appeals to incentives of food, drink, and female company, although with vastly different implicit consequences. In this respect, the simpleton demonstrates the importance of character formation, for his desires might be steered in a productive direction, although as long as he remains caught up in his own simplicity, any attempt to seek wisdom will go unfulfilled (1:28).[40]

The simpleton's problem is less psychological malfunction, as in the case of the fool, but rather psychological immaturity. Formation is still possible; the simpleton can learn, and he can learn through his desires. Thus Wisdom offers him not only rebuke, but the promise of satisfaction in her food, drink, and attention. Of course, the foolish woman and the strange woman offer these promises, as well, which is precisely the point. Desire is a crucible of formation for the simpleton, and the desires he chooses to indulge will dictate whether he becomes wise or falls into foolishness. "Let the simple enter here!" proclaim both Wisdom and the foolish woman (מי־פתי יסר הנה, 9:4, 16),[41] and much is vested in whose invitation he accepts.

---

[39] The particular figure who walks near the strange woman is a "boy without sense" (נער חסר־לב), although he comes from a group of simpletons.

[40] Like the simple, the scoffer (לץ) also seeks wisdom, but without success (14:6). Like the fool, the scoffer also has confused emotional reactions. The scoffer delights in his own scoffing (1:22) and disdains rebuke (15:12), in which one should delight (cf. 9:8).

[41] For the rather unusual use of מי as introducing a generalizing relative clause (i.e., "whoever is simple ..."), see P. Joüon and T. Muraoka, *A Grammar of Biblical Hebrew* (2nd ed.; Rome: Gregorian & Biblical Press, 2009), §144fa.

## The Righteous, the Wise, and Woman Wisdom

If the character of the wicked is the epitome of moral and psychological confusion, the righteous one is the embodiment of right desire, for his senses of pleasure and pain are in accord with the moral order. The righteous one hates deceit (13:5), and he delights in justice: "doing justice is a joy to the righteous but terror to evildoers" (21:15; see also 29:27). Moreover, his desires lead to satiety. "The righteous eats until his appetite (נפשו) is full," proclaims Prov 13:25, "but the belly of the wicked is empty (תחסר)." Similarly, Prov 10:3 observes that "YHWH will not let the appetite of the righteous go hungry, but he denies the desire of the wicked" (לא־ירעיב יהוה נפש צדיק והות רשעים יהדף). In contrast to the righteous, the wicked are ensnared by their desires, such that the only satiety to which they lead is death or destruction. As Prov 10:24 insists, "the terror of the wicked overtakes him (תבואנו), but the desire of the righteous is granted (תואות צדיקים יתן)" (see also 10:28; 11:5, 7; 12:21; 14:32; 15:6; 21:7). These contrasting depictions serve an important pedagogical function. Lyu notes that although correct desire cannot be taught, per se, "we can hope to induce desire *by showing what is desirable.* Moral instruction is in essence a process of persuasion and, to put it bluntly, a form of seduction. And seduction requires a lure, a prospect of palpable gain."[42] By presenting the contrasting consequences of the desires of the righteous and the wicked, Proverbs is, in effect, teaching the student to desire. Further, the portrayal of the righteous as one who desires rightly also serves to provide a paradigm for the student's own desires. As Lyu explains, "the rhetorical function of the discourse of praising the righteous person is to instill in its readers a desire to emulate the idealized character of the righteous person. Intellectual assent is not a sufficient ground for change of behavior; for the latter, one has to desire to emulate the ideals."[43] Indeed, the depiction of the righteous one's desires portrays both the character of the righteous and the objects of his desire as worthy of the student's own desire.

Proverbs makes surprisingly few explicit statements about the desires of the wise one (חכם). He loves the one who rebukes him (9:8), indicating a desire for discipline, and he seeks knowledge (18:15). Yet even though the desires of the wise are not mentioned in the book explicitly as often as one might expect, Proverbs presents the positive objects of desire as habits of

---

[42] Lyu, *Righteousness in the Book of Proverbs,* 62; emphasis in original.
[43] Ibid.

the wise, worthy of emulation by the student. In this respect, the book itself is a manual of wise desires. For example, understanding (בינה, תבונה) is figured as an enticing possession that the wise ought continually to seek, and the wise person is able to recognize its inherent desirability, a capacity that fools lack (18:2). In this sense, the wise are equipped with a faculty of perception that enables them to perceive the right objects as desirable and, consequently, to seek them out.

Woman Wisdom is the ultimate embodiment of positive desire, for she is herself an upstanding character who not only is an object of desire but who has her own desires. The depiction of woman Wisdom calls on multiple semantic fields of desire within the book, including the mention of desirable attributes, an experience of absence or lack, and the dynamics of pursuit. Wisdom presents herself as alluring and affluent (8:17–19), although she promises to be just beyond the grasp of those who desire her (1:28). In this sense, she embodies both absence and presence as vital elements of desire that impel the student to continue to seek her out. The desire for wisdom is in a certain respect insatiable. She calls out to the simple, scoffers, fools, and all humanity, seeking after them and prompting them to seek after her (1:20; 8:4–5; 9:4). Her goal is to win the love of the simple, and she promises to love them in turn (8:17). Wisdom is an embodiment of the virtues extolled by the father and an example of one who has attained the virtues that elsewhere the student is advised to seek, such as knowledge and foresight (8:12; cf. 1:4).

The psychology of desire evident in woman Wisdom's language communicates an essential feature of the search for wisdom. Woman Wisdom's discourse of desire illustrates what Carson calls the "axis of paradox" on which desire is poised. Its poles are absence and presence, she writes, "love and hate its motive energies."[44] Likewise, love and hatred are the poles with which Wisdom frames the stakes for her own desirability. "All who hate me love death!" she proclaims (8:36a). Moreover, Wisdom proves an elusive lover who is both absent and present to the object of her affections. In fact, this is part of the rhetoric of enticement, akin to the activity of the beloved in the Song of Songs or the lovers in ancient Egyptian love poetry. The postponement of satiation – i.e., continued absence – provokes greater desire, even as a foretaste of the lover's presence leaves the desirer wanting more. As personified Wisdom proclaims in Ben Sira, "those who eat of me will hunger for more, and those who drink of me will thirst for more" (Sir 24:21).

---

[44] Carson, *Eros*, 11.

Similarly, Proverbs indicates that the nature of the search for wisdom is itself elusive and prolonged, for it both offers and resists full satiation, leaving the student desiring more. Thus the summons to pursue wisdom never ends. The concept of wisdom's elusiveness is slightly different than in Job or Qoheleth, where it has more to do with a suspicion about the intelligibility of order in the cosmos and the human ability to comprehend it (cf. Job 28:12–13; Qoh 7:23–24). Within Proverbs, wisdom's elusiveness is not indicative of a frustration or complaint, but it functions to impel the continued search for wisdom. The book assumes that humans are capable of seeking wisdom and, in fact, never lose the need to seek more wisdom. Thus woman Wisdom is both accessible and yet remains playfully just out of reach to her students, bidding them to wait daily by her doors and linger at her gates (8:34).

Furthermore, not only does Wisdom impel the absent student to seek her presence, but she also seeks the presence of the student. In this sense, the poetry envisions a reciprocal desire between Wisdom and student. While the student ought to seek out Wisdom, Wisdom herself is eager to be sought, even providing a banquet feast, as if to attract the beloved one (9:2–5). Fox suggests that in the reciprocal love of wisdom and the wise, Proverbs expresses the idea that even as the student learns to love wisdom, wisdom may show itself open to being loved. While the beginner may feel overwhelmed by the vast amounts of knowledge she has yet to master, as she progresses in her learning she gains greater understanding of the underlying structures of knowledge that allow her to make further advances. Fox explains, "[A] learner may have the sensation that the field of knowledge is cooperating in clarifying itself, at least in the territory one has already traversed."[45] At the same time, the elusive nature of wisdom continues to impel the learner, whatever her degree of learning, to seek more knowledge, which is, in fact, one of the central goals of the book, such that "the wise hears and gains more teaching" (1:5).

In sum, the wise and the righteous, as they are presented throughout the book, demonstrate that certain students can desire rightly, while the simpleton indicates that the education of one's desires is critical to character formation. Some characters are beyond the pale of discipline; in fact, their desires are warped such that they have an aversion to the very thing they should seek. However, desire can be directed toward productive ends should the student heed the instruction of his teachers. To this end, the book itself participates in educating the desires of its student, directing the student toward the desires and the ends that the sages promote.

[45] Fox, *Proverbs 1–9*, 276.

## The (Poetic) Patterning of Desire

Proverbs is not simply a catalog of good and bad desires, but rather the book participates in shaping the desires of its student as it patterns various desires and desirers over the course of the poems and proverbial sayings. In this respect, the book itself functions to shape the desires and, consequently, the character of the student. As Wayne C. Booth argues with respect to fiction, if literature is to affect the reader's character, it must engage her desires, for "the most powerful effect on my ethos, at least during my reading, is the concentration of my desires and fears and expectations, leading with as much concentration as possible toward some further, some *future* fulfillment: I am made to want something that I do not yet have enough of."[46] Booth argues that different narratives will pattern the reader's desire differently, by which he means that each will shape the reader's desires so that she seeks more of what the work offers in order to keep her turning its pages. One thus acquires from different stories a "desire to become a different kind of desirer," for each work fashions a reader's desire in a slightly different way.[47] In comparing various narratives and the desires they engender, one can determine the patterns of desire that are best, for "we try out each new pattern of desire against those that we have found surviving past reflections, and we then decide, in an explicit or implicit act of ethical criticism, that this new pattern is or is not an improvement over what we have previously desired to desire."[48] Likewise, Christine McKinnon, who writes from the perspective of moral philosophy, also highlights the role of evaluating desires and appropriating good desires in character formation. Desire provides a motivating source that is vital for the cultivation of character, she explains, because "the agent wants to *be* a certain way, and that means

---

[46] Wayne C. Booth, *The Company We Keep: An Ethics of Fiction* (Berkeley: University of California Press, 1988), 201; emphasis in original.

[47] Ibid., 272. For example, Booth considers the opening vignette in Peter Benchley's *Jaws* (1974), which describes the circling of a shark in dark water and foreshadows a violent scene between this creature and an amorous couple on the beach. Booth describes the way in which the scene simultaneously engages the reader's desire in a particular way to keep her turning the pages of the book *and* also shapes those desires toward particular beliefs and commitments: "Already I can hardly wait for the promised bloody encounter between such a primitive brain and such a sexy thrasher. But if I move on to enjoy that, I do not do so with the mere passive curiosity that keeps me browsing in that anthology of literary anecdotes. I am both fearing spectacular bloodshed and desiring it, enjoying the prospect of bloody death for those who don't matter, hoping for (and fully expecting) final safety for the good guys (who don't matter much more) and learning – learning all the while – both that happiness for these characters is defined as escape from danger and that happiness for me is watching people fall into danger and then, sometimes, miraculously fall out of it" (ibid., 202–03).

[48] Ibid., 272.

that she wants certain desires to be central to her motivational economy. She wants to perceive the world, and she wants to act, in ways characteristic of those desires."[49]

In a similar fashion, Proverbs patterns the student's desire as part of its pedagogical goal to shape his character. Proverbs of course presents the desires it favors as the best and most worthy desires, yet it admits that there are compelling alternatives to these desires, if only for short-sighted gain. It is striking that Proverbs does not suppress the desires it considers to be negative by refusing to speak of them, but instead it prompts the student to dismiss them by viewing them against the sanctioned desires. Booth writes that "all stories will produce a practical patterning of desire, so long as I stay with them. And each pattern, in itself narrow as compared with all the other possible patterns, will imply that it is the best."[50] Within Proverbs, the patterning of desire occurs in the juxtaposition of positive and negative desires, both of which admit a certain appeal. Yet Proverbs ultimately undermines the desires it considers to be dangerous, and in this way it implies that the sanctioned desires are indeed the best. This particular presentation of disparate desires further functions to shape the student's self and to affirm the community's social norms. N. J. H. Dent explains that conflicting desires

> would seem to provide a central occasion for the gradual establishing of this more stable sense of significance. Particularly where someone was in feeling inclined to attribute equal and great importance to two exclusive courses of action, he could hardly not be caused to consider which was overall the more material to him.[51]

Such a situation causes one to measure different desires against his conception of the well-lived life, and this process reinforces the enduring value of that moral vision. In this fashion, the book of Proverbs presents two ways of desire as a pedagogical tool to solidify the sanctioned desires of the community and to shape the student's character in their likeness.[52]

---

[49] Christine McKinnon, *Character, Virtue Theories, and the Vices* (Orchard Park: Broadview Press, 1999), 66–67.

[50] Booth, *The Company We Keep*, 204.

[51] N. J. H. Dent, "Desires and Deliberation," in *The Virtues: Contemporary Essays in Moral Character* (eds. Robert B. Kruschwitz and Robert C. Roberts; Belmont: Wadsworth Publishing Company, 1987), 114–15.

[52] For a discussion of the worldview implicit in the metaphorical system of the two ways and women in Prov 1–9, see Raymond C. Van Leeuwen, "Liminality and Worldview in Proverbs 1–9," *Semeia* 50 (1990): 111–44. Van Leeuwen argues that the fundamental reality behind these metaphors, including and especially metaphors related to women and erotic love, is a recognition of cosmic boundaries. Those who respect and live within such cosmic limits pursue the

The way in which the book of Proverbs patterns desire cannot be fully understood apart from how its function is realized through poetic form. It does not issue staid descriptions of desirable objects, but it appeals to the breadth of the student's senses, prompting not only cognitive analysis of various desires but also sensory perception as a means of evaluation. The use of sensory imagery and figurative language is a vital part of how the text makes meaning and contributes to shaping the desire of the student. Proverbs indicates that desire is not shaped strictly by appeal to the rational analysis of the intellect, but it relies on the senses of taste, touch, smell, vision, and hearing.

The patterning of desire in Proverbs is developed to the most elaborate extent in chapters 1–9, which will be sampled later, but even many of the proverbial sayings in the rest of the book evidence a subtle shaping of desire that privileges sensory appeal, draws distinctions between disparate desires, and promotes a particular way of viewing the world. In each case, their form, including their brevity, choice of words, and use of figurative language, contributes to affirming or undercutting the virtue or vice in question. Proverbs 24:13–14 and 20:17, for example, appeal to the desire of food in order to shape the student's view of the desires of wisdom or deceit, respectively.

### Proverbs 24:13–14

Eat honey, my son, for it is good – sweet drippings[53] on your palate!
Know this: such is wisdom for your soul;[54] if you find it, there is a future,
And your hope will not be cut off.

אכל־בני דבש כי־טוב ונפת מתוק על־חכך
כן דעה חכמה לנפשך אם־מצאת ויש אחרית ותקותך לא תכרת

Honey has a discernible taste, which this saying expounds through appeal to the senses, and in so doing, it uses taste perception to foster

---

good, while those who transgress them represent evil. Implicit in this metaphorical system is "the bi-polar human *eros* for the beauty of Wisdom, who proscribes life within limits, or for the seeming beauty of Folly, who offers bogus delights in defiance of created limits.... Literal erotic love in these chapters is a symbol, in the proper sense, of cosmic eros for good or evil" (ibid., 116).

[53] נפת, "honey," may imply honey that is flowing or dripping from the comb, especially if one understands it to derive from the root נוף. See Prov 5:3 and Song 4:11, where the term is used with the verb נטף, "to drip," and Ps 19:11, נפת צופים, "flowing honey."

[54] נפש, "soul" or "appetite," here implies one's very self or being. As Fox explains, "The learning spoken of here is not merely intellectual storage of information ... but learning *for your nepeš* – a deep appropriation of wisdom to yourself, making it your own" (Michael V. Fox, *Proverbs 10–31: A New Translation with Introduction and Commentary* [AB 18B; New Haven: Yale University Press, 2009], 749).

one's desire toward what is lacking – not honey, but wisdom.[55] The first line employs a literal directive for the student to savor the sweet substance, the taste of which is embellished in the second half of the line. Here the parallel structure specifies and advances the "goodness" (טוב) of the honey: its taste is sweet; it flows abundantly; and it is located on the student's tongue. The image is rich, visceral, and immediate – on *your* palate. Yet the second line transforms the literal image into a metaphor of wisdom's properties, and the link between the two images is subtly underscored by syntax and sound. דבש and חכמה are parallel terms in the two lines, and there is a clear sound play between the final terms in verses 13b and 14a: ʿal-ḥikkekā and lĕnapšekā. The very attributes that make one salivate are applicable to wisdom: it has a tangible quality that affects the student directly ("for *your* soul"), and it flows with abundance. The use of a triplet line in verse 14 extends the image of flowing honey to a metaphor of wisdom's inexhaustible rewards. In fact, such rewards extend even beyond the bounds of the expected couplet! As the triplet breaks the established pattern of balanced couplet lines, it implicitly highlights the import of the line that the promised future "will not be cut off." The saying operates with sensory perception, identifying wisdom's desirability by its taste, and the opening description of nature's honey makes the saying more pressing and tangible than if it simply said, "wisdom is good for your soul, if you find it there is a future." Instead, the pleasures of wisdom are conveyed through another desirable image.

*Proverbs 20:17*
Tasty[56] is bread of deceit to the man, but afterwards his mouth is filled with gravel.

ערב לאיש לחם שקר ואחר ימלא־פיהו חצץ

The taste buds are not always a reliable guide to wisdom, as Prov 20:17 indicates, and this saying hints in some measure toward the destabilizing nature of desire.[57] This saying also appeals to a sensory description of taste,

---

[55] For a discussion of the literal and figurative use of honey imagery in the Hebrew Bible, see Tova Forti, "Bee's Honey – From Realia to Metaphor in Biblical Wisdom Literature," *VT* 56.3 (2006): 327–41. For a discussion of the honey image in the metaphor DISCOURSE IS FOOD, see Brown, "The Didactic Power of Metaphor," 144.

[56] ערב, "pleasant," that is, sweet, tasty, or appetizing.

[57] Even the metaphors used and the arrangement of the terms in this saying are in some sense destabilizing. Brown notes that in both colons of the line, the final terms (שקר, "deceit," and חצץ, "gravel") are both unexpected, for the metaphors used at the beginning of each colon lead the reader to anticipate a rather conventional conclusion. Yet "the proverbial punch is thrown only at the end" (Brown, "The Didactic Power of Metaphor," 144). Furthermore, Brown notes that "[t]he proverb

in this case the appealing taste of bread and the biting texture of gravel,[58] but it transforms the image into a metaphor for deceitful practices. It acknowledges that bread of deceit, that is, the spoils gained by deceit, have a certain appeal.[59] Yet its appeal is fleeting, quickly turning sour. Deception is in fact deceptively desirable to those who fail to consider its long-term consequences. The saying thus captures an implicit problem of desire, that is, what appears desirable may in fact prove undesirable in the end, a point which is nicely underscored by the balance of the line, beginning with *appetizing* (ערב) and ending with *unappetizing* (חצץ). The line may also employ a subtle word play between חצץ, a rare word that occurs only here in Proverbs, and the more common חפץ ("delight"). Indeed, the advice of the saying is ultimately that one must not confuse חפץ and חצץ. Without due caution, one's desires can lead to one's undoing.

While these sayings do not depict the sexy, even racy, aspects of desire that are more commonly found in ancient love poetry, as well in as Prov 1–9, they do point to the magnetic pull of desire to influence human behavior, drawing a person toward the desirable object that is found to be lacking. This is, of course, both a problem and an opportunity for pedagogy, depending on the ends toward which it leads. The desire for an appetizing taste can lead to satisfaction or to a mouth full of gravel; desire requires the discernment to know the difference. Further, coupled with the language of rebuke and motivation, these sayings pattern the student as one who wishes to choose rightly. Proverbs 23:13–14 positions the hearer as the son to whom advice is given directly, pointing him to the ultimate motivation of life, while Prov 20:17 functions as an implicit rebuke of the one who chose an ephemeral treat. Although these opposing pictures of desire are not as elaborately developed as in the poems of chapters 1–9, they nonetheless illustrate that even at the level of individual sayings, desire is a tool that is used to shape perception, and it is a way of speaking about the inherent attraction of various paths, whether for good or for ill. The language of the sayings invokes the reader's desire to a certain extent by its appeal to sensory imagery, but it also functions to pattern the

masterfully enlists two opposing source domains (food and stones) to target the effects of deceptive discourse," as opposed to other sayings that consistently use metaphors of food and fruit to convey the benefits of right speech (ibid.). With such turns in its syntax and unusual combination of metaphorical source domains, the saying, in a certain sense, enacts the destabilizing aspect that its content communicates.

[58] This is also an image of touch, perhaps appealing to the roughness or harsh texture of pebbles (cf. Lam 3:16, "he crushed my teeth on gravel," ויגרס בחצץ שני). In this respect, one could also understand ערב to refer to the pleasant texture or consistency of the bread.

[59] Fox suggests that the image is both bread gained by deceit and bread that itself deceives (Fox, *Proverbs 10–31*, 671).

student's desire, subtly teaching him to discern what is ultimately desirable, in the sages' view.

The patterning of the student's desire reaches particular heights in the poetry of the first nine chapters of the book. The pedagogy of Prov 1–9 hinges on the articulation of two competing patterns of desire, which are developed over the course of the poems by appeal to a range of the student's senses, desires, and motivations. For this reason, the motif of desire cannot be separated from its realization through the poetic medium. The form of poetry allows each pattern to become more immediate than a prose description would otherwise permit, and this feature is a vital part of the pedagogical function of these poems. While the father offers his sagely advice, the strange woman and woman Wisdom both entice the student through direct address, promising him riches, luxuries, and delight. Furthermore, as part of one collection, the poems together function to provide a practicum in desire for the student, as they enact alternate patterns of desire by means of direct appeal from various speakers to the student.[60]

The book makes clear that the two primary patterns of desire, while both compelling in their own right, are not equal, yet their disparity is often presented more implicitly than explicitly. While the father's voice certainly indicates his perspective on the alternative paths of Wisdom and the strange woman, the most revealing evidence for or against them is the subtle way in which they either advance or undermine the virtues that the book endorses. In this way, the father's counsel offers a means of evaluation by which the student is led to measure the alternatives as the two patterns are developed alongside one another over the course of the poems in the first nine chapters. In fact, this too is part of the pedagogical function of the poems, for they lead the student to embrace the sanctioned path by evaluating opposing perspectives, not by refusing to admit of alternatives. Moreover, the form of poetry offers a particular means of appeal and evaluation. This is no detached, cognitive analysis of opposing arguments. Rather, it is the emotional and aesthetic appeal, not simply the logical cogency, of the claims that is compared.

The shifting voices of first-person address are one of the chief means that the poems in chapters 1–9 use to promote the formation of character. These poems are not disinterested descriptions, but are presented as the unique perspective of particular characters, which has a decisive

---

[60] For a discussion of a chiastic structure of speeches in Prov 1–9, see Gale A. Yee, "'I Have Perfumed My Bed with Myrrh': The Foreign Woman (*'iššâ zārâ*) in Proverbs 1–9," *JSOT* 43 (1989): 55.

impact on the goal of character formation of the one who is addressed. As Carl Dennis argues, "the argument of the first-person poem is primarily an ethical argument, based on the *ethos* or moral qualities exhibited by the speaker."[61] Like Booth, Dennis speaks of the influence of the character of the speaker on the character of the reader as an interaction akin to engagement with a friend. "The central experience of reading a poem," he argues, "is that of making contact with a whole human being, not only with arguments and opinions but with a complex of emotional, ethical, and aesthetic attitudes expressed with the kind of directness and openness that we experience in the frank speech of a friend."[62] Within Proverbs, as the character of these speakers – and the associated desires that they offer – are figured positively or negatively throughout the poems, the student is invited to align his own character with the speakers who offer wisdom and wise counsel. The student encounters various voices throughout the chapters who address him directly, and the poems position the hearer in the subject position of one who hears the counsel of the father as an authority figure and one who experiences directly the enticing speech of Wisdom and the strange woman. As the poems unfold over the course of the collection, they shape his character in the likeness of one who reveres the parent's voice and has the ability to resist the pull of harmful desires. For this reason, attending to how each of these poems portrays the *ethos* of the speakers illumines how they function to shape the character of the student.

With the motif of desire, the didacticism *and* the lyricism of Proverbs' poetry are on full display. Like Hebrew love poetry, these poems develop the motif of seeking and finding as a game between lovers; they make extensive use of first-person speech; they appeal to sensory imagery; they

---

[61] Carl Dennis, *Poetry as Persuasion* (Athens: University of Georgia Press, 2001), 17. Dennis draws on Booth's work to ask of its particular implications for poetry. In fact, Dennis suggests that the metaphor of friendship that Booth introduces to speak of the relationship between literature and the reader "is perhaps even more appropriate for poetry than it is for fiction, for in a poem we seem to enter into a direct relation with the speaker, without the indirection of a mediating narrative" (ibid., 11). Dennis, more than Booth, is interested in the particular strategies that literature (poetry, specifically) employs to engage the reader in certain kinds of friendship. Whereas prose may appeal to evidentiary reasoning, poetry utilizes a "primarily ethical argument, based on the *ethos* or moral qualities exhibited by the speaker, and only secondarily an appeal to particular evidence" (ibid., 17). Dennis explores the particular virtues a poem's speaker must exhibit to be a compelling, authoritative voice whom the reader will want to befriend. In this sense, poetry has a different means of addressing the reader than does prose. It does not develop a linear, logical argument to appeal to the reader's intellect, but it "is based more on *ethos* than on *logos*, more on the character of the speaker than on logical proof" (ibid., 2). It seeks to persuade the reader with a speaker whose compelling character wins her attention.

[62] Ibid., 6.

flash between different scenes, often without any clear connection or intervening narrative arc. Yet Proverbs uses these lyrical features to didactic ends. Its interest is not simply to describe the dynamic between lovers or even to evoke desire in the student through appeal to sensory language and imagery. Rather, the ultimate concern of Prov 1–9 is to educate the student's cognitive, emotional, and aesthetic sensibilities such that he can discern the way of wisdom from the way of foolishness and make appropriate choices to pursue it.

For this reason, the form of poetry is crucial to the function of pedagogy. Proverbs does not seek only to educate the student's mind with clearly developed lectures that advance logical conclusions, as if rational argument alone would suffice. Rather, it uses the poetic medium to invoke and to educate the student's emotions and desires, as a range of enticing choices are displayed before him, many of which have particular sounds, tastes, smells, and appearances.[63] While these dynamics are operative throughout chapters 1–9, I will examine the poems in Prov 4 and Prov 7 as key examples. In these poems, as in the rest of the book, the use of direct speech, vivid imagery, and appeal to desire function didactically as they delight poetically.

*Proverbs 4:1–9*

*1*  Listen, students,[64] to a father's discipline,
         and pay attention to know understanding.
*2*  For good teaching I give to you.
         Do not abandon my instruction!
*3*  For I was a son to my father,
         precious and dear to my mother;
*4*  He taught me, saying to me,
         Let your heart grasp my words!
         Keep my commands, and live!
*5*  Possess[65] wisdom! Possess understanding!
         Do not forget – do not stray from the words of my mouth!

---

[63] See Chapter 3 for a discussion of the genre of Proverbs' poetry and its connection to the Hebrew love lyric.

[64] בנים, literally, "sons," yet I choose to translate as "students" in order to capture the sound play in this verse between בנים and בינה, "understanding." "Son" is a frequent designation for student in ancient Near Eastern wisdom texts and does not necessarily imply biological relationship, although this poem plays with the figure of the father as both the teacher of sons and the son of his own father and mother.

[65] The verb קנה can imply a variety of transactions, including physical acquisition (e.g., Gen 4:1), intellectual acquisition or understanding (e.g., Prov 1:5), economic purchase (e.g., Isa 43:24), transfer of ownership (e.g., Gen 47:20), and marriage, that is, the acquisition of a wife (e.g., Ruth 4:5). Several of these senses are operative in this poem, thus the rather ambiguous translation, "possess."

6  Do not abandon her, and she will keep you.
     Love her! And she will guard you.
7  The beginning of wisdom – possess Wisdom![66]
     Above all of your possessions,[67] possess Understanding!
8  Adore her,[68] and she will exalt you –
     She will honor you, if you embrace her.
9  She will set upon your head a wreath of grace,
     a magnificent crown[69] she will gift you.

As this poem subtly underscores the authority and trustworthiness of the father's voice, it functions to make his voice more compelling than the other voices that the student will encounter over the course of the other poems. The authority of the father's voice is grounded in direct appeal to a previous generation, the wisdom that he received from his own father. As the father reports the counsel that was delivered to him, the ambiguity of the second-person imperatives underscores the timelessness of this wisdom. The imperatives simultaneously function as a report of past wisdom *and* as a present address to the student.[70] The father echoes his own father in addressing the son, lending greater weight to his words.

The poem also endows the father's voice with a persuasive passion through the rhythmic cadence of its syntax. The constant repetition of imperatives binds together the lines and lends them a driving urgency, which grows greater as the poem advances. The opening lines of the poem

---

[66] While the personification (or lack thereof) of wisdom is ambiguous in the earlier use of חכמה in the poem (v. 5), here it likely envisions wisdom as a person, given the directive in verse 6 to "love her," coupled with the promise that she will guard the youth. The personification becomes clearer as the poem unfolds, particularly in the last verses as she is a figure who can be embraced and adored and who will bestow honor herself.

[67] The construction ובכל־קנינך could be rendered several ways. If the preposition ב is understood to mark a price (cf. Gen 23:9; GKC §119.3.b.6), then it could be understood as, "*with* (i.e., *at the cost of*) all of your possessions ..." It is also possible, however, that here ב has a comparative sense (see Mitchell J. Dahood, who notes the comparative use of ב in biblical Hebrew and Ugaritic [Mitchell J. Dahood, "Hebrew-Ugaritic Lexicography I," *Biblica* 44 (1963): 299–300]), and thus I translate, "*above* (i.e., *more than*) all of your possessions ..." This translation accords with the larger point of wisdom's supreme value, which surpasses other possessions (cf. Prov 3:14–15).

[68] סלל occurs in the *pilpel* only here, perhaps meaning to honor or make high. Arnold B. Ehrlich translates as "eng anschmiegen" ("snuggle tightly"), based on its use in rabbinic Hebrew (Arnold B. Ehrlich, *Randglossen zur Hebräischen Bibel: textkritisches, sprachliches und sachliches*, vol. 6 [Leipzig: Hinrichs, 1913], 23–24); see also Berend Gemser, who notes that it may mean to hug or embrace, its meaning connected to the weaving or entangling of vines on a branch (cf. Jer 6:9, סלסלות) (Berend Gemser, *Sprüche Salomos* [Tübingen: J.C.B. Mohr, 1937], 24).

[69] עטרת תפארת, literally a "crown of glory."

[70] There is some differentiation between the two, for the father's address is in the second-person plural (vv. 1–2), while the speech he reports is in the second-person singular (vv. 3–9). Yet even this shift from plural to singular address subtly functions to position the listener as the sole recipient of the tradition.

establish a pattern of two verbs per verse (4:1–3), yet the pattern doubles to four verbs per verse in verses 5, 6, and 8, which quickens the rhythm of the lines and highlights the urgency of the address: "Possess! Possess! Do not forget! Do not stray!" (4:5). The frequent repetition of the sounds /ī/ and, especially, /ā/ throughout the poem also construct a decisive rhythm that binds the whole poem together yet grows more frequent in the second part of the poem.[71] Dennis argues that a poem's rhythm is a vital factor in what makes its voice compelling.[72] Rhythm, he insists, "is not an adornment of a statement but one of its elements. It shapes it, giving it focus and clarity. It endows it with a specific weight that helps define its value."[73] In Prov 4, the building rhythm underscores the authority and urgency of the father's counsel. His is the voice of value.

In this poem, the motif of desire is a central tenet of the father's pedagogical appeal, operative in its metaphors and images, and emphasized by its building rhythm and parallel lines. The exhortation in verse 4, "let your heart grasp my words" (יתמך־דברי לבך), hints toward the fulfillment of desire motif, followed by the double imperative to possess (קנה) wisdom and understanding in verse 5. Behind these phrases is the metaphor WISDOM IS AN OBJECT, something that can be physically obtained (grasped) and acquired, whether it is figured as words of instruction or as the concepts of wisdom and understanding. Here the metaphors have a loose connection to the motif of desire, insofar as these objects are worthy of pursuit by the student. By verse 6, however, the motif of desire becomes more transparent when the metaphor WISDOM IS AN OBJECT combines with the metaphor WISDOM IS A BELOVED. Personified Wisdom is not only a worthy object of pursuit and desire, but she promises to receive and to return the affections of the student, as the father exclaims, "Love her! (אהבה) … Adore her! (סלסלה) … Embrace her! (תחבקנה)," for she will protect, exalt,

---

[71] Compare, for example, the first verse, in which /ā/ figures in four of seven words (and only once as final -â), with verses 6 and 8, in which the sound is present in nearly every word:

> šimʿû bānîm mûsar ʾāb wĕhaqšîbû lādaʿat bînâ (4:1)
> ʾal-taʿazbehā wĕtišmĕrekkā ʾĕhābehā wĕtiṣṣĕrekkā (4:6)
> salsĕlehā ûtĕrômĕmekkā tĕkabbēdkā kî tĕhabbĕqennâ (4:8)

[72] Dennis argues that passion is one of the essential characteristics of a persuasive speaker. He explains that the speaker must demonstrate that he cares deeply for the subject: "to seem passionate the speaker must give the impression that his words express a deep-seated conviction, that he stands behind what he is saying" (Dennis, *Poetry as Persuasion*, 17). While there are a variety of rhetorical techniques to convey this sense, Dennis suggests that the most important is rhythm – not only the pattern of stressed and unstressed syllables but also the general flow of the lines. Rhythm, he explains, "makes us feel the presence of a speaker behind the words" (ibid., 18).

[73] Ibid., 21.

and honor the student in exchange. The full import of these metaphors comes to a crescendo in verse 7 with the threefold repetition of the root קנה: "*Possess* Wisdom! Above all of your *possessions, possess* Understanding!" By this point, the term has acquired more than an economic meaning as it combines with the language of affection and emotion. This is an impassioned image of emotional and even *physical* possession.

The pedagogy of this poem is a blend of the models of motivation and desire. Seeking wisdom and obeying the parent's teaching promise life, protection, and honor as incentives for the student's adherence. Yet while the motivations serve to figure Wisdom as desirable, the deeper significance of the desire theme pertains to the way in which – not just *why* – the student should pursue her. Wisdom is not simply a means to an end, but is something to be cherished and embraced as a beloved.[74] It is a disposition toward learning that the father imparts through metaphors of physical affection, which qualify the motivational discourse. Learning is not simply a matter of economic exchange or calculation of benefits.

*Proverbs 7:1–27*

*1* My son, keep my words and shelter[75] my commands with you.

*2* Keep my commands and live! And my teaching as the sparkle[76] of your eyes!

*3* Bind them on your fingers – write them on the tablet of your mind!

*4* Say to Wisdom, "you are my sister," and call Understanding, "companion,"[77]

*5* To keep you from a strange woman, from a foreigner – her words flatter.

*6* When in the window of my house, through my lattice, I gazed,

*7* I saw among the simple, I perceived among the pupils,[78] a boy without a mind

---

[74] Personified Wisdom is depicted in this poem as a beloved figure, although not necessarily because of erotic appeal. It is her ability to protect and grace the student that makes her worthy of the student's love. Here she is more a mother than a lover, although this too can be a relationship of tender affection and emotion, a possibility that is first introduced in verse 3: רך ויחיד לפני אמי.

[75] The verb צפן can denote both the act of storing up (e.g., Ps 31:20) and of concealing, such as an object one wishes to protect or treasure (e.g., Exod 2:2; Ps 27:5). Both senses may be operative here.

[76] כאישון עיניך, literally "as the pupil of your eyes." The אישון is the center of one's eye, and thus the object likened to it is central to one's vision and something worthy of protection, just as one would protect the eye itself from harm (see also Deut 32:10; Ps 17:18). The image also connotes special favor or honored status that the object or person holds in the bearer's eyes (Deut 32:11, 13–14), and so I choose to translate "sparkle of your eyes" (cf. NRSV and NJPS: "the apple of your eye").

[77] מדע, a distant relative or acquaintance (see Ruth 2:1; 3:2); cf. Ugaritic *mdd*, "beloved friend"; Akkadian *mūdû*, "experienced," or "intelligent" person. Here the term, in parallel to אחות, implies the name of a relative that is used as an epithet for a beloved one (cf., e.g., Song 4:9).

[78] Note the consonance of אבינה בבנים.

*8* Passing through the street beside her corner, stepping in the path of her house

*9* At twilight – day's evening, in the black[79] of night and darkness.

*10* Then a woman to call him – a harlot's garment, of veiled mind,[80]

*11* Turbulent, defiant is she – in her own house, her feet[81] do not linger –

*12* A foot[82] in the street, another in the squares – beside every corner she lurks.

*13* Then she seizes him and kisses him! With a brazen face she tells him,

*14* "Completed sacrifices for me! Today I made my vows complete.[83]

*15* Then I went out to call you – to seek your face! And I found you!

*16* I prepared coverings for my couch, colored cloth, Egyptian linen,

*17* I sprinkled my bed – myrrh, aloes, cinnamon!

*18* Come! Let's imbibe lovemaking until morning! Let's gorge ourselves on love!

---

[79] Some propose reading אשׁון, "time," as opposed to אישׁון, "pupil," following Qere in Prov 20:20 (K: אישׁון) (see Roland E. Murphy, *Proverbs* [WBC 22; Nashville: Thomson Nelson, 1998], 42), but this is unnecessary. Here אישׁון refers to the darkness of the eye's pupil as a description of the blackness of the night (see Fox, *Proverbs 1–9*, 243).

[80] ונצרת לב, literally "of guarded mind." The strange woman's intent is hidden from the youth (although surely not from the father or, by extension, the reader!), which is part of her danger. In fact, her mysteriousness is part of what may entice the young man, just like her promiscuous garments.

[81] For a discussion of the cognitive metaphors implicit in the bodily description of the strange woman, see M. Beth Szlos, "Body Parts as Metaphor and the Value of a Cognitive Approach: A Study of the Female Figures in Proverbs via Metaphor," in *Metaphor in the Hebrew Bible* (ed. P. van Hecke; BETL 187; Leuven: Leuven University Press, 2005), 185–95. Szlos points out that while the strange woman's oral body parts are named in Prov 5, 7 (פה,לשׁון,חך,שׂפה), usually as a metaphor both for her speech and sexual appeal, her palms, hands, and arms are not described. Unlike the description of the אשׁת חיל in Prov 31, the strange woman does "not have the body parts associated with labor or social power or physical strength" (ibid., 193).

[82] פעם may denote an occurrence or time, as well as a step or foot, thus many translations render "*now* in the street, *now* in the squares" (see NRSV; NJPS; NIV; Fox, *Proverbs 1–9*, 238; Murphy, *Proverbs*, 41). However, the translation "foot" maintains the image of her restless feet (רגלים) in the previous line.

[83] The initial words of the strange woman's speech are rather cryptic, and perhaps deliberately so. The term זבחי שׁלמים is often understood to imply the kind of sacrifices that the woman offers, either peace- or well-being offerings (see NJPS; Fox, *Proverbs 1–9*, 245–46; Murphy, *Proverbs*, 43–44; Crawford H. Toy, *The Book of Proverbs* [ICC; Edinburgh: T&T Clark, 1899], 150–51; cf., e.g., Lev 7:11–21). For a discussion of Prov 7 in relation to sacred prostitution, see Karel Van der Toorn, "Female Prostitution in Payment of Vows in Ancient Israel," *JBL* 108 (1989): 193–205. That the strange woman offers sacrifices of שׁלמים is in any case ironic since in the father's eyes she surely presents nothing of peace or well-being. Yet the word play with שׁלמתי, "I made complete," in the second half of the line may underscore another quality of the sacrifices, their completeness. That is, she indicates that she has already offered the sacrifices, and presumably she then has meat to share. The term resonates with more than one meaning, but I choose to translate "completed sacrifices" in order to preserve in English the word play with שׁלמתי in the second half of the line.

*19* For the man is not in his house, he walks on a distant path.[84]

*20* He took the moneybag in his hand; not until the new moon will he enter his house."

*21* She sways him with her great teaching,[85] with her smooth lips she seduces him –

*22* He follows her blindly,[86] like a bull to slaughter, like a dancing fool to punishment[87]

*23* Until the arrow pierces his liver, like a bird rushing to a trap, not knowing his life is in it.[88]

*24* Now my sons, listen to me – pay attention to the words of my mouth!

---

[84] While she most likely refers to her husband, the term הָאִישׁ is ambiguous, and here could also refer to the boy himself. He is not at home but strays on a distant road, a point that underscores the father's message of danger in straying from home and familiar paths (cf. vv. 25–27). The ambiguity is resolved in the following line, however, as she continues to describe the man who took his wallet and will not return soon, which must be the husband.

[85] It is interesting that the strange woman also offers a teaching (לקח), which highlights the nature of her rival discourse – like the father's speech, it is a kind of instruction (cf. 4:2). His teaching may be good (4:2, כי לקח טוב נתתי לכם), but hers is great (רב לקחה) in its power to sway and entice.

[86] MT has פתאם, "suddenly," although LXX may be reading פתאים. It translates κεπφωθείς, a rare term meaning to be easily enticed or ensnared (i.e., to be ensnared like a κέπφος, a "feather-brained" person, according to H. G. Liddell and R. Scott, *A Greek-English Lexicon* [rev. ed.; Oxford: Clarendon Press, 1996]). Even if one reads with MT, it is likely that the term is playing off of פתאים (see 7:7). Thus, the term may imply both the speed with which the boy follows the woman, as suggested by the image of a bird rushing to a trap (v. 23), *and* his foolishness or naïveté in doing so, a failure to consider the lasting implications, as suggested by the image of a bull going to slaughter.

[87] MT is extremely difficult here: וכעכס אל־מוסר אויל. Following LXX, many interpreters emend to כְּעֶכֶס אֶל מוֹסַר אַיָּל, "as a stag bounds to fetters" (see Fox, *Proverbs 1–9*, 249; Murphy, *Proverbs*, 41; William McKane, *Proverbs: A New Approach* [OTL; Philadelphia: Westminster Press, 1970], 221). G. R. Driver suggests that when עכס is used as a verb, it refers not to the jangling of bracelets but to the manner of gait (G. R. Driver, "Hebrew Notes," *VT* 1 [1951]: 241; cf. 11QPsᵃ 5, וברחובות תפארתך יעכסו, in which עכס describes the action of rejoicing in Zion). Given the other images in this sequence, another animal comparison seems likely here. However, a reference to a fool is not out of the question, especially if one discerns an implicit or explicit reference to an attribute of simpletons in the first half of the verse. If כעכס is understood as a verb, referring to a festive quality of gait (cf. Isa 3:16, in which it describes the merry way in which the haughty women who are adorned with anklets [עֶכֶס] walk), it is possible to make sense of the MT, "as a fool dances to punishment." While this does not preserve the threefold animal image as in the LXX, it does serve to bridge the two senses of the surrounding animal images, which underscores the multivalency of פתאם. That is, the fool proceeds merrily to his own punishment and demise (v. 23a) without considering the consequences, much as the bull to slaughter; moreover, he does not simply tread solemnly, but with joyful, decadent movement, like the flitting bird.

[88] The ambiguity of the antecedent of נפשו further highlights the comparison between the senseless one, the bull, the fool, and the bird. נפשו could refer to any of them, and in fact refers to all of them. None are aware of the consequences of their actions, a point which lends additional credence to interpreting פתאם as the naïveté of the one who follows the strange woman, not only the speed with which he does it.

25 Do not let your senses[89] stray towards her ways; do not stumble on her paths.

26 For many are the pierced she has toppled, and numerous those she has killed.

27 The ways of Sheol: her house – leading down to the chambers of death.[90]

Proverbs 7 is a veritable apprenticeship in desire, schooling the student in the discernment of desire as the poem unfolds. By use of first-person voice and second-person address, the poem alternatively figures the hearer first as the son of the father, the one to whom he offers counsel, but secondly as the simpleton to whom the strange woman appeals directly. The poem concludes, however, by situating the hearer once again as the father's student, admonished to avoid the temptress at all costs. The poem manipulates the subject position of the hearer and in so doing, patterns his desire – first setting before him the desirability of wisdom, which promises life (v. 2) and protection (v. 5), two of the most important motivations in the book, and then positioning him as one who is sought directly by the strange woman and invited to gaze on her desirability. Yet her speech is ultimately undermined by the poem's framework.[91] The student's gaze is through the father's window, and this orientation, which is again made explicit at the conclusion of the poem, functions as a commentary on the strange woman's speech. Although the poem indicates that the paths of wisdom and the strange woman are both desirable to some extent, the question of which is the sanctioned path is never ambiguous.

At the same time, however, the paradox of desire, bringing both pleasure and pain, defies simplistic choices between two paths, and in this poem the difficulty of choosing the sanctioned path is never underestimated. Indeed, the strange woman may well prove even more attractive than woman Wisdom given her elaborate promises of sensual delights, the description of her seductive appearance, and the smoothness of her

---

[89] Within Proverbs, לב connotes the center of intellectual powers ("mind"), as well as emotions ("heart"). Within the context of this poem, לב here refers not just to one's mind but to all of one's senses. The strange woman's teaching is not simply a cognitive argument; she also appeals to the youth's sight, sound, smell, and taste. The father warns that the sons should not allow any of their faculties to lead them astray.

[90] The very form of the final lines highlights the meaning. The poem quite literally leads to *death*, its final word.

[91] For an analysis of the structure and dynamic movement of this poem, see Robert Alter, *The Art of Biblical Poetry* (New York: Basic Books, 1985), 55–61.

speech.[92] The invocation of erotic desire complicates everything, and the evocative language sets a sensory dilemma before the student. Carson suggests that erotic desire sparks a crisis of the senses that stifles one's ordinary power of rational control: "decision is impossible and action a paradox when eros stirs the senses."[93] Furthermore, she insists, "moral evaluation also fractures under pressure of paradox, splitting desire into a thing good and bad at the same time."[94] Indeed, within Prov 7 (and chapters 1–9 as a whole), desire is split into something thoroughly paradoxical, offering both the most sensual of pleasures and the gravest of pains. Scott C. Jones suggests that in this respect, the text "mirrors something of the confusing nature of reality, as both erotic and repulsive description point to the same Strange Woman."[95]

This paradoxical dynamic is evident in the conflict between how the strange woman and the father frame the satiation of desire. The promise of satiation is the linchpin of the woman's appeal. She offers a night of passion that bodes to overwhelm the senses. The would-be lovers will not just *sample* delights, she proclaims, but they will *gorge themselves* (רוה, עלס, v. 18). On the other hand, the father also alludes to the satiation of desire, although he points to its devastating consequences. In fact, to satisfy this desire will bring the end of all desire: death itself (v. 27). The Song of Songs also links death and desire (Song 8:6), and although the contexts are very different, both point to the paradox of desire – pleasure and pain – that, in effect, constitutes a threat to the self. As Carey Ellen Walsh explains with reference to the Song, desire "is partly about self-transcendence or loss of self, the urge toward annihilation of identity."[96] That is, complete satiation consists, in some measure, of a losing of oneself to the desired object, which promises both pain and pleasure.[97]

---

[92] The father concedes that the strange woman's words are appealing – literally, they "make smooth" (אמריה החליקה, 7:5), and with her "smooth lips" she sways (בחלק שפתיה, 7:21). Her poetic speech underscores the smoothness of her words. She speaks in balanced lines and makes effective use of sound and word play to bind her lines together. For example, the first line she speaks uses the repetition of שלם in each half of the verse and rhyme in the final word of each half (*ʿālāy; nĕdārāy*) to bind the two halves of the line together and offer a rhythm pleasing to the ear.

[93] Carson, *Eros*, 8.

[94] Ibid., 8–9.

[95] Jones, "Wisdom's Pedagogy," 66.

[96] Carey Ellen Walsh, *Exquisite Desire: Religion, Erotic, and the Song of Songs* (Minneapolis: Augsburg Fortress, 2000), 169.

[97] Citing Georges Bataille, Dollimore notes: "it is through eroticism that we are seduced by the pull of annihilation; we really do want death to 'wreak its havoc at our expense.' Death is experienced most intensely as desire" (Dollimore, *Death, Desire and Loss*, 251). Dollimore's observation suggests that even in its likeness to death, love contains elements of pain and pleasure. Even as humans resist death, its promise of transcendence is attractive. So too, even as we may resist the chaotic

And this is precisely why the pedagogical risk of desire is high. To be sated with the strange woman's wares is to lose the self entirely, for her ways "lead down to the chambers of death" (v. 27).

The shifting speaking voices in this poem also point to the destabilizing nature of desire and the problems that this raises for moral discernment. While the poem begins by positioning the youth as a benefactor of the father's counsel and a confidant of Wisdom, the poem allows the student to enter deeply into precisely the nefarious desire that the father warns against.[98] In this sense, the addressee of the poem is given a different identity at the point when erotic desire is most intense, becoming the object of the strange woman's own pursuit. The shifting speaking voices in the poem prove a destabilizing effect for the subject position of the addressee, which shifts from loyal student, to onlooker, to simpleton caught in the woman's trap, and finally back to student. Within Proverbs, erotic desire is destabilizing not in the sense that it causes physical illness – as evident in the Song of Songs or the Egyptian poems (see earlier discussion) – but in the sense that it causes moral illness, impairing one's ability to choose wisely.

---

forces of love, we long for the pleasure of losing ourselves in the object of desire. Allowing the reader to experience both the bitter and the sweet of desire, Prov 7 and the Song provide witnesses to that force which is "destructively insatiable, a permanent lack whose attempted fulfillment is at once the destiny of the self and what destroys it, leading the poet to cry, in Shakespeare's Sonnet 147, 'I desperate now approve / Desire is death'" (ibid., 12).

[98] Jones argues that the pedagogical function of displaying both the alluring and repulsive aspects of the strange woman is to guide the student "to discern not between dualistic opposites, but between various shades of good and bad. Through this instruction, the son gains the skills to deconstruct the Strange Woman's speech and reveal the shadow-side of her smooth words, thereby exposing her true character" (Jones, "Wisdom's Pedagogy," 74–75). Jones provides a fruitful comparison with the presentation of the wicked woman in 4Q184. Although this text draws heavily on Prov 7, it in effect removes the indeterminacy of the strange woman's depiction. Instead, it makes more explicit the darkness, corruption, and evil that surround this figure. There is nothing desirable about the wicked woman in 4Q184. Her eyes are iniquitous; her hands seize the pit; her legs work wickedness; her bed is corruption. Jones notes that "it is clear that this female figure is not a tool to spur the student on to inductive reasoning or complex processes of differentiation. While the Wicked Woman herself represents the chaos of the underworld, her description is regularized, categorized, and determinate" (ibid., 78) Moreover, the wicked woman does not speak in 4Q184. Whereas the strange woman makes a seemingly desirable appeal in her own voice, the wicked woman is not permitted direct speech. Her speech is only reported by a third party. As Jones points out, "The objectification of the Wicked Woman's speech betrays a reticence to present this outsider in all her allure" (ibid., 77). The discrepancy between the presentations of the women in these texts reflects a fundamental difference in pedagogical strategy and view of the moral world. Jones explains: "the instructor at Qumran displays an antipathetic posture toward indeterminacy in pedagogical method, fearing that the student might be unable to distinguish between good and bad.... The father of Proverbs vii, on the other hand, recognizes that such seemingly disparate structures ... are not so easily distinguished. Reality, then, is construed indeterminately. In such a pedagogical task, both the father and the son must wield all their intellectual and imaginative powers to live wisely in a world of harshly ambiguous foes" (ibid., 79).

And yet as these different characters raise their voices and address the student over the course of the poem, they function to enact the process of discernment that the wise student must carry out. The lesson unfolds with the poem. Katharina Volk suggests that a prominent feature of Latin didactic poetry is what she terms "poetic simultaneity," the notion that the poet is crafting the poem before the reader's eyes,[99] and she also observes a related concept, "mimetic simultaneity," in which the poem is presented as simultaneous to external events.[100] Proverbs 7 evidences a similar phenomenon, insofar as the father's instructions unfold as the poem advances and prove themselves particularly pressing as they are delivered while a cautionary tale is unfolding outside of the father's window. In addition, the strange woman's speech implicates the student in her schemes as a common endeavor, for she proclaims, "*Let us* gorge ourselves on love!" (v. 18). Furthermore, as the poem uses a shift to the strange woman's first-person voice to place the student in the middle of the scene, so it returns him to the father's counsel in verse 21, implicitly positioning the student as one who has successfully resisted the strange woman's claims. The student is left with no choice but to imbibe the lesson.[101] The poem positions the hearer as a successful student, one who has perhaps dallied with the strange woman, yet in the end has chosen wisely.

## Desire and the Moral Self

The poetic articulation of desire within Proverbs reveals a holistic view of the moral self. There is no sharp distinction between reason and passion, intellect and emotion, mind and heart.[102] Rather, the book indicates that knowledge equally arises from and is influenced by cognitive, emotional, and sensory activity. Knowledge is not solely the product of rational calculation. Accordingly, the formation of the moral self is more than an intellectual project, but also requires the cultivation of one's emotions,

[99] Katharina Volk, *The Poetics of Latin Didactic: Lucretius, Vergil, Ovid, Manilius* (New York: Oxford University Press, 2002), 13. See my discussion in Chapter 3.

[100] Ibid., 182. For example, in Ovid's *Fasti*, the progress of the poem is depicted as concurrent with the passing of the year. See also Katharina Volk, "*Cum carmine crescit et annus*: Ovid's *Fasti* and the Poetics of Simultaneity," *TAPA* 127 (1997): 287–313.

[101] Note that the simpleton whom the strange woman addresses is never permitted to speak. In this way, he is not differentiated from the listener. Only the father differentiates the student from the one to whom the strange woman speaks.

[102] Yoder affirms that the parent of Proverbs "advocates a holistic understanding of the human: he teaches to and for the whole person, and he resists distinctions and dichotomies between the rational, the emotional and the passionate as he fosters certain beliefs in the youth" (Yoder, "The Shaping of Erotic Desire," 162).

senses, and desires. Proverbs demonstrates that the evaluation of desire is not a purely rational act. Proverbs patterns desire not only by appealing to logical reasoning, but more often by invoking the student's emotion to love and long for certain objects or embellishing its descriptions with aesthetic appeal. In this way, Proverbs suggests a more complex view of the human person that demands a more complex pedagogy. Logical argument alone will not suffice, as if humans were moral automatons, incapable of being moved by beauty, longing, and desire. Moreover, in Proverbs' view, humans' innate capacity for desire is not something that must be resisted entirely, but can be channeled toward wisdom and the good. In this respect, Fox is surely correct to insist that "wisdom is by nature cognitive *and* emotional *and* aesthetic. … Only together and inseparably can all these acts of mind and heart be wisdom."[103]

The implicit claim of Proverbs is that what one desires has the potential to shape one's character, for good or for ill, because one's very self is formed in the likeness of the desirable objects that one pursues. For this reason, desire has ethical implications, as one's desires reflect the people, virtues, or ideas that one finds valuable, and in turn, these desires inform the actions and identity of the one who desires them.[104] Desire is operative at the bounds between oneself and the desired object, each separated by a condition of lack. Carson notes that erotic desire is an exploration of boundaries, as the lover seeks to dissolve the divide between himself and his beloved. Desire is in part a quest for the loss of oneself in the transcendence of this boundary.[105] Such a dynamic is also true of other kinds of desire. If one is consumed with the desire for wealth, for example, she may undertake habits to redress this lack, whether morally worthy (e.g., industry, perseverance) or otherwise (e.g., fraud, theft); her moral character is thus shaped by her relation to wealth itself. Given the influence of desire on the formation of character, one of the primary pedagogical goals of Proverbs is the formation of the student's moral self in the likeness of wisdom.

---

[103] Fox, *Proverbs 10–31*, 976. He elaborates: "No one can be wise who desires the good but does not engage his mind in absorbing and understanding it. No one can be wise who knows what is good but does not desire it. No one can be wise who knows what is good but does not feel its beauty and love it" (ibid.).

[104] A similar view is found in Plato's *Symposium*. Frisbee C. C. Sheffield argues that for Plato, "our desires embody our values and beliefs about what is worth having or doing. Insofar as they do so they are an important part of our ethical lives. What and whom one desires determine the choices that one makes and the kind of person one turns out to be" (Frisbee C. C. Sheffield, *Plato's Symposium: The Ethics of Desire* [New York: Oxford University Press, 2006], 3–4).

[105] Carson, *Eros*, 39–40.

In Proverbs, the desire of wisdom serves to reorient the student toward the object of his desire and to reshape his identity in terms of the love of wisdom. Having desired Wisdom, the young man is no longer the same person. Of course, the same is true of the fool's desire for the strange woman, which is why that particular desire is so dangerous. Such a union threatens his very self, for he gains a new identity infected by her dangerous wiles. Carson observes that "desire *changes* the lover.... The change gives him a glimpse of a self he never knew before."[106] To illustrate this idea of a new-found self, Carson cites a passage from Virginia Woolf's *The Waves* about a young man, Neville, watching his friend Bernard approach, noting the pain and self-reflection that comes when love mixes the self with another:

> Something now leaves me; something goes from me to meet that figure who is coming, and assures me that I know him before I see who it is. How curiously one is changed by the addition, even at a distance, of a friend. How useful an office one's friends perform when they recall us. Yet how painful to be recalled, to be mitigated, to have one's self adulterated, mixed up, become part of another. As he approaches I become not myself but Neville mixed with somebody – with whom? – with Bernard? Yes, it is Bernard, and it is to Bernard that I shall put the question, Who am I?[107]

In similar fashion, the love of Wisdom changes the lover of Wisdom. The metaphors of desire have a pedagogical function, for the student is encouraged to seek Wisdom because she possesses the virtues that the parent sanctions. A union with her will shape the student's self toward the virtues that the parent advances and will give him the ability to see in Wisdom a new reflection of himself, asking Wisdom, "Who am I?" Thus, the desire of Wisdom is a means of discipline, forming the student in the likeness of Wisdom herself.[108] Consider, for example, Wisdom's poem in chapter 8.[109]

## Proverbs 8:1–21

*1* Doesn't Wisdom call? And Understanding raise her voice?

*2* At the top of the heights, beside the path, at the crossroads,[110]

---

[106] Carson, *Eros*, 37; emphasis in original.

[107] Ibid., 36.

[108] This idea of a new creation of identity may resonate with the interlude of creation imagery in chapter 8. In a certain sense, a new creation is formed from the mutual desire of Wisdom and the student.

[109] Proverbs 8 is one long poem, only the first part of which is translated here. Thematically, the poem can be divided into three sections: a) vv. 1–21, in which Wisdom's voice is introduced and she makes her first appeal; b) vv. 22–31, in which Wisdom explains her relationship to YHWH at creation; and c) vv. 32–36, in which Wisdom again exhorts the students to seek her.

[110] בית נתיבות, literally "house of paths," which may refer to a meeting point of various paths at a public intersection (Franz Delitzsch, *Biblical Commentary on the Proverbs of Solomon* [trans. M. G.

*3* Beside[III] the gates, at the entrance of the city,[112] at the entryways she cries,

*4* "To you, O men, I call! My voice – to humanity's students![113]

*5* Learn savvy, you simpletons! And fools – gain sense![114]

*6* Listen! For I speak lofty things;[115] from the entry of my lips – straightness![116]

*7* For my mouth utters truth – the abomination of my lips is wickedness.

*8* With righteousness: all of the words of my mouth – there is nothing twisted or crooked in them!

*9* All of them are plumb[117] to the one who understands, and straight to those who find knowledge.

*10* Take my discipline! Not money! And knowledge above choice gold!

*11* For Wisdom is better than jewels, no delights can equal her.

*12* I, Wisdom, dwell with savvy, and knowledge, shrewdness I find

---

Easton; 2 vols.; Edinburgh: T&T Clark, 1874], 1:173), or "between paths," if בית is understood to mean "between," as in Aramaic (feminine form of בין; see 2 Kgs 11:15; Ezek 41:9; Job 8:17; cf. LXX Prov 8:2 [ἀνὰ μέϛον δὲ τῶν τρίβων] and Vulgate [*in mediis semitis*]).

[III] For דיל as "beside," see also 1 Sam 19:3.

[112] The reference to the opening, literally the "mouth of" (לפי) the city, nicely foreshadows the importance of Wisdom's mouth and openings later in the poem (see vv. 6, 8; cf. v. 13).

[113] Or "sons of humanity," בני אדם. Here Wisdom emphasizes the object of her appeal: human students.

[114] The imperative הבינו לב implies a directive to acquire the faculty of discernment, which is a task of mind, emotion, and sense perception.

[115] The form נגידים is only used here in this sense. If understood as the plural form of נגיד, "ruler," it may connote noble or lofty things (cf. LXX: ϛεμνὰ, "honorable things"). A reference to "high" or "lofty" things nicely echoes Wisdom's position at the heights (v. 2), as well as her endowment of rulers (v. 16). It also provides a contrasting metaphor of spatial dimension with the description of her words in the second half of the verse, מישרים. Wisdom's words are both *high* (a vertical dimension) and *straight* (a horizontal dimension), that is, they are both lofty and true. If understood as a nominal form of נגד, however, it may imply apparent or honest things, i.e., that which is *before* a person (cf. Fox's translation: "candid things" [Fox, *Proverbs 1–9*, 269]). In this case, it is a synonym of מישרים and suggests the integrity of Wisdom's words, a point that is elaborated in the following verses.

[116] Straightness, or "uprightness" (מישרים), denotes an attribute of order and the ability to speak and act in ways that promote order. Wisdom acts in accord with such order and grants her students the ability to discern order in the world (v. 9). The translation "straightness" preserves the aesthetic and spatial dimension of the metaphor, which also appears in the metaphors of verse 8 as Wisdom insists that her words are not twisted or crooked.

[117] The adjective נכחים indicates something that is "straight" or "before" a person (cf. the preposition נכח, "before," which may offer a parallel for deriving נגידים in verse 6 from נגד). It is often used in a metaphorical sense to imply something that is straightforward or true (cf. Prov 24:26; 2 Sam 15:3; Isa 26:10; 57:2; Amos 3:10). I choose the translation "plumb" in order to maintain the metaphor of the aesthetic dimension of Wisdom's words, which are "high" and "straight," neither "twisted" nor "crooked." The wise person can discern the correct measurements of her words.

*13* Fear of YHWH[118] is hatred of evil: pride and pretension,[119] the way of evil, and a mouth of crooked schemes, I hate.[120]

*14* Counsel and competence are mine! I have understanding – might is mine.

*15* With me, rulers reign, leaders proscribe righteousness.

*16* With me, princes rule, nobles and all judges of righteousness.

*17* I love those who love me[121] and those who seek me will find me.

*18* Riches and honor are with me! Great wealth and righteousness!

*19* My fruit is better than gold, even pure gold, and my produce than choice silver.

*20* I walk on the path of righteousness, in the midst of paths of justice

*21* To endow those who love me; I will fill their storehouses.

With this construction of Wisdom's desirability, the poem promotes the virtues that the parent considers fundamental to moral character. These virtues are packaged in the first-person speech of Wisdom, a form that has significant overlap with the strange woman's own appeal but also quite revealing departures. Like the strange woman, woman Wisdom calls from the public spaces; she addresses the same clientele: simpletons and fools. With direct speech, she promises surpassing delight and offers fine luxuries (vv. 10–11). Wisdom, too, is an attractive woman, yet her speech, appearance, and manner are not as overtly sexual as the strange woman's.[122] On the contrary, Wisdom's chief desirability abides in the virtues she possesses. Her beauty, surpassing fine jewels, is figured as the straight

---

[118] יראת יהוה may function with both the previous line and the present line as simultaneously the object of what Wisdom finds (v. 12) and the subject of the verbless clause "the fear of YHWH is hatred of evil." The word order in verse 12 leaves slightly ambiguous which objects follow which verbs. In fact, one could even read the three nouns ערמה ודעת מזמות as the objects of שכנתי, and יראת יהוה as the sole object of אמצא. That is, "I dwell with savvy and knowledge [and] shrewdness. I find the fear of YHWH." In this reading, the rest of the terms in verse 13 would be the objects that Wisdom hates. All of the previous lines in this poem are end-stopped (although note vv. 20–21), and an enjambed line would be a significant departure from the established pattern. It thus likely makes most sense to understand a syntactical break between the two lines, as most modern translations do, but nonetheless, there is a subtle ambiguity in the arrangement of the words.

[119] Note the sound play of cognates גאה וגאון.

[120] The only triplet line in this section of the poem draws attention to the disjuncture between praiseworthy Wisdom and the things that she hates. The form is literally and figuratively at odds with the rest of the encomium.

[121] Reading with Qere: אהבי (K: אהביה).

[122] Yoder notes that only Wisdom's hands, lips, and mouth are named (see also 1:24; 3:16), while there are many more references to the strange woman's body and mannerisms (Yoder, "The Shaping of Desire," 158).

words that issue from her lips (vv. 6–9), the valuable knowledge she offers (vv. 10, 12, 14), and her possession of savvy, shrewdness, and wise counsel (v. 12). Yet the figurative description of these virtues is not without elements that allude to erotic desire, as Wisdom promises to love those who love her and be found by those who seek her (v. 17). Interestingly enough, this language reverses the dynamic of the poem in chapter 7, in which the strange woman is the one who seeks the simpleton and offers him love (7:15, 18). Her speech positions him as the passive recipient of what she offers, while Wisdom's speech presumes the student's volition in seeking her out, even as she calls to him.

In the presentation of Wisdom as a desirable figure, the poem functions to shape desire itself, for it expounds on her attractiveness in relation to virtues of character – righteousness, savvy, shrewdness, wise counsel, and the like. She is to be desired not for her seductive secrecy, fragrant bed linens, or stealthy embrace, but for the virtues that adorn her. She is a model of the desirable, and she calls her students to gaze on her desirability in order to learn what virtues are worthy of their admiration. As Wisdom becomes an object of pursuit for the student, she in turn will shape his character as she mirrors back to him the virtues she possesses. Whether or not this model is ultimately compelling – particularly if its primary audience is adolescent boys – is a different question. Will a youth truly be persuaded to prefer the virtues of wisdom to the passions of sex? While it is impossible to say, the significant pedagogical risk that Proverbs takes should not be minimized. Indeed, the comparison between personified Wisdom and her dangerous counterparts is depicted with much less ambiguity in later texts such as 4Q184, which makes the strange woman a thoroughly repulsive figure.[123]

Nonetheless, woman Wisdom's virtue must exceed her sex appeal in the sages' eyes because of the way in which desire can serve as an important gauge of the moral self. As desire is a condition of lack, so it reveals what is lacking in the self. Carson suggests that the act of desiring is a process of self-discovery, for feelings of desire expose both what is whole and what is lacking in oneself when viewed against the object of desire. She explains:

> All at once a self never known before, which now strikes you as the true one, is coming into focus. A gust of godlikeness may pass through you and for an instant a great many things look knowable, possible, and present. Then the edge asserts itself. You are not a god. You are not that enlarged self. Indeed, you are not even a whole self, as you now see. Your

---

[123] See discussion in Jones, "Wisdom's Pedagogy."

new knowledge of possibilities is also a knowledge of what is lacking in the actual.[124]

This dynamic suggests why desire is such a prominent category for the book of Proverbs, which advances a model of educated moral selfhood, the notion that the moral self is formed by both internal and external agency.[125] The objects that one desires, which are external to the self, participate in shaping that self, insofar as they mirror a new vision of wholeness. At the same time, however, it is the self's pursuit of those objects that shapes it in their likeness. There is a reciprocal element of desire that is akin to the model of formation implicit in Proverbs. Yoder, noting the prominence of desire in chapters 1–9, insists that positive desire "empowers one's moral agency" because it makes a person look outward and turn away from the self.[126] Thus, righteous desire for wisdom, she explains, prompts justice and compassion.[127] On the other hand, foolish or evil desires "result in isolation and alienation from others."[128] She finds that desire for the strange woman, for example, is harmful because it is merely a means for selfish pleasure for both the woman and the fool. "Neither party," she states, "regards the other as a person of wholeness and identity."[129]

Yet negative desires may pose an even greater threat to the formation of the self than does sheer selfishness because any kind of desire reshapes the self in relation to the desired object. It is not that evil desires cause one to retain one's gaze on the self, but rather the problem is that they shift the student's gaze to a harmful object, prompting him to refashion the self in a destructive image. In Carson's words, the change that desire causes within a person "gives him a glimpse of a self he never knew before."[130] In this sense, the student who is enticed by negative desires glimpses his own potential to become a person formed in the likeness of the wicked or foolish objects he desires, which is precisely what the sages want their students to resist. Thus Prov 13:20 advises, "whoever walks with the wise becomes wise,[131] but the friend of fools is harmed."

---

[124] Carson, *Eros*, 36. See also Yoder, who notes that "erotic love *opens* a person. Inherent is the perception that one is limited, even incomplete, and in need of the other for wholeness" (Yoder, "The Objects of Our Affections," 83).

[125] See discussion in Chapter 4.

[126] Yoder, "The Shaping of Erotic Desire," 155.

[127] Ibid.

[128] Ibid., 151.

[129] Ibid., 160.

[130] Carson, *Eros*, 17.

[131] Reading with Qere: הולך את־חכמים יחכם (K: הלוך את־חכמים וחכם).

Within Proverbs, desire aids discipline because it can spark the knowledge that makes one aware of the need for wisdom. Proverbs utilizes the poetry of desire in order to set the youth at the edges of the self and the edges of wisdom. At this boundary, the malleable student is able to "hear discipline and become wise" (8:33), for, as Carson notes, "the self forms at the end of desire."[132] Insofar as the student desires Wisdom, she reflects to him what he lacks and should pursue: knowledge, shrewdness, righteousness. William P. Brown affirms that Wisdom describes herself as the ideal inquirer who is characterized by desirable virtues and, in so doing, "invites appropriation via imitation so that the human self can be recast in the *imago sapientiae*."[133] Yet should the youth fall prey to the negative desires of the strange woman, it threatens to shape his self in the likeness of death and destruction, for according to the book, this is what she represents. The conclusion of Prov 8 indicates the profound consequences of consummating one's desire for Wisdom – or failing to do so.

### Proverbs 8:32–36

32 Now, sons, listen to me: fortunate are those who keep my ways!
33 Listen to discipline and be wise! Do not spurn it!
34 Fortunate is the one who listens to me, vigilant by my doors day after day, guarding the entrance of my gates.
35 For the one who finds me finds life and obtains favor from YHWH.
36 But the one who rejects[134] me harms his very self – all who hate me love death.

Pursuing Wisdom and keeping vigil at her door results in divine favor and *life*, the ultimate goal of the book. On the other hand, rejecting Wisdom is akin to the desire of death, and this desire constitutes severe harm to the student's self (נפשׁ). It is a threat to the core of his being, for his נפשׁ is adulterated with death (see also 7:23, 27). The speeches of both women situate

---

Ibid., 39.
133 William P. Brown, *Wisdom's Wonder: Character, Creation, and Crisis in the Bible's Wisdom Literature* (Grand Rapids: Eerdmans, 2014), 49.
134 Murphy suggests that "miss the mark" is a fitting translation for חטא here, for "sin can be directed only against the Lord" (Murphy, *Proverbs*, 54; see also Delitzsch, *Proverbs of Solomon*, 195; Toy, *The Book of Proverbs*, 179). But it is not simply "missing" or even "offending" Wisdom (see Fox, *Proverbs 1–9*, 291) that is at issue here. Love and hatred are the poles of Wisdom's rhetoric. Failing to pursue Wisdom is equivalent to loving death, a love with which the desire of Wisdom is entirely incompatible. Wisdom is a beloved who demands an all-consuming desire from the student, who is to adhere to her ways and constantly keep watch by her gates. Spurning Wisdom is an emotional affront to the beloved. Yet this rejection is also a moral offense, tantamount to rejecting YHWH, the one in whom Wisdom delights (8:30).

the student at the edges of desire, differentiating the listener from themselves yet also calling him to mix his self with theirs. Wisdom reminds the student of the consequences for his self should he fail to pursue her.

The student's very self is at stake in the pursuit and consummation of desire, for the objects of one's desire will reflect a particular kind of lack and shape the student's self in their resemblance. It is thus no surprise that both Wisdom and the strange woman explicitly address the simpleton, for he is a malleable student whose moral self is contested. The simpleton can become wise or foolish, which is partly dependent on which desires he pursues. Proverbs indicates that desire, which is an innate capacity of all humans, whether wise or foolish, righteous or wicked, can be educated, and at stake in the education of desire is the formation of the moral self. As it talks about desire and even participates in shaping the desire of the student, the book provides a practicum in the evaluation of desire, teaching the student to measure various voices, tastes, and scents against the rubric of the father's guiding voice. In the process, character is formed, for to shape the student's character, Proverbs indicates, one must first shape his desires.

CHAPTER 7

# *The Model of Imagination*

> We must cultivate moral imagination by sharpening our powers of discrimination, exercising our capacity for envisioning new possibilities, and imaginatively tracing out the implications of our metaphors, prototypes, and narratives.[1]

> It is the cultivation of imagination which should be the chief aim of education.[2]

Imagination is indispensable to human reasoning. Imagination can take many forms, ranging from the creation of simple mental images to the construction of genuinely new ways of perception. It facilitates the exploration of yet unrealized possibilities and permits the creation of alternative worlds. Imagination is a capacity to "see as," as David J. Bryant says, which enables a person to make sense of the world and perceive human experience as meaningful.[3] Bryant thus insists that that "imagination is a sine qua non of human life."[4] The imagination's role in meaning making also makes it a profoundly important category for moral reflection. Thus Mark Johnson insists that imagination is a vital capacity for moral reasoning because it allows one to apply moral principles in unforeseen situations. "Moral principles without moral imagination," he explains, "become trivial, impossible to apply, and even a hindrance to morally constructive action."[5] On the other hand, "[m]oral imagination without principles or some form of grounding ... is arbitrary, irresponsible, and harmful."[6]

---

[1] Mark Johnson, *Moral Imagination: Implications of Cognitive Science for Ethics* (Chicago: University of Chicago Press, 1993), 198.
[2] Mary Warnock, *Imagination* (Berkeley: University of California Press, 1976), 9.
[3] David J. Bryant, *Faith and the Play of Imagination* (Studies in American Biblical Hermeneutics 5; Macon: Mercer University Press, 1989), 88.
[4] Ibid.
[5] Johnson, *Moral Imagination*, x.
[6] Ibid.

In Johnson's view, imagination and principles must go hand-in-hand in moral reasoning.

At first glance, it may seem that there is little room for imaginative thought in the proverbial worldview. The sages tread a well-worn path and disdain the road less traveled. At the same time, however, they indicate that wisdom is less a function of instruction absorbed as it is a product of instruction applied, an outcome that arises from deep understanding that allows one to evaluate correctly the surrounding world, with its attendant desires, characters, and situations of moral complexity. Accordingly, the book of Proverbs is comprised of a variety of literary forms that serve to expand the student's moral imagination and equip one with the acumen not only to understand moral precepts but to apply them correctly in new situations. In this respect, the book itself is an exemplar of imaginative moral reasoning. Within Proverbs, the imagination functions on several different levels and is most clearly evident in the development of cognitive prototypes, the extensive use of metaphor, and the use of vibrant imagery that appeals to a range of sense perceptions.

## Proverbs and the Imagination

The book of Proverbs indicates that the cultivation of imagination is vital to moral reasoning, and for this reason, it is a central aspect of the book's pedagogy. The enduring prominence in biblical wisdom scholarship of the simplicity thesis – the notion that Proverbs' wisdom is simplistic or naïve – may give one the false impression that the Israelite sages suffered from a severe lack of imagination. As Amos Wilder observes, "When imagination fails doctrines become ossified, witness and proclamation wooden, doxologies and litanies empty, consolation hollow, and ethics legalistic,"[7] a sentiment that sounds remarkably similar to the conclusions of many wisdom scholars. Yet such an impression of the sages would be as misleading as the simplicity thesis itself. To the contrary, the book of Proverbs, with its wealth of figurative language and variety of literary forms, evidences immense imagination on the part of the sages who produced it and handed it on.

Imagination, at its most basic level, has often been described simply as the capacity to create mental images. But imagination is also an essential part of the creation of meaning. More than the mere formation of images,

---

[7] Amos Wilder, *Theopoetic: Theology and the Religious Imagination* (Philadelphia: Fortress Press, 1976), 2.

the imagination is a capacity of perception insofar as it involves organizing such images into meaningful structures that allow one to make sense of the world. As Mary Warnock states, the imagination is "our means of interpreting the world,"[8] for imagination involves attaching significance to what is perceived, even to the point of creating entirely new meanings or worldviews from the innovative combination of various images. In short, imagination may refer either to the simple formation of images, a kind of reproduction, or to the production of genuinely new ways of looking at the world.[9]

Within moral reasoning, imagination has a crucial evaluative function because it allows one to project and explore various possible outcomes of a given situation. A critically important imaginative activity, John Kekes explains, is "the mental exploration of what it would be like to realize particular possibilities."[10] In this sense, the imagination can become *moral* imagination, that is, the capacity to utilize the faculty of perception to consider various possible outcomes of a particular situation and to evaluate their moral worth. In this respect, imagination is vital to moral reasoning because it allows one to foresee the potential consequences of certain actions without bringing them to full fruition. John Dewey argued that this kind of imaginative deliberation

> is an experiment in finding out what the various lines of possible action are really like. It is an experiment in making various combinations of selected elements of habits and impulses, to see what the resultant action would be like if it were entered upon.... Thought runs ahead and foresees outcomes, and thereby avoids having to await the instruction of actual failure and disaster. An act overtly tried out is irrevocable, its consequences cannot be blotted out. An act tried out in imagination is not final or fatal. It is retrievable.[11]

With the imagination, deliberation is *retrievable* – a point which illumines one of the central pedagogical values of the imagination for Proverbs. In this respect, the variety of actions, situations, and characters portrayed within the book constitute a tutorial for the student's imagination,

---

[8] Warnock, *Imagination*, 194.
[9] John Kekes suggests that "[t]he history of thought about imagination is the history of conflicts between these two views" (John Kekes, *The Enlargement of Life: Moral Imagination at Work* [Ithaca: Cornell University Press, 2006], 16).
[10] John Kekes, *The Morality of Pluralism* (Princeton: Princeton University Press, 1993), 101.
[11] John Dewey, *Human Nature and Conduct: An Introduction to Social Psychology* (New York: Henry Holt, 1922), 190. For a discussion of imaginative deliberation in Dewey's thought, see Steven Fesmire, *John Dewey and Moral Imagination: Pragmatism in Ethics* (Bloomington: Indiana University Press, 2003), 69–91.

exploring various possible outcomes and supplying their implications, all the while removing the threat of actual failure and disaster.

The association between Israelite wisdom and the imagination is not a new observation, although the significance of imagination for the peda-gogical function of the book has not been fully appreciated. Leo G. Perdue has pointed to the constitutive role of the imagination in the construc-tion of the sapiential worldview. Israelite sages, he explains, "made their way in the world, at least in part, by using common imagination to form, classify, organize, combine, and synthesize the images indirectly derived from their sense experience to articulate in the artful presentation of lan-guage their character and substance."[12] Yet imagination is not just a mat-ter of classification, but also involves the formation of a particular view of the world. In this respect, "the sages used their creative imagination in the shaping of a world view that provided the context of wise living and being."[13] In other words, the sapiential worldview of divine justice and order in the cosmos is an imaginative construction, for it involves the arrangement of various images – wise, righteous, fool, wicked, etc. – in meaningful configurations.

But the role of the imagination in Proverbs involves more than just the creation and promotion of a particular worldview; it extends to the nature of moral reasoning itself. The form of the book of Proverbs indicates that moral reasoning is fundamentally imaginative. Proverbs suggests that moral reasoning relies not on the literal application of rigid doctrines or rules, as if memorizing the book would guarantee wisdom, but instead it presumes that the proper application of one's knowledge requires the mental acuity to discern how known concepts apply to new and unforeseen situations, which is essentially an imaginative enterprise. In this respect, insights from the fields of neuroscience and cognitive linguistics can illumine some of the implicit assumptions within this ancient literature.

## Cognitive Science, Ethics, and the Moral Imagination

According to cognitive linguist Mark Johnson, human moral reasoning is fundamentally *imaginative*. It is not governed by the application of

---

[12] Leo G. Perdue, *Wisdom and Creation: The Theology of Wisdom Literature* (Nashville: Abingdon Press, 1994), 50. Perdue distinguishes between what he terms "common imagination," and "creative imagination," which is involved in the creation of a worldview. Creative imagination may have sev-eral levels, from simply placing images into a meaning system to putting images in new, innovative configurations (ibid., 50–51).

[13] Ibid., 52.

ultimate moral rules, whether they derive from divine law, human reason, or utilitarian good, but rather "our moral understanding depends in large measure on various structures of imagination, such as images, image schemas, metaphors, narratives, and so forth."[14] Johnson contends that this view of moral reasoning challenges the basic assumptions about moral reasoning in the Western philosophical tradition. In contrast to what he terms the "Moral Law folk theory," which measures moral dilemmas by moral laws that tell one what is the "right thing to do," Johnson insists that imaginative structures are fundamental to the nature of moral reasoning, not simply alternative ways to express moral laws. He explains:

> Moral reasoning is thus basically an imaginative activity because it uses imaginatively structured concepts and requires imagination to discern what is morally relevant in situations, to understand empathically how others experience things, and to envision the full range of possibilities open to us in a particular case.[15]

When confronted with a moral dilemma, imagination allows one to reason by perceiving the range of possible responses, extending known concepts or laws to new applications, projecting the implications of various possibilities, and discerning the best course. Johnson charges that the Moral Law folk theory, which is implicit in both theological and rationalist ethical traditions, is both narrow and simplistic, for it presumes a divide between cognition and embodied experience, indicates that reason governs passion, and implies that reasoning is basically a matter of knowing which moral laws to apply in which situation.[16] Johnson, however, examines the imaginative nature of the very common ways in which humans reason.

Cognitive prototypes are one of the basic conceptual structures that reveal the necessity of the imagination in moral reasoning. Research in cognitive science has suggested that humans understand categories based not by a list of features that each member of the category equally possesses, but by the measure of prototypes, in which certain elements of a category are more central than others.[17] In the category of a bird, for example, the bluebird may be more conceptually central to one's understanding of the category than other members, such as penguins or ostriches, which are still part of the category, although their features depart from the prototype

---

[14] Johnson, *Moral Imagination*, ix.
[15] Ibid., ix-x.
[16] Ibid., 7.
[17] See ibid., 78–79; 267, note 1.

to greater or lesser degrees. As a structure of moral categories, prototypes point to the complexity of moral concepts and the imaginative reasoning that most moral dilemmas require. Prototypes, Johnson argues, account for both the stability of ethical concepts *and* their indeterminacy, which requires discernment to apply such concepts to those cases that do not fit soundly at their center. Consider, for example, the category of lying. At the center of the concept are non-factual statements delivered with the intent to deceive and that, as such, are morally suspect. But what are the ethical implications of a "white lie," an exaggeration, or an honest mistake, all of which depart in varying degrees from the prototype? Such deliberation, Johnson claims, is a type of imaginative reasoning, for the solution is not clearly prescribed but requires the application of imaginative structures.

The existence of cognitive prototypes severely challenges the view of morality as a set of fixed, universal rules. Johnson argues that moral absolutism disavows

> the possibility that the fundamental moral concept (or any subsidiary concepts) might be relatively indeterminate and would thus be open to possible alternative interpretations relative to a context, set of purposes, or complex of interests. For this would mean that clarifying or determining a concept in a given context would require an evaluative decision. That, of course, would destroy the kind of objectivity that is the defining and motivating force of moral absolutism.[18]

Yet this is not the way human cognition works, Johnson suggests. It is not simply propositional and syllogistic, as absolutism presumes. Rather, as Steven Winter explains, "Propositional legal rules promise determinate answers; the imaginative and metaphoric structure of thought yields a different pattern of decision-making," which allows greater room for indeterminacy.[19] The daily encounter with non-prototypical events requires imaginative extensions of known prototypes, which defies the determinacy that moral absolutism requires.

Johnson also points to the pervasiveness of metaphor as another indication of the thoroughly imaginative nature of moral reasoning.[20]

---

[18] Ibid., 89.

[19] Steven Winter, "Transcendental Nonsense, Metaphoric Reasoning, and the Cognitive Stakes for Law," *University of Pennsylvania Law Review* 137.4 (1989): 1196; cited in Johnson, *Moral Imagination*, 102.

[20] In this work, Johnson uses the term "imagination" in contrast to the literal absoluteness of the Moral Law folk theory. All metaphor is thus imaginative, in this sense. Elsewhere, Johnson and George Lakoff refer to "imaginative metaphors" as a specific type of metaphor, which involves

Throughout the Western philosophical tradition, as well as contemporary cultural parlance, the most basic moral concepts are conceptualized by metaphor, not by literal proscriptions or absolute moral laws. For example, he argues, the metaphor MORAL INTERACTIONS ARE COMMODITY TRANSACTIONS governs how we understand the nature of obligation, responsibility, and moral value. This primary metaphor (also known as the MORAL ACCOUNTING metaphor) is realized in such expressions as "with your kindness you have *enriched* my life," which uses the metaphor WELL-BEING IS WEALTH, or "she *owes a debt* to society for her crime," which uses the metaphor IMMORAL DEEDS ARE DEBTS. Johnson insists that such metaphors are not simply conventions of language but provide the basic structure of moral understanding. "They are constitutive," he argues, "of our modes of reasoning, evaluation, and moral exploration. They are truly 'metaphors we live by.' "[21] For the metaphors by which one understands a situation will govern how one evaluates that situation and discerns how to respond to it.[22] Even moral traditions that purport to be thoroughly rational, Johnson claims, are in fact deeply imaginative in nature, for they are built on metaphors.[23]

Not only is metaphor employed in some of the most basic ways of expressing certain concepts, but moral reasoning itself is metaphorical, Johnson insists. It is metaphor that enables one to make moral judgments, for it provides differing ways of conceptualizing moral concepts and serves as the basis for applying those concepts to new situations. For example, the application of a particular prototype to a non-prototypical situation is a metaphorical extension of the concept, for a literal, one-to-one

---

innovative blends of primary metaphors, those which are part of the standard conventions of a language (George Lakoff and Mark Johnson, *Metaphors We Live By* [Chicago: University of Chicago Press, 1980], 53).

[21] Johnson, *Moral Imagination*, 52.

[22] Winter makes the interesting observation that the operative metaphors in legal reasoning have profound consequences for the interpretation of the law. As an example, he considers the case *NLRB v. Jones and Laughlin Steel Corp.*, which concerned federal oversight of labor relations in manufacturing. Winter notes that the authors of the act used the metaphor COMMERCE IS A STREAM to argue the perspective that government oversight would burden and *obstruct* the free *flow* of commerce by *controlling the flow* of raw materials or processed items into the *channels of commerce*. By this rationale, the role of the federal government is to avoid obstructions of the flow of commerce. The judge, however, used a different metaphor of COMMERCE IS A JOURNEY, reasoning that commerce is a *great movement* of goods along defined *paths*. Commerce, then, must be *protected* as it *moves along the path*, as a traveler protected along a journey. Accordingly, the government may have a role in commerce at any point along its journey, even at the "start" of the journey within the bounds of states (thus, before the goods become part of the *flow* of interstate commerce). In this sense, the JOURNEY metaphor provided the rationale for a far more expansive role of government (see Winter, "Transcendental Nonsense," and discussion in Johnson, *Moral Imagination*, 204–07).

[23] For example, see Johnson's analysis of Kant (ibid., 65–76).

correspondence is impossible. In this respect, the conceptualization and evaluation of moral dilemmas is fundamentally metaphorical. "It is principally metaphoric reasoning," Johnson suggests, "that makes it possible for us to learn from our experience. Such reasoning is necessary if we are to draw out the implications of our previous experiences for a present situation. We must be able to project beyond clear cases that are morally unproblematic to those that are either nonprototypical or completely novel in our experience."[24]

Of course the Israelite sages responsible for Proverbs were not cognitive linguists, yet the literary forms within the book suggest that the sages might agree with Johnson that "human beings are fundamentally *imaginative* moral animals."[25] The book of Proverbs is built on some of the very same imaginative structures that Johnson observes, and they suggest a primary role for moral imagination in human reasoning. Moreover, the structures within the book indicate that the cultivation of moral imagination is a central goal of the book's pedagogy. From the pervasiveness of metaphor to the presence of prototypes to the significant role of passion and emotion in discernment, Proverbs constantly resists a rigid, axiomatic application of universal moral laws. To the contrary, it enjoins the student to engage the full range of his cognitive powers – mind, body, emotion, desire – in imaginative modes of moral reasoning.

## Proverbs and Moral Prototypes

Proverbs is saturated with imaginative structures, and one of the most prominent is the prototype, which is fundamental to the way in which the book asks its student to reason. In fact, the pervasiveness of prototypes in the book has been one factor in the power of the simplicity thesis, for the constant repetition of prototypical situations and characters may leave the impression that the sages of Proverbs conceived of a black-and-white world in which the righteous always prosper and the wicked always get their just deserts. It is true that the majority of the sayings and poems in the book are situated squarely in the center of the prototype and describe a world in which the righteous and the wise are valorized, while the wicked and the fools suffer disgrace. Yet as Johnson explains, prototypes are not equivalent to absolute categories. Prototypes do provide an essential coherence and stability to moral concepts, yet they also permit some indeterminacy

[24] Ibid., 3.
[25] Ibid., 1.

in that their bounds are not rigid.[26] Situations and characters can adhere to the prototype to greater and lesser degrees. In fact, within the book of Proverbs there are several sayings that indicate an awareness of situations that are not prototypical or are on the periphery of the prototype. Such sayings are in the minority; they function to construct proverbial prototypes by delineating the edges of their bounds. Their presence underscores both the stability and the indeterminacy of the prototype. In this respect, the development of a moral prototype in Proverbs points to the implicit complexity of moral concepts.

To a certain extent, the book of Proverbs can be understood as the articulation of a single overarching moral prototype. It has many facets, to be sure, comprised of various characters, actions, and situations, yet each of these is part of a larger prototype that envisions the nature of order in the cosmos. The center of the cf. prototype consists of the sapiential understanding of the regular operation of the world. Consider, for example, the following sayings:

> *Prov 13:1* A wise son – a father's discipline;[27] but a scorner never heard rebuke.
>
> *Prov 14:24* The crown of the wise – their wealth; the foolishness[28] of fools – foolishness.
>
> *Prov 18:15* The heart of the discerning acquires knowledge, and the ear of the wise seeks knowledge.
>
> *Prov 10:3* YHWH will not let the righteous soul starve, but he will disrupt[29] the desire of the wicked.

---

[26] See ibid., 88–89.

[27] BHS proposes emending אב to אהב (cf. 12:1, אהב מוסר אהב דעת), but this is unnecessary. The juxtaposition of two images is frequent in Proverbs. Michael V. Fox also cites this saying as an example of "blunt juxtaposition" (Michael V. Fox, *Proverbs 10–31: A New Translation with Introduction and Commentary* [AB 18B; New Haven: Yale University Press, 2009], 561); see also James G. Williams, "The Power of Form: A Study of Biblical Proverbs," *Semeia* 17 (1980): 40–41.

[28] BHS proposes ולוית instead of אולת; cf. 4:9, where לוית and עטרת are parallel terms. See also the LXX: ϛτέφανος ϛοφῶν πανοῦργος ἡ δὲ διατριβὴ ἀφρόνων κακή, "a crown of the wise is cleverness, the habit of fools is foolishness." The emended text, "the garland of fools is foolishness," makes good sense, yet one could also make sense of the tautology within the MT: the foolishness of fools is pure foolishness (see also Roland E. Murphy, *Proverbs* [WBC 22; Nashville: Thomson Nelson, 1998], 102, 106). Moreover, the parallelism between עטרת and אולת subtly suggests that fools may wear their foolishness as a badge of honor or mistake it for something it is not (cf. 12:15; 26:5), yet it proves irredeemable. Foolishness is nothing more than foolishness. The terms עטרת and אולת have greater sound and rhythm resonance than if the text were to be emended, which supports reading with the MT, and the sound and rhythm of the saying in fact support the meaning. Given the close parallelism between the first two terms of each half – עטרת חכמים and אולת כסילים – the rhythm leads one to expect a term that sounds like עשרם to conclude the second colon. But instead, the last term strikes a discordant note, akin to foolishness itself.

[29] Literally, to "push away" or "thrust out" (הדף).

*Prov 10:7* The memory of the righteous, a blessing; but the name of the wicked rots.

*Prov 10:30* The righteous will never totter, but the wicked will not dwell on earth.

Each of these sayings describes some aspect of the prototype. Hearing wisdom, seeking wisdom, and receiving rebuke all lead to wisdom. Wisdom, in turn, is associated with wealth, success, and prosperity. On the other hand, fools are those who do not hear wisdom, seek wisdom, or profit from rebuke. Consequently, they are often poor, troubled, and unsuccessful. Similarly, the righteous – those who speak rightly, uphold justice, and trust in YHWH – will enjoy protection, satiety, and enduring renown, while the wicked – the ones who speak falsely, deceive others, and trust in their own powers – will fall in calamity, suffer devastation, and fade into oblivion. According to the prototype, the world is characterized by a regular pattern in which the cosmos rewards moral worth and impedes moral failure.

Yet this is not a rigid axiom, for while it may characterize how things *usually* work or are *supposed* to work, there is ample evidence that reality does not always function so smoothly. Toward the periphery of the moral prototype are partial failures of the moral mechanisms that normally ensure the reliable operation of the cosmos. As Prov 14:6a reports, "a scoffer seeks wisdom – but no result." Indeed, one can hear wisdom but not accept it, seek wisdom and not find it, or receive rebuke and not profit from it (e.g., 17:10; 27:22; 29:1). In such cases, the normal means to acquire wisdom prove ineffective. Toward the periphery of the prototype are also situations in which the wicked appear to prosper or the righteous experience hardship, even if only temporarily:

*Prov 11:8* The righteous is delivered from trouble, and the wicked goes in place of him.

*Prov 24:16* Seven times the righteous falls and rises, but the wicked stumbles in trouble.

*Prov 28:28* When the wicked rise up, humans are hidden, but when they die, the righteous increase.

*Prov 29:2* When the righteous increase, the people rejoice, but when the wicked rule, the people groan.

Within the gaps of these sayings, the non-prototypical appears. While the righteous will be delivered, they may know trouble. Although the wicked will not prevail, they may rise for a time. Such situations are ultimately still within the framework of the larger prototype. While the reversal of fortune may endure for a moment, in the final analysis, the wicked will falter and the righteous will prevail. Yet these scenarios indicate that the prototype is not a rigid axiom; it accommodates the fact that not all situations will fit solidly within its center.

While the majority of the sayings in Proverbs testify to the workings of the prototype, there are certain references to non-prototypical events. Proverbs 25:26, for example, indicates that the righteous do not always prevail: "A muddied spring[30] and a ruined fountain is the righteous tottering before the wicked." Yet even evidence of the non-prototypical functions to promote the general reliability of the prototype itself, for such events are depicted as clearly outside of the norm. Proverbs 17:15, for example, affirms that the subversion or confusion of the proper distinction between righteous and wicked is repugnant to God: "making righteous of the wicked or wicked of the righteous – both are an abomination to YHWH." The non-prototypical also serves to identify elements that are not essential to the center of the prototype. For example, Prov 28:11 indicates that wealth is not a reliable guide to wisdom, for the foolish too may possess fortune: "Wise in his own eyes, a man of wealth, but the discerning pauper (דל מבין) can search him out." The association between wisdom and wealth, in other words, is not an inviolable aspect of the prototype.

The construction of the moral prototype throughout the book has a pedagogical function, for it encourages the development of the student's moral imagination. As it familiarizes the student with the contours of the prototype, it equips him to make moral judgments in a world in which events do not always correspond evenly to the prototype. In this respect, moral reasoning is a function of the imagination, for it requires improvisation in the application of known moral paradigms to unforeseen events. As Johnson explains, prototypes themselves are inherently malleable and must undergo imaginative extensions if they are to be applied to actual moral dilemmas.[31] In this respect, a central aspect of moral development is the imaginative use of prototypes, for "each prototype has a definite structure, yet that structure must undergo gradual imaginative transformation as new situations arise."[32] Similarly, the development of the moral prototype in Proverbs is indicative not of a dogmatic, black-and-white worldview that cannot accommodate the fluctuations of reality, but rather it suggests that the complexities of reality require a thorough education in

---

[30] That is, a spring that has been trampled in (nip'al רפש; cf. Akk. rapāsu[m], to smite, thresh) and soiled.

[31] See Johnson, *Moral Imagination*, 190–92.

[32] Ibid., 192.

the prototypical moral features of the cosmos in order to equip a person to encounter ever new situations with wisdom.

The promotion of the prototype further functions to construct a particular view of the world in which the workings of the cosmos mirror and legitimate the vision of social structure that the book advances. In other words, it is not that the prototype is based on empirical reality, necessarily, nor that the prototype's depiction of the cosmic engine should be understood literally. Rather, it expresses a perspective that is linked to a social vision in the scribal community in which much is vested in hierarchy and the practices that lend themselves to the stability of that structure. Thus the prototype vests authority in the hands of God and parental teachers, and it depicts as non-prototypical both the reversal of that authority (e.g., 26:1; 30:21–23) and the failure of figures of authority (e.g., 13:24a). In a certain sense, then, the prototype does not function descriptively but prescriptively.

## Metaphor and Moral Reasoning

The pervasiveness of metaphors in Proverbs also points to the imaginative nature of moral reasoning. Metaphors are not simply poetic embellishments or an interesting way to say what could be said otherwise. Rather, metaphors participate in shaping a view of the world. Metaphors, Perdue observes, "become the semantic building blocks in the linguistic construction of reality."[33] Yet the significance of metaphor in Proverbs extends beyond the creation of a sapiential worldview; it reveals something about the nature of moral reasoning itself. As Johnson explains, "the metaphoric character of our moral understanding is precisely what makes it possible for us to make appropriate moral judgments."[34] He points out that the conceptual system of morality is structured by a complex web of metaphorical mappings, which, in turn, inform how humans make moral judgments. Metaphors provide different ways of conceptualizing situations and understanding the nature of morality.[35] Thus moral reasoning, Johnson concludes, is fundamentally imaginative in the sense that it is not strictly governed by the literal application of absolute moral laws but proceeds by metaphorical understanding of morality and social interaction.

---

[33] Perdue, *Wisdom and Creation*, 60.
[34] Johnson, *Moral Imagination*, 10.
[35] For example, see Winter's discussion of the influence of two different metaphors to conceptualize the role of government in intrastate commerce (note 22).

In their study *Philosophy in the Flesh: The Embodied Mind and Its Challenge to Western Thought,* George Lakoff and Mark Johnson likewise indicate that the analysis of the metaphorical nature of common moral concepts reveals significant insights about the nature of moral understanding and the implicit logic on which moral systems within a culture are based.[36] They insist that no moral concept can be understood apart from its metaphorical mapping on common human experience, and that understanding the range of and disjunction between certain metaphorical mappings will itself shape moral reasoning. Although Lakoff and Johnson refer particularly to moral reasoning as understood in the modern era and within the larger tradition of Western philosophy, their insights are relevant to Israelite wisdom literature, which is as thoroughly metaphorical as the later traditions that they study. In fact, many of the basic moral metaphors that Lakoff and Johnson enumerate are also found in Proverbs.

Metaphor, not the application of absolute laws or rigid doctrine, constitutes the basic building blocks of moral reasoning within Proverbs. The interlocking metaphorical webs within the book are part of schooling the student in the nature of moral reasoning. Moreover, the logic of these metaphors reveals some implicit assumptions about the nature of the moral world in the sapiential imagination. A comprehensive survey of metaphors in the book is beyond the scope of this project,[37] but the following brief survey of some of the primary generating metaphors in Proverbs will provide a representative sampling of the many metaphors used to conceptualize certain characters and concepts within the book.

### Moral Accounting

One of the primary ways in which Proverbs conceptualizes moral understanding is through the MORAL ACCOUNTING metaphor, which governs how the sages depict relations between people, the value of wisdom, and the nature of well-being. Through this metaphorical concept, which is actually a network of related metaphors, virtuous acts are conceptualized as commodity transactions. Accordingly, within Proverbs, wisdom and other values are figured as commodities that can be bought or sold. For example, Prov 23:23 admonishes the student "*buy* (קנה) truth and *do not*

---

[36] George Lakoff and Mark Johnson, *Philosophy in the Flesh: The Embodied Mind and Its Challenge to Western Thought* (New York: Basic Books, 1999), 290–334.

[37] For a thorough treatment of metaphor in wisdom literature, see Nicole Lynn Tilford, " 'Taste and See': The Role of Perception in Israelite and Early Jewish Sapiential Epistemology," (PhD diss., Emory University, 2013).

*sell* it – wisdom, discipline, and understanding!" Similarly, Prov 17:16 asks "what is *money* in the hand of a fool *to purchase* wisdom without a mind?"

The MORAL ACCOUNTING metaphor relies on the underlying metaphor WELL-BEING IS WEALTH, which is based on the notion that morality constitutes enhancing the well-being of another such that increasing another's well-being is conceived as a gain or gift to that person, while decreasing another's well-being is understood as taking something of cost from that person. As a modern example, consider the common expression, "I *owe you* one!" as a response to a kind gesture, or the belief within the justice system that a criminal is *paying his debt* to society by serving a prison sentence. Doing moral or immoral acts places one in the position of a creditor or debtor to others.[38] Within Proverbs, acting with virtue or with vice likewise places one in a position of financial gain or loss. This metaphor permeates Proverbs and, in fact, is the basis for much of the motivational pedagogy of the book.[39] Thus the father implores his son to follow the way of wisdom because it (she) will endow him with riches (e.g., 3:10, 16; 4:9). Similarly, virtuous character or activities result in wealth, while vice leads to poverty, a metaphor for the decrease in well-being (e.g., 10:4).

According to the MORAL ACCOUNTING metaphor, doing virtuous acts places one in a social network of financial exchange in which debts are owed and repaid. Thus virtuous and wicked deeds are reimbursed. For example, Prov 17:13, "one who repays (מֵשִׁיב) evil in place of good – trouble will never depart[40] from his house," conveys that those who do an evil act will be *repaid* in kind, even when they themselves transgress the moral balance – repaying a debt of good with evil, the incorrect currency. This metaphor also governs the sapiential view of God's dealings with humans, for "the one who guards your life knows, and he will repay (וְהֵשִׁיב) a person according to his work (כְּפָעֳלוֹ)." In other words, God balances the moral accounts. Indeed, this is part of the natural order of the moral universe. In fact, one can even become a creditor to YHWH by doing moral acts. Proverbs 19:17, for example, relies on the MORAL ACCOUNTING metaphor as a rationale for concern for the poor: "one who is generous to the poor *makes a loan* (מַלְוֵה) to YHWH; he will *repay* him his due (וּגְמֻלוֹ יְשַׁלֶּם־לוֹ)."[41]

[38] See Lakoff and Johnson, *Philosophy in the Flesh*, 292–98.
[39] See Chapter 5.
[40] Reading with Qere: תמיש (K: תמיש).
[41] For a discussion of the economic metaphors used for almsgiving in Proverbs, as well as in the wider biblical and post-biblical tradition, see Gary A. Anderson, *Sin: A History* (New Haven: Yale University Press, 2009), especially 139–40.

The implications of the MORAL ACCOUNTING metaphor extend to the concept of honor and shame within Proverbs. As Lakoff and Johnson explain, "Honor is a form of social capital that people get because they are the kind who pay their moral debts. Dishonor is a form of social debt that one accrues by not paying moral debts."[42] People must have confidence in the stability of the currency system and the ability to recoup debts if the financial economy is to function smoothly, and the same is true of the moral economy. Consequently, those who jeopardize the economy earn dishonor within the community. For this reason, Proverbs emphasizes that crooked dealings – and crooked currency – are abominable to God. Thus Prov 11:1: "false scales are an abomination to YHWH, but an honest weight (ואבן שלמה) his delight." In Prov 3:27–32, the concept is taken further as the father enumerates a list of dishonorable things, each of which involves dishonest or unfair exchange:

27 Do not withhold good from one owed (מבעליו) when you have the power to act.
28 Do not say to your friend, "Come back, I'll give it tomorrow," when it is with you.
29 Do not plot evil against your friend who lives in trust with you.
30 Do not litigate[43] with a person without cause when you received no trouble (אם־לא גמלך רעה).
31 Do not envy a lawless man or choose any of his ways;
32 For the crooked (נלוז) is an abomination to YHWH, but the straight are his confidant.

Each of these injunctions is predicated on a principle of just, fair transaction. Do not withhold what one is owed, and do not repay trust with violence, for such earns dishonor from God. In this sense, the concepts of honor and shame function to preserve smooth moral transactions.

### Moral Strength

The metaphor of MORAL STRENGTH informs the way in which Proverbs depicts the nature of the wise person and the utility of discipline. Like the MORAL ACCOUNTING metaphor, the MORAL STRENGTH metaphor is comprised of a series of related metaphors. In this case, the relevant metaphors are organized around the concept of strength as a trope for moral

---

[42] Lakoff and Johnson, *Philosophy in the Flesh*, 295.
[43] Reading with Qere: תריב (K: תרוב).

virtue. Lakoff and Johnson suggest that there are two primary forms of moral strength within this complex of metaphors. Strength is both the ability to maintain an upright moral posture (e.g., the metaphors BEING MORAL IS BEING UPRIGHT / BEING IMMORAL IS BEING LOW) and the ability to overcome evil, which relies on the related metaphor EVIL IS A FORCE.[44] Furthermore, moral strength can connote either moral courage (i.e., the ability to overcome external forces) or willpower (i.e., the ability to overcome internal forces, such as temptations or desires).[45] All of these aspects of the metaphorical complex are evident in Proverbs, and indeed both the righteous and the wise are embodiments of moral strength. Thus Prov 10:30a exclaims that "the righteous will never totter," while Prov 24:5–6 indicates that a wise person's strength of mind surpasses military might: "the wise is mightier than the strong, and one of knowledge more than one of great power,[46] for you should make war with strategy, and victory is in many counselors."

The clearest articulation of this metaphor is the subsidiary metaphor BEING MORAL IS BEING STRAIGHT. Within Proverbs, the Hebrew term יָשָׁר refers both to a person who is vertically straight in posture (versus one who is bowed over or low, e.g., 14:19) and one who is horizontally straight, that is, who travels on the straight path.[47] Thus the "upright" (יְשָׁרִים) are those with the moral fortitude to withstand countervailing forces, as in Prov 12:6, "the words of the wicked are a bloody ambush, but the mouth of the upright saves them" (see also 2:20–22; 11:6; 16:17). In addition, יָשָׁר can also refer to those who have received protection, a kind of strength, from wisdom, instruction, or the divine (e.g., 3:6; 4:11). Within Proverbs, this metaphor implies that strength is moral virtue, yet this kind of strength is not innate within the human person. It must be cultivated through discipline or gifted from a figure of authority.

The MORAL STRENGTH metaphor thus coheres with the strong emphasis on discipline within Proverbs, for the function of discipline is to strengthen a person as a moral agent. Lakoff and Johnson argue that

---

[44] Lakoff and Johnson, *Philosophy in the Flesh*, 300.

[45] Ibid.

[46] Reading חֲכַם־יָמָאֵם תַּעֲד־שִׂיאוֹ זַעַם סָכָה־רָבָג, as do some commentators (see Fox, *Proverbs 10–31*, 744; but cf. Murphy, *Proverbs*, 178). The LXX reflects comparative מִן: κρείςςων ςοφὸς ἰχςυροῦ καὶ ἀνὴρ φρόνηςιν ἔχων γεωργίου μεγάλου, "the wise is better than the strong, and a man of insight than one who owns a great field" (see also the Targum, אנישע זמ אמיכח ארבג בט ). The MT has חֲכ־יָמָאֵם תַּעֲד־שִׂיאוֹ זוֹעַב סָכָה־רָבָג (הילייחב זירוד זמ אתעידיד ארבגו ), "the wise man is in might, and a man of knowledge strengthens power," which also figures wisdom and knowledge as strength, although the emendation makes better sense of the line.

[47] The metaphor thus often combines with the LIFE IS A PATH metaphor.

because moral strength must be built, it must be cultivated through discipline and self-denial, just as physical strength is built through careful discipline and training. Accordingly, they explain, one consequence of the MORAL STRENGTH metaphor "is that punishment can be good for you when it is in the service of moral discipline."[48] Lakoff and Johnson point to the way in which the conceptual understanding of discipline relates to the metaphorical expression, which is grounded in human experience. Furthermore, it contains implicit assumptions about the nature of the world. As they explain, "Reward and punishment are moral in this scheme, not just for their own sake, but rather because they help the child succeed in a world of struggle and competition. To survive and compete, children must learn discipline and must develop strong character."[49] So too in Proverbs, discipline is a primary virtue that reflects a view of a fraught moral world in which only the strong survive.

Within this moral worldview, discipline is required in order to withstand countervailing forces, whether those come from internal or external temptations. The metaphor EVIL IS A FORCE infuses the entire book and is a fundamental component of how the sages understand the world. This metaphor is developed most elaborately with the figure of the strange woman, who is conceptualized as a pressing threat to the student. She is a force that acts on men, even to the point of death (e.g., 7:26). The strange woman is the personification of threatening forces that exist in the world. Yet this metaphor is operative throughout the book, implicit in such sayings as "a mallet,[50] a sword, a sharpened arrow – one who gives false witness against his fellow" (25:18), and "one who guards his mouth protects his life; one who widens[51] his lips – his ruin" (13:3).[52] The understanding of such evil forces is one of the main reasons that the motivation of security is so prominent within Proverbs. The allure of wisdom is that it offers protection from the evil forces that threaten to assault the student. Wisdom is itself a moral strength that defends its student. For this reason, the father adjures his son to attain wisdom and knowledge, for "shrewdness (מְזִמָּה) will *protect* you, and discernment will *guard* you. It will *save* you from the way of evil men" (2:11–12a).

---

[48] Lakoff and Johnson, *Philosophy in the Flesh*, 300.

[49] Ibid., 314.

[50] Reading מֵפֵץ (MT מֵפִיץ).

[51] The rare term פשק may have connotations of illicit behavior. See Ezek 16:25 (*piʿel*), where it refers to a harlot "spreading wide" her legs.

[52] Lakoff and Johnson explain that the EVIL IS A FORCE metaphor can include both internal and external forces (Lakoff and Johnson, *Philosophy in the Flesh*, 299). In the case of this saying, speech impulses (conveyed through the metonymies of "tongue" and "mouth") are figured as internal forces that one must *guard against*, for they have the capacity to *destroy* a person.

The pervasiveness of metaphors related to MORAL STRENGTH illumines a central assumption about the moral world, according to Proverbs. Virtuous character requires strength because the world itself is full of oppressive forces that threaten to assault the student and the sage alike. Furthermore, as Lakoff and Johnson explain, "by the logic of the metaphor, moral weakness is in itself a form of immorality.... A morally weak person is likely to fall, to give in to evil, to perform immoral acts, and thus to become part of the forces of evil. Moral weakness is thus nascent immorality – immorality waiting to happen."[53] This nicely accounts for a similar assumption within Proverbs and explains why the fool represents such a danger to the community. Although he may not have the nefarious intent of the wicked, nonetheless his propensity to succumb to prevailing evil forces makes him extremely liable to become part of those forces. Indeed, this is precisely why the father counsels his son to avoid their company, for fools themselves become an evil force that may lead the young son astray. As Prov 13:20 observes, "whoever walks with the wise becomes wise,[54] but the friend of fools is harmed" (see also 14:7; 26:4).

## Moral Authority

The MORAL AUTHORITY metaphor constitutes the backbone of the pedagogical logic of Proverbs and informs the guiding assumptions of the pedagogical worldview. This complex of metaphors accounts for authority in the moral world based on patterns of dominance in the physical world. The moral authority of parent over child, for example, is modeled on the physical power of adults over youth. As Lakoff and Johnson explain, "This is not a might-makes-right literal model," but rather it is a metaphorical model that grounds the logic of moral authority in physical realities.[55] While the book of Proverbs is couched in the guise of an address from a literal father to a literal son, the father's voice acquires authority based on the related metaphors A MORAL AUTHORITY IS A PARENT and A MORAL AGENT IS A CHILD. These metaphors stand behind the constant enjoinders for the student to obey the voice of the teacher, such as Prov 4:1–2, "Listen sons, to a father's discipline, and pay attention to know understanding. Good teaching I give to you. Do not abandon my instruction!" It is the figuring of the speaker's voice as a father – and the underlying metaphor

---

[53] Lakoff and Johnson, *Philosophy in the Flesh*, 300.
[54] Reading with Qere: הולך את־חכמים יחכם (K: הלוך את־חכמים וחכם).
[55] Lakoff and Johnson, *Philosophy in the Flesh*, 301.

that a father is not just another person but a moral authority – that is the logic behind this appeal.

It is evident within Proverbs that the use of these metaphors is more than figurative embellishment, but actually structures how the sages understand and view the world. In this respect, the book's hierarchical orientation is based on a metaphorical model of moral authority. Thus parents and teachers are the sources of valid instruction. The book does entertain the possibility that a parent may be inadequate to the task of his authority (e.g., 13:24), but this is a serious deviation from the expected order. Moreover, such metaphors account for the primary value of obedience in the book. Within this complex of metaphors, obedience is a figure for the moral life itself. Proverbs 30:17 puts it most vividly: "An eye that mocks father or rejects obedience to mother – ravens of the valley will peck it out and the vulture's young devour it." In other words, disobedience is the gravest form of vice.

Through the use of these metaphorical concepts, Proverbs implicitly insists that its vision of moral authority is enshrined in the natural order. Lakoff and Johnson point out that this larger metaphor, which they term the metaphor of MORAL ORDER, "legitimizes a certain class of existing power relations as being natural and therefore moral."[56] Accordingly, the metaphor implicitly suggests that other ways of configuring power relations are in fact unnatural and counter to the moral order. Proverbs 30:21–23, for example, envisions the reversal of certain power relations to be unbearable to the natural order:

21 Earth shudders at three things, and four it cannot bear:
22 A slave that becomes king, and a fool that is sated with food,
23 A despised woman who marries, and a servant who succeeds her mistress.

Furthermore, Proverbs spends a great deal of time depicting those who shame their parents as moral deviants, bringing grief and turmoil to their parents (e.g., 10:1; 15:20; 17:21, 25; 19:13; 20:20; 23:22; 28:7, 24; 30:11). Proverbs 19:26, for example, uses the language of violence to depict one who disgraces his parents: "*Assaults* father (משדד־אב) and *chases* (בריח) mother is the son who brings shame and disgrace (מביש ומחפיר)." For this

---

[56] Lakoff and Johnson give a very suspicious appraisal of this implicit logic: "The consequences of the metaphor of Moral Order are sweeping, momentous, and, we believe, morally repugnant. The metaphor legitimizes a certain class of existing power relations as being natural and therefore moral. In this way it makes certain social movements, such as feminism, appear to be unnatural and therefore counter to the moral order" (Lakoff and Johnson, *Philosophy in the Flesh*, 304).

reason, the use of metaphorical moral models in Proverbs is an important aspect of its pedagogy. Without explicitly declaring as much, the book advances a powerful argument for its own moral worldview as not simply the opinion of learned sages, but instead deriving from the nature of order itself.

## Moral Nurturance

Although Proverbs certainly advances a model of strict discipline based on metaphors of MORAL STRENGTH and MORAL AUTHORITY, other concepts, such as nurture and nourishment, are not foreign to its view of the moral world, although they imply fairly different assumptions about the nature of that world. Indeed, even as the father's words of instruction are figured as a means of protection against external forces, they are also a healing balm: "for they are life to those who find them, healing for the whole body (4:22) "(ולכל־בשׂרו מרפא; see also 16:24). Similarly, wisdom has the power to heal: "it will be healing for your body and tonic for your bones" (3:8); and acting with wisdom is also described with medicinal properties: "the tongue of the wise is healing" (12:18b). The metaphor WELL-BEING IS HEALTH is part of the operative logic of these sayings. Accordingly, wisdom or doing virtuous acts constitutes a restorative elixir. Conversely, foolishness, wickedness, and other various vices are a threat to one's health. Proverbs 14:30, for example, indicates that "a healing heart is life to the flesh, but passion is rot to the bones." Furthermore, just as wisdom has the potential to heal the body, so also it nourishes and sustains. Thus wisdom is figured as rich food (e.g., 23:13–14), and both wisdom and righteousness are called a "fountain of life" (מקור חיים, 10:11; 14:27; 16:22; see also 13:14).

This complex of metaphors provides a slightly different way of conceptualizing the nature of the moral world than do those metaphors associated with authority, strength, and order. As opposed to the logic of financial exchange or obedience to authority, the metaphors of health and nourishment understand the moral world in terms of nurture. Lakoff and Johnson argue that the metaphor of MORAL NURTURANCE is based on a model of the family in which the role of parents is to nurture, love, care for, feed, and protect their children.[57] The metaphor, they explain, "maps this practical necessity for nurture onto a moral obligation to nurture

---

[57] They contrast this with the "strict father" model of the family, which privileges the top-down authority and strict discipline of the paternal figure (ibid., 313–16).

others."⁵⁸ This model of the family is thus projected onto society as a whole, which results in a different conception of moral obligation. Rather than remuneration or respect for hierarchical authority, the relationship between people is governed by a mutual obligation to care for and promote the health of others, as parents do for their children. This model tends to emphasize empathy and care more than equity and authority.

Within Proverbs, even as obedience and honest dealings are central values, there is evidence that MORAL NURTURE is a meaningful concept in understanding a certain facet of societal relations. Thus the emphasis on right speech is described in terms of its healing capacity, not simply its conformance to an established rule. The ethic of care for the poor is based, in part, on placing oneself in the other's position. Thus Prov 21:13, "One who shuts his ear to the cry of the poor will cry out himself and not be answered" (see also 29:7). In this sense, motivation for moral action comes not from collecting what one is owed, but from envisioning the plight of another.

Indeed, the diversity of metaphors within the book – and the differing conceptions implicit within them – indicates a certain complexity inherent in the sage's view of the moral world. Proponents of the simplicity thesis often emphasize the presence of a "doctrine of retribution" in the book, which operates with the MORAL ACCOUNTING metaphor, but that metaphor, although prominent within Proverbs, does not have exclusive domain. This is not to say, however, that all metaphors are equally weighted. Within a coherent moral system, certain metaphors are inevitably privileged over others, yet this does not require that the system as a whole be entirely uniform. With respect to modern moral systems, Lakoff and Johnson insist:

> We do not have a monolithic, homogeneous, consistent set of moral concepts. For example, we have different, inconsistent, metaphorical structurings of our notion of well-being, and these are employed in moral reasoning. Which one we use, such as Well-Being Is Wealth versus Well-Being Is Health, will depend on the hierarchical structuring imposed by family-based moral systems as well as our purposes, interests, and the particular context we find ourselves in. There is no single, internally consistent concept of well-being that incorporates both of these metaphorical structures.⁵⁹

Within Proverbs, too, there is not a monolithic set of concepts, although ultimately the book's moral understanding is organized by the hierarchical

⁵⁸ Ibid., 310.
⁵⁹ Ibid., 330.

model, which privileges metaphors of MORAL STRENGTH, MORAL AUTHOR-
ITY, and MORAL ORDER, more than MORAL NURTURANCE. Even so, the
presence of other metaphors indicates that Proverbs' moral world is more
complex than first meets the eye.

The abundance of moral metaphors throughout Proverbs, both in
chapters 1–9 and the sayings, reveals the thoroughly metaphorical nature
of sapiential moral understanding and its attendant complexity. Although
there is a high degree of coherence among the metaphors, not all are
entirely consistent with one another. In fact, the particular metaphorical lens through which one views a specific situation may result in dramatically different conclusions. For example, some sayings advise restraint
in speech, figuring the tongue as a powerful and potentially destructive
force, as in "the one who *guards* (שמר) his mouth and his tongue *protects*
(שמר) himself from trouble" (21:23). Proverbs 25:15 speaks of the power of
even a restrained tongue, "with patience a ruler is persuaded (יפתה), for a
soft tongue breaks bone." However, other sayings emphasize the healing
nature of right speech; for example, Prov 15:4a, "the tongue's balm (מרפא
לשון) is a tree of life."[60] By the logic of this metaphor, withholding such
speech may be detrimental to the patient. What, then, is a person to do?
Is the tongue destructive or healing? Of course, it can be both. Yet in any
given situation, such differences cannot be entirely reconciled; one must
privilege one metaphor over the other. In this respect, Proverbs seeks to
form not moral automatons, but those who have the moral acuity to discern the proper course of action – and the proper metaphors to privilege –
for a given situation.

## Imagining Alternatives

The role of imagination in Proverbs is not limited to its function in prototypes and metaphors, but it also extends to the nature of discernment.
Throughout the book, discernment requires the evaluation of competing
possibilities and perspectives. This is particularly evident in the binary
oppositions that pervade the sayings, as well as the presentation of opposing women characters in chapters 1–9. Moreover, the way in which the
book advances these alternatives is a significant pedagogical tool in fostering discernment, which requires a vibrant imaginative capacity, within the
student. The imagination allows, as Kekes says, "the mental exploration of

---

[60] The second half of the line employs the metaphor of the tongue's destructive potential, "but devi-
ousness (סלף) in it breaks the spirit."

*what it would be like* to realize particular possibilities."[61] That is, one can envision the consequences without actualizing them. As Dewey explained, one of the chief attributes of imaginative reasoning is that various possibilities can be considered, yet are ultimately "retrievable."[62]

In this sense, the form of Proverbs functions to educate the student's imagination, for it enacts the consequences of wisdom and foolishness as it guides the student to evaluate the various possibilities in a way that aligns with the sages' viewpoint. This technique is particularly evident in the extended descriptions of liaisons with various women through the poems of chapters 1–9. Not only do the poems present strikingly different possibilities before the student, but the vibrant depiction of these alternatives through vivid imagery and sophisticated use of metaphor enhances the tangibility of each prospect. As an example, I will consider Prov 5, which juxtaposes the figures of two women: the strange woman and the wife of one's youth (אשת נעוריך). Yet these possibilities are not merely set alongside one another, leaving the reader without any guidance to evaluate their competing claims. Rather, the way in which the poem weaves images and metaphors between the two alternatives leads to moral evaluation. Indeed, this poem displays the "thinking process" of poetry.[63]

*Proverbs 5*

*1* My son, pay attention to my wisdom! Toward my understanding bend your ear!

*2* So to keep shrewdness – let your lips guard knowledge!

*3* For the lips of a strange woman are dripping honey; her mouth is smoother than oil.

*4* But afterwards – bitter as wormwood, sharp as a double-edged sword![64]

*5* Her feet go down to death, her steps seize Sheol –

*6* Lest she tread[65] the path of life – her tracks wander, she does not know.

---

[61] Kekes, *The Morality of Pluralism*, 101; emphasis added.

[62] Dewey, *Human Conduct*, 190.

[63] See Chapter 3.

[64] חרב פיות, literally a "sword of mouths." Fox explains that a blade of a sword is thought of as a "mouth" that "eats" its victims (see Judg 3:16; Fox, *Proverbs 10–31*, 192). See also Joshua Berman, "The 'Sword of Mouths' (Jud. III 16; Ps. CXLIX 6; Prov. V 4): A Metaphor and Its Ancient Near Eastern Context," *VT* 53 (2002): 291–303.

[65] The interpretation of פן־תפלס is difficult. The verb פלס means either to observe (see v. 21; cf. Akk. *palāsu*, "to see") or to make way (see Isa 26:7; Ps 78:50; cf. Akk. *palāšu*, "to pierce, break in to"). תפלס could be analyzed either as a second- or third-person form. Thus the phrase may imply either that the strange woman is the one who avoids either walking in or gazing on the straight path *or* that she impedes the youth ("you") from doing so. Indeed, the Hebrew permits ambiguity, and both resonances may very well be operative. Yet the collage of images in verses 5–6 emphasizes the strange woman's activity and her deliberate avoidance of the path of life. Fox thus translates, "she

*7* Now my sons listen to me! Do not turn from the words of my mouth!

*8* Keep your path far from her – don't near the opening[66] of her door!

*9* Lest you give your vigor to others or your years to a cruel one,

*10* Lest strangers sate themselves on your strength as you toil in a foreigner's house.

*11* You will groan afterwards when your flesh and blood[67] are consumed.

*12* Then you will say, "How I hated discipline! My heart rejected reproof!

*13* I did not listen to the voice of my teacher, I did not bend my ear towards my instructor!

*14* How quickly I am in every trouble in the midst of the whole assembly."[68]

*15* Drink water from your own cistern, flowing water from your own well!

*16* Your streams are scattered about – channels of water in the squares:[69]

*17* May they be for you alone – no strangers with you!

*18* May your fountain be blessed: take joy in the wife of your youth,

*19* A loving doe, a graceful goat – may her breasts saturate you in every season, in her love may you always grow drunk![70]

*20* Why would you be intoxicated with a strange woman, my son? Cling to the foreigner's bosom?

*21* For the ways of a man are before the eyes of YHWH, he watches all of his tracks.[71]

*22* The iniquities of the wicked trap him, seized in the ropes of his sin.

*23* He will die without discipline, drunk on his great foolishness.

The visceral description of the strange woman in this poem endows her with a certain measure of appeal, facilitating, at least at first glance, a

---

refuses to go straight in the path of life" (Fox, *Proverbs 1–9*, 192–93). On the other hand, the ambiguity of the form תפלס may foreshadow the explicit address to the sons in the following verse. So Murphy, "lest you observe the path of life" (Murphy, *Proverbs*, 30).

[66] פתח, here a double entendre for the "opening" of the house, i.e., the door, and the "opening" of the body, a euphemism for genitalia.

[67] בשׂרך ושׁארך, literally "your flesh and your body."

[68] בתוך קהל ועדה, literally "in the midst of assembly and congregation," but here a hendiadys for the entire assembly.

[69] Some translations interpret the line as an implicit question, i.e., "Should your springs be scattered abroad, streams of water in the streets?" (NRSV; see also Murphy, *Proverbs*, 30), yet the line is not marked as such (cf. v. 20). In this way, it implicitly indicts the student as if he had already propagated his promiscuous waters.

[70] The verb שׁגה means to stagger from intoxication or, metaphorically, to err, i.e., to stumble from the right path (see Ps 119:21, 118). Here it has a positive connotation of imbibing on the drink of one's wife's love, yet the negative overtones of the term are operative in the other two occurrences of the root (vv. 20, 23).

[71] With the repetition of פלס and מעגלת, the image echoes verse 6, while turning it on its head. Here פלס has the meaning "to see," as YHWH observes the tracks of the human. The strange woman, meanwhile, walks in tracks that lead one astray.

rather generous concession to her potential to entice. Within the discourse of the poem, this character is not an abstraction or even a completely unambiguous caricature. She is depicted, at least momentarily, with a measure of legitimate appeal. Moreover, her appeal is not simply a utilitarian offer of wealth or well-being, but a sensual enticement that leads the student to evaluate her texture and taste. Her lips drip with honey, and even the sound of the Hebrew phrase is pleasing to the ear: נפת תטפנה שפתי זרה, the resounding /n/, /t/, /f/, and /â/ sounds allowing the words themselves to drip smoothly off of the tongue. The image is almost identical to that of the desired beloved in Song 4:11, "Honey drips from your lips, O bride (נפת תטפנה שפתותיך כלה); honey and milk are under your tongue." The second half of verse 3 extends the image of dripping liquid to oil, providing another visceral image of the texture of her speech. Yet the sweetness and smoothness of the strange woman are ephemeral. Verse 4 also employs vivid imagery to turn the tastes and textures of verse 3 on their head; sweet becomes bitter, and smooth becomes sharp; honey turns to wormwood, and oil to a sword. With two lines, the poem evokes the range of touch and taste sensations. This is not dry description, but language of bodily experience that draws on the senses in appeal to the student's imagination.

The father's commentary provides certain constraints on the way in which the strange woman is envisioned in an effort to educate the student's moral imagination. Although she is envisioned with some measure of appeal,[72] she is ultimately granted little legitimacy, for the father controls the way in which she is imagined. In so doing, he in effect educates the student's imagination to view her one particular way and not another. Indeed, one of the subtle ways in which the poem forms the student's imagination of the strange woman is the use of certain metaphors to envision the implications of following her path. The strange woman is a moral deviant, for her path departs from the straight course and leads to death (vv. 5–6). In turn, the father admonishes the son to keep his own path far from her (v. 8), for to do otherwise would be to give one's very life to another (פן־תתן לאחרים הודך). Here the MORAL ACCOUNTING metaphor, which is operative in the notion that one's הוד is something of value that is *given away*, combines with the metaphor LIFE IS A PATH, using familiar concepts of paths and financial exchange to conceptualize the cost of the strange woman's ways.

---

[72] The wicked woman in 4Q184, by contrast, is imagined with no appeal whatsoever. For a discussion, see Scott C. Jones, "Wisdom's Pedagogy: A Comparison of Proverbs VII and 4Q184," *VT* 53 (2003): 65–80.

By the midpoint of the poem, the MORAL STRENGTH metaphor comes to the forefront, implying that one who succumbs to the strange woman will wish he had developed greater strength to withstand her ways (v. 12). If only he had submitted to discipline! As the poem unfolds, the metaphors layer on top of one another, providing multiple images of the consequences, costs, and dangers of this woman.

However, when a second woman – the wife of one's youth – is introduced (v. 15) a different set of metaphors colors the way in which this new possibility is imagined. The poem shifts from the complex of MORAL ACCOUNTING and MORAL STRENGTH metaphors to those of NOURISHMENT. In verse 15, a complex of water metaphors is used to speak of the fulfillment of lovemaking with one's own wife, as sexuality is figured as a substance that one can *drink*. Here again, the imagery of the poem is strikingly similar to that of the Song of Songs. Compare Song 4:15, in which the beloved calls his lover "a garden spring, a well of living water, and flowing streams from Lebanon" (cf. Song 4:12). Verse 19 elaborates further, describing the wife as lovely animals; her breasts provide nourishment, satiation, and intoxication. While the first half of the poem used metaphorical language of the loss of physical and financial prowess to convey the danger of sexual liaison, the water metaphors convey the nourishment and satisfaction that it can bring. In so doing, the poem provides two strikingly different ways for the student to conceptualize women and lovemaking. In this sense, the lesson is in the metaphor. One possibility *costs*, while the other *nourishes*.

When the NOURISHMENT metaphor combines with a metaphor of INTOXICATION (i.e., LOVEMAKING IS INTOXICATION[73]) in the final verses of the poem, it draws attention to the divergent ways of these two women and leads to the direct point of evaluation. With verse 19, the use of a triplet line – the only one in the entire poem – signals a shift in the use of the NOURISHMENT metaphor. Not only does a wife's love nourish and give life in its abundance, but it becomes an intoxicating substance: "may her breasts *saturate* you (דדיה ירוך) in every season, in her love may you always *grow drunk* (תשגה)." Here drunkenness is a figure of satiation, abundant nourishment, and delight. However, the threefold repetition of שגה in the last five lines of the poem points to the ambiguity of the metaphor. Intoxication can also be dangerous, a figure for impaired judgment, leading to the very opposite of healthy nourishment: death. Verse

---

[73] This metaphor is realized differently depending on whether the image is drawing on satisfaction or impairment as properties of intoxication.

20a functions as a hinge in the second half of the poem, for the same form of the verb is repeated again (תשׁגה) yet the final term of the clause – בזרה – turns the meaning on its head: "Why do you grow drunk, my son – *with a strange woman?*" Suddenly intoxication has become a trope for foolishness, which is underscored by the final line of the poem: "he will die without discipline, drunk (ישׁגה) on his great foolishness." Indeed, the figure of health has become its very opposite: death.

The metaphors are a tool of evaluation throughout the poem, serving as an imaginative lens through which the student will view the alternative possibilities. In fact, the dominant metaphors of the first half of the poem return in these last lines, melding with the metaphor of INTOXICA-TION to underscore the multiple dangers that the foreign woman's path presents. The MORAL STRENGTH metaphor is implicit in verse 21, as the iniquities are figured as forces with the ability to seize the wicked person,[74] who lacks the ability to disentangle himself, and the PATH metaphor becomes a cipher not just for the habits of the strange woman but of the measure by which God evaluates humanity. In this respect, the poem thoroughly mixes the two dominant sets of metaphors – NOURISHMENT and STRENGTH – that had been thematic structuring devices to separate two primary sections of the poem. The shifting nuances in the metaphors subtly indicate that careful discernment is required in moral reasoning, for metaphors themselves are multivalent.

As a whole, the poem functions as an imaginative exercise in exploring alternative possibilities. By its use of vivid imagery, it appeals to the student's senses; by its metaphorical reasoning, it guides the student to conceptualize the sanctioned way differently than the alternative. The poem relies on the form and the figures of poetry to make its argument and lead the student toward the desired evaluation. Its "logic" unfolds by metaphor, imagery, and allusion, not simply by the presentation of theses and refutations. In this respect, the poetic form is central to the way in which the book appeals to the imagination and, consequently, its pedagogical method.

This technique is certainly not isolated to chapter 5. Indeed, within each collection alternative situations, characters, and actions are stationed next to one another, while the particular images, metaphors, and language that are used to envision them subtly – or not so subtly – lead the student to the moral evaluation sanctioned by the sages. In Prov 1–9 as a whole,

---

[74] The metaphor is underscored by the repetition of the root תמך, which occurs here and in verse 5 with reference to the strange woman's steps that "seize" Sheol.

for example, the juxtaposition of the strange woman and woman Wisdom points to the stark distinctions between them and the consequences of following one path or the other, even as their depictions have enough similarity in language and image to invite comparison.

## The Moral Imagination of Proverbs as Didactic Poetry

While particular examples of individual sayings and poems have been the focus of this chapter, genres as a whole evidence and advance moral commitments. Thus far, I have examined the ways in which specific texts in Proverbs function to appeal to and expand the student's moral imagination, but one can also consider the moral imagination of the genre of the book – namely, that of didactic poetry. Historically, didactic literature has won few admirers among literary critics and moral philosophers. So much so, in fact, that very little work has been devoted to the particular ways in which the generic conventions of didactic literature function to promote particular moral commitments. Most of the work that has been done, moreover, has focused on didactic narrative, and while this is a useful starting point from which to consider the moral imagination of Proverbs, it has certain limits in illuminating the particular features of didactic poetry.

Didactic narrative privileges coherence at the expense of multivalency and absoluteness at the expense of ambiguity, promoting itself as a unitary and authoritative form of truth. In turn, it positions the reader as its receptive student, leaving little alternative to imbibing its view of the moral landscape. Carol A. Newsom, relying on the work of literary critic Susan Rubin Suleiman, explains that "[w]ithin the world of didactic narrative, truth is neither plural nor elusive nor contestable but is unitary, unambiguous, and absolute. Voices of authority, clearly marked within the text, convey truth to the presumptively compliant reader."[75] Accordingly, didactic literature values coherency of the moral world and uses its literary form to create such an effect. To this end, it often eliminates extraneous details and privileges structures of redundancy, such as repetition of the same events happening to multiple characters or the same commentary by the narrator repeated over the course of the work.[76]

---

[75] Carol A. Newsom, *The Book of Job: A Contest of Moral Imaginations* (New York: Oxford University Press, 2003), 42. See also Susan Rubin Suleiman, *Authoritarian Fictions: The Ideological Novel as a Literary Genre* (New York: Columbia University Press, 1983).

[76] For an extensive typology of various structures of redundancy, see ibid., 159–70.

Anything that would threaten the coherency of the moral world, such as the introduction of alternative voices or perspectives, is either excluded from view or soundly dismissed. "Much is invested," Newsom notes, "in simply not seeing what does not fit."[77]

Within Proverbs, one can certainly see the propensity toward coherence and redundancy in that the frequent repetition of terminology, characterizations, and commentary serves to reinforce the validity of its content. In this manner, Proverbs creates a world of coherence that privileges consistency, obedience, and clarity. Furthermore, Proverbs indicates that its truth corresponds to reality and is a reliable guide for action in the world. It also prizes the hierarchical relationship of parent to child, which allows the text to promulgate a coherent moral world established by the singular voice of the parent. In this respect, moral truth is unitary in Proverbs. While other perspectives are at times acknowledged, their legitimacy is ultimately undermined by the parent's guiding voice. For this reason, it indeed has "a necessarily authoritarian relationship to meaning."[78]

Didactic narrative also advances the absoluteness of its unitary moral truth, and for this reason it privileges principle, not situation, in moral reasoning. Newsom states that within didactic literature, "[t]ruth is propositional, and good and successful conduct is in the broadest sense a matter of knowing and applying the rules, that is, the fundamental principles that are not dependent on context."[79] Here, however, Proverbs departs from one of the main features of didactic narrative in its extraordinary emphasis on context, not simply principle, in moral action. Proverbs privileges the moral discernment that changing contexts constantly require. Truth may be "propositional" to the extent that wisdom is a matter of having deep understanding of the moral order and acting accordingly, yet the rote application of rules will not suffice. Kathleen M. O'Connor thus notes that the literary form of Proverbs draws attention to the ambiguous nature of reality and the limitations of absolute principles. In setting contradictory sayings side-by-side, presenting riddles, or openly acknowledging the limits of human wisdom, the book "requires that readers enter

---

[77] Newsom, *The Book of Job,* 46. Suleiman refers to this feature of didactic literature as "repressive righteousness." It is repressive in its authoritarian disposition. In didactic literature, she explains, "the 'correct' interpretation of the story is inscribed in capital letters, in such a way that there can be no mistaking it" (Suleiman, *Authoritarian Fictions,* 10). At the same time, it is righteous in the sense that it advances its claims as the best or true or right interpretation.
[78] Newsom, *The Book of Job,* 42.
[79] Ibid., 46.

into the ambiguity themselves and discover their own resolutions to the conflict of truths."[80] She elaborates:

> According to wisdom, life is not a simple set of truths to be followed scrupulously, but a continual encounter with conflicting truths, each making competing claims upon the seeker. Wisdom views life as paradoxical, requiring discernment from situation to situation of how, when and if one should act.[81]

It is precisely in the poetic form of the text that Proverbs resists the absoluteness of didactic narrative. This is not to say, of course, that Proverbs creates a world of incoherent ambiguity. Its coherence rests in the reliable and discernible nature of the moral order it depicts. However, its very form points toward the limits of that order.

Didactic literature enshrines the unitary nature of its truth in voices of hierarchical authority. Within didactic literature, one does not find truth for oneself, but it is mediated through a hierarchical relationship. For this reason, the parent-child metaphor is often employed in didactic literature, and Newsom suggests that this implies certain constraints on the development of the child as moral agent: "Moral maturity within this perspective would consist of receptively internalizing the values of the authorizing voices, not becoming an autonomous and critical moral agent."[82] The high regard for authority within Proverbs raises the question of the extent to which Proverbs "infantilizes" the reader.[83] Newsom suggests that within didactic narrative, moral maturity is realized by internalizing the voices of authority. Imaginative or critical thought is not valued. On the one hand, Proverbs certainly encourages the student to internalize the father's counsel. Yet at the same time, the form of the text may subtly permit the development of a more independent capacity of moral agency. As O'Connor writes:

> Proverbial wisdom assumes that people are capable of choosing, are free to choose, indeed, must choose their own course of action in life. The reason for this emphasis is that life is ambiguous and multivalent. No predetermined recipe, blueprint or teaching can prepare one for all the turns and permutations of life. Though some of the proverbs are quite dogmatic and

---

[80] Kathleen M. O'Connor, *The Wisdom Literature* (Message of Biblical Spirituality 5; Collegeville: Liturgical Press, 1988), 20.

[81] Ibid., 19.

[82] Newsom, *The Book of Job*, 46.

[83] By placing the reader in the subject position of a child schooled by an authority figure, Suleiman argues, didactic narrative in effect "infantilizes the reader" in exchange for the stability and security of paternal assurance (Suleiman, *Authoritarian Fictions*, 10–11).

prescriptive in tone, appearing to contradict this claim, few teach behaviors
that are universally applicable.[84]

Proverbs does not suggest the possibility of completely innovative
moral agency apart from the wisdom of received instruction. Yet as
it acknowledges the limits of wisdom and employs imaginative – and
indeterminate – literary structures such as metaphors and prototypes, it
implies that the authoritarian relationship to meaning is not absolute,
which permits some degree of room for the development of the student
as moral agent, not simply ignorant infant.

Although it shares similar features, didactic poetry, at least in the case
of Proverbs, has a slightly different manner of moral perception than does
didactic narrative, and to confuse the genres leads to mistaken assumptions about the nature of Proverbs. Some of the standard approaches to
the book of Proverbs have read it with the generic conventions of didactic
narrative in mind, which has produced the impression of greater determinacy than is actually warranted by the text. Suleiman suggests that a
popular plot model within works of didactic fiction is what she terms the
"apprenticeship model," in which the main character of the story moves
from ignorance to knowledge and from passivity to action.[85] Many scholars have read Proverbs as a book with a similar scheme in mind. However,
as we have seen, this is inadequate to the form of the book.[86] There is no
clear resolution at the end of the book, as if the neophyte addressed in
chapter 1 is a full-fledged sage by chapter 31. To the contrary, the poetic
form of the book prohibits resolution and linear progression. Moreover,
the lack of a coherent narrative plot across the book results in a different
moral imagination. Rather than absolute coherency, the poetic medium
presents episodic situations and highly contextual admonitions, not all
of which are entirely consistent with one another. Far from simplicity or
doctrinaire rigidity, the poetic form requires of its student the imagination
and perception to become a moral agent who can navigate the episodicity
of the moral world.

[84] O'Connor, *The Wisdom Literature*, 40.
[85] Suleiman, *Authoritarian Fictions*, 65.
[86] See discussion in Chapter 2 and Chapter 3.

# PART III

# Narrative, Poetry, and Personhood

CHAPTER 8

# Narrative, Poetry, and Personhood

Narrative writing centers on a sequence of events, or in the quan-
titative version, a sequence of variables. This sequence of events or
variables explains the phenomenon of interest. By contrast, lyrical
writing centers on an image or images. These are viewed in different
ways, through different lenses, to evoke the sources of the writer's
emotional reaction.[1]

The poetic form of Proverbs is a vital aspect of how the text makes meaning and thus how it shapes the moral universe of its readers. As Gerhard
von Rad so aptly observed decades ago, "in no circumstances can [the
poetry] be considered to be an insignificant, external feature. Indeed, this
peculiarity cannot be separated from the intellectual process as if it were
something added later; rather, perception takes place precisely in and
with the poetic composition."[2] The text uses the resources of its poetry to
achieve its pedagogical goals of character formation. Discipline is both discussed and enacted as the poems cultivate the student's faculty of perception by appealing to the senses, emotions, desires, and imagination. While
for heuristic purposes I have separated Proverbs' modes of formation into
discrete categories – rebuke, motivation, desire, imagination – these models work in concert. Each impinges on the others and contributes to a
holistic view of the moral self. Moreover, Proverbs resists a strongly narratival conception of character in which character is viewed as the outcome
of a quest or the conclusion of a plot. In this respect, Proverbs offers a
unique contribution to the articulation of character not only within biblical literature but, more broadly, in the character ethics project writ large.

[1] Andrew Abbott, "Against Narrative: Preface to a Lyrical Sociology," *Sociological Theory* 25 (2007): 76.
[2] Gerhard von Rad, *Wisdom in Israel* (trans. James D. Martin; London: SCM Press, 1972; repr.,
Harrisburg: Trinity Press International, 1993), 24.

## The Emplotment of Character

Central to many approaches to character ethics is the assumption that character has meaning primarily – even *only* – through narrative, a linear sequence of events that are meaningfully connected into a coherent plot. Narrative, in this sense, refers to a kind of rationality that provides the lens through which character, virtue, and personhood are articulated.[3] Alasdair MacIntyre, for example, maintains that "[n]arrative history of a certain kind turns out to be the basic and essential genre for the characterization of human actions."[4] In this sense, "narrative" refers not necessarily to a particular literary form by which the events of a person's life are told, but, more broadly, to the way in which human action is characterized: as part of a series of events in a larger plot. Not only is narrative the privileged rationality for MacIntyre, but it defines the way in which selfhood is understood. Thus, MacIntyre insists that "the unity of a virtue in someone's life is intelligible only as a characteristic of a unitary life, a life that can be conceived and evaluated as a whole."[5] For this reason, the conception of selfhood that he advances is characterized by "a self whose unity resides in the unity of a narrative which links birth to life to death as a narrative beginning to middle to end."[6] Similarly, Stanley Hauerwas and David B. Burrell go so far as to say that "character and moral notions *only* take on meaning in narrative."[7] Their conception of character involves a teleological trajectory toward a particular end, which is known and communicated through narrative.[8] Thus they argue that character is "the cumulative source of human actions. Stories themselves attempt to probe that source and discover its inner structure by trying

---

[3] See the discussion in Chapter 2.

[4] Alasdair MacIntyre, *After Virtue: A Study in Moral Theory* (2nd ed.; Notre Dame: University of Notre Dame Press, 1984), 208. He explains, "We place the agent's intentions, I have suggested, in causal and temporal order with reference to their role in his or her history; and we also place them with reference to their role in the history of the setting or settings to which they belong. In doing this, in determining what causal efficacy the agent's intentions had in one or more directions, and how his short-term intentions succeeded or failed to be constitutive of long-term intentions, we ourselves write a further part of these histories" (ibid.)

[5] Ibid., 205.

[6] Ibid.

[7] Stanley Hauerwas with David B. Burrell, "From System to Story: An Alternative Pattern for Rationality in Ethics," in Stanley Hauerwas et al., *Truthfulness and Tragedy: Further Investigations in Christian Ethics* (Notre Dame: University of Notre Dame Press, 1977), 15; emphasis added.

[8] They define narrative as "a connection among elements (actions, events, situations) which is neither one of logical consequence nor of mere sequence. This connection seems rather designed to move our understanding of a situation forward by developing or unfolding it. We have described this movement as gathering to a point" (ibid., 28).

to display how human actions and passions connect with one another to develop a character."[9] By the logic of Hauerwas, Burrell, MacIntyre, and others, narrative gives particular insight about the human person and in fact serves as the organizing paradigm of selfhood.[10]

Similarly, Paul Ricoeur draws a close connection between narrative and selfhood, although he makes a greater distinction between narrative as literary fiction and the stories enacted in actual experience. Literary fiction provides an organizational paradigm for human life and, in this sense, provides an opportunity for ethical reflection. As Ricoeur explains,

> It is precisely because of the elusive character of real life that we need the help of fiction to organize life retrospectively, after the fact, prepared to take as provisional and open to revision any figure of emplotment borrowed from fiction or from history. In this way, with the help of narrative beginnings which our reading has made familiar to us, straining this feature somewhat, we stabilize the real beginnings formed by the initiatives (in the strong sense of the term) we take. And we also have the experience, however incomplete, of what is meant by ending a course of action, a slice of life. Literature helps us in a sense to fix the outline of these provisional ends.[11]

Narrative becomes an organizational scheme because, in fact, much of human life resists the clear construction of a plot's beginning and ending. As Ricoeur acknowledges, a narrative beginning of one's life is "lost in the hazes of early childhood" and both one's birth and one's death are recounted only in the stories of others.[12] Narrative plot thus provides a form that lends coherence to character; it is what mediates between the contingency of experiences and the unity of a character.[13] For Ricoeur, narrative is what holds together the concordance of character – its essential

---

[9] Ibid., 29.

[10] See also Charles Taylor, who argues that humans understand their lives in a narrative because they make sense of their lives as a larger trajectory toward the good: "because we cannot but orient ourselves to the good, and thus determine our place relative to it and hence determine the direction of our lives, we must inescapably understand our lives in narrative form, as a 'quest'" (Charles Taylor, *Sources of the Self: The Making of the Modern Identity* [Cambridge: Harvard University Press, 1989], 51–52). In addition, see Paul Ricoeur, *Time and Narrative* (trans. Kathleen McLaughlin and David Pellauer; Chicago: University of Chicago Press, 1990), trans. of *Temps et récit* (Paris: Seuil, 1983–1985); and Anthony Paul Kelby, *Narrative and the Self* (Studies in Continental Thought; Bloomington: Indiana University Press, 1991).

[11] Paul Ricoeur, *Oneself as Another* (trans. Kathleen Blarney; Chicago: University of Chicago Press, 1992), 162.

[12] Ibid., 160.

[13] Ricoeur defines character as "the set of distinctive marks which permit the reidentification of a human individual as being the same" (ibid., 119).

unity or sameness – and the discordance of human action. Through the plot of a story, contingent events take on temporal connection and significance. Thus, "the narrative constructs the identity of the character, what can be called his or her narrative identity, in constructing that of the story told. It is the identity of the story that makes the identity of the character."[14]

Yet this narrative mode of rationality has certain limitations and need not be the only mode through which one views the moral life. Narrative rationality is sequential, with a beginning, middle, and end. It has a plot that gives meaning to one's character and is the lens through which the integrity of the moral life is evaluated. However, Galen Strawson counters that one can also have an episodic sense of rationality, in which events are not necessarily connected to the past or the future.[15] Such an episodic perspective can, Strawson argues, be deeply moral, although it tends to privilege present experience apart from any connection it may have to past or future.[16] Likewise, Dan Zahavi suggests that narrative as a paradigm of selfhood has certain limitations.[17] It is inadequate, he argues, to capture a first-person experiential component of the self, for narrative tends to subsume the perspective of the individual to that of the larger community that inevitably shapes the story one tells about oneself.[18] He insists, "an account of self which disregards the fundamental structures and features of our experiential life is a non-starter, and a correct description and account of the experiential dimension must necessarily do justice to the first-person perspective and to the primate form of self-reference that it entails."[19] For both Zahavi and Strawson, the linear trajectory of narrative rationality proves unsatisfactory because it minimizes the episodic and individual experience, favoring instead the shape of the larger arc of a plot to lend meaning to human action. Zahavi and Strawson

---

[14] Ibid., 147–48.

[15] Galen Strawson, "Against Narrativity," *Ratio* 17 (2004): 428–52.

[16] Ibid., 433. Strawson insists that all moral traits can have both episodic and diachronic modes of expression and that both are equally moral. Diachronicity, he insists, is not the sole realm of the moral life (Galen Strawson, "Episodic Ethics," in *Narrative and Understanding Persons* [ed. Daniel D. Hutto; Royal Institute of Philosophy Supplement 60; Cambridge: Cambridge University Press, 2007], 98).

[17] Dan Zahavi, "Self and Other: The Limits of Narrative Understanding," in *Narrative and Understanding Persons* (ed. Daniel D. Hutto; Royal Institute of Philosophy Supplement 60; Cambridge: Cambridge University Press, 2007), 179–201.

[18] He explains, "When I interpret myself in terms of a life story, I might be both the narrator and the main character, but I am not the sole author. The beginning of my own story has always already been made for me by others and the way the story unfolds is only in part determined by my own choices and decisions" (ibid., 181).

[19] Ibid., 200.

point to an alternative mode of rationality, insisting that both narrative and non-narrative modes have integrity as means to view the moral life. One is no less moral than the other; they are simply different perspectives through which to understand the moral self. Yet they present two genuine alternatives that color the prism through which moral selfhood acquires meaning, whether in the scope of a larger plot or the particularity of discrete episodes. The question remains whether a non-narrative mode of rationality has traction in character ethics. That is, does character have meaning other than through a narrative plot?

## The Emplotment of Proverbs

The book of Proverbs is an interesting place to explore this question, for it illumines both the value and the limits of narrative rationality as a lens for understanding character. Strawson and Zahavi emphasize the elements of selfhood that a narrative rationality does not privilege or accommodate. And while they would both concede that narrative does provide a valid framework for ethical analysis, they critique the notion that moral selfhood acquires meaning only through narrative. As Zahavi insists, "narratives play an important role in the constitution of a certain dimension or aspect of selfhood. However, I would oppose the exclusivity claim, that is, the claim that *the* self is a narratively constructed entity and that *every* access to the self and other are mediated by narratives."[20] Yet Strawson and Zahavi spend more time critiquing such claims of exclusivity than they do offering constructive alternative models. The book of Proverbs, however, provides an example of such an alternative. Within Proverbs, the coherence of character comes not from its place in a larger linear frame but from particular actions and emotions displayed in discrete circumstances. One's moral identity is evident in the actions, reactions, emotions, and desires that one exhibits. Proverbs 15:28, for example, suggests that one's circumspection (or lack thereof) is an indication of character: "a righteous heart contemplates a reply (יהגה לענות), but the wicked gush with evil things." Proverbs 13:16 indicates that one's character is exposed in one's actions: "Every clever one (ערום) acts with knowledge, but the dunce displays folly (כסיל יפרש אולת)."

Throughout the book, character is not linked to a larger narrative arc. It is not grounded in a larger story through which one makes sense of moral identity. In this respect, Proverbs is distinct from other texts in the

---

[20] Ibid., 184.

Hebrew Bible. Compare Proverbs' perspective with, for example, Deut 7, where Moses presents identity in relation to the addressee's belonging to the people of God:

> For you are a people holy to YHWH your God; YHWH your God chose you to be a treasured people above all of the peoples on earth. Not because you were more numerous than all of the peoples did YHWH love you and choose you, for you were the smallest of the peoples. It was because YHWH loved you and kept the vow he swore to your fathers that YHWH brought you out with a strong hand and delivered you from the house of slavery, from the hand of Pharaoh the king of Egypt. So know that YHWH your God is God, the faithful God who keeps the covenant faithfully to the thousandth generation of those who love him and keep his commandments. (Deut 7:6–9)

Deuteronomy 7 is rooted in historical experience and connected to the continuity of the community in past, present, and future generations.

Certainly, narratival elements are not entirely lacking in Proverbs' conception of selfhood, and the character ethics approach is particularly helpful in drawing these out. For example, the father's appeal to the wisdom of the grandparent in Prov 4 seeks to incorporate the youth into a chain of authority that stretches from past into the present. Thus one could say that the construction of the authority of one's elders and the student's relation to the hierarchy is in some sense narratival; he is figured in relation to a story that the father tells of the wisdom that his own father handed on to him.[21] In this sense, character is embedded in a larger familial or communal context.

The path metaphor within Proverbs is, to some extent, another narratival aspect of character within the book and provides a way to conceptualize the development of character. The language of the path in Proverbs is a figure of speech that often describes a particular condition – it is indicative of foolish action (e.g., 2:12–13) or of wisdom in analyzing a situation (e.g., 14:18). At the same time, the path itself does not always predict or determine one's end. Only the path of the foreign woman (נכריה) is said to set a person on a path from which one cannot return (2:19), but it is never assumed that one cannot digress from the path of wisdom or righteousness. Rather, Proverbs' advice is directed to the student as if in any one situation he could choose among multiple paths. Thus the father's counsel in guiding his student on the way of wisdom includes instruction not to walk in the ways of the wicked (e.g., 4:14–15). In this sense, one is always

---

[21] See the discussion of Prov 4 in Chapter 6.

at a crossroads between competing paths. Accordingly, within Proverbs the process of formation is not a linear process, with a beginning, middle, and end. It is a cyclical journey, always circling back on itself. Wisdom resists attainment; it is not a destination at which one can finally arrive, as if one could travel far enough along wisdom's way that one does not encounter alternative paths at every step.

The character ethics approach has been a tremendously helpful lens for highlighting the concept of character and character's formation in Proverbs. It affirms that particular virtues – e.g., righteousness, wisdom, shrewdness – provide a language for character and that one can grow in and be formed by these virtues. However, the model of character in Proverbs also suggests that a narrative notion of character is not entirely sufficient, for Proverbs does not, by and large, operate with this narrative model of selfhood. Rather, it privileges discrete episodes, conjures up the emotions evoked by particular moments, and features a string of isolated situations that are not of necessity connected into a coherent whole. Although the familiar characters of the wise one, the righteous, the simpleton, and the fool reappear throughout the book, it is not clear that it is one consistent person mentioned in each instance. In other words, Proverbs does not present the tale of Joseph the wise one or Eli the fool, who reappear in various situations. Rather, we witness an indeterminate חכם or כסיל who appears in isolated instances; the figure's wisdom or foolishness is with reference to the particular problem or situation he negotiates.

Thus while the pursuit of wisdom orients the shaping of character, the moral self is not conceptualized as a narrative story within Proverbs. It does not figure in the larger arc of a plot that can be traced from birth to death or naïveté to maturity, strictly speaking. Instead, Proverbs displays snapshots of character throughout the book that are largely unconnected to previous events. The path metaphor provides a way of characterizing particular situations and characters (i.e., the "way of wickedness" or the "way of wisdom"), but it does not function as an organizational scheme to construct selfhood, as in Ricoeur's concept of the "emplotment" of the self. In this way, although character ethics is quite congenial to the notion of character in Proverbs, its emphasis on viewing selfhood primarily or exclusively through narrative plot is less helpful and suggests a narrative rationality that is not native to the text.

Nonetheless, the pervasiveness of narrative within character ethics has impacted interpretation of the book. The concept of emplotment has colored how scholars have read the book of Proverbs as a whole, often resulting in an effort to construct a plot for the book at large. William

P. Brown, for example, uses a narrative framework to explain the development of character over the course of the book. In this reading, the book begins with the student situated within the confines of the home (Prov 1–9), then "the youth moves out from the household to the Grand Central Stations of urban life"[22] (chapters 10–29), before returning home with his proper wife (Prov 31). Brown is careful to say that the book of Proverbs is not narrative in genre, but he insists that "there is a narrative-like resolution given in the last chapter of the book."[23] While it began with the silent son who hears the father's injunctions, it ends with an adult male who has fulfilled them in finding the capable wife praised in chapter 31. In the framework of the book as a whole, "the narratival shape of Proverbs fleshes out, socially and ethically, the primordial journey of the male from child to adult as he finds union with his mate."[24] Yet the son addressed in Prov 1–9 need not be the husband of the woman of valor in Prov 31. Indeed, throughout the book בן is an indeterminate term, which facilitates the pedagogical function of the book, allowing the reader to become the child who is addressed. Moreover, it is vital to the book's pedagogy that the reader is positioned differently in different episodes – at times as a wise person, at others as a simpleton, and in yet other instances addressed as among the wicked. In this way, the addressee is always renegotiating character.

Other scholars who have searched for a coherent organizing principle of the book also presume an implicit conception of narrative rationality in which Proverbs as a *book* must have some kind of linear framework. Christopher B. Ansberry, for example, observes a progression in the literary form of the book as the wisdom contained therein grows from simplistic to increasingly complex.[25] Further, Ansberry describes the final collection in the book (31:1–31) as the conclusion to which the entire book has been building: "The *concluding* composition represents the *culmination* of the book's pedagogical program and the *consummation* of the

[22] William P. Brown, *Wisdom's Wonder: Character, Creation, and Crisis in the Bible's Wisdom Literature* (Grand Rapids: Eerdmans, 2014), 64.
[23] Ibid., 65.
[24] Ibid., 66. While Brown reads the book as a progressive journey from child to adult, he also finds that the end of the book echoes the beginning, in effect circling back to the familial context (ibid., 192).
[25] Christopher B. Ansberry, *Be Wise, My Son, and Make My Heart Glad: An Exploration of the Courtly Nature of the Book of Proverbs* (BZAW 422; Berlin: De Gruyter, 2011). See the discussion in Chapter 5. See also Brown's argument about thematic developments and growing complexity as the proverbial collections advance in Prov 10–31 (William P. Brown, "The Pedagogy of Proverbs 10:1–31:9," in *Character and Scripture: Moral Formation, Community, and Biblical Interpretation* [ed. William P. Brown; Grand Rapids: Eerdmans, 2002], 150–82).

addressee's moral formation; it marks the *completion* of the quest for wisdom, a journey of character that finds its concrete expression in the world of the court."[26] Here the book is figured as a particular kind of plot: a quest whose consummation is the final proverbial collection.

Both Brown and Ansberry draw attention to certain distinctions among the proverbial collections within the book and offer helpful ways to understand the collections as a part of a larger sequence. The sayings in the later collections more often seem to stand at the periphery of the prototypes established in earlier collections (see discussion in Chapter 7), and the poem in Prov 31:10–31 shares certain literary features in common with the poems in chapters 1–9, providing a frame to the book as a whole. The book of Proverbs thus holds coherence as a loose sequence. However, it is difficult to make an argument for a clear plot of the book that emerges from the text itself.

In this respect, Proverbs stands in contrast to other wisdom texts from the ancient Near East, which are often prefaced with a prose framework that situates their wisdom in a particular narrative context. For example, the *Instruction of Ankhsheshonqy* begins with the story of the circumstances leading to its instruction, and the *Instruction of Any* concludes by recording a conversation between the student and his father concerning what he has and has not learned, a framework which figures Any's recalcitrant student Khonshotep as the figure addressed throughout the text.

Proverbs also differs from the mode of presentation that is found elsewhere in the Hebrew Bible. The book of Genesis, for instance, is constructed in part by following Abraham, Sarah, and other particular characters through a series of connected events. Genesis 12 is based on an unfolding series of events in which Abraham (Abram) is called by God, responds, and encounters a series of situations as he travels through various geographical regions. More broadly, the larger plot of the Abraham cycle that unfolds over several chapters is based on a model of linear plot that traces Abraham's birth, marriage (Gen 11:26–29), divine calling (Gen 12:2–3), and the threat to that calling in the absence of progeny and other complications. The plot moves toward resolution in the fulfillment of the covenant promise in the birth of Isaac, and the story of Abraham's lineage continues in the stories of his descendants. While the Abraham cycle does chronicle the experience of the person Abraham, it is told not from his own perspective but from third-person narration that rather objectively describes the scenes. Consequently, its emotional register is different than if it were

---

[26] Ansberry, *Be Wise, My Son, and Make My Heart Glad*, 175; emphasis added.

told in Abraham's own voice. This is certainly not to say that emotion is for-eign to any narrative or this narrative in particular. Indeed, there may be no more gripping a scene in all of biblical literature than Isaac's near sacrifice in Gen 22. Yet the inner emotional life of these characters is not privileged; instead, it is left largely to the reader's imagination.

The lack of plot within Proverbs is not incidental to its import, but has to do with its claims about the nature of wisdom and the process of formation. With its literary form, it enacts a cyclical process of formation that resists consummation. In this way, the poems themselves keep the student ever in the midst of the pursuit of wisdom. Proverbs 5, for instance, speaks of the consequences that will befall the one who follows the strange woman, but the vignette does not function as a structuring device to build a larger plot. Instead, as Robert Alter argues, it has an intensifying effect to build a series of images across the course of the poem.[27] Such intensification has didactic purpose, for the imagery functions not to set the scene but to enact the les-son. For example, Alter observes that the cluster of orificial images associated with the strange woman contrasts with the metaphors of well and womb used to describe the wife. Across the course of the poem, these images make a larger point that "man as an erotic creature is drawn by the powerful allure of ecstasy, but there are both salutary and destructive channels for the fulfill-ment of that urge."[28] In so doing, it evokes those allures by lingering over sensual imagery that appeals to the student's imagination; the women are constructed before the student's eyes.[29] Moreover, the poem provides a win-dow into the presumed anguish of the wayward in his own voice – "*How I hated discipline!*" (5:12–14) – as a cautionary lesson to the student. In all of these ways, the poem offers an "imaginative plunge into the experiential enactment of moral alternatives."[30]

[27] Robert Alter, *The Art of Biblical Poetry* (New York: Basic Books, 1985), 181. He explains that, in a wisdom poem, "[i]magery functions differently because it can be elaborated and amplified from line to line and linked with clusters of associated images. Narrativity is not limited to thumbnail illustrative plots, because it can be carried forward in stages, sometimes with the introduction of dramatic dialogue" (ibid., 183).

[28] Ibid.

[29] By contrast, consider Gen 22, which provides little detail as to the characters' appearance, emotion, motives, or interrelation. Did Isaac question his father about the sacrificial animal out of naïve curiosity or fearful suspicion? Did Abraham draw the knife with hesitation, confidence, expectation of deliverance, or disbelief? In fact, it is precisely these gaps that have led to such a rich interpre-tive history from this passage. Accordingly, various commentators have pictured Isaac as a young, frightened boy or an older, confident man. The lack of imagistic detail leaves ambiguous crucial details that influence the import of the text. For a variety of interpretations of this text in the his-tory of reception, see the essays in Ed Noort and Eibert Tigchelaar, eds., *The Sacrifice of Isaac: The Aqedah (Genesis 22) and Its Interpretations* (Themes in Biblical Narrative 4; Leiden: Brill, 2002).

[30] Alter, *The Art of Biblical Poetry*, 184.

Proverbs makes an important contribution to the larger character ethics project in two specific ways. First, it offers an example of a text that shapes character in a distinctly poetic way. That is, it uses the particular resources of its poetic form – for example, episodicity, direct address, appeal to the senses – to shape the moral identity of its student. While character ethicists have drawn attention to the rhetorical function of literature, especially narrative fiction, to shape the character of the reader, they have not always attended to the capability of poetry to do the same. Proverbs highlights the merit of examining poetry *qua* poetry within the scope of character ethics. Second, Proverbs provides a counterpoint to the notion that narrative is the only lens through which character has meaning. The character ethics approach often assumes that narrative – whether the literary form or the stories that a community tells about itself – is the defining orientation of the self. Yet Proverbs offers a compelling example of a text that is not narrative in literary form and does not conceive of personhood in a narratival way. While this does not negate the insights of Hauerwas and MacIntyre that certain conceptions of character and the moral life have a narrative arc, it does qualify their totalizing claims that character *only* takes on meaning in narrative.

The book of Proverbs provides a non-narrative way of articulating character that does not rely on a linear plot but is instead revealed in discrete moments and particular situations. In this respect, it bears some resemblance to a rule-based ethic that privileges acts, not character. At the same time, however, Proverbs' emphasis remains on the quality of the agent rather than the act itself, for individual episodes provide windows into the quality of character displayed, whether wise or foolish. Accordingly, Proverbs presents a complex moral discourse that eschews neat classification. Even as it does not follow a simplistic act-consequence scheme akin to a rule-based ethic, it also qualifies the strictly narrative orientation of character in a character ethic. Proverbs conceptualizes character in a meaningful way apart from a strong narrative lens.

## The Emplotment of the Wisdom Tradition

Recognizing the non-narrative nature of Proverbs also illumines significant aspects of the larger Israelite wisdom tradition. Narrative as a conceptual category has influenced readings of other wisdom texts, yet Job and Qoheleth hardly prove more conducive to its claims. This narrative understanding is particularly evident in analyses of Job, which is not surprising given that the prose framework does function to create a general plot, although the relationship between this framework and the rest of the book is notoriously difficult to determine. For Brown, a narrative rationality informs his understanding of the trajectory of the book of Job. Brown argues that Job begins with the traditional, normative conception of character (represented by Job 1:1–2:13), which is quickly challenged and deconstructed in the dialogue with the friends (Job 3:1–31:39). By the conclusion of the book, normative character has been re-formed through the speeches of Elihu, God, and Job himself (Job 32–42). Much like the silent son of Prov 1–9 traveled into the larger world and eventually returned home with a virtuous wife by the end of the book, argues Brown, so Job is driven from the confines of his home, embarks on a journey of wonder and discovery, and returns home with new compassion for his cosmic community. "Like the son-turned-family-man at the conclusion of Proverbs," Brown observes, "Job, the patriarch-turned-citizen of the cosmos, returns to his domicile."[31] This linear, narrative structure is central to Brown's understanding of character within both books, although he emphasizes the complexity in Job's character that the poetic dialogues introduce. Even as the epilogue of the book returns to Job and his family life, "it cannot beat a path back to Job's flat character. By shifting the reader's perception, the dialogues have made sure that there is no return."[32]

Despite its prose framework, Job does not display a greater degree of narrative rationality than does Proverbs. Charles Davis Hankins has argued that the character ethics approach is ill suited to the book of Job because it obscures the radical discontinuity that Job experiences when he is ruptured from his past life.[33] Hankins critiques Brown's emphasis on the continuity and development of Job's character throughout the book.[34] Rather, Hankins emphasizes the radical subjectivity of Job's situation and the disjuncture that Job experiences from his previous life: "Job's ethical subjectivity is not generated out of the unfolding, dialogical interactions between his present experiences, past history, personal convictions, and community's values. Instead, Job emerges as an ethical subject at the moment of traumatic experience of rupture from his present and his past."[35] Part of what Hankins is resisting is the linear trajectory and narrative orientation of character ethics, for he does not find that Job's character has an essential continuity with his past. In fact, Hankins argues,

---

[31] Brown, *Wisdom's Wonder*, 135.
[32] Ibid., 129.
[33] Charles Davis Hankins, "Job and the Limits of Wisdom" (PhD diss., Emory University, 2011), 430–44.
[34] Hankins's critique appeared before the revised edition of *Character in Crisis*, but many of these issues are nuanced in Brown's more recent publication, *Wisdom's Wonder*.
[35] Hankins, "Job and the Limits of Wisdom," 430.

this radical discontinuity is at the heart of the book's argument about the ethical act.[36] Yet Hankins's critique may be ameliorated, at least in part, by the way in which Proverbs qualifies the character ethics approach in demonstrating that narrative rationality need not be the only rationality. Indeed, the book of Job provides another example of non-narrative rationality insofar as it privileges Job's subjective experience and takes the reader into Job's deeply personal engagement with the reality of suffering, the counterarguments of his community, and the divine response to his complaints. Although it offers strikingly different form and content than Proverbs, Job presents another example of a text that resists a narrative scheme. In fact, the radical discontinuity between Job's experiences of prosperity and emptiness, as well as his perception of those experiences versus the conclusions of his friends, defies resolution. Rather, they sit in tension across the book as discrete experiences that cannot be reconciled or connected meaningfully into a larger whole.

A non-narrative mode of rationality is also present in the book of Qoheleth and is in fact vital to its meaning. Challenging the linearity of past, present, and future is a central premise of the book. Indeed, the teacher Qoheleth disavows the value of both the past, which is already gone, leaving no remembrance of those who have come before (Qoh 1:11), and the future, which is unreliable and unknowable (Qoh 8:16–17; 9:11–12). Instead, Qoheleth emphasizes the present moment; everything else is futile (הבל, Qoh 1:2, 12–14).[37] One of the larger points of the book is thus that a narrative rationality is bankrupt! As Brown notes, Qoheleth is deeply suspicious about the prospects for the advance of knowledge and understanding, for the cosmos itself resists a linear trajectory:

> the pursuit of wisdom is no journey at all; wisdom is a destination that dissipates like mist once the first steps are taken toward it. Qoheleth finds inherited tradition, the wisdom of the ages, to be a *fata morgana*: progress, growth, and fulfillment are all mirages of the same illusions. The workings of the cosmos, in which no real purpose or direction can be discerned, only confirm the ephemerality of wisdom.[38]

---

[36] He explains, "There is a lack of unity or incoherence, a dislocated or excessive element that is present within a situation in order for ethical conduct to occur. Like Job to his friends, this component will never be visible to those who read through the lens of character ethics" (ibid., 440).

[37] The term הבל, usually translated as "vanity" but, literally, "vapor" or "breath," occurs thirty-eight times in the book and is a *leitmotif* throughout. For a discussion of the meaning and interpretation of this term in Qoheleth, see Douglas B. Miller, "Qohelet's Symbolic Use of הבל," *JBL* 117 (1998): 437–54; and Michael V. Fox, "The Meaning of *Hebel* for Qohelet," *JBL* 105 (1986): 409–27.

[38] William P. Brown, *Character in Crisis: A Fresh Approach to the Wisdom Literature of the Old Testament* (Grand Rapids: Eerdmans, 1996), 125.

This conception is at odds with a narrative rationality in which there is a meaningful connection between events, building a larger plot. For Qoheleth, no such plot exists.

## The Moral Landscape of Israelite Wisdom

A narrative rationality has also influenced the way in which scholars conceptualize the relationship between these wisdom books. Thus the two most common typologies with which the books are characterized both promote an overarching linear scheme, whether from the simplicity of Proverbs to the complexity of Job and Qoheleth or from the conventional view of wisdom in Proverbs to the "crisis" of wisdom found in Job and Qoheleth.[39] Yet both of these frameworks unfairly position Proverbs as the inferior prototype in relation to the other two books. Proverbs is characterized as a model that is eventually proven inadequate to or outmoded for changing climes. However, a different relationship among the books is present when their non-narrative modes are understood. Rather than part of one linear trajectory, the books ask different questions and privilege different moments, their relationship more akin to lyric episodes than linear trajectory.

The differences among the wisdom books have less to do with increasing complexity or the experience of crisis than with distinctions between their driving assumptions and governing questions. For Proverbs, Job, and

[39] For a discussion of the "simplicity thesis" in wisdom scholarship, see the discussion in Part II. The notion of a "crisis" of wisdom is usually connected to the presumed social and cultural contexts of the wisdom books, Proverbs representing the stability of the preexilic period and Job or Qoheleth reflecting the inadequacy of Proverbs' doctrines after the exile and associated crises. For example, Rainier Albertz associated the "crisis" of wisdom in Job with the experience of exile and its aftermath: "Now the book of Job as a whole bears witness that this personal theology of the upper class underwent a serious crisis. The reason for this is ... the severity of the crisis which shook the community of Judah in the second half of the fifth century.... The optimistic promises of their personal theology and the bitter social experiences that they underwent became hopelessly incompatible" (Rainer Albertz, *A History of Israelite Religion in the Old Testament Period, Vol. 2: From the Exile to the Maccabees* [Louisville: Westminster John Knox, 1994], 514). For a critique of this concept of a crisis of wisdom, see Hankins, "Job and the Limits of Wisdom," 61–63. For a discussion of the crisis of wisdom as evident in Qoheleth, see Aare Lauha, "Die Krise des religiösen Glaubens bei Kohelet," in *Wisdom in Israel and in the Ancient Near East* (ed. M. Noth and D. Winton Thomas; VTSup 3; Leiden: Brill, 1955), 183–91; Hartmut Gese, "The Crisis of Wisdom in Koheleth," in *Theodicy in the Old Testament* (Issues in Religion and Theology 4; ed. James L. Crenshaw; Philadelphia/London: Fortress/SPCK, 1983), 141–53, trans. by Lester L. Grabbe from "Die Krisis der Weisheit bei Koheleth," in *Les sagesses du Proche-Orient ancient: Colloque de Strasbourg, 17–19 Mai, 1962* (Paris: Presses Universitaires de France, 1963), 139–51. See also the critique in James L. Crenshaw, *Old Testament Wisdom: An Introduction* (rev. ed.; Louisville: Westminster John Knox, 1998), 184–96; Roland E. Murphy, "Qoheleth's 'Quarrel' with the Fathers," in *From Faith to Faith* (ed. D. Y. Hadidian; PTMS 31; Pittsburgh: Pickwick, 1979), 235–45.

Qoheleth, motivation and desire emerge as central issues, yet each book has different presumptions about their respective roles in the formation of character. It is not that Job and Qoheleth somehow find the ideas of Proverbs to be inadequate, but rather they begin with different assumptions, which lead to different animating questions and conclusions. While an exhaustive treatment is beyond the scope of the present discussion, a very brief comparison of how the books treat the concepts of motivation and desire will demonstrate the nature of the distinctions.

As we have seen, Proverbs assumes that motivation plays a fundamental role in character formation. Thus the book figures its wisdom with language of incentive and value. Furthermore, desire of various kinds is understood as a vital and ever-present part of the human person. Motivation and desire are crucial aspects of Proverbs' moral vocabulary. Accordingly, much of the book turns on the pursuit of character with these elements of the person in mind.

By contrast, the role of motivation is not a given in Qoheleth. In fact, this book hinges on the utter meaninglessness of motivation, for the pursuit of wisdom, wealth, and security ultimately leads nowhere, as Qoheleth admits from his own experience: "I turned to all that my hands had made, to the labor that I labored to do – but it was all futile, chasing wind. There is no true gain (יתרון)[40] under the sun!" (Qoh 2:11). As in Proverbs, desire is assumed to be a fundamental aspect of human nature. Qoheleth recognizes the inherent attraction of wealth, food, drink, and love as things in which humans take pleasure. In fact, he admits that these pleasures are the only rightful portion of the human: "This, I have seen, is truly good: it is right that one should eat and drink and experience what is good[41] in all the toil that he toils under the sun for the number of the days of his life that God gives him, for that is his portion" (Qoh 5:17 [Eng. v. 18]). Similarly, the teacher admonishes the student to enjoy life's pleasures:

> Go, eat your bread with joy and drink your wine with a glad heart; for God has already been pleased with your works. Let your garments always be white and your head never lack oil. Enjoy life with the woman you love

---

[40] The term יתרון, which occurs ten times in Qoheleth, may have been a commercial term for a "profit"; the root יתר means "to surpass or exceed." C. L. Seow notes that the term "means 'profit' in the sense of something additional, and not 'profit' merely as 'benefit.' In other words, *yitrôn* in this case is not just 'a plus' (something positive) but 'a surplus' (an advantage). It is not that toil has no benefit whatsoever, but that toil does not give one any additional 'edge'" (C. L. Seow, *Ecclesiastes: A New Translation with Introduction and Commentary* [AB 18C; New York: Doubleday, 1997], 103–04).

[41] Literally, "to see good" (ולראות טובה). For ראה as "to experience," cf. Ps 34:13; Job 9:25; see also Ps 89:49 (to "see death").

all of the days of your fleeting life (כל ימי הבלך) that have been given to you under the sun – all your fleeting days. For that is your portion in life and your labor in which you labored under the sun. (Qoh 9:7–9)

Yet unlike Proverbs, in Qoheleth such desires have no motivational teeth, for they lead to no reward, either material or immaterial. The great irony, Qoheleth finds, is that a wise person spends his life laboring to build his fortune, and yet it can all be lost in a moment or may be passed on to a fool who will squander it (Qoh 5:12–13). One of the driving questions of this book, then, concerns the shape and meaning of human life in the absence of motivation.

On the other hand, the book of Job is predicated on the vacuum of desire. Job, having possessed the best of human desires that are so common within Proverbs – wealth, love, progeny, health – loses it all. With this frame, the book takes up the question of whether there is any motivation to fear YHWH in the absence of such desires, as the ṣātān asks, "Does Job fear God for naught?" (Job 1:9).[42] Within Proverbs, motivation and desire are closely linked, the promise of certain desires serving as a powerful motivational incentive for the student to follow the sanctioned path. Job, however, crystallizes the question of motivation differently by removing desire from the equation. In this respect, Job and his friends talk past each other, for the friends presume a principle of motivation that is predicated on the reality and attainability of human desire (cf. Job 8:5–7; 11:13–19). As David J. A. Clines argues, the issue within Job is not strictly one of motivation; rather, the question is the causal link from piety to prosperity or, conversely, prosperity to piety. Consequently, "it is because the prosperity is intertwined with the piety that the prosperity must be removed in order to uncover the relationship between the two."[43] In this respect, Job takes several elements that are present in Proverbs – motivation, desire (and prosperity), fear of YHWH – but dissects them from a different angle.

These wisdom books construe the connection between motivation and desire in distinct ways and, consequently, ask different questions. It is not that Proverbs is less complex than the other books or ill equipped to deal with a later "crisis" of the tradition. It is unlikely that Job or Qoheleth would rebuke the sages of Proverbs because of their naïveté. Rather the

---

[42]  See the discussion of disinterested piety in Matitiahu Tsevat, "The Meaning of the Book of Job," *HUCA* 37 (1966): 73–106.

[43]  David J. A. Clines, *Job 1–20* (WBC 17; Dallas: Word Books, 1989), 28.

nature of their debate concerns, at least in part, the relationship between desire and motivation. All three books treat desire and motivation as important aspects of their moral vocabulary, but they reserve different roles for each. In this sense, these books can be understood as lyric modes within the larger wisdom tradition, offering distinct perspectives, rather than as a series that is connected in a linear, evolutionary trajectory.

Accordingly, although long viewed with a certain amount of disdain for its alleged simplicity or naïveté, the book of Proverbs presents a lasting contribution to the Israelite wisdom tradition and to the contemporary character ethics conversation. It is sophisticated poetic literature that resists the emplotment of the self, instead making a claim about the often elusive nature of wisdom and the cultivation of its desire that is fundamental to the formation of character. Indeed, through its poetic form, Proverbs is not a single hue of rose-colored glass, but a kaleidoscope of images and metaphors that indicate a much more agile and complicated vision of the moral world than has often been assumed. Proverbs presents a sophisticated understanding of the role of emotion, desire, and imagination in the formation of the moral self, thus suggesting that character formation requires educating all of the senses, not simply the cognitive faculties. In fact, the book gives an astounding degree of attention to the desires and emotions that animate human action in an effort to shape one's moral imagination. Proverbs offers a compelling example of a text that is not narrative in literary form and also does not conceive of personhood in a narratival way. Poetry is a vital aspect of how Proverbs makes meaning, how it conceptualizes the human person, and thus how it shapes the moral universe of its readers.

# Bibliography

Abbott, Andrew. "Against Narrative: Preface to a Lyrical Sociology." *Sociological Theory* 25 (2007): 67–99.

Adams, Samuel L. *Wisdom in Transition: Act and Consequence in Second Temple Instructions*. Supplements to the Journal for the Study of Judaism 125. Leiden: Brill, 2008.

Albertz, Rainer. *A History of Israelite Religion in the Old Testament Period, Vol. 2: From the Exile to the Maccabees*. Louisville: Westminster John Knox, 1994.

Albright, William F. "Some Canaanite-Phoenician Sources of Hebrew Wisdom." Pages 1–15 in *Wisdom in Israel and in the Ancient Near East: Presented to Professor Harold Henry Rowley*. Edited by M. Noth and D. Winton Thomas. Vetus Testamentum Supplements 3. Leiden: Brill, 1955.

*From the Stone Age to Christianity: Monotheism and the Historical Process*. Baltimore: Johns Hopkins Press, 1940.

Aletti, J. N. "Seduction et Parole en Proverbes I-IX." *Vetus Testamentum* 27(1977): 129–44.

Alt, "Die Weisheit Salomos," *Theologische Literaturzeitung* 76 (1951): 139–44.

Alter, Robert. *The Art of Biblical Poetry*. New York: Basic Books, 1985.

Altieri, Charles. "Lyrical Ethics and Literary Experience." Pages 30–58 in *Mapping the Ethical Turn: A Reader in Ethics, Culture, and Literary Theory*. Edited by Todd F. Davis and Kenneth Womack. Charlottesville: University Press of Virginia, 2001.

Anderson, Francis I., and David Noel Freedman. *Micah: A New Translation with Introduction and Commentary*. Anchor Bible 24E. New York: Doubleday, 2000.

Anderson, Gary A. *Sin: A History*. New Haven: Yale University Press, 2009.

Annas, Julia. "Virtue Ethics." Pages 515–36 in *The Oxford Handbook of Ethical Theory*. Edited by David Copp. New York: Oxford University Press, 2007.

Ansberry, Christopher B. *Be Wise, My Son, and Make My Heart Glad: An Exploration of the Courtly Nature of the Book of Proverbs*. Beihefte zur Zeitschrift für die alttestamentliche Wissenschaft 422. Berlin: De Gruyter, 2011.

"What Does Jerusalem Have to Do with Athens? The Moral Vision of the Book of Proverbs and Aristotle's *Nicomachean Ethics*." *Hebrew Studies* 51 (2010): 157–73.

Anscombe, G. E. M. "Modern Moral Philosophy." *Philosophy* 33.124 (1958): 1–19.

Aristotle. *Nicomachean Ethics*. Translated by Roger Crisp. Cambridge: Cambridge University Press, 2000.

Arnold, Bill T., and John H. Choi. *A Guide to Biblical Hebrew Syntax*. Cambridge: Cambridge University Press, 2003.

Bahti, Timothy. "Figure, Trope, Scheme." Pages 90–93 in *The New Princeton Handbook of Poetic Terms*. Edited by T. V. F. Brogan. Princeton: Princeton University Press, 1994.

Bartholomew, Craig G. *Ecclesiastes*. Baker Commentary on the Old Testament Wisdom and Psalms. Grand Rapids: Baker Academic, 2009.

Bartholomew, Craig G., and Ryan P. O'Dowd. *Old Testament Wisdom Literature: A Theological Introduction*. Downers Grove: InterVarsity Press, 2011.

Barton, John. *Understanding Old Testament Ethics: Approaches and Explanations*. Louisville: Westminster John Knox, 2003.

Ethics and the Old Testament. Harrisburg: Trinity Press International, 1998.

"Reading for Life: The Use of the Bible in Ethics and the Work of Martha C. Nussbaum." Pages 66–76 in *The Bible in Ethics: The Second Sheffield Colloquium*. Edited by John Rogerson et al. Journal for the Study of the Old Testament: Supplement Series 207. Sheffield: Sheffield Academic Press, 1995.

Benson, Hugh H. *Socratic Wisdom: The Model of Knowledge in Plato's Early Dialogues*. New York: Oxford University Press, 2000.

Berlin, Adele. *The Dynamics of Biblical Parallelism*. Rev. and enl. ed. Grand Rapids: Eerdmans, 2008.

Berman, Joshua. "The 'Sword of Mouths' (Jud. III 16; Ps. CXLIX 6; Prov. V 4): A Metaphor and Its Ancient Near Eastern Context." *Vetus Testamentum* 53 (2002): 291–303.

Bernat, David. "Biblical *Wasfs* Beyond Song of Songs." *Journal for the Study of the Old Testament* 28 (2004): 327–49.

Birch, Bruce. *Let Justice Roll Down: The Old Testament, Ethics, and the Christian Life*. Louisville: Westminster John Knox, 1991.

Birch, Bruce, and Larry Rasmussen. *Bible and Ethics in the Christian Life*. Rev. ed. Minneapolis: Augsburg, 1989.

Black, Jeremy. *Reading Sumerian Poetry*. Ithaca: Cornell University Press, 1998.

Blenkinsopp, Joseph. "The Social Context of the 'Outsider Woman' in Prov 1–9." *Biblica* 72 (1991): 457–73.

Bondi, Richard. "The Elements of Character." *Journal of Religions Ethics* 12.2 (1984): 201–18.

Booth, Wayne C. "Ethics and Criticism." Pages 384–86 in *The New Princeton Encyclopedia of Poetry and Poetics*. Edited by A. Preminger and T. V. F. Brogan. New York: MJF Books, 1993.

The Company We Keep: An Ethics of Fiction. Berkeley: University of California Press, 1988.

Boström, Gustav. *Paronomasi i den äldre hebraiska Maschalliteraturen*. Lund: Gleerup, 1928.

Boström, Lennart. *The God of the Sages: The Portrayal of God in the Book of Proverbs.* Coniectanea biblical: Old Testament Series 29. Stockholm: Almqvist & Wiksell International, 1990.

Botterweck, G. Johannes, and Helmer Ringgren. *Theological Dictionary of the Old Testament.* Translated by J. T. Willis, G. W. Bromiley, and D. E. Green. 8 vols. Grand Rapids: Eerdmans, 1974.

Brenner, Athalya. "Proverbs 1–9: An F Voice?" Pages 113–30 in *On Gendering Texts: Female and Male Voices in the Hebrew Bible.* Edited by Athalya Brenner and Fokkelien van Dijk-Hemmes. Leiden: Brill, 1993.

Briant, Pierre. *From Cyrus to Alexander: A History of the Persian Empire.* Translated by Peter T. Daniels. Winona Lake: Eisenbrauns, 2002.

Brickhouse, Thomas C., and Nicholas D. Smith. *Socratic Moral Psychology.* Cambridge: Cambridge University Press, 2010.

Brown, William P. *Wisdom's Wonder: Character, Creation, and Crisis in the Bible's Wisdom Literature.* Grand Rapids: Eerdmans, 2014.

———. "To Discipline without Destruction: The Multifaceted Profile of the Child in Proverbs." Pages 63–81 in *The Child in the Bible.* Edited by Marcia J. Bunge. Grand Rapids: Eerdmans, 2008.

———. "The Didactic Power of Metaphor in the Aphoristic Sayings of Proverbs." *Journal for the Study of the Old Testament* 29 (2004): 133–54.

———, ed. *Character and Scripture: Moral Formation, Community, and Biblical Interpretation.* Grand Rapids: Eerdmans, 2002.

———. "The Pedagogy of Proverbs 10:1–31:9." Pages 150–82 in *Character and Scripture: Moral Formation, Community, and Biblical Interpretation.* Edited by William P. Brown. Grand Rapids: Eerdmans, 2002.

———. *Character in Crisis: A Fresh Approach to the Wisdom Literature of the Old Testament.* Grand Rapids: Eerdmans, 1996.

Bryant, David J. *Faith and the Play of Imagination.* Studies in American Biblical Hermeneutics 5. Macon: Mercer University Press, 1989.

Bryce, Glendon. "Another Wisdom-'Book' in Proverbs." *Journal of Biblical Literature* 91 (1972): 145–57.

Budge, E. W. *Second Series of Facsimiles of Egyptian Hieratic Papyri in the British Museum.* London: British Museum, 1923.

Buss, Martin J. *Biblical Form Criticism in Its Context.* Journal for the Study of the Old Testament: Supplement Series 274. Sheffield: Sheffield Academic Press, 1999.

Calvin, John. *Institutes of the Christian Religion.* Translated by F. L. Battles. 2 vols. Library of Christian Classics 20. Louisville: Westminster John Knox, 1960.

Camp, Claudia V. "What's So Strange about the Strange Woman?" Pages 17–31 in *The Bible and the Politics of Exegesis: Essays in Honor of Norman K. Gottwald on His Sixty-Fifth Birthday.* Edited by David Jobling et al. Cleveland: Pilgrim Press, 1991.

———. *Wisdom and the Feminine in the Book of Proverbs.* Bible and Literature Series. Decatur: Almond Press, 1985.

Carr, David. "Gender and the Shaping of Desire in the Song of Songs and Its Interpretation." *Journal of Biblical Literature* 119 (2000): 233–48.

Carroll R., M. Daniel. "'He Has Told You What Is Good': Moral Formation in Micah." Pages 103–18 in *Character Ethics and the Old Testament: Moral Dimensions of Scripture*. Edited by M. Daniel Carroll R. and Jacqueline E. Lapsley. Louisville: Westminster John Knox, 2007.

Carroll R., M. Daniel, and Jacqueline E. Lapsley, eds. *Character Ethics and the Old Testament: Moral Dimensions of Scripture*. Louisville: Westminster John Knox, 2007.

Carson, Anne. *Eros: The Bittersweet*. Princeton: Princeton University Press, 1986. Repr., Champaign: Dalkey Archive Press, 2009.

Childs, Brevard S. *Biblical Theology in Crisis*. Philadelphia: Westminster Press, 1970.

Clements, Ronald E. *A Century of Old Testament Study*. Rev. ed. Cambridge: Lutterworth Press, 1983. Repr. 1992.

Clifford, Richard J. "Reading Proverbs 10–22." *Interpretation* 63 (2009): 242–53.
    *Proverbs: A Commentary*. Old Testament Library. Louisville: Westminster John Knox, 1999.

Clines, David J. A. *Job 1–20*. Word Biblical Commentary 17. Dallas: Word Books, 1989.
    "The Parallelism of Greater Precision: Notes from Isaiah 40 for a Theory of Hebrew Poetry." Pages 77–100 in *Directions in Biblical Hebrew Poetry*. Edited by Elaine R. Follis. Journal for the Study of the Old Testament: Supplement Series 40. Sheffield: JSOT, 1987.

Coleridge, Samuel Taylor. *Poems of Coleridge*. Edited by Arthur Symons. Whitefish: Kessinger Publishing, 2004.

Collins, Billy. *Sailing Alone Around the Room: New and Selected Poems*. New York: Random House, 2001.

Crenshaw, James L. *Old Testament Wisdom: An Introduction*. Rev. and enl. ed. Louisville: Westminster John Knox, 1998.

Dahood, Mitchell J. "Poetic Devices in the Book of Proverbs." Pages 7–17 in *Studies in Bible and the Ancient Near East Presented to Samuel E. Loewenstamm on his Seventieth Birthday*. Edited by Y. Avishur and J. Blau. Jerusalem: Rubinstein, 1978.
    "Hebrew-Ugaritic Lexicography I." *Biblica* 44 (1963): 289–303.

Dalzell, Alexander. *The Criticism of Didactic Poetry: Essays on Lucretius, Virgil, and Ovid*. Toronto: University of Toronto Press, 1996.

Davies, Graham. "The Ethics of Friendship in Wisdom Literature." Pages 135–50 in *Ethical and Unethical in the Old Testament: God and Humans in Dialogue*. Edited by Katharine J. Dell. New York: T&T Clark, 2010.

Davis, Ellen F. *Scripture, Culture, and Agriculture: An Agrarian Reading of the Bible*. New York: Cambridge University Press, 2009.
    "Preserving Virtues: Renewing the Tradition of the Sages." Pages 183–201 in *Character and Scripture: Moral Formation, Community, and Biblical Interpretation*. Edited by William P. Brown. Grand Rapids: Eerdmans, 2002.

*Proverbs, Ecclesiastes, Song of Songs.* Westminster Bible Companion. Louisville: Westminster John Knox, 2000.

de Boer, P. A. H. "The Counsellor." Pages 42–71 in *Wisdom in Israel and in the Ancient Near East: Presented to Professor Harold Henry Rowley.* Edited by M. Noth and D. Winton Thomas. Vetus Testamentum Supplements 3. Leiden: Brill, 1955.

Delitzsch, Franz. *Biblical Commentary on the Proverbs of Solomon.* Translated by M. G. Easton. 2 vols. Edinburgh: T&T Clark, 1874.

Dell, Katherine J. "Does God Behave Unethically in the Book of Job?" Pages 170–86 in *Ethical and Unethical in the Old Testament: God and Humans in Dialogue.* Edited by Katharine J. Dell. New York: T&T Clark, 2010.

*"Get Wisdom, Get Insight": An Introduction to Israel's Wisdom Literature.* Macon: Smyth & Helwys, 2000.

Dennis, Carl. *Poetry as Persuasion.* Athens: University of Georgia Press, 2001.

Dent, N. J. H. "Desires and Deliberation." Pages 106–20 in *The Virtues: Contemporary Essays in Moral Character.* Edited by Robert B. Kruschwitz and Robert C. Roberts. Belmont: Wadsworth Publishing, 1987.

Dewey , John. *Human Nature and Conduct: An Introduction to Social Psychology.* New York: Henry Holt, 1922.

Di Vito, Robert A. "Here One Need Not Be Oneself: The Concept of 'Self' in the Hebrew Scriptures." Pages 49–88 in *The Whole and Divided Self.* Edited by David A. Aune and John McCarthy. New York: Crossroad Publishing, 1997.

Dobbs-Allsopp, F. W. "Space, Line, and the Written Biblical Poem in Texts from the Judean Desert." Pages 19–61 in *Puzzling Out the Past: Studies in Northwest Semitic Languages and Literatures in Honor of Bruce Zuckerman.* Edited by Marilyn J. Lundberg et al. Culture and History of the Ancient Near East 55. Leiden: Brill, 2012.

"The Psalms and Lyric Verse." Pages 346–79 in *The Evolution of Rationality: Interdisciplinary Essays in Honor of J. Wentzel van Huyssteen.* Edited by L. Schultz. Grand Rapids: Eerdmans, 2006.

"Poetry, Hebrew." Pages 550–58 in vol. 4 of *The New Interpreter's Dictionary of the Bible.* Edited by Katherine Doob Sakenfeld. 5 vols. Nashville: Abingdon Press, 2009.

*Lamentations.* Interpretation: A Bible Commentary for Preaching and Teaching. Louisville: Westminster John Knox, 2002.

Dollimore, Jonathan. *Death, Desire, and Loss in Western Culture.* New York: Routledge, 1998.

Driver, G. R. "Hebrew Notes." *Vetus Testamentum* 1 (1951): 241–50.

"Problems in the Hebrew Text of Proverbs." *Biblica* 32 (1951): 173–97.

Driver, S. R. *An Introduction to the Literature of the Old Testament.* Rev. ed. New York: Charles Scribner's Sons, 1920.

Duff, David. *Romanticism and the Uses of Genre.* New York: Oxford University Press, 2009.

Ehrlich, Arnold B. *Randglossen zur Hebräischen Bibel: textkritisches, sprachliches und sachliches.* 7 vols. Leipzig: Hinrichs, 1908–14.

Eichrodt, Walther. *Theology of the Old Testament*. Translated by J. A. Baker. 2 vols. Old Testament Library. Philadelphia: Westminster Press, 1967.

   *Man in the Old Testament*. Translated by K. and R. Gregor Smith. Studies in Biblical Theology. London: SCM Press, 1951. Repr. 1959.

Eissfeldt, Otto. *Der Maschal im Alten Testament. Eine wortgeschichtliche Untersuchung nebst einer literargeschichtlichen Untersuchung der לשׁמ genannten Gattungen "Volkssprichwort."* Beihefte zur Zeitschrift für die alttestamentliche Wissenschaft 24. Giessen: Töppelmann, 1913.

Eliot, George. *The Mill on the Floss*. Edited by Carol T. Christ. New York: Norton & Company, 1994.

Elmslie, W. A. L. *Studies in Life from Jewish Proverbs*. London: James Clark & Co., 1917.

Erman, Adolf. "Eine ägyptische Quelle der 'Spruch Salomos.'" *Sitzungsberichte der Preussischen Akademie der Wissenschaften* 15 (1924): 86–93.

Exum, J. Cheryl. *The Song of Songs*. Old Testament Library. Louisville: Westminster John Knox, 2005.

   "How Does the Song of Songs Mean? On Reading the Poetry of Desire." *Svensk Exegetisk Arsbok* 64 (1999): 47–63.

Fagin, Larry. *The List Poem: A Guide to Teaching & Writing Catalog Verse*. New York: Teachers & Writers Collaborative, 2000.

Fesmire, Steven. *John Dewey and Moral Imagination: Pragmatism in Ethics*. Bloomington: Indiana University Press, 2003.

Finkelstein, Louis. *The Pharisees: the Sociological Background of their Faith*. Philadelphia: Jewish Publication Society of America, 1938.

Fishbane, Michael. *Text and Texture: Close Readings of Selected Biblical Texts*. New York: Schocken, 1979.

Fitzgerald, Chloë, and Peter Goldie. "Thick Concepts and Their Role in Moral Psychology." Pages 219–36 in *Emotions, Imagination, and Moral Reasoning*. Edited by Robyn Langdon and Catriona Mackenzie. New York: Psychology Press, 2012.

Fokkelman, J. P. *Reading Biblical Poetry: An Introductory Guide*. Translated by Ineke Smit. Louisville: Westminster John Knox, 2001.

Fontaine, Carole. R. "Proverbs." Pages 153–60 in *Women's Bible Commentary: Expanded Edition*. Edited by Carol A. Newsom and Sharon H. Ringe. Louisville: Westminster John Knox, 1998.

   *Traditional Sayings in the Old Testament*. Sheffield: Almond Press, 1982.

Forti, Tova L. *Animal Imagery in the Book of Proverbs*. Vetus Testamentum Supplements 118. Leiden: Brill, 2008.

   "The *Isha Zara* in Proverbs 1–9: Allegory and Allegorization." *Hebrew Studies* 48 (2007): 89–100.

   "Bee's Honey – From Realia to Metaphor in Biblical Wisdom Literature." *Vetus Testamentum* 56 (2006): 327–41.

Fowl, Stephen E., and L. Gregory Jones. *Reading in Communion: Scripture and Ethics in the Christian Life*. Grand Rapids: Eerdmans, 1991.

Fox, Michael V. *Proverbs 10–31: A New Translation with Introduction and Commentary*. Anchor Bible 18B. New Haven: Yale University Press, 2009.

"The Rhetoric of Disjointed Proverbs." *Journal for the Study of the Old Testament* 29 (2004): 165–77.

*Proverbs 1–9: A New Translation with Introduction and Commentary*. Anchor Bible 18A. New York: Doubleday, 2000.

"Who Can Learn? A Dispute in Ancient Pedagogy." Pages 62–77 in *Wisdom, You Are My Sister: Studies in Honor of Roland E. Murphy, O. Carm., on the Occasion of His Eightieth Birthday*. Edited by Michael L. Barré. Catholic Biblical Quarterly Monograph Series 29. Washington, DC: The Catholic Biblical Association of America, 1997.

"The Pedagogy of Proverbs 2." *Journal of Biblical Literature* 113 (1994): 233–43.

*Qohelet and His Contradictions*. Journal for the Study of the Old Testament: Supplement Series 71. Sheffield: Almond Press, 1989.

"The Meaning of *Hebel* for Qohelet." *Journal of Biblical Literature* 105 (1986): 409–27.

*The Song of Songs and the Ancient Egyptian Love Songs*. Madison: University of Wisconsin Press, 1985.

Frost, Robert. "The Figure a Poem Makes." Pages 439–442 in *The Robert Frost Reader: Poetry and Prose*. Edited by E. C. Lathem and L. R. Thompson. New York: Henry Holt and Co., 2002.

Frydrych, Tomáš. *Living under the Sun: Examination of Proverbs and Qoheleth*. Vetus Testamentum Supplements 40. Leiden: Brill, 2002.

Gemser, Berend. "The Instructions of 'Onchsheshonqy and Biblical Wisdom Literature." Pages 134–60 in *Studies in Ancient Israelite Wisdom*. Edited by James L. Crenshaw. New York: KTAV, 1976. Repr. from *Congress Volume: Oxford, 1959*. Edited by G. W. Anderson. Vetus Testamentum Supplements 7. Leiden: Brill, 1960.

"The Importance of the Motive Clause in Old Testament Law." Pages 50–66 in *Congress Volume, Copenhagen 1953*. Vetus Testamentum Supplements 1. Leiden: Brill, 1953.

*Sprüche Salomos*. Tübingen: J.C.B. Mohr, 1937.

Gerstenberger, Erhard. *Wesen und Herkunft des "apodiktischen Rechts."* Wissenschaftliche Monographien zum Alten und Neuen Testament 20. Neukirchen-Vluyn: Neukirchener Verlag, 1965.

Gese, Hartmut. "The Crisis of Wisdom in Koheleth." Pages 141–53 in *Theodicy in the Old Testament*. Edited by James L. Crenshaw. Issues in Religion and Theology 4. Philadelphia/London: Fortress/SPCK, 1983. Translated from "Die Krisis der Weisheit bei Koheleth." Pages 139–51 in *Les sagesses du Proche-Orient ancient: Colloque de Strasbourg, 17–19 Mai, 1962*. Paris: Presses Universitaires de France, 1963.

*Lehre und Wirklichkeit in der alten Weisheit. Studien zu den Sprüchen Salomos und zu dem Buche Hiob*. Tübingen: Mohr, 1958.

Gillingham, S. E. *The Poems and Psalms of the Hebrew Bible*. Oxford: Oxford University Press, 1994.

Goldingay, John. "The Arrangement of Sayings in Proverbs 10–15." *Journal for the Study of the Old Testament* 61 (1994): 75–83.

Gordon, Edmund I. "A New Look at the Wisdom of Sumer and Akkad." *Bibliotheca orientalis* 17 (1960): 122–52.

*Sumerian Proverbs: Glimpses of Everyday Life in Ancient Mesopotamia.* Philadelphia: University Museum, University of Pennsylvania, 1959.

Gordon, R. N. "Motivation in Proverbs." *Biblical Theology* 25 (1975): 49–56.

Gottwald, Norman K. *A Light to the Nations: An Introduction to the Old Testament.* New York: Harper, 1959.

Graham, M. Patrick. "A Character Ethics Reading of 1 Chronicles 29:1–25." Pages 98–120 in *Character and Scripture: Moral Formation, Community, and Biblical Interpretation.* Edited by William P. Brown. Grand Rapids: Eerdmans, 2002.

Greenspahn, Frederick E. "The Number and Distribution of *hapax legomena* in Biblical Hebrew." *Vetus Testamentum* 30 (1980): 8–19.

Greenstein, Edward L. "How Does Parallelism Mean?" Pages 41–70 in *A Sense of Text: The Art of Language in the Study of Biblical Literature: Papers from a Symposium at the Dropsie College for Hebrew and Cognate Learning, May 11, 1982.* Jewish Quarterly Review Supplement. Winona Lake: Eisenbrauns, 1982.

Gregory of Nyssa, *Commentary on the Song of Songs.* Translated by Casimir McCambley. Brookline: Hellenic College Press, 1987.

Hankins, Charles Davis. "Job and the Limits of Wisdom." PhD diss., Emory University, 2011.

Harris, Scott L. *Proverbs 1–9: A Study of Inner-Biblical Interpretation.* Society of Biblical Literature Dissertation Series. Atlanta: Scholars Press, 1995.

Hatton, Peter T. H. *Contradiction in the Book of Proverbs: The Deep Waters of Counsel.* Burlington: Ashgate, 2008.

Hauerwas, Stanley. *A Community of Character: Toward a Constructive Christian Social Ethic.* Notre Dame: University of Notre Dame Press, 1981.

*Character and the Christian Life: A Study in Theological Ethics.* San Antonio: Trinity University Press, 1975. Repr. 1985.

Hauerwas, Stanley, and L. Gregory Jones, eds. *Why Narrative? Readings in Narrative Theology.* Grand Rapids: Eerdmans, 1989.

Hauerwas, Stanley, with Richard Bondi, and David B. Burrell. *Truthfulness and Tragedy: Further Investigations in Christian Ethics.* Notre Dame: University of Notre Dame Press, 1977.

Hays, Richard B. *The Moral Vision of the New Testament: Community, Cross, New Creation: A Contemporary Introduction to New Testament Ethics.* New York: HarperCollins, 1996.

Heim, Knut M. *Poetic Imagination in Proverbs: Variant Repetitions and the Nature of Poetry.* Bulletin for Biblical Research Supplement 4. Winona Lake: Eisenbrauns, 2013.

"A Closer Look at the Pig in Proverbs XI 22." *Vetus Testamentum* (2008): 13–27.

*Like Grapes of Gold Set in Silver: An Interpretation of Proverbial Clusters in Proverbs 10:1–22:16.* Beihefte zur Zeitschrift für die alttestamentliche Wissenschaft 273. Berlin: Walter de Gruyter, 2001.

Hempel, Johannes. *Das Ethos des Alten Testaments*. Beihefte zur Zeitschrift für die alttestamentliche Wissenschaft 67. Berlin: Verlag von Alfred Töpelmann, 1938; 2nd ed., 1964.

"Ethics in the OT." Pages 153–61 in vol. 2 of *The Interpreter's Dictionary of the Bible*. Edited by G. A. Buttrick. 4 vols. Nashville: Abingdon Press, 1962.

"Pathos und Humor in der israelitischen Erziehung." Pages 63–81 in *Von Ugarit nach Qumran: Beiträge zur alttestamentlichen und altorientalischen Forschung: Otto Eissfeldt*. Edited by Johannes Hempel et al. Beihefte zur Zeitschrift für die alttestamentliche Wissenschaft 77. Berlin: Verlag Alfred Töpelmann, 1958.

*Die althebräische Literatur und ihr hellenistisch-jüdisches Nachleben*. Wildpark-Potsdam: Akademische Verlagsgesellschaft Athenaion, 1930.

*Gott und Mensch im Alten Testament*. Beiträrage zur Wissenschaft vom Alten und Neuen Testament 3.2. Stuttgart: Kohlhammer, 1926.

Hermisson, Hans-Jürgen. *Studien zur israelitischen Spruchweisheit*. Wissenschaftliche Monographien zum Alten und Neuen Testament 28. Neukirchen: Neukirchener Verlag, 1968.

Hildebrandt, Ted. "Motivation and Antithetic Parallelism in Proverbs 10–15." *Journal of the Evangelical Theological Society* 35 (1992): 433–44.

"Proverbial Pairs: Compositional Units in Proverbs 10–29." *Journal of Biblical Literature* 107 (1988): 207–24.

"Proverbs 22:6a: Train Up a Child?" *Grace Theological Journal* 11 (1988): 3–19.

Hunter, James Davison. *The Death of Character: Moral Education in an Age without Good or Evil*. New York: Basic Books, 2000.

Hurowitz, Victor. "The Seventh Pillar – Reconsidering the Literary Structure and Unity of Proverbs 31." *Zeitschrift für die alttestamentliche Wissenschaft* 113 (2001): 209–18.

Hursthouse, Rosalind. *On Virtue Ethics*. Oxford: Oxford University Press, 1999.

Huwiler, Elizabeth Faith. "Control of Reality in Israelite Wisdom." PhD diss., Duke University, 1988.

Irvine, William B. *On Desire: Why We Want What We Want*. New York: Oxford University Press, 2006.

Jakobson, Roman. "Linguistics and Poetics." Pages 18–51 in *Selected Writings, vol. 3: Poetry of Grammar and Grammar of Poetry*. Edited by Stephen Rudy. New York: Mouton Publishers, 1981.

Janowski, Bernd. "Die Tat kehrt zum Täter zurück: Offene Fragen im Umkreis des >>Tun-Ergehen-Zusammenhangs<<." *Zeitschrift für Theologie und Kirche* (1994): 247–71.

Janzen, Waldemar. *Old Testament Ethics: A Paradigmatic Approach*. Louisville: Westminster John Knox, 1994.

Johnson, Mark. *Moral Imagination: Implications of Cognitive Science for Ethics*. Chicago: University of Chicago Press, 1993.

Johnson, Samuel. "Preface to Shakespeare (1765)." Pages 9–63 in *Johnson on Shakespeare: Essays and Notes*. Edited by Walter Raleigh. London: Henry Frowde, 1908.

Johnson, Timothy. "Implied Antecedents in Job XL 2b and Proverbs III 6a." *Vetus Testamentum* 52 (2002): 278–84.

Johnson, W. R. *The Idea of Lyric.* Berkeley: University of California, 1982.

Jones, L. Gregory. "Alasdair MacIntyre on Narrative, Community, and the Moral Life." *Modern Theology* 4 (1987): 53–69.

Jones, Scott C. "Wisdom's Pedagogy: A Comparison of Proverbs VII and 4Q184." *Vetus Testamentum* 53 (2003): 65–80.

Joüon, P., and T. Muraoka. *A Grammar of Biblical Hebrew.* 2nd ed. Rome: Gregorian & Biblical Press, 2009.

Kaiser, Walter C. *Toward Old Testament Ethics.* Grand Rapids: Zondervan, 1983.

Kass, Leon R. *The Hungry Soul: Eating and the Perfecting of Our Nature.* New York: Free Press, 1994.

Katz, Albert N. "Figurative Language and Figurative Thought: A Review." Pages 3–43 in *Figurative Language and Thought.* Edited by Albert N. Katz et al. New York: Oxford University Press, 1998.

Kautzsch, E., ed. *Gesenius' Hebrew Grammar.* Translated by A. E. Cowley. 2nd ed. Boston: A. I. Bradley & Co., 1898.

Kayatz, Christa. *Studien zu Proverbien 1–9: Eine form- und motivgeschichtliche Untersuchung unter Einbeziehung ägyptischen Vergleichmaterials.* Wissenschaftliche Monographien zum Alten und Neuen Testament 22. Neukirchen-Vluyn: Neukirchener Verlag, 1966.

Keel, Othmar. *Goddesses and Trees, New Moon and Yahweh: Ancient Near Eastern Art and the Hebrew Bible.* Journal for the Study of the Old Testament: Supplement Series 261. Sheffield: Sheffield Academic Press, 1998.

Kekes, John. *The Enlargement of Life: Moral Imagination at Work.* Ithaca: Cornell University Press, 2006.

⸻. *The Morality of Pluralism.* Princeton: Princeton University Press, 1993.

Kelby, Anthony Paul. *Narrative and the Self.* Studies in Continental Thought; Bloomington: Indiana University Press, 1991.

Kelly, Ursula. *Schooling Desire: Literacy, Cultural Politics, and Pedagogy.* New York: Routledge, 1997.

Koch, Klaus. "Is There a Doctrine of Retribution in the Old Testament?" Translated by Thomas H. Trapp. Pages 57–87 in *Theodicy in the Old Testament.* Edited by James L. Crenshaw. Issues in Religion and Theology 4. Philadelphia: Fortress, 1983. Translation of "Gibt es ein Vergeltungsdogma im Alten Testament?" *Zeitschrift für Theologie und Kirche* (1955): 1–42.

Koehler, Ludwig, Walter Baumgartner, and Johann J. Stamm. *The Hebrew and Aramaic Lexicon of the Old Testament: Study Edition.* 2 vols. Leiden: Brill, 2001.

Krispenz, Jutta. *Spruchkompositionen im Buch Proverbia.* Europäische Hochschulschriften 23. New York: Peter Lang, 1989.

Krüger, Thomas. *Qoheleth: A Commentary.* Hermeneia. Minneapolis: Fortress Press, 2004.

Kugel, James L. *The Idea of Biblical Poetry: Parallelism and Its History.* New Haven: Yale University Press, 1981.

Laird, Martin L. "Under Solomon's Tutelage: The Education of Desire in the *Homilies on the Song of Songs.*" *Modern Theology* 18.4 (2002): 507–25.

Lakoff, George, and Mark Johnson. *Philosophy in the Flesh: The Embodied Mind and Its Challenge to Western Thought.* New York: Basic Books, 1999.

*Metaphors We Live By.* Chicago: University of Chicago Press, 1980.

Lakoff, George, and Mark Turner. *More Than Cool Reason: A Field Guide to Poetic Metaphor.* Chicago: University of Chicago Press, 1989.

Lang, Bernhard. *Die weisheitliche Lehrrede. Eine Untersuchung von Sprüche 1–7.* Stuttgarter Bibelstudien 54. Stuttgart: KBW, 1972.

Lanham, Richard A. *A Handlist of Rhetorical Terms: A Guide for Students of English Literature.* Berkeley: University of California Press, 1968.

Lapsley, Jacqueline E. *Can These Bones Live? The Problem of the Moral Self in the Book of Ezekiel.* Beihefte zur Zeitschrift für die alttestamentliche Wissenschaft 301. Berlin: Walter de Gruyter, 2000.

Lauha, Aare. "Die Krise des religiösen Glaubens bei Kohelet." Pages 183–91 in *Wisdom in Israel and in the Ancient Near East.* Edited by M. Noth and D. Winton Thomas. Vetus Testamentum Supplements 3. Leiden: Brill, 1955.

Lichtenstein, Murray H. "Chiasm and Symmetry in Proverbs 31." *Catholic Biblical Quarterly* 44 (1982): 202–11.

Lichtheim, Miriam. *Late Egyptian Wisdom Literature in the International Context: A Study of Demotic Instructions.* Orbis Biblicus et Orientalis 52. Göttingen: Vandenhoeck & Ruprecht, 1983.

*Ancient Egyptian Literature: A Book of Readings.* 3 vols. Berkeley: University of California Press, 1973–80.

Liddell, Henry George, and Robert Scott. *A Greek-English Lexicon.* Rev. ed. Oxford: Clarendon Press, 1996.

Linafelt, Tod, and F. W. Dobbs-Allsopp, "Poetic Line Structure in Qoheleth 3:1." *Vetus Testamentum* 60 (2010): 249–59.

Lowth, Robert. *Lectures on the Sacred Poetry of the Hebrews.* Translated by G. Gregory. 2 vols. London: Ogles, Duncan, and Cochran, 1816.

Lucretius. *De Rerum Natura: The Nature of Things, a Poetic Translation.* Translated by David R. Slavitt. Berkeley: University of California Press, 2008.

Lyu, Sun Myung. *Righteousness in the Book of Proverbs.* Forschungen zum Alten Testament II. Tübingen: Mohr Siebeck, 2012.

MacIntyre, Alasdair. *After Virtue: A Study in Moral Theory.* 2nd ed. Notre Dame: University of Notre Dame Press, 1984.

Marcus, Ralph. "The Tree of Life in Proverbs." *Journal of Biblical Literature* 62 (1943): 117–20.

McCreesh, Thomas P. *Biblical Sound and Sense: Poetic Sound Patterns in Proverbs 10–29.* Journal for the Study of the Old Testament: Supplement Series 128. Sheffield: JSOT Press, 1991.

"Wisdom as Wife: Proverbs 31:10–31." *Revue biblique* 92 (1985): 25–46.

McKane, William. *Proverbs: A New Approach.* Old Testament Library. Philadelphia: Westminster Press, 1970.

McKinnon, Christine. *Character, Virtue Theories, and the Vices.* Orchard Park: Broadview Press, 1999.

Meinhold, Arndt. *Die Sprüche.* Zürcher Bibelkommentare 16. 2 vols. Zürich: Theologischer Verlag, 1991.

"Gott und Mensch in Proverbien III." *Vetus Testamentum* 37 (1987): 468–77.

Mieder, Wolfgang. *Proverbs: A Handbook.* Westport: Greenwood Press, 2004.

ed. *A Dictionary of American Proverbs.* New York: Oxford University Press, 1992.

Miller, Douglas B. "Qohelet's Symbolic Use of הבל." *Journal of Biblical Literature* 117 (1998): 437–54.

Miller, Patrick D. *Interpreting the Psalms.* Philadelphia: Fortress Press, 1986.

Miner, Earl. *Comparative Poetics: An Intercultural Essay on Theories of Literature.* Princeton: Princeton University Press, 1990.

Munro, Jill M. *Spikenard and Saffron: The Imagery of the Song of Songs.* Journal for the Study of the Old Testament: Supplement Series 203. Sheffield: Sheffield Academic Press, 1995.

Munro, Thomas. *Form and Style in the Arts: An Introduction to Aesthetic Morphology.* Cleveland: Case Western Reserve University, 1970.

Murphy, Roland E. *Proverbs.* Word Biblical Commentary 22. Nashville: Thomson Nelson, 1998.

*The Song of Songs: A Commentary on the Book of Canticles or the Song of Songs.* Edited by S. Dean McBride, Jr. Hermeneia. Minneapolis: Fortress Press, 1990.

"Wisdom and Eros in Proverbs 1–9." *Catholic Biblical Quarterly* 50 (1988): 600–03.

"Wisdom's Song: Proverbs 1:20–33." *Catholic Biblical Quarterly* 48 (1986): 456–60.

*Wisdom Literature: Job, Proverbs, Ruth, Canticles, Ecclesiastes, and Esther.* Forms of the Old Testament Literature 13. Grand Rapids: Eerdmans, 1981.

"Qoheleth's 'Quarrel' with the Fathers." Pages 235–45 in *From Faith to Faith.* Edited by D. Y. Hadidian. Pittsburgh Theological Monograph Series 31. Pittsburgh: Pickwick, 1979).

"The Kerygma of the Book of Proverbs." *Interpretation* 20 (1966): 3–14.

Nagel, Thomas. *The Possibility of Altruism.* Princeton: Princeton University Press, 1978.

Nel, Philip Johannes. *The Structure and Ethos of the Wisdom Admonitions in Proverbs.* Beihefte zur Zeitschrift für die alttestamentliche Wissenschaft 158. Berlin: Walter de Gruyter, 1982.

Newsom, Carol A. "Models of the Moral Self: Hebrew Bible and Second Temple Judaism." *Journal of Biblical Literature* 131 (2012): 5–25.

"Spying Out the Land: A Report from Genology." Pages 437–50 in *Seeking Out the Wisdom of the Ancients: Essays Offered to Honor Michael V. Fox on the Occasion of His Sixty-Fifth Birthday.* Edited by Ronald L. Troxel et al. Winona Lake: Eisenbrauns, 2005.

*The Book of Job: A Contest of Moral Imaginations.* New York: Oxford University Press, 2003.

"Narrative Ethics, Character, and the Prose Tale of Job." Pages 121–34 in *Character and Scripture: Moral Formation, Community, and Biblical Interpretation.* Edited by William P. Brown. Grand Rapids: Eerdmans, 2002.

"Woman and the Discourse of Patriarchal Wisdom: A Study of Proverbs 1–9." Pages 142–60 in *Gender and Difference in Ancient Israel.* Edited by P. Day. Minneapolis: Augsburg Fortress, 1989.

Newton, Adam Zachary. *Narrative Ethics.* Cambridge: Harvard University Press, 1995.

Noort, Ed, and Eibert Tigchelaar, eds., *The Sacrifice of Isaac: The Aqedah (Genesis 22) and Its Interpretations.* Themes in Biblical Narrative 4. Leiden: Brill, 2002.

Nussbaum, Martha C. *Upheavals of Thought: The Intelligence of Emotions.* Cambridge: Cambridge University Press, 2001.

"Virtue Ethics: A Misleading Category?" *The Journal of Ethics* 3.3 (1999): 163–201.

*The Therapy of Desire: Theory and Practice in Hellenistic Ethics.* Martin Classical Lectures 2. Princeton: Princeton University Press, 1994.

*Love's Knowledge: Essays on Philosophy and Literature.* New York: Oxford University Press, 1990.

"Recoiling from Reason" (review of Alasdair MacIntyre, *Whose Justice? Which Rationality?*). *New York Review of Books,* December 7, 1989, 36–41.

"Narrative Emotions: Beckett's Genealogy of Love." *Ethics* 98.2 (1988): 225–54.

O'Connor, Kathleen M. *The Wisdom Literature.* Message of Biblical Spirituality 5. Collegeville: Liturgical Press, 1988.

Oesterley, W. O. E. *The Book of Proverbs.* New York: E.P. Dutton and Company, 1929.

Ollenburger, Ben C. "'Seeing the Truth': Proverbial Wisdom and Christian Ethics." *Direction* 9.2 (1980): 23–31.

Otto, Eckart. *Theologische Ethik des Alten Testaments.* Stuttgart: Kohlhammer, 1995.

Overland, Paul. "Did the Sage Draw from the Shema? A Study of Proverbs 3:1–12." *Catholic Biblical Quarterly* 62 (2000): 424–40.

Ovid. *The Art of Love.* Translated by Henry T. Riley. Edited by Walter S. Keating. New York: Stravon Publishers, 1949.

Pardee, Dennis. *Ugaritic and Hebrew Parallelism: A Trial Cut ('nt 1 and Proverbs 2).* Vetus Testamentum Supplements 39. Leiden: Brill, 1987.

Perdue, Leo G. *The Sword and the Stylus: An Introduction to Wisdom in the Age of Empires.* Grand Rapids: Eerdmans, 2008.

*Wisdom and Creation: The Theology of Wisdom Literature.* Nashville: Abingdon Press, 1994.

Perry, T. A. *Wisdom Literature and the Structure of Proverbs.* University Park: Pennsylvania State University Press, 1993.

Pincoffs, Edmund L. *Quandaries and Virtues: Against Reductivism in Ethics.* Lawrence: University Press of Kansas, 1986.

Pope, Marvin H. *Song of Songs: A New Translation with Introduction and Commentary.* Anchor Bible 7C. Garden City: Doubleday, 1977.

Postel, Henry John. *The Form and Function of the Motive Clause in Proverbs 10–29.* PhD diss., University of Iowa, 1976.

Reif, C. "Dedicated to חנך." *Vetus Testamentum* 22 (1972): 495–501.

Richards, I. A. *The Philosophy of Rhetoric.* New York: Oxford University Press, 1965.

Ricoeur, Paul. *Oneself as Another.* Translated by Kathleen Blarney. Chicago: University of Chicago Press, 1992.

    *Time and Narrative.* Translated by Kathleen McLaughlin and David Pellauer. Chicago: University of Chicago Press, 1990. Translation of *Temps et récit.* Paris: Seuil, 1983–1985.

    "Biblical Hermeneutics." *Semeia* 4 (1975): 29–148.

Robert, André. "Les Attaches Littéraires Bibliques de Prov. i-ix." *Revue biblique* 43 (1934): 42–68, 172–204, 374–84; *Revue biblique* 44 (1935): 344–65, 502–25.

Robinson, T. H. "Basic Principles of Hebrew Poetic Form." Pages 438–50 in *Festschrift Alfred Bertholet zum 80. Geburtstab gewidment von Kollegen und Freunden.* Edited by Walter Baumgartner et al. Tübingen: J.C.B. Mohr (Paul Siebeck), 1950.

Rodd, Cyril S. *Glimpses of a Strange Land: Studies in Old Testament Ethics.* Old Testament Studies. Edinburgh: T&T Clark, 2001.

Rogerson, John. *Theory and Practice in Old Testament Ethics.* Edited by M. Daniel Carroll R. New York: T&T Clark, 2004.

Rosati, Connie S. "Moral Motivation." *The Stanford Encyclopedia of Philosophy (Fall 2008 Edition).* Edited by Edward N. Zalta. No pages. Cited 28 February 2012. Online: <http://plato.stanford.edu/archives/fall2008/entries/moral-motivation/>.

Roth, Wolfgant. *Numerical Sayings in the Old Testament: A Form-Critical Study.* Vetus Testamentum Supplements 13. Leiden: Brill, 1965.

Ruf, Frederick J. "The Consequences of Genre: Narrative, Lyric, and Dramatic Intelligibility." *Journal of the American Academy of Religion* 62 (1994): 799–818.

Rylaarsdam, J. Coert. *The Proverbs, Ecclesiastes, the Song of Solomon.* Layman's Bible Commentary 10. Richmond: John Knox, 1964.

Sakenfeld, Katherine Doob. *The Meaning of Hesed in the Hebrew Bible: A New Inquiry.* Harvard Semitic Monographs 17. Missoula: Scholars Press, 1978.

Sandoval, Timothy J. *The Discourse of Wealth and Poverty in the Book of Proverbs.* Biblical Interpretation Series 77. Leiden: Brill, 2006.

Sauer, Georg. *Die Sprüche Agurs: Untersuchungen zur Herkunft, Verbreitung und Bedeutung einer biblischen Stilform unter besonderer Berücksichtigung von Proverbia c. 30.* Beiträge zur Wissenschaft vom Alten und Neuen Testament 5.4. Stuttgart: Kohlhammer, 1963.

Schloen, J. David. *The House of the Father as Fact and Symbol: Patrimonialism in Ugarit and the Ancient Near East.* Winona Lake: Eisenbrauns, 2001.

Schmid, Hans Heinrich. *Wesen und Geschichte der Weisheit: Eine Untersuchung zur altorientalischen und israelitischen Weisheitsliteratur.* Beihefte zur Zeitschrift für die alttestamentliche Wissenschaft 101. Berlin: Verlag Alfred Töpelmann, 1966.

Schroeder, Timothy, Adina L. Roskies, and Shaun Nichols. "Moral Motivation." Pages 74–78 in *The Moral Psychology Handbook.* Edited by John M. Doris et al. New York: Oxford University Press, 2010.

Schwáb, Zoltán S. *Toward an Interpretation of the Book of Proverbs: Selfishness and Secularity Reconsidered.* Winona Lake: Eisenbrauns, 2013.

Scott, R. B. Y. "Folk Proverbs of the Ancient Near East." Pages 417–26 in *Studies in Ancient Israelite Wisdom.* Edited by James L. Crenshaw. New York: KTAV, 1976. Repr. from *Transactions of the Royal Society of Canada* 55.3 (1961): 47–56.

*The Way of Wisdom in the Old Testament.* New York: Macmillan, 1971.

*Proverbs – Ecclesiastes.* Anchor Bible 18. Garden City: Doubleday & Company, 1965.

Seow, C. L. "An Exquisitely Poetic Introduction to the Psalter." *Journal of Biblical Literature* 132 (2013): 275–93.

*Ecclesiastes: A New Translation with Introduction and Commentary.* Anchor Bible 18C. New York: Doubleday, 1997.

Sheffield, Frisbee C. C. *Plato's Symposium: The Ethics of Desire.* New York: Oxford University Press, 2006.

Shupak, Nili. "Female Imagery in Proverbs 1–9 in the Light of Egyptian Sources." *Vetus Testamentum* 61 (2011): 310–23.

"The Instruction of Amenemope and Proverbs 22:17–24:22 from the Perspective of Contemporary Research." Pages 203–20 in *Searching Out the Wisdom of the Ancients: Essays Offered to Michael V. Fox on the Occasion of His Sixty-Fifth Birthday.* Edited by Ronald L. Troxel et al. Winona Lake: Eisenbrauns, 2005.

Skehan, Patrick W. "The Seven Columns of Wisdom's House in Proverbs 1–9." Pages 9–14 in *Studies in Israelite Poetry and Wisdom.* Edited by Patrick W. Skehan. Catholic Biblical Quarterly Monograph Series 1. Washington, DC: The Catholic Biblical Association of America, 1971. Repr. and rev. from *Catholic Biblical Quarterly* 9 (1947): 190–98.

Slote, Michael A. *The Impossibility of Perfection: Aristotle, Feminism, and the Complexities of Ethics.* New York: Oxford University Press, 2011.

Smith, Barbara Herrnstein. *Poetic Closure: A Study of How Poems End.* Chicago: University of Chicago, 1968.

Smith, Neil G. "Family Ethics in the Wisdom Literature." *Interpretation* 4 (1950): 453–57.

Sneed, Mark. "'White Trash' Wisdom: Proverbs 9 Deconstructed." *Journal of Hebrew Scriptures* 7.5 (2007): 1–10.

Sonsino, Rifat. *Motive Clauses in Hebrew Law: Biblical Forms and Near Eastern Parallels.* Chico: Scholars Press, 1980.

Sorabji, Richard. "Aristotle on the Role of the Intellect in Virtue." Pages 201–20 in *Essays on Aristotle's Ethics.* Edited by A. O. Rorty. Major Thinkers Series. Berkeley: University of California Press, 1980.

Spiegelman, Willard. *The Didactic Muse: Scenes of Instruction in Contemporary American Poetry*. Princeton: Princeton University Press, 1989.

Steiert, Franz-Josef. *Die Weisheit Israels – ein Fremdkörper im Alten Testament? Eine Untersuchung zum Buch der Sprüche auf dem Hintergrund der ägyptischen Weisheitslehren*. Freiburger theologische Studien 143. Freiburg: Herder, 1990.

Stevenson, William B. "A Mnemonic Use of Numbers in Proverbs and Ben Sira." *Glasgow University Oriental Society, Transactions* 9 (1938–39): 26–38.

Stewart, Susan. *Poetry and the Fate of the Senses*. Chicago: University of Chicago Press, 2002.

Stone, Jon R., ed. *The Routledge Book of World Proverbs*. New York: Routledge, 2006.

Story, Cullen I. K. "The Book of Proverbs and North West Semitic Literature." *Journal of Biblical Literature* (1945): 319–37.

Strawn, Brent A. "Comparative Approaches: History, Theory, and the Image of God." Pages 117–42 in *Method Matters: Essays on the Interpretation of the Hebrew Bible in Honor of David L. Petersen*. Edited by Joel M. LeMon and Kent Harold Richards. Atlanta: Society of Biblical Literature, 2009.

——— "Lyric Poetry." Pages 437–46 in *Dictionary of the Old Testament: Wisdom, Literature, and Writings*. Edited by Tremper Longman III and Peter Enns; Downers Grove: InterVarsity Press, 2008.

Strawson, Galen. "Episodic Ethics." Pages 85–115 in *Narrative and Understanding Persons*. Edited by Daniel D. Hutto. Royal Institute of Philosophy Supplement 60. Cambridge: Cambridge University Press, 2007.

——— "Against Narrativity." *Ratio* 17 (2004): 428–52.

Suleiman, Susan Rubin. *Authoritarian Fictions: The Ideological Novel as a Literary Genre*. New York: Columbia University Press, 1983.

Szlos, M. Beth. "Body Parts as Metaphor and the Value of a Cognitive Approach: A Study of the Female Figures in Proverbs via Metaphor." Pages 185–95 in *Metaphor in the Hebrew Bible*. Edited by P. van Hecke. Bibliotheca ephemeridum theologicarum lovaniensium 187. Leuven: Leuven University Press, 2005.

——— "A Portrait of Power: A Literary-Critical Study of the Depiction in Proverbs 31:10–31." *Union Seminary Quarterly Review* 54 (2000): 97–103.

Tan, Nancy Nam Hoon. *The "Foreignness" of the Foreign Woman in Proverbs 1–9: A Study of the Origin and Development of a Biblical Motif*. Beihefte zur Zeitschrift für die alttestamentliche Wissenschaft 381. Berlin: Walter de Gruyter, 2008.

Taylor, Charles. *Sources of the Self: The Making of the Modern Identity*. Cambridge: Harvard University Press, 1989.

Tilford, Nicole Lynn. " 'Taste and See': The Role of Perception in Israelite and Early Jewish Sapiential Epistemology." PhD diss., Emory University, 2013.

Toy, Crawford H. *The Book of Proverbs: A Critical and Exegetical Commentary*. International Critical Commentary 13. Edinburgh: T&T Clark, 1899.

Trible, Phyllis. "Wisdom Builds a Poem: The Architecture of Proverbs 1:20–33." *Journal of Biblical Literature* 94 (1975): 509–18.

Tsevat, Matitiahu. "The Meaning of the Book of Job." *Hebrew Union College Annual* 37 (1966): 73–106.

Van der Toorn, Karel. "Female Prostitution in Payment of Vows in Ancient Israel." *Journal of Biblical Literature* 108 (1989): 193–205.

Van Leeuwen, Raymond C. "Wealth and Poverty: System and Contradiction in Proverbs." *Hebrew Studies* 33 (1992): 25–36.

"Liminality and Worldview in Proverbs 1–9." *Semeia* 50 (1990): 111–44.

*Context and Meaning in Proverbs 25–27.* Society of Biblical Literature Dissertation Series 96. Atlanta: Scholars Press, 1988.

Vendler, Helen. *Poets Thinking: Pope, Whitman, Dickinson, Yeats.* Cambridge: Harvard University Press, 2004.

Volk, Katharina. *The Poetics of Latin Didactic: Lucretius, Vergil, Ovid, Manilius.* New York: Oxford University Press, 2002.

"*Cum carmine crescit et annus*: Ovid's *Fasti* and the Poetics of Simultaneity." *Transactions of the American Philological Association* 127 (1997): 287–313.

von Hallberg, Robert. *Lyric Powers.* Chicago: University of Chicago Press, 2008.

von Oyen, Hendrik. *Ethik des Alten Testaments.* 2 vols. Gütersloh: Gütersloher Verlagshuas Gerd Mohn, 1967.

von Rad, Gerhard. *Wisdom in Israel.* Translated by James D. Martin. London: SCM Press, 1972. Repr., Harrisburg: Trinity Press International, 1993.

Walsh, Carey Ellen. *Exquisite Desire: Religion, Erotic, and the Song of Songs.* Minneapolis: Augsburg Fortress, 2000.

Waltke, Bruce K. *The Book of Proverbs: Chapters 1–15.* Grand Rapids: Eerdmans, 2004.

"Lady Wisdom as Mediatrix: An Exposition of Proverbs 1:20–33." *Presbyterion* 14.1 (1988): 1–15.

Warnock, Mary. *Imagination.* Berkeley: University of California Press, 1976.

Washington, Harold C. *Wealth and Poverty in the Instruction of Amenemope and the Hebrew Proverbs.* Society of Biblical Literature Dissertation Series 142. Atlanta: Scholars Press, 1994.

Wenham, Gordon J. *Story as Torah: Reading the Old Testament Ethically.* Old Testament Studies. Edinburgh: T&T Clark, 2000.

Whybray, R. N. *The Book of Proverbs: A Survey of Modern Study.* History of Biblical Interpretation 1. Leiden: Brill, 1995.

*The Composition of the Book of Proverbs.* Journal for the Study of the Old Testament: Supplement Series 168. Sheffield: JSOT Press, 1994.

*Wealth and Poverty in the Book of Proverbs.* Journal for the Study of the Old Testament: Supplement Series 99. Sheffield: Sheffield Academic Press, 1990.

*Wisdom in Proverbs: The Concept of Wisdom in Proverbs 1–9.* Studies in Biblical Theology 45. London: SCM Press, 1965.

"The Concept of Wisdom in Proverbs I–IX." DPhil diss., Oxford, 1962.

Wierzbicka, Anna. "Metaphors Linguists Live By: Lakoff & Johnson Contra Aristotle." *Papers in Linguistics* 19.2 (1986): 287–313.

Wilder, Amos. *Theopoetic: Theology and the Religious Imagination.* Philadelphia: Fortress Press, 1976.

Williams, Anne. *Prophetic Strain: The Greater Lyric in the Eighteenth Century.* Chicago: University of Chicago Press, 1984.

Williams, Bernard. *Ethics and the Limits of Philosophy.* Cambridge: Harvard University Press, 1985.

*Moral Luck: Philosophical Papers 1973–1980.* New York: Cambridge University Press, 1981.

Williams, James G. "The Power of Form: A Study of Biblical Proverbs." *Semeia* 17 (1980): 35–58.

Wilson, F. P., ed. *The Oxford Dictionary of English Proverbs.* 3rd ed. Oxford: Oxford University Press, 1970.

Winter, Steven. "Transcendental Nonsense, Metaphoric Reasoning, and the Cognitive Stakes for Law." *University of Pennsylvania Law Review* 137.4 (1989): 1105–1237.

Wolters, Al. "Proverbs XXXI 10–31 as Heroic Hymn: A Form-Critical Analysis." *Vetus Testamentum* 38 (1988): 446–57.

Wordsworth, William. *Lyrical Ballads with Pastoral and Other Poems in Two Volumes.* London: T.N. Longman, 1802.

Wright, Christopher J. H. *Old Testament Ethics for the People of God.* Downers Grove: InterVarsity Press, 2004.

Yee, Gale A. " 'I Have Perfumed My Bed with Myrrh': The Foreign Woman (*'iššâ zārâ*) in Proverbs 1–9." *Journal for the Study of the Old Testament* 43 (1989): 53–68.

Yoder, Christine Roy. "Contours of Desire in Israelite Wisdom Literature." Paper presented at the annual meeting of the SBL. Chicago, IL, 17 November 2012.

"The Shaping of Erotic Desire in Proverbs 1–9." Pages 148–62 in *Saving Desire: The Seduction of Christian Theology.* Edited by J. Henriksen and L. Shults. Grand Rapids: Eerdmans, 2011.

*Proverbs.* Abingdon Old Testament Commentaries. Nashville: Abingdon Press, 2009.

"The Objects of Our Affections: Emotions and the Moral Life in Proverbs 1–9." Pages 73–88 in *Shaking Heaven and Earth: Essays in Honor of Walter Brueggemann and Charles B. Cousar.* Edited by Christine Roy Yoder et al. Louisville: Westminster John Knox, 2005.

"Forming 'Fearers of Yahweh': Repetition and Contradiction as Pedagogy in Proverbs." Pages 167–83 in *Seeking Out the Wisdom of the Ancients.* Edited by Ronald Troxel et al. Winona Lake: Eisenbrauns, 2005.

*Wisdom as a Woman of Substance: A Socioeconomic Reading of Proverbs 1–9 and 31:10–31.* Beihefte zur Zeitschrift für die alttestamentliche Wissenschaft 304. Berlin: de Gruyter, 2001.

Zahavi, Dan. "Self and Other: The Limits of Narrative Understanding." Pages 179–201 in *Narrative and Understanding Persons.* Edited by Daniel D. Hutto. Royal Institute of Philosophy Supplement 60. Cambridge: Cambridge University Press, 2007.

Zimmerli, Walther. "Concerning the Structure of Old Testament Wisdom." Translated by Brian Kovacs. Pages 175–207 in *Studies in Ancient Israelite Wisdom.* Edited by James L. Crenshaw. New York: KTAV, 1976. Translation of "Zur Struktur der alttestamentlichen Weisheit." *Zeitschrift für die alttestamentliche Wissenschaft* 51 (1933): 177–204.

# Index of Names

Abbott, Andrew, 203n1
Adams, Samuel L., 103n8
Albertz, Rainier, 216n39
Albright, W. F., 88n22
Alter, Robert, 4, 37, 39, 40, 41, 50, 52n90, 65n138, 158n91, 212
Anderson, Gary A., 183n41
Annas, Julia, 13n11
Ansberry, Christopher B., 6, 7, 75, 77, 118, 210, 211

Bahti, Timothy, 52n92
Bartholomew, Craig G., 29n3
Barton, John, 3, 13–14, 15, 15n18, 16n23, 19n40, 82, 102, 103, 118n42
Berlin, Adele, 37n31
Berman, Joshua, 192n64
Birch, Bruce, 16
Blenkinsopp, Joseph, 137n29
Bondi, Richard, 19n38, 19n39
Booth, Wayne C., 19, 20, 20n41, 24, 25–26, 68, 145, 146, 151
Boström, Lennart, 103n8
Brickhouse, Thomas C., 128n66
Brown, William P., 3, 11n1, 12–13, 16, 17n33, 19, 27, 55, 75n19, 85n18, 95n48, 98n58, 136n25, 148n55, 148n57, 168, 210, 210n25, 211, 214, 215
Bryant, David J., 170
Bryce, Glendon, 32
Burrell, David B., 19n38, 22, 23, 204, 205
Buss, Martin J., 34n23

Calvin, John, 16n22
Camp, Claudia V., 137n29
Caquot, A., 83n13
Carroll R., M. Daniel, 17, 18n37
Carson, Anne, 130n2, 131–32, 143, 159, 162, 163, 166, 167, 168
Clifford, Richard J., 34n22
Clines, David J. A., 119n47, 218
Coleridge, Samuel Taylor, 46

Collins, Billy, 47
Crenshaw, James L., 72, 82, 216n39

Dahood, Mitchell J., 153n67
Dalzell, Alexander, 42, 55, 60
Davis, Ellen F., 39
De Boer, P. A. H., 91n34
Delitzsch, Franz, 49n77, 163n110, 168n134
Dell, Katharine, 74
Dennis, Carl, 151, 154
Dent, N. J. H., 146
Dewey, John, 172, 192
Dobbs-Allsopp, F. W., 37–38, 39
Dollimore, Jonathan, 130n1, 135n21, 159n97
Driver, G. R., 48n67, 121n51, 157n87
Driver, S. R., 41
Duff, David, 55n107, 225

Ehrlich, Arnold B., 153n68
Eichrodt, Walther, 16n22
Eissfeldt, Otto, 30
Eliot, George, 71n1, 72
Erman, Adolf, 31n110
Exum, J. Cheryl, 63n131, 65, 65n136, 66, 134

Fagin, Larry, 36n28
Fesmire, Steven, 172n11
Fishbane, Michael, 39n41
Fitzgerald, Chloë, 72n5
Fokkelman, J. P., 40n42
Fontaine, Carole R., 64n132
Forti, Tova, 137n29, 148n55
Fox, Michael V., 6, 7, 15n17, 31n12, 32n16, 34, 45n53, 48, 49n76, 63, 63n127, 64n132, 64n133, 78, 81n6, 84n14, 85n17, 86n19, 87n20, 87n21, 88n23, 89n24, 93, 94n42, 94n44, 96n49, 103n8, 104n9, 118n43, 120n48, 120n49, 121n52, 122n53, 125n63, 127, 132n12, 134n19, 137n29, 139, 144, 147n54, 149n59, 156n79, 156n82, 156n83, 157n87, 162, 164n115, 168n134, 178n27, 185n46, 192n64, 215n37

# Index of Scripture and Ancient Sources